THE SALONIKA BAY MURDER

Other Books by Edmund Keeley

FICTION

The Libation
The Gold-Hatted Lover
The Impostor
Voyage to a Dark Island
A Wilderness Called Peace

NONFICTION

Modern Greek Writers
   (ed. with Peter Bien)
Cavafy's Alexandria
Modern Greek Poetry: Voice and Myth
R. P. Blackmur: Essays, Memoirs, Texts
   (ed. with Edward Cone and Joseph Frank)

POETRY IN TRANSLATION

Six Poets of Modern Greece
   (with Philip Sherrard)
George Seferis: Collected Poems
   (with Philip Sherrard)
C. P. Cavafy: Passions and Ancient Days
   (with George Savidis)
C. P. Cavafy: Selected Poems
   (with Philip Sherrard)
Odysseus Elytis: The Axion Esti
   (with George Savidis)
C. P. Cavafy: Collected Poems
   (with Philip Sherrard and George Savidis)
Angelos Sikelianos: Selected Poems
   (with Philip Sherrard)
Ritsos in Parentheses
The Dark Crystal/Voices of Modern Greece
   (with Philip Sherrard)
Odysseus Elytis: Selected Poems
   (with Philip Sherrard)
Yannis Ritsos; Exile and Return, Selected Poems 1968–74

FICTION IN TRANSLATION

Vassilis Vassilikos: The Plant, the Well, the Angel
   (with Mary Keeley)

THE SALONIKA BAY MURDER

COLD WAR POLITICS AND THE POLK AFFAIR

EDMUND KEELEY

Princeton University Press, Princeton, New Jersey

Published by Princeton University Press, 41 William Street, Princeton,
New Jersey 08540

This book has been composed in Linotron Trump

Clothbound editions of Princeton University Press books are printed on
acid-free paper, and binding materials are chosen for strength and durability
Paperbacks, although satisfactory for personal collections, are
not usually suitable for library rebinding

Printed in the United States of America by Princeton University Press,
Princeton, New Jersey

Library of Congress Cataloging-in-Publication Data
Keeley, Edmund.
The Salonika Bay murder: cold war politics and the Polk
affair / Edmund Keeley.
p. cm.
Bibliography: p.
Includes index.
ISBN 0-691-05565-3 (alk. paper)
1. Murder—Greece—Thessalonikē—Case studies. 2. Polk, George.
3. Victims of crimes—Greece—Thessalonikē—Case studies. 4. Journalists—
Greece—Thessalonikē—Case studies. 5. Greece—Politics
and government—1935–1967. I. Title.
HV6535.G83T45   1989
364.1/523/094956—dc19   88-34039

For James H. Keeley and Robert V. Keeley,

ἀγαθοὶ πρεσβευταί

All of us, whether guilty or not, whether young or old, must accept the past. We are all affected by the consequences and liable for it. . . . We . . . must look truth straight in the eye—without embellishment and without distortion. . . . There can be no reconciliation without remembrance.
—Richard von Weizsäcker, president of West Germany, Bittenburg, 1985

Contents

Illustrations

Acknowledgments

I AM GRATEFUL first of all to the Fulbright Program in Washington and to William Ammerman of the U.S. Educational Foundation in Athens for granting me three part-time research fellowships between 1985 and 1987 to work on this book, and I am also grateful to the Hellenic Studies Program at Princeton for a summer fellowship in 1988 and other support for the same purpose. Many people have helped me during the course of my work by offering suggestions, opinions, gossip, background information, leads and misleads, but my most consistent personal source for authoritative commentary on the political context of this study has been Professor John O. Iatrides, who reviewed my work from start to finish with unusual devotion and patience (but who is not to be held responsible for the use I made of his valuable assistance). I want to thank Ben Sonnenberg for drawing my attention to the latest phase of the Polk affair by asking me to do a piece on Gregory Staktopoulos's 1984 book about that journalist's role in the affair; Mr. Sonnenberg is not to be blamed for my having extended his request for forty pages to nearly four hundred pages. A number of people were good enough to tolerate my solicitations and questions, either in person or over the phone: Rea Polk first of all, Gregory Staktopoulos, Kosta Hadjiargyris, William Polk, William E. Colby, Homer Bigart, Anthony Cave Brown, William van den Heuvel, Bruce Lansdale, Louis Buol, Nicholas Gage, Stelios Papathemelis, and several others who preferred to remain nameless. The staff of the Sterling Memorial Library of Yale University assisted me amply in my review of the Walter Lippmann papers housed there. I am grateful to Kati Marten for allowing me full access to the William Donovan papers while they were in her possession at the Gannett Center for Media Studies. I owe special thanks to Laura Goldin and Georges Borchardt for keeping faith in this enterprise through the long haul of it and to my wife, Mary, for never once complaining about what my obsession with the Polk affair may have cost her. Joanna Hitchcock, Beth Gianfagna, and their colleagues at Princeton University Press demonstrated exceptionally dedicated enterprise in bringing the manuscript to publication in a timely fashion. I hope the book provides some recompense for the generosity of those who kept me from losing heart as I made my way on a journey that in any case had its just measure of adventure and discovery in a Cavafian mode.

The Polk Case: Dramatis Personae

FREDERICK AYER: special investigator assigned by secretary of state to Polk case

MARY BARBER: journalist in Athens, wife of Stephen

STEPHEN BARBER: British journalist in Athens

WILLIAM O. BAXTER: assistant chief of State Department's Division of Greek, Turkish, and Iranian Affairs

HOMER BIGART: correspondent for the *New York Herald Tribune*

WINSTON BURDETT: CBS correspondent covering the Polk case

RANDALL COATE: British information officer in Salonika

WILLIAM E. COLBY: member of Donovan's law firm during Polk case

CARL COMPTON: teacher and eventually president of Anatolia College in Salonika

WAIDE CONDON: U.S. Information Service officer in Salonika

PANAYOTIS CONSTANTINIDIS: attorney general for the Greek Court of Appeals

WILLIAM J. ("WILD BILL") DONOVAN: New York lawyer, former head of OSS, counsel to Overseas Writers Special Committee ("Lippmann Committee")

GERALD DREW: American delegate to UNSCOB in Salonika

GEORGE DROSSOS: deputy Greek liaison officer to UNSCOB

THEODORE ECONOMOU: Staktopoulos's lawyer for a time

ANGELOS EVERT: chief of Athens police

RALEIGH GIBSON: American consul general in Salonika

HENRY GRADY: American ambassador in Greece during Polk case

DWIGHT P. GRISWOLD: head of the American Mission for Aid to Greece

KOSTA HADJIARGYRIS: Athens journalist and *Christian Science Monitor* correspondent

JAMES KELLIS: assistant to Donovan early in Polk investigation

ALEXANDER KENDRICK: CBS correspondent at Polk trial

MATHEW DIMITRIOU KOKKONIS: Rea Polk's father

CHRISTOS KOMOTOUROS: inquiry magistrate in Salonika

CHRISTOS LADAS: Greek minister of justice assassinated May 1, 1948

THEODORE LAMBRON: replaced James Kellis as assistant to Donovan

ERNEST K. LINDLEY: Washington bureau chief for *Newsweek*, president of the Overseas Writers

WALTER LIPPMANN: American foreign affairs columnist, chairman of Overseas Writers Special Committee ("Lippmann Committee")

GEORGE C. McGHEE: State Department coordinator for aid to Greece

LINCOLN MacVEAGH: American ambassador in Athens, 1943–48

HELEN MAMAS: Associated Press stringer in Salonika

GEORGE MARSHALL: U.S. secretary of state during Polk case

COLONEL MARTIN: British Police Mission officer in Salonika

DONALD MATCHEN: correspondent for York, Pennsylvania, *Daily Gazette*

ROBERT G. MINER: second secretary of American embassy in Athens

ANNA MOLYVDA: Adam Mouzenidis's sister-in-law

NICOLAOS MOUSKOUNDIS: chief of the Salonika Security Police

CHRISTOS MOUSTAKIS: attorney general for the Salonika Court of the First Instance

ADAM MOUZENIDIS: Communist guerrilla leader accused of Polk's murder

STYLIANOS (STELIOS) MOUZENIDIS: Adam's brother

EDWARD R. MURROW: CBS radio commentator and friend of Polk

YANNIS PANOPOULOS: director of town police in Ministry of Public Order under Rendis

STELIOS PAPATHEMELIS: Staktopoulos's lawyer for his 1979 appeal

DREW PEARSON: columnist for the *Washington Post*

GEORGE POLK: CBS correspondent in Greece and Middle East

REA POLK (née Renée Cocconis or Kokkonis): George Polk's widow

WILLIAM POLK: George's younger brother, represented Newsmen's Commission at Polk trial

CONSTANTINE POULOS: correspondent of Overseas News Agency, represented Newsmen's Commission at Polk trial

RUPERT PROHME: U.S. Information Service officer in Salonika

KARL RANKIN: chargé d'affaires of the American embassy in Athens

CONSTANTINOS RENDIS: Greek minister of public order

A.G.R. ROUSE: chief of British Information Department in Athens

JOHN SECONDARI: CBS correspondent covering the Polk case

ALEXANDER ("SHAN") SEDGWICK: *New York Times* correspondent in Athens

THEMISTOCLES SOPHOULIS: prime minister of Greece during Polk case

ADRIANI STAKTOPOULOS: Gregory's sister

ANNA STAKTOPOULOS: Gregory's mother

GREGORY STAKTOPOULOS: Salonika journalist and Reuters stringer

ELEFTHERIOS STAVRIDIS: Salonika journalist who testified at Polk trial

DANIEL THRAPP: correspondent for United Press in Greece and Italy

CONSTANTINE TSALDARIS: Greek prime minister at time of Truman Doctrine

IORDANIS VAFIADIS: one of the two defense lawyers at Polk trial

MARKOS VAFIADIS ("MARKOS"): Communist guerrilla general

NICOLAOS ("NIKOS") VASSILIKOS: one of the two defense lawyers at Polk trial

EVANGELOS ("VANGELIS") VASVANAS: Communist guerrilla leader accused of Polk's murder

DESPINA VROUTSI: Polk's maid in Athens

SIR CHARLES WICKHAM: chief of British police and prison mission to Greece

APOSTOLOS XANTHOPOULOS: Salonika chief of police

NIKOS ZACHARIADIS: secretary general of the Greek Communist Party

THE SALONIKA BAY MURDER

Prologue

On a May Sunday in 1948, the clothed body of a man in his mid-thirties was spotted by a boatman and two boys out for a pleasure ride in Salonika Bay not far from the fifteenth-century prison tower that is the city's landmark. The boatman towed the body to the harbormaster's dock and helped lay it out on the pier. The hands and feet were loosely bound by hemp rope covered with cuttlefish eggs, and much of the exposed flesh—face, neck, hands—had become soapy and whitish from days underwater. There was a bullet hole in the back of the head. The bullet had evidently come out cleanly through the victim's nose because the coroner found no other wound on the body. The clothing was intact—camel's-hair jacket, officer's surplus green trousers, shirt open at the neck, shoes laced—and clean of bloodstains or other telling evidence except for an ample residue of sand wherever it could settle. The pockets of the jacket and trousers still held money and other personal effects. On one wrist the watch had stopped at 12:20, and on the other there was a white metal identity bracelet bearing the name GEORGE POLK. A wedding ring carried the inscription "Renée Cocconis" and the numerals "9/11/47, K. 18."[1]

The authorities who were called to the pier knew immediately that they had come upon a difficult case, more than they surely cared to handle, given the problems they already had in dealing with the Communist insurgents who were still threatening the very suburbs of the city. From the various identity cards in the pockets, they gathered that the body belonged to an American, and not just an ordinary American but the CBS correspondent who had been missing for a week and whose press identity card had been mailed in by somebody to the Third Police Precinct five days earlier, the man named Polk recently arrived from Athens and reported by the local papers to have been looking for a way to interview the Communist guerrilla leader Markos Vafiadis.

The evidence of the bullet wound and the trussing seemed to point not to a routine murder but to an assassination. That in turn suggested politics in one form or another, and politics involving an American, especially now that the U.S. aid program under the Truman Doctrine

3

was beginning to make a difference in the Greek civil war, could only mean serious trouble. The guerrilla threat approaching the outskirts of the city was cause enough for alarm, but now there was also the problem of a change in the foreign factor, the British leaving Greece and the Americans moving in. Finding the culprits who had murdered an American correspondent on Greek soil at the outset of the Truman Doctrine and the Marshall Plan could be more than a question of solving an awkward crime; given the inevitable publicity, a bad press at home and abroad could endanger the aid program.

For all their sensitivity to the ominous, what the officials at the pier could not have predicted was that the discovery of George Polk's body on May 16, 1948, would initiate not only a difficult case with international repercussions but what would eventually become an "affair" that is now seen by many as the Greek equivalent of the Dreyfus affair, one still capable of rousing passionate debate in Greece about the processes of justice and the influence of foreign agencies forty years after the fact. There have been other cases in the region that still occasion debate, for example, the Lambrakis murder case of 1963, which became an international cause célèbre when it was made into the French film Z at the time of the Colonels' dictatorship, but the Polk affair is taken to have revealed an even more complicated and pernicious mix of domestic and foreign misbehavior, and the case has remained more of a mystery because it is still considered by most to be unsolved. The quality of passion it stimulates is a legacy of the most bitter period in modern Greek history, a civil war that is still fought with only slowly dying ardor in the minds of those who remember it and that has bequeathed murky prejudices to those who don't.

I first heard about the case in the spring of 1949, when a favorite college professor of mine suggested that it would be folly for me to postpone graduate work in order to teach at an American secondary school in Salonika under the Fulbright Program. "You'll end up in Salonika Bay, just like George Polk," he told me. I didn't know what he was referring to, and in any case I didn't take his advice. I thought of Salonika as one of my home cities in those days. I had spent three years there before World War II, while my father was the American consul in Salonika, and for me it still had the aura of a vividly remembered, if rapidly vanishing, paradise. That was in part because it was the last place I could remember where I had been prince of my own domain, with Greeks, Armenians, Jews, Turks, and a variety of other foreign residents for companions in territory where all fields were green and where the son of a diplomat—especially an American diplomat—was not simply an exotic but was normally treated with such deference by the local care-takers that he could come to think the fields he played in were his by some unspecified divine right. The particular region that it appeared the gods had granted me, my brothers, and my motley friends to command, anyway on the lowest level, was called the American Farm School, an oasis on the outskirts of Salonika that provided fresh vegetables from its gardens and fresh milk from an imported herd of Guernsey cows and ample grounds for games or mischief invented by a wealth of nation-alities.

I had returned to Greece after World War II, in the summer of 1947—by then my father was counselor of embassy in Athens—and I had spent the best part of my time not in the capital but in Salonika trying to recapture something of that prewar mood. Of course that was out of the question. I had forgotten so much of the language and had evidently turned so foreign to Greek eyes that it seemed at first I would never be able to communicate with those few old companions who had made it through the wars and were still on the scene. And as an American with Athens embassy connections—though still in my teens—I found myself treated by others either with too much courtesy or too much suspicion. I was in any case no longer prince of anything, and with the Greek civil war still very much in progress, it was almost impossible to explore those outlying regions where the old Greece had provided a village cul-ture so hospitable to foreigners that a child might live for a while with the illusion that he was native to that generous climate.

My return to Salonika in 1949—and it was at the American Farm School that I went to teach—was partly motivated by a lingering need to become comfortable again with the country that I had once loved with unquestioning energy. And with the civil war still not over, there was adventure in the air, maybe even a chance to report on the American presence in Greece from close to the front lines. The image of George Polk was a latent influence in this fantasy. I had been intrigued enough by my professor's comment on the CBS correspondent's demise to dig up what I could about him from the American newspaper accounts of his murder. He turned out to be a glamorous figure to my young mind, with much to recommend him in his biography—World War II navy pilot, war correspondent, White House reporter, friend of Edward R. Murrow, au-thor of articles on the Near East, a journalist known for his courage in traveling wherever it was necessary to get the news and then telling it as it was. He had also become a Greek specialist in his last days, newly married to a beautiful Alexandrian Greek not yet twenty who had been an airline hostess, and the two had settled in Athens for some months before his fatal trip to Salonika. By that time I thought of myself also as an aspiring specialist on Greece, anyway on life in Macedonia, and since I too aspired to be some sort of writer, I felt more affinity for George Polk as I headed back to Salonika in 1949 than now seems rational.

The feeling did not last long. When I reached the city in the summer of that year, the Polk case appeared to be dead. Nobody in the American community was talking about it, though the consul general in town (my father's prewar position had been upgraded and was now filled by a seasoned gentleman named Raleigh Gibson) had apparently been much involved in the investigation of the murder. He and others who knew about the case were evidently keeping their own counsel. All I remember hearing is that the murder had been solved that spring when a Greek journalist who was once a member of the Communist party had confessed to complicity in the crime, which had actually been committed by two Communist co-conspirators, on instructions from higher up, in order to embarrass the Americans and threaten their aid program through the bad publicity it would occasion in the United States. It seemed there was nothing more to be said. One could still hear talk among some local Greeks about open questions that remained from the April trial—contradictions in the confessions that had solved the case and rumors that one of the Communists who had been sentenced to death in absentia was reported to have been already dead at the time of the murder—but the governing sentiment was that the case had been justly laid to rest. And since the civil war turned out to be in its final phase by the fall of 1949, American Helldiver bombers under General Van Fleet now using napalm effectively to clean out the last guerrilla nests in the Pindos mountains south of Albania, the Communist threat itself appeared to be close to a dead issue.[2]

It was not entirely a dead issue at the American Farm School, where there was still much excited talk about the civil war "event" that had suddenly put the school on the world stage for a day the past winter. On a Friday night in late January, 1949, one of the coldest nights of the season, a band of some twenty Communist guerrillas (known as "andartes") reached the small cemetery at the edge of the school grounds after trekking for three days across enemy territory from their mountain hideout. They spread out and crept through the school grounds to the trees opposite the main dormitory building (called "Princeton Hall"), and when they saw the lights go out in the dormitory, they moved in quickly to round up thirty-three boys from the senior class, four from the junior class, and four young staff members sleeping in a ground-floor dormitory room, told them to dress quickly, pick up a blanket, and line up in the corridor because they were heading for the mountains to join the forces of Free Greece. The students were sleepy, thought it a joke, sat up in bed and stared at these oddly uniformed soldiers. Then guns came out, so they dressed quickly and lined up, and then they filed out, led past the kitchen so that they could each pick up a loaf of bread before they went into the night.[3]

Some of the new "recruits" got away within the first few kilometers beyond the school by dropping off into the darkness. More would ease out of line whenever the group crossed a road or riverbed where there were gullies for hiding. Within the first twenty-four hours, twenty-five had made it back to the school, and most others drifted back during the first week, escaping whenever there was a skirmish with the Greek army. The last senior—son of a guerrilla fighter—came back two months later, well before spring graduation, which was granted him in any case more for courage than aptitude. It had not been easy for the late "deserters" among the "recruits" because they had been lectured on what would happen to them if they tried to escape, and once they had been made to watch while a "deserter" from another group was shot for his effort; but they had taken advantage of the growing confusion that had come with increased activity by the Greek army in guerrilla territory. Those who had gotten away the first night said that they had found it remarkably easy to fall out of line and hide, maybe, some thought, because the guerrilla band had been afraid to reveal themselves by firing at the new recruits inside enemy territory, maybe, others thought, because the guerrillas were exhausted from their travels and the fighting and themselves dropped out along the way.

The raid on the school was seen in the Greek government press as an audacious act of desperation, a failed attempt on the part of the guerrilla forces to show that Salonika itself was still vulnerable to the insurgents despite their losses elsewhere. Others found it evidence of an alarming weakness in the army's defense of the city's outskirts, especially in an area so close to the military airport—a weakness equal to that which had permitted the downtown area of the city to come under artillery fire from the guerrillas earlier in the civil war.

There may have been truth in both views, but neither seemed of much moment by the fall of 1949, when the guerrilla forces were in full retreat. The principal legacy of the event was the celebrative aura that could be felt at the school long after the senior class had graduated. The four juniors who had taken part in the action were already established as local heroes by the time my classes started in the fall, designated leaders of the unruly, restless in fame, impossible to be taught anything. But on graduation two of them found a way of carrying their young notoriety to America, where they eventually went to college and ended up minor millionaires. One of the others served for a while as an instructor at the school, and the fourth, true to his original mission, became the leading chicken farmer of his generation in Macedonia.

I sent in no reports from the front that year. The glamour of playing George Polk diminished under the harsh demands of a first attempt at teaching English to high-spirited adolescent boys not much younger than I was who would have preferred to learn the exotic American sport called basketball on a full-time basis and go home illiterate in foreign languages to cultivate their fields. And after the civil war ended that winter, travel by jeep in any direction beyond the city became all the high adventure one could want, especially when a young American reaching the remoter northern villages was received and honored as though he were General George Marshall's son. In the folk imagination, America had by then fully replaced Britain as Greece's savior, and the disillusionment that inevitably undoes the charitable image of a patron nation among those who become dependent upon it was still some years away. So was the now generally accepted view that America played a pernicious role in the Polk affair, along with its British ally.

I came back to the case with more than nostalgic interest when I was asked in the mid-1980s to review a recent book in Greek by the man who had been sentenced to life imprisonment by the Salonika court in 1949 as an accomplice in Polk's murder along with two Communist co-conspirators and who had subsequently been released after serving eleven years of his sentence. The claims of this man, Gregory Staktopoulos, a Salonika journalist who had been the local stringer for Reuters at the time of the murder, had been before the public for some years and had resulted in a failed appeal to the Greek Supreme Court for a retrial in 1979, but the book he wrote spelled out the role he had played in the case with the kind of personal detail that was convincing enough in its horror to draw me back into a reexamination of the whole affair.[4] The essence of Staktopoulos's position was that he had been a scapegoat, innocent of any crime connected with the Polk murder, having had nothing whatsoever to do with it. He claimed that the trial which had sentenced him to life imprisonment had been rigged by collusion between the prosecution and the defense under orders from higher up, and the confessions which had served as the basis for his conviction and that of his presumed Communist co-conspirators had been obtained by extended torture at the hands of one Major Mouskoundis and the Salonika General Security Police, torture that he described in all its particularized agony.

Staktopoulos's view of who had in fact been responsible for the murder was based in large measure on another book on the Polk affair that had appeared in Greek a decade earlier,[5] written by one of the former suspects in the case, an Athenian journalist named Kosta Hadjiargyris, who had been George Polk's Athens assistant and who had reviewed the case persistently after 1949. His research was meant to prove in the first instance that he had nothing to do with the murder, but in addition he provided what evidence he could to support his opinion that the crime had been the result of a hurriedly organized plot hatched in Salonika by the British Intelligence Service in order to embarrass the newly arrived American patrons of Greece who were, in British eyes, presumably too eager to assume the prerogatives of power that the British once had in Greece, Palestine, and elsewhere. The plot, according to Hadjiargyris, had been executed by a British agent in Salonika named Randall Coate who had been working under cover of being the local British information officer and who had left the city permanently on reassignment to Norway a few days before Polk's body was recovered from Salonika Bay. Hadjiargyris also argued that American officials, in cooperation with higher British officials, had played a major role in directing the murder investigation away from the true culprits and toward others who were not guilty at all—first, Hadjiargyris himself, then Polk's widow Rea, and finally Gregory Staktopoulos and two absent Communist leaders presumably then hiding out in the mountains.

According to this account, the Americans were implicated first through excessive pressure exerted by Washington on the Greek authorities to find a culprit, second, through the manipulation of the case by diplomatic officials in Athens and Salonika—in particular, the chargé d'affaires of the Athens embassy, Karl Rankin (who had replaced my father in 1948), Salonika Consul General Raleigh Gibson, and a former FBI agent named Frederick Ayer, appointed by the State Department as a special investigator in the case—and third, most surprisingly, through a collaborative effort with these officials on the part of representatives of the American press who had been sent to Greece to take part in the investigation: Winston Burdett and John Secondari of CBS and General William J. "Wild Bill" Donovan, wartime director of the OSS. The latter was acting as counsel for the Special Committee of Inquiry of the Overseas Writers, a group of distinguished journalists under the chairmanship of Walter Lippmann (known as the Lippmann Committee), created specifically to follow the investigation in Greece, with State Department backing, in an effort to ensure that justice was done in a case involving the murder of a fellow journalist.

Hadjiargyris regarded the outcome of the Lippmann Committee's work as grossly suspect, even pernicious, not only in its having accepted a miscarriage of justice in the case of Staktopoulos but in its having contributed essentially to a cover-up of a rigged trial in Salonika. In this opinion he was echoing an allegation first published by I. F. Stone in a 1952 series that challenged the Lippmann Committee's formal report on the case,[6] and he was later supported by two journalists specializing in Greece, Yannis Roubatis and Elias Vlanton, who, in 1977, dipped into the newly released State Department archives to find some evidence in the Polk file of collusion between American officials and American press representatives in promoting the "Staktopoulos solution" that put the Polk case temporarily to rest.[7] General Donovan was pictured as a particular villain in having pressured Greek officials at one point to make an arrest and then having steered his committee, and American opinion more generally, toward accepting the guilt of Staktopoulos and his presumed Communist co-conspirators despite the many unanswered questions raised by Staktopoulos's continually revised confession and the Salonika trial that convicted him. But Roubatis and Vlanton also pictured Donovan's assistant, a former OSS operator named Colonel James Kellis, as having made a conscientious effort, during his forty-five days in Greece, to turn the investigation in other directions, including toward the extreme Right, before he was abruptly taken off the case. Their account, though provocative, was clearly incomplete—especially regarding Kellis's role—and it so emphasized foreign villainy and the influence of rightist elements as to appear slanted.

Much in these various accounts of the Polk affair provided grounds for skepticism. Aspects of the literature on the story, whether characters, plot, or motivation, seemed unreal, not quite plausible for either history or fiction, possibly appropriate to a post-Watergate vision of things, but not to that of a presumably more innocent post–World War II period when Americans and their allies (anyway in the West) were still sharing the afterglow of having triumphed in a just cause. It was true that by 1948, after Truman had declared his excessively broad-based Doctrine, what innocence America had left was already being severely threatened by our new role as a world power dedicated "to support free peoples who are resisting subjugation by armed minorities or by outside pressures"[8] anywhere in the world, a self-assigned mission that in the practice of it could lead all too readily to hubris and, as it did in time, to the kind of debacle we knew in Vietnam and Cambodia. But to most, the first testing of the Truman Doctrine in the war against the Communist guerrillas in Greece seemed legitimate, even necessary in the context of the times, and I was not ready without further evidence to believe that innocence dies as easily as these accounts suggested it had done in that part of our first test known as the Polk affair, even if it did appear that disproportionate power had been placed in the hands of limited men, whether well-meaning or not.

The known literature did not entirely convince me that a sort of American hubris was at the heart of the case. For one, the sources for the story were predominantly Greek, sometimes revealing what could be taken for an anti-American bias. And the literature did not sufficiently answer key questions raised by the version of events it promulgated. What motive, for instance, would a British spy pretending to be an information officer in Salonika have for killing an American correspondent who arrived in town for a few days during that season? And if he was acting unofficially, out of some private anti-American passion, why was a loose gun of that kind reassigned by his superiors to official positions elsewhere for a number of years? And would American and British officials then cooperate in a cover-up of what had happened? Would Greek officials allow themselves to be pressured into cooperating with the wishes of one or the other foreign patron to the extent of torturing an innocent Greek into confessing complicity in the murder? And would the Greek system of justice tolerate a solution of that kind? In any case, how could a trial be rigged and then be passed off as legitimate when there were so many observers, official and unofficial, in the courtroom to see what was going on? And if the trial had led to a miscarriage of justice in which American officials had participated, why would American press representatives work hand in hand with those officials in promoting the falsehood that justice had been done? Under our system of government, was it not the accepted role of the Fourth Estate to protect the public against excess in government by exposing it? Finally, wasn't this version of events too often based on the speculation of one suspect who may have had reason to be self-protective and on the revised testimony of another suspect who had been convicted after offering false testimony several times revised for presentation in court?

I would have to admit that some of this skepticism was subjective, rooted in a certain personal nostalgia. Even in a post-Watergate decade, I still believed that the American Foreign Service was generally made up of honest men who might be working under more and more constraints but who were professionally committed to upholding the principles of government, including civil liberties, that their oath pledged them to and who were both sophisticated and relatively independent in their judgment of political events. My father had been such a man, perhaps too outspoken against policies that he considered unjust, but not prepared to manipulate others or be manipulated by them against the terms of his oath, even in the name of what others might perceive to be the national interest. And my brother, a career diplomat, was such a man too, as were many colleagues of his that I had met over the years.

I also still believed that American journalists, the good ones, were committed to the truth first of all, like any writer worth the name. Toward government officials who worked in secret, I carried the negative prejudices of those in my generation who continued to prefer open political discourse and conduct to secret debate and covert action, but I knew this to be an outdated and impractical position, and I wasn't prepared to think of such officials as entirely unnecessary or corrupt by nature. As for Greek officials and journalists, some nostalgia was at work there too, though I had lived in Greece too often during the past forty years not to have passed from adoration for all things Greek to a muted philhellenism that allowed for moments of keen despair. In any case, I was still fully prepared to grant most Greek officials and journalists their just degree of pride and professionalism, and I no longer felt that as an American I had any more right to judge them than the next man— perhaps less, since my primary allegiance was to my own country.

If these subjective assumptions appeared still valid to me late in the century, I found it hard to believe that officials and press of whatever nationality had behaved some forty years earlier as the known literature on the Polk case indicated they had. Yet that literature disturbed me enough to compel a review of both the case—the affair—and its larger context, and my interest focused from the start, again perhaps for subjective reasons, on America's role in the affair. To attempt to get to the bottom of that, I decided that my richest resource would be the State Department archives that had come into the public domain in the seventies, all—anyway, almost all—the once-secret or confidential communications between diplomats in the field and the Department of State concerning the Polk case, only partially explored by Roubatis, Vlanton, and other Greek journalists. And as I went through those archives— some hundreds of documents in the National Archives building in Washington—I found that there were also ample records of testimony taken by Greek officials, trial proceedings, and summarized newspaper accounts, enough to provide a context for what the Americans were saying to each other in private. Beyond that archive, there were a few declassified CIA documents, some once-secret material from British government archives, some valuable letters, reports, and other documents among the Donovan papers held by the General's law firm, the Greek newspaper accounts of the Polk affair through the years, the various historical commentaries on the period, and the recollections of those still alive who had actually been a part of the affair, including such principals as Gregory Staktopoulos, Kosta Hadjiargyris (who died in December 1986), George Polk's widow Rea, and his brother William.

What follows is the story that I have reconstructed from these various sources. That too much of my initial skepticism about possible misconduct by officials and press was ill-founded will become apparent as the story unfolds. If the version I emerge with seems colored at times by an excess of passion and my own kind of prejudice, I hope that will be seen as the excusable consequence of a progressive sense of outrage. I have tried in any case to tell the story as candidly as I am able and as completely as these still partial sources permit.

The Victim

THE FIRST GREEK OFFICIAL with proper authority to be called to the harbormaster's dock in the delicate matter of George Polk's body surfacing in Salonika Bay was Major Nicolaos Mouskoundis, head of the local branch of the General Security Police, an investigative unit under the Ministry of Public Order. Mouskoundis was known to be a man who got things done. A career officer preparing to retire after twenty-five years of service, he was overweight, bald, but still straitlaced, a man who kept to himself, a bit short on diplomacy at times but with a strong reputation for producing what was needed when there was a difficult case.[1] And fanatically anti-Communist, along with most of the police officers he commanded.

Major Mouskoundis had worked closely with the British over the years; he prided himself on knowing the psychology of Anglo-Saxons, which now included the Americans—less skilled and predictable than the British, it seemed, more naive, but also more forthright. And he appeared to be fully aware of how important this case was from the Greek point of view, the dangers that bad publicity could create in Greece and abroad when a newsman was involved and when American aid to Greece was being put to the test. But for all his reputed shrewdness, it is unlikely that Major Mouskoundis could have predicted that there would be those in Greece—Communist sources most vociferously but not exclusively—who would hold that the discovery of George Polk's body in Salonika Bay could not have come as any surprise to Major Mouskoundis, since it was either his own men or some other branch of the local forces of law and order that had put the correspondent's body out to sea in the first place.

In any case, the major's quick assumption of command after the body was recovered gave no sign of this. The first thing he did on arriving at the scene was to notify the American consulate that the body of the missing CBS newsman had now surfaced. The second thing he did was order an immediate autopsy—a rather precipitous move, some came to think. The autopsy was performed by Constantine Eliakis, Ordinary Professor of Legal Medicine and Toxicology at Salonika University, and it demonstrated that the body had been in the water for approximately seven days, that there was no evidence of a struggle before the shooting and no other signs of ill-treatment.[2] The nose proved to be boneless, but that was clearly the result of a previous injury. The quantity of water in the lungs led the professor to conclude that the victim was still alive when he was thrown into the bay, though the severe damage to brain tissue and the evidence of hemorrhaging indicated that he was unconscious at the time he hit the water. The only unusual fact revealed by the autopsy in addition to the bullet hole was the contents of the victim's stomach: four and a half pounds of solid food consisting of lobster, peas, some meat and brown bread—all mostly unchewed—and a small quantity of alcohol. The autopsy report stated that the lobster remnants were rather large and had not "undergone in any way the influence of digestion," and most of the green peas were whole. George Polk's last meal was luxuriously substantial if evidently consumed with inadequate leisure.

The first American to enter the case was Consul General Raleigh Gibson—tall, oval-faced, only a fringe of thin hair, neatly trimmed moustache, nearing the end of his career in the Foreign Service—who did not know George Polk personally but who was able to identify the victim from old surgical scars and from the paraphernalia that he found with the body at the Central Hospital, where the autopsy had taken place. Another American official who actually knew Polk, Waide M. Condon of the Salonika Information Office, confirmed the identification.[3] A cable was sent that day to the Department of State reporting that the recovered body of missing CBS correspondent George Polk, which had been in the water for some days, showed that he had been shot in the head and that his arms and legs had been trussed. "Local authorities are carrying on intensive investigation with aid of British police mission officials."[4]

Following the identification, Consul General Gibson accompanied Major Mouskoundis and other police officials to the Astoria Hotel, where Polk had taken a room on the Friday before he disappeared and where his Greek wife of eight months, Rea (née Renée Cocconis), had come to join him for a vacation trip midway through the week that he turned out to be missing. Gibson reported that, fortunately, they did not find Rea in Room 25 of the Astoria Hotel.[5] What they did find was a letter from Polk to Edward R. Murrow of CBS, a letter from Polk to his mother, a number of personal effects including Polk's camera, typewriter, and toilet articles, and a few of Rea's dresses.

In the letter to Edward R. Murrow, Polk spoke of his having "come north to Salonika for a last look around" and "frankly . . . to get into some kind of direct, really-business-like contact with the Markos government crowd," not having had, since 1946, a contact with the Greek Communist party "that I believed was a real contact." Many people had claimed to speak authoritatively but, said Polk, "I think they all were phonies." Now, "with a contact through a contact," Polk told Murrow that he'd "like to get in touch with persons who count," would go outside Salonika to do so if he had to, go to "any other town or village 'they' may designate" with the aim of eventually reaching the Markos headquarters—"even blindfolded, if necessary"—so that he could put the guerrilla leader "on the air from his secret radio station and have the BBC record." That, Polk felt, might make a good story. He concluded: "I've offered to let them write the script on every word Markos says while I'll just give him cues and do the translating. Then—when I come 'outside' I'd be able to tell any story I'd care to."

Given the violence and complexity of the Greek civil war then rising to its apex in the northern regions, many Americans reading a letter of this kind would consider a reporter's motive in wanting to visit the secret mountain headquarters of the leading Communist guerrilla, "General" Markos Vafiadis, as smart journalism, even gutsy journalism, especially in view of the news to be made and the danger involved. Polk's line, "Might make a good story," severely understates the case—a clue to his casual approach, at least when addressing a fellow newsman as distinguished as Murrow. And another line in the letter reveals that touch of journalistic integrity, some would say naive integrity, that no doubt was one reason the two men became friends: "Most of us have done an awful lot of talking and writing about the objectives of the Markos gang, yet few of us have really factual information."

But both the American and the Greek officials on the scene responded otherwise to Polk's self-appointed mission. A few days before Polk's body was discovered, Consul General Gibson, cabling Washington that Polk's War Department press identity card and a Pan Am advertisement (sometimes described in official documents as a calendar card or schedule) had reached the Third Police Precinct in a plain envelope "under circumstances as yet unexplained," added that Polk had expressed a desire to contact Communist elements within or outside Salonika but was "familiar with security regulations" and "had made no request for permission to visit military zone."[6] From the official American point of view, no request for permission presumably meant no trip to Markos, and in light of this, it is highly unlikely that any such permission from the Greek authorities would have been effectively solicited on his behalf by the consulate had Polk put in a request. During his two days in Salonika before he disappeared, every American official he approached for help in realizing his ambition to interview "the other side" in the civil war thoroughly discouraged him from trying, so that he must have concluded that he either had to make the attempt alone unofficially or give up the story.

The Greek officials on the scene when the Murrow letter was discovered must have responded to its contents with something between dismay and barely concealed rage—perhaps in particular the man who was to play the lead in the Polk affair among the local Greek participants. Major Mouskoundis was thought to have felt—and he was evidently not alone in this—that no American correspondent had any business even contemplating a trip to the enemy's headquarters, and if one or another chose to do so, he would likely get exactly what he deserved, a point of view that some in Greece who remember the circumstances still hold to this day. The problem now was how to deal with the consequences of what seemed to these officials at best a foolhardy and at worst a treacherous reason for earning a young death, but this problem was not one for Raleigh Gibson and Major Mouskoundis alone; from the start it became a major problem for their superiors in Athens—the top embassy officials on the American side, the ministers of justice and public order on the Greek side—so that within hours after Polk's body was discovered, Prime Minister Themistocles Sophoulis himself felt that he had to meet the foreign press to state that finding the "authors" of "this loathsome crime" was now "a question of honor for Greece."[7]

The fact is that most Greek officials and much of the Greek press thought it more than a matter of honor. In the climate of those days, it seemed likely to many on the scene that a failure to find the perpetrators of the crime would raise a major protest in America—especially in the American press—that could threaten the continuation of military aid in support of the Greek army's rejuvenated campaign against the Communist insurgency and the economic aid program for rebuilding Greece after the devastation of World War II and the earlier phases of the civil war. The need was desperate; to many, the potential threat in this murder case appeared enormous.

As for the Salonika police investigators specifically, neither honor nor the country's salvation seems to have been as much on their minds as the need to perform credibly enough to keep both the Americans and the Athenian politicians off their backs until the Greek army succeeded in defeating the guerrilla forces, surely only a matter of time now that Truman had declared his Doctrine of protecting Greece and Turkey from Communist aggression. The Salonika authorities had a particular difficulty to cope with beyond that of dealing with the new American factor:

the aura of political dissension mixed with arrogance that emanated from Athens. To many in the north, the government then seated in the capital must have seemed a shaky construction made up of disparate elements from the extreme Right to the somewhat left of center, created largely under American persuasion in order to show the world a less reactionary face than that of the government it had replaced. And to supplement the traditional rivalry and lingering animosity between police officials in Salonika and Athens, there was now some sort of internecine rivalry between the two more liberal representatives in the government who also had most to do with police matters, Minister of Justice Melas and Minister of Public Order Rendis. The Salonika authorities must have felt that they not only had to cover their flanks, one of which was under surveillance by the Americans and the other by the still present British police advisers, but also their backs, open to attack at any moment by one or another rival faction in Athens out to promote its own interests. The possibilities for embarrassment on a grand scale were immense, even of disaster—and disaster had to be prevented at all cost, given the dangerous times and the anomalies in the national political environment. It must have seemed to Major Mouskoundis and his colleagues that it was up to the Salonika authorities to establish at the start a firm line consistent with their own politics and acceptable to their foreign patrons, this both for their own protection and to promote the final victory against the Communist insurgents.

Along with the American and Greek officials who found the Murrow letter in Polk's hotel room, there was a British official present, a "liaison officer" and adviser to the local police, first identified in State Department archives as "Major Martin Thomas" and later as "Colonel Martin." His name appears regularly during the investigation of the Polk case, and this foreign adviser was evidently permitted to follow developments without restriction and at one point to evaluate them formally. The archives do not show what Colonel Martin thought of the Murrow letter, but his attendance at the search that turned it up and his subsequent participation in the case helped to create a "British factor" in the Polk affair that continues to haunt it almost as persistently as the American presence. The other British official involved in the case anyway before the body was recovered, British Information Officer Randall Coate, remains the presumed key to the British factor. We know that after reaching Salonika Polk asked Coate—as he had a number of others—for help in establishing a contact with the guerrilla "persons who count." There are contradictory stories about Coate's response to this request—one that he nearly threw Polk out of his office when the American became too insistent,[8] and the other that Coate received him cautiously but amiably, in fact tested Polk's sincerity by suggesting that he might be of assistance to him before finally refusing to help.[9] But whatever actually took place during this recorded meeting and other suspected meetings, Coate was transferred from Salonika to Oslo a few days after Polk disappeared, and his secretary moved on to Australia at the same time, effectively closing the British Information Office in Salonika, anyway for the moment. The only word from Coate thereafter was a comment he was reported to have made to an American official who got in touch with him in Norway after Polk's body surfaced in Salonika Bay, namely, that "he [Coate] might well have been the last person to have met Mr. Polk before the latter's death."[10] For forty years, the rest has been silence.

The transfer and subsequent inaccessibility of Randall Coate has been made much of over the years, but there is evidence that the transfer had been ordered by his superiors some months before Polk reached Salonika. The remaining mystery is whether his superiors speeded up his departure after Polk's identity card appeared at the Third Police Precinct. Once-secret British archives suggest that this was not the case,[11] but to judge the reliability of that source one should have available all the relevant evidence in the affair.

Polk's meeting with Coate is in any case only one of many curious moments in the itinerary of Polk's fatal Salonika trip as it was reconstructed and finally recorded on June 15 by two of his colleagues at CBS, Winston Burdett and John Secondari, who arrived in Salonika two days after Polk's body was recovered.[12] The itinerary is full of odd encounters and unexplained gaps. We learn that Polk was originally headed toward the Macedonian town of Kavalla with his wife Rea and his Athens assistant, Kosta Hadjiargyris, the latter also to be accompanied by his wife: a final vacation jaunt by the two couples to several northern towns, with newsgathering only a secondary motive, since the Polk couple was scheduled to leave for the States two weeks later and Polk's Middle East duties for CBS about to end because he hoped to take up a Nieman Fellowship at Harvard (the fellowship was still pending at the time of his death). Rea and the Hadjiargyris couple decided not to join Polk for the trip north, more or less at the last minute, Rea because of what she called "a spat" with her husband, the Hadjiargyris couple because of other domestic complications. A first stop in Salonika apparently occurred when the Kavalla airport proved to be rained out, but there are differing views of exactly when Polk changed his plans, some suggesting not until the plane touched down at the military airport in Salonika, others before he left Athens. According to Burdett and Secondari, Hadjiargyris told them that Kavalla was still Polk's first destination the night before he left Athens, but Mrs. Hadjiargyris said that Polk announced to her that he was heading for Salonika first, and Burdett and Secondari also report that Polk told Don Matchen, "roving correspondent of a York, Pennsylvania daily [sic]" whom he met at the Athens airport, that he was going to Salonika "for four days, taking a last swing through the north."

Still, however casual the decision to visit Salonika may have been, Polk was quick to pick up on the possibility of using the stopover for a last attempt to reach the guerrilla leader Markos, though he also became interested in the question of whether village children were being abducted across the northern border by the Communist forces, a question then being explored by a United Nations Special Commission on the Balkans (UNSCOB) that was housed in Salonika at the time. During his first morning in the city, Polk worked on both fronts. After a brief call on his friend Rupert Prohme, the United States Information Service officer, he met with one "Colonel Miller" of the American consulate[13] to see if the colonel might suggest a way for him to get in touch with the guerrillas and was strongly advised against making the attempt. He then approached Gerald Drew, acting American delegate to UNSCOB—a man he was meeting for the first time—and brought up the question of a possible trip to Markos. Drew, according to his later sworn testimony, indicated to Polk that it would be a great mistake for him to try to make a contact of that kind "because it would have established a [sic] favorable propaganda for Markos."[14]

Polk then apparently turned his attention to the child abduction question, using Colonel Miller to get an introduction to one Dr. Ahmed, Hindustani press officer of UNSCOB. After a talk on the subject, he lunched with Dr. Ahmed, a "leisurely affair," according to the Burdett-Secondari report. Polk and "the tiny Hindu" sat at a sidewalk table, "ate slowly and deliberately, talked of everything except Communism and looked at the open bay of Salonika on the opposite side of the Street," about at the point where Polk's body was to end up some thirty-six hours later.

After lunch Polk ran into a young Greek-American woman named Helen Mamas whom he had met previously in Athens and who was in Salonika for the moment as a stringer for the Associated Press. Polk apparently asked Helen Mamas point-blank if she could help him get in touch with the guerrillas and was told no. At least so Helen Mamas later testified, and she also testified that at one point she had herself explored the possibility of visiting Markos's mountain headquarters, only to give up the idea when a high-ranking Greek army officer told her—disingenuously, it would seem—that Markos's headquarters were not on Greek soil. Despite her persistent denials of having been involved in Polk's Salonika plans, Helen Mamas found herself drawn more and more deeply into the Polk affair during the months of investigation that followed her colleague's murder, no doubt in part because she was one of the few people Polk encountered during his last hours who had no official connection and who had only her American citizenship to fall back on—a thing that finally worked to protect her.

Polk then was lost sight of for some four hours, during which time, according to the itinerary report, he returned to his hotel and told the manager that he was expecting "one or more people" and that they should be shown right up to his room. No one at the hotel could remember whether anybody came in to see Polk that Friday afternoon. At 6:00 P.M. he sent a telegram to his wife Rea saying that he was staying on in Salonika "because uninations story upshaping on child abductions" and that he might continue on to Kavalla on Monday or Tuesday before returning to Athens. The itinerary report tells us that by 7:30 that Friday evening his friend Rupert Prohme—"dragging" Don Matchen and Robert Crosby (an Athens consular official) with him—came into the Mediterranean Hotel bar to find Polk there chatting with Helen Mamas. They stayed in the bar for an hour and a half, "a gay group," the report says, George "at his raconteur best," telling anecdotes "of his life in half a dozen Middle Eastern countries during the past two years," but no mention of Greece, in fact, no mention of any controversial subject, a particularly interesting fact according to Burdett and Secondari, because "George by nature was not one to avoid controversial subjects either at cocktails, dinner, or any time."

Why Polk chose to avoid talk of Greece and other "controversial" subjects during the cocktail hour, after spending much of the earlier part of the day doing the opposite, the report does not tell us, but it mentions an episode during this hour that was later to become one of the focal points of the police investigation. Dr. Ahmed of UNSCOB came into the bar briefly with two Greek companions and brought them over to Polk's table. We are told that Helen Mamas then introduced the two Greek gentlemen to Polk. One was a liaison officer with UNSCOB who remains unnamed in the report (possibly an official who appears later in archival sources as George Drossos), and the other was a "journalist of Salonika named Statopoulos"—actually, the local Reuters stringer, Gregory Staktopoulos. These were the only Greek nationals that Polk was seen talking to during his two days in Salonika, and brief though this encounter with Staktopoulos was, the fact that he was a local journalist fluent in English (Polk knew little if any Greek) led police officials to give special importance first to this meeting and then, as they developed their reading of the case, to Staktopoulos's possible role in the Polk affair more generally.

The itinerary report tells us that the original cocktail group eventually went off to dinner at the Olympus-Naoussa restaurant, and during the course of the dinner Helen Mamas was called to the phone and came back to the table to say that it had been Staktopoulos asking for the exact spelling of the names of the visiting American journalists (presumably Polk and Matchen) so that he could put news of their arrival in the local paper he worked for, *Makedonia*—a "usual" journalistic courtesy in Salonika, according to Burdett and Secondari, which implies that those preparing the itinerary report a month after the fact did not themselves find grounds for giving Staktopoulos more than passing attention at the time they sent in their report.

The dinner party at the Olympus-Naoussa broke up at 11:00. Don Matchen escorted Helen Mamas to the Cosmopolite Hotel where they were both staying, the others walked down the quay toward the British consulate where Prohme and Crosby lived, said good night there in the light rain, and Polk was seen to turn down a street that led to his hotel, the Astoria. The hotel porters testified that Polk was not spotted coming into the hotel until 1:00 A.M., almost two hours later. There is no explanation of this time gap from any source.

On Saturday morning Polk was out of his room before 8:00, according to the hotel chambermaid, but again it was almost two hours before anyone saw him. Around 9:30 he stopped in on Prohme at the consulate, and when Prohme invited him to dinner that evening, Polk said he was busy that night and "had 'something on' Sunday night" but would see Prohme for dinner on Monday. Polk then went on, says the report, to visit British Information Officer Randall Coate for the purpose we have seen. Gerald Drew testified that he ran into Polk by chance around noon at the Mediterranean Hotel and invited him to have a drink at his apartment that evening. Polk evidently tried to find Don Matchen for lunch but missed him, and he was not seen again until he met Drew that evening at 7:00. Back in his hotel room during the afternoon, Polk asked not to be disturbed, apparently wrote the letters to his mother and Edward R. Murrow, and at 6:00 P.M. sent a second telegram to Rea telling her that he was planning to fly to Kavalla and suggesting that she join him there "via greek airlines wednesday or thursday." This meant that he had decided to stay in Salonika two days longer than he had indicated in the telegram he sent Rea the previous afternoon, and there is reason to believe, especially in view of what he says in the Murrow letter, that by this time he had met somebody who promised—whether truthfully or not—to put him in touch with a contact who would presumably help him in due course to realize his ambition of visiting Markos in the guerrilla leader's mountain headquarters. There is also reason to believe that the meeting with the contact was scheduled for some time that Saturday evening, either during or after the dinner hour, or at the very least, that the dinner was intended to explore in some concrete way the possibility of Polk's finding an appropriate contact.

Polk met Gerald Drew and his wife promptly at 7:00, clean-shaven, wearing an ascot. The two men again talked about the Markos trip—in private, on the balcony—and Polk asked Drew, according to the latter's testimony, whether Drew "knew of any local communists who could help put him in contact with Markos."[15] Drew replied that he did not, and he adds in his testimony that Polk "declared to me that he was going to make a contact with Markos, but I did not come to the conclusion from our conversation that he had previous contact with persons in a position to bring him to contact with Markos"—though the implication of the letter that Polk wrote to Murrow that afternoon is that Polk had already met with someone who had at least promised to find him an appropriate contact. In any case, Drew and his wife appear to have been the last Americans to have seen Polk alive. Just before Polk left them at 8:15, Mrs. Drew invited Polk to stay for dinner; he thanked her but said that "he had an appointment with others," others he didn't name, and he agreed instead to come for lunch the following day (Sunday). According to the Burdett-Secondari report, the only others claiming to have seen Polk alive subsequently were some of the "hotel people" who "have proven so unreliable in their testimony" and who reported that Polk returned to the Astoria Hotel at 11:00 P.M., went out again at 11:15 P.M., then returned an hour and a half later. Nobody reported seeing him after 12:45 A.M. on Sunday.

A number of questions are left unanswered by the Burdett-Secondari itinerary. Who, if anybody, visited Polk in his hotel room on Friday afternoon? Where did he go between 11:15 and 1:00 that evening and between 8:00 and 9:30 the next morning? Did he lunch with anybody that Saturday or visit anybody Saturday afternoon? And on any of these occasions did he actually encounter the "contact through a contact" that he mentions in the Murrow letter or any one of those called "them" in his curious statement that "I've offered to let them write the script on every word Markos says while I'll just give him cues and do the translating." Finally, perhaps most important of all, whom did he dine with

Saturday evening, sharing a large meal of lobster and peas, which is hardly traditional Greek fare, and eating with such speed from anticipation or exhilaration or possibly fear as to swallow the best part of the meal without first chewing what he ate? These are among the questions that the investigators, local and foreign, worked over during the weeks that followed the discovery of Polk's body and that spawned contradictory theories about who had murdered Polk early on Sunday morning of May 8, 1948, the one unverified time and date in the Polk's Salonika itinerary that all investigators appear to have accepted as its terminus.

The early Security Police reconstruction of the murder, directed by Major Mouskoundis and reported by Burdett and Secondari[16]—what they themselves call "a purely tentative picture of what we suppose happened" that "may be far from the truth" but is in any case "the image of the crime which the police have in their minds" a month after the fact—has George Polk leaving his hotel room in apparent haste at some point during the night of Saturday-Sunday in order to meet "his long-sought second contact" (his first contact was made at some earlier point, according to the Security Police perception of things, most likely in Athens). This meeting may not have been perceived by Polk as the actual start of a long fifty-mile sea voyage across the Thermaic Gulf to guerrilla-held territory on the opposite coast in Pieria, north of Mount Olympus, but perhaps for the presumed purpose of conferring about that journey. The conference was set to take place during a dinner either in a restaurant or on board a small Greek cargo vessel called a caique (normally something between 30 and 120 feet), the former seemingly more likely since "a luxury dish" combining lobster and peas, unusual fare for Greeks, "could not easily be prepared and served aboard a caique." Yet the short time-gap between Polk's last meal and his drowning (both "a little time" and "immediately" after eating, according to the autopsy report), led the investigators to point strongly toward the possibility that the crime was committed on the water and that Polk took his last meal on the water as well.

As the Security Police saw it, Polk may well have boarded a caique along with his contact or contacts, gone below decks into the tiny cabin that caiques normally provide, there eaten "tremendously and obviously with great appetite," as a man might who feels "great relief in the company of people whom he understands he can trust." And in the heat of that crowded cabin, he could well have removed the ascot or scarf he was reported to be wearing when last seen or the tie missing from his wardrobe, again the act of a man "who feels 'at home.' " Major Mouskoundis summarized this image of Polk's last moments by declaring that

"George Polk was murdered by 'gentlemen.' They put him completely at his ease."

Wherever the last meal, the Security Police felt certain that Polk was shot in a boat. Why so? Because they thought it almost impossible that a man whose hands and feet were bound and whose head was bleeding profusely could have been carried through a street in Salonika to be dumped into the bay (why his hands and feet were necessarily tied up for the street journey is not explained), though it would have been easy enough for him, at some point before he was shot, to climb into a rowboat along the quay, crowded on any night with small boats used for transport to the larger caiques anchored offshore. Also, according to the Security Police, the slightly downward path of the bullet could have been caused by the rocking motion of a boat. In any event, Burdett and Secondari conclude that "it seems almost certain that George was shot within sight of the busy Salonika waterfront," and nothing now in the records contradicts that hypothesis, though others prefer to think of Polk as having been shot on land before his body was dropped into the sea.

The rest of their reconstruction, the CBS correspondents tell us, is "mechanical and bound to be correct." After shooting Polk—whether inside the cabin of a caique or elsewhere—the killers bound Polk's hands and feet, took out his wallet and removed his press identity card (no mention of why they also removed something as innocuous as a Pan Am calendar-advertisement that Polk evidently had in his wallet), got rid of his "tell-tale address book and note-book," then threw Polk, still alive and breathing, into the bay. According to this account, shortly after the crime one of the killers must have returned to shore to mail the identity card and the Pan Am advertisement to the Third Police Precinct in an unstamped envelope, no later than Monday morning. From the record it appears that at no point during the police investigation or the trial that followed it did anyone consider the possibility that the identity card (one of several that Polk carried) and the Pan Am advertisement were dropped by Polk's killers as they searched his body or at some other time and were found accidentally by someone not involved in the murder at all.

What Burdett and Secondari see as the most striking feature of the crime is its "deliberately sensational character," that is, the fact that, according to their reconstruction and the police hypothesis it reflects, it was important for the murderers not only to kill Polk but to make known the fact of his murder, first by mailing the identity card (and—for some reason they do not explain—the Pan Am advertisement), then by leaving other means of identification on the unweighted body so that when "the gases generated by decomposition lifted it again to the surface," Polk's identity would be unmistakable and, trussed up as he was, the murder would be seen as an "execution." Since "a dead body rises in from eight to fourteen days, depending on the temperature of the water," the murderers could count on at least a week's grace before the body would be discovered.

The other striking feature of the crime, according to Burdett and Secondari, was the speed with which it was prepared and committed: within forty-eight hours after Polk reached Salonika. Even if the Security Police were correct in their assumption that Polk had already made a first contact in Athens for his trip to Markos's headquarters and the projected interview that he apparently told friends in Athens could turn out to be "the story of the year" (so the *New York Herald Tribune* reported the day after his body was recovered), it would have been difficult for him to make a second contact in Salonika with the kind of "persons who count" in the Communist hierarchy who would be in a position actually to arrange the trip he had in mind on such short notice. Burdett and Secondari tell us that Communists in Salonika were under strict police surveillance and worked through "cells" that normally consisted of a single man. The CBS representatives therefore conclude that the Communists would not have introduced Polk to important persons in the hierarchy without "the greatest caution and most extensive checking." They also conclude that the likeliest possibility was that Polk walked into a trap which, in view of the short time it took him to find a Salonika "contact," must have been prepared well in advance by an organization in place and ready, but taking orders from "higher up" outside Salonika, surely from a place where Polk's movements and plans were known: "almost certainly, from Athens."

Burdett and Secondari emphasize that these conclusions are still "in the realm of surmise." It is still possible that Polk got in touch with bona fide Communists who really meant to take him to guerrilla territory and that the murder was an impromptu act that occurred either because Polk mistrusted his contacts (and presumably showed it), or because they mistrusted him, or maybe because his contacts decided he was too hot to handle. The presumption in any case is that the murder was political and that the organization best able to carry it out was the Communist Party (known locally as the KKE), "probably operating through one of its terrorist or sabotage branches," presumably on orders from the Communist hierarchy outside Salonika. The two other possibilities are one or another branch of the Greek police itself and "the small, ultra-right and royalist terrorist body known as 'X'," the latter weak in organization and amateurish in sabotage. Of the four branches of the police—gendarmerie, National Security, General Security (Mouskoundis's investigative branch), and the military police—the first three were then responsible for the investigation and were thought by the head of the British Police Mission in Salonika, Colonel Martin, to be so "well commanded and well-disciplined" as to "practically exclude the possibility of some inside 'conspiracy.'" Colonel Martin had considerable confidence in the men who headed these three branches; about the military branch he would "say only that he is 'not so sure.'" In any case, the colonel's confidence appears to have been persuasive with Burdett and Secondari.

Obviously from the local police perspective, the weight of suspicion fell on the Left rather than the Right, though Burdett and Secondari offered a possible motive for each, the motive of the former that of shifting the blame for the crime onto the government and—in the words of one police chief—thus blackening the name of Greece, the motive of the latter "to execute, as a warning to others, one of the most courageous and outspoken critics of the present Greek regime." As the Security Police saw it, the Communists still had an active organization in Salonika despite heavy police raids, and Salonika was the city closest to the guerrilla front. The Communists were also expert at sabotage. In fact, Major Mouskoundis claimed to have learned that in early May a right-hand aide of Markos known as "the Colonel" (later identified as Evangelos Vasvanas) came into Salonika for the purpose of sabotage and "pulled out" of town—as Burdett and Secondari put it—on May 8, the very day on which Polk disappeared. And the Security Police also had a report from Athens indicating that a query had been sent from Communist headquarters in the capital to their people in the north asking why Polk had been murdered and on whose instructions—though a similar report also appeared in what Burdett and Secondari call "the wholly untrustworthy Athens press," a fact which "may or may not make [the report] less true." Finally, the local police maintained that shooting a victim through the head from behind was "the standard practice of Communist executioners," and they were unable to recall a rightist murder carried out in that way.

The Burdett and Secondari report tells us that at this early stage of the investigation the local police were privately convinced that they were confronted by a Communist murder. But the police also insisted—and, the report says, "our feeling is that they are sincere in insisting"—that they did not exclude other possibilities and would follow all trails wherever they might lead. Burdett and Secondari conclude their tentative picture of the case by saying that they are personally satisfied that the

Salonika police are doing their best to find Polk's murderers—and "their best is reputedly very good," especially under the leadership of Major Mouskoundis, who has "the highest respect of American and British observers."

Part of the story of George Polk's last hours that doesn't appear in the Burdett-Secondari report or other State Department documents belongs to Rea Polk, as does much of the story of the days between Polk's murder and the discovery of his body. Rea Polk, a Greek citizen while married to Polk but later a naturalized American, is now a woman in her late fifties, twice widowed, mother of a son by her second husband, and though suffering from increasingly severe multiple sclerosis, still a woman who gives off the aura of strength and beauty that made her seem quite remarkable as Polk's bride at nineteen and his widow eight months later—what one early observer called a dark Mediterranean synthesis of Gene Tierney and Hedi Lamarr, but with larger, unprovocative eyes. As Rea Polk now recalls those days[17] (and her recollection has the lacunae one might expect to find almost forty years after an event that she would have every reason to want to push into the more obscure corners of her memory), she did not go to Kavalla as Polk had suggested in his telegram because the airport was still flooded but headed straight for Salonika on Wednesday ("Was it Wednesday? It must have been if the records say so.") and went to the Astoria Hotel to find her husband. What she actually found alarmed her immensely: two telegrams that she had sent her husband still unopened in Polk's mail slot at the hotel and his room there a complete mess. "George was so neat. He simply wouldn't have left his room that way."

It didn't occur to her immediately that somebody else must have left it that way, because the first thought that struck her as she looked around the room was that her husband couldn't have gone far since he'd left so much behind: all his extra clothes, his toilet articles, his camera, a scarf ("He never went out for long without his scarf because he had a chronic throat irritation. And he always carried his camera on an important news assignment.") She figured that whenever he had gone out, he must have planned on coming back soon. And then she found his three-day alarm clock, set as usual for waking at 6:30, still running, though it stopped soon after that. The undelivered telegrams worried her. And the unmailed letters she found dated May 8, the carbon copies still on the radiator. She decided she'd better notify the consulate.

Then, later that day, the news came that her husband's press identity card had turned up at a local police station, mailed in by somebody unidentified. And that night ("Or was it the following night?"), at 3:00

in the morning, two men in what appeared to be bloodstained shirts entered her room without warning, saying they were policemen, and they searched the room for a list of names that they said her husband must have left behind. They searched and searched, didn't find what they were looking for, and left her lying there, now scared to death. "I never did find out who those intruders were," Rea reports. Nor, evidently, did the police—at least not officially, not so that it would show in the record. One has to assume that these "policemen" were looking for evidence that would be useful either in helping or hindering the investigation. If the former, their method was crude, to say the least, as it was generally in their early encounters with Rea Polk. If the latter, they were part of a local conspiracy that no one following the case chose to pursue.

After this intrusion, Rea knew something was very wrong, something terrible must be happening, maybe had already happened, but she did her best to put up a brave front. She was aware that her husband's life had been threatened in many countries and that recently he'd sometimes received threats over the phone in Athens—though she always passed him the receiver when the call was for him, so she never knew what was said on the other end of the line or what kind of voice had done the threatening. And her husband was a man who had always lived dangerously whether in wartime or peacetime. He always had a gun at his bedside, and he never sat in a restaurant with his back to the door.

Rea consoled herself by thinking that maybe George Polk had gone off to meet the Communist leader Markos as the letter to Edward R. Murrow suggested—but would he have done so without the things he normally took with him on a trip of that kind? And if a newsgathering trip, what connection could that have with these awful-looking men who had come in to search his hotel room while he was gone? She now became afraid that her husband's terrible temper may have gotten him into serious trouble. Or his honesty—because not long before his trip north he had met with the leader of the right-wing Populist party in the coalition government, Constantine Tsaldaris, and had "blown his top," had threatened to expose Tsaldaris and what the right wing was up to in Greece, actually selling arms to their enemies the rebels and rigging the distribution of aid supplies and God knows what else. Maybe they had thought her husband was an enemy, as in the past they had thought other American correspondents to be enemies. She was only seventeen at the time—"Or was I eighteen?" (the State Department archive makes her out to have been twenty)—and she had to work hard to be brave, but that is what she tried to be during the days that followed, until Consul

General Raleigh Gibson appeared on Sunday and told her—rather undiplomatically, she thought—that her husband had been found, and when she'd asked: "Where? Where is he?" Raleigh Gibson had said: "He's dead."

Apparently Rea Polk appeared a bit too brave for some tastes. The day after Polk's body was recovered, Waide Condon of the United States Information Service in Salonika reported confidentially to Raleigh Gibson that during Rea's daily visits to his office after she reached the city she did not seem to him much perturbed about her husband's absence during that week.[18] She told him that her husband had regarded their vacation trip north as useful only for background purposes, and though she was now ready to believe that he may have gone "into rebel territory," she did not know of any connections he may have had with Communist guerrillas. She also confirmed what the consulate had learned from Herbert Lansdale of the American Mission in Athens: that Polk was suffering from old nose and head wounds and had been taking penicillin, in fact was afraid that he might have to be hospitalized in Salonika, as he certainly expected he would be when he and Rea returned to the United States later in the month. The implicit question was: would Polk have chosen to go on a mission as dangerous as that of visiting Markos with such a health problem on his mind? The likely answer from those who knew George Polk best was: certainly.

In his memorandum to Gibson, Waide Condon also revealed that after being notified of her husband's murder, Rea said that she believed "perhaps the Government could be behind his death" because of strong anti-government pieces Polk had written and because he had told Tsaldaris what his feelings were to the man's face. She was also reported to have said that her husband had often expressed his belief that he would die in the not-too-distant future, that he would never see California again but was not worried because "he had lived a much fuller life than had most young men of his age." According to Condon, Rea had remained optimistic through the Saturday before her husband's body surfaced and had not authorized an official investigation because she felt that even if her husband had found a way into rebel territory, "in due time he would return."

Condon sent Gibson a second confidential memorandum on Rea the following day, this one based on information his wife had picked up in conversation with her.[19] Rea again told Mrs. Condon that she was convinced the Greek government was responsible for her husband's death. For one, the Greek ambassador in Washington had tried to "get" Polk's job after he had furnished information to Drew Pearson for a broadcast in January "castigating the Greek Government." And Polk had complained to the authorities when packages from the U.S. were withheld from all Communist families in Greek villages, a thing that he had felt was wrong not from a political point of view but because those deprived were women and children. Finally, according to Condon's memorandum, Rea claimed that her husband had been "threatened many times— by the police." As far as she was concerned, Polk's body was "a definite 'plant,'" presumably by the police or other government agents, since in her view the Communists would never have let his body be found, anyway not before they had used a stone—every Greek boat carries one—"to skin" the body. And they would have taken his valuables, knowing that they would in any case be blamed for the murder. Also, why would the Communists have bothered to mail her husband's press identity card to the police? That too must have been a plant by the real murderers.

Rea Polk's early theory that some goverment agency was responsible for George Polk's murder found little support from any local quarter, domestic or foreign. State Department archives reveal that from the very start the most important Greek officials in Salonika expressed their preference for what came to be known as "the Communist angle" and gave little thought or credence to either "the right-wing angle" or "the British factor." And in this they assumed—not without reason—that they would find sympathy for their preference among the Americans, whose increased presence in Greece was, after all, a result of the Truman Doctrine, promulgated and financed with the specific aim of confronting Communist ambitions in Greece. But, as we have seen, from the start there was also an attempt by local officials to assure the Americans that the investigation of the Polk case would consider all angles and all factors.

The Salonika official who took on the crucial role of communicating with the American consulate about the Polk case, Attorney General for the Court of Appeals Panayotis Constantinidis, was the man who ended up serving as public prosecutor in the court case that emerged from the investigation that Major Mouskoundis conducted and that Constantinidis himself supervised. The attorney general has been described by acquaintances as a short, stocky, Edward G. Robinson type of old-time district attorney, but without Robinson's expressiveness and with a closer physical resemblance to Telly Savalas, head bald, face stony, eyes often blanked by wire-rimmed glasses, a man whose occasionally brusque manner revealed a tension in him between arrogance and insufficient self-confidence.

Five days after Polk's body surfaced, Constantinidis sought out Raleigh Gibson to give the consulate an updated account of the Polk investigation, and, by the way, to respond to what the attorney general took to be critical comments by one of the news associations (evidently quoted in the U.S. during a CBS broadcast) to the effect that the Salonika police had so far investigated only Communist suspects in the Polk case.[20] Constantinidis stated that in fact no Communists had been queried—an equally peculiar bit of news—and he assured Consul General Gibson that all avenues were being fully explored, on the basis of one of the four established hypotheses as to the origins of the crime: (1) right-wing extremists, (2) Communists, (3) Zionists, (4) a love affair. The latter two were being given "small importance," according to Gibson's secret cable report to the secretary of state, and there was no recorded mention here of a hypothetical "British factor" or a hypothetical government agency.

Constantinidis offered his belief that though one could not ignore the possibility that the right wing had murdered Polk, this possibility should be excluded because "Polk was murdered according to the typical way Communists execute their victims," by which he presumably meant what was to become a recurrent police argument in support of "the Communist angle," namely, that the assassin had shot his victim from behind rather than confronting his victim face to face. The attorney general stated that "no crime of the Right-wing was known to have been committed in the way that Polk was murdered." That it might have been committed in that way exactly in order to cover the Right and cast suspicion on the Left was evidently not among the hypothetical possibilities that either the attorney general or the consul general was prepared to entertain.

Mr. Constantinidis obviously preferred what Gibson himself labeled "the Communist angle." But the attorney general added a fifth hypothesis: professional jealousy. Maybe someone "desired Mr. Polk's position." Here he clearly had in mind Polk's assistant in Athens, *Christian Science Monitor* correspondent Kosta Hadjiargyris. The attorney general wondered why Hadjiargyris, who was Polk's closest friend in Athens, hadn't rushed to Salonika to be with Mrs. Polk as soon as word was received that Polk had disappeared. Hadjiargyris had shown up only after the body was recovered. And with this hypothesis, Constantinidis introduced for the first time what became his abiding candidate for an Athenian connection to the murder, a presumption reinforced in due course by explorations into Hadjiargyris's leftist background.

But it was "the Communist angle" more generally that dominated this early conversation with the American consul general. Constantinidis cited as further evidence in support of this supposition the fact that nobody had come forth to claim the 25 million drachma reward ($2,500) that had been offered for information regarding the murder. He argued that if the Communists knew that the right wing had committed the murder as their guerrilla radio and their various newspapers insisted, "some one of them would have rushed forward to claim the reward and expose the rightists to the world." Gibson remarks: "It can be seen that the Attorney General does not want to believe that the murder was caused by the Right-wing, and I am of the opinion that he is endeavoring to convince himself of the fact. However, I do not believe that he will suppress any information that would show that the Right-wing had committed the murder." He adds that a recent visitor to Salonika, Sir Charles Wickham, chief of the British Police and Prison Mission to Greece, fully agrees with him. Gibson concludes his report with the personal opinion that the investigation is being efficiently handled by the Security Police under Major Mouskoundis. The confidence in the local authorities, Greek and British, that these concluding remarks suggest has to be seen, anyway in retrospect, as our first evidence that Raleigh Gibson was either so naive as to be easily duped or so eager to cooperate with the Salonika authorities that he was less than sufficiently eager to scrutinize their detective work with objectivity and cunning.

Fortunately for the Salonika authorities, American officials in Athens not only appeared to share Gibson's confidence but evidently agreed with Attorney General Constantinidis's preferred hypothesis. Karl Rankin, chargé d'affaires of the American embassy, signed a duplicate of Gibson's secret cable without alteration,[21] and a few days later (May 25), the head of the American Mission for Aid to Greece, Dwight P. Griswold, then in Washington for consultation, gave a *New York Times* reporter his own personal opinion regarding the murder, evidently derived from secondary sources: "I feel that certain Communists are to blame." Those who focused on "the Communist angle" seemed to share the explanation of Communist motives that Greek officials offered from the start: killing Polk would serve to embarrass the Greek government and its new patron through negative publicity in the United States that the Communists hoped would so compromise American aid under the Truman Doctrine and the Marshall Plan as to neutralize its influence on the progress of the civil war, which some guerrilla leaders mistakenly thought they were close to winning decisively.

But there were others in Greece who held no office—along with Rea Polk, some local reporters and American journalists interested in the case—who thought it equally likely that Polk had been killed by agents or terrorists of the political Right, possibly with the connivance of the government in power (or anyway its right wing, as Rea Polk had suggested), possibly in cooperation with certain foreign interests—the British and even the newly arrived Americans not entirely excluded. The killing was presumed to have had the general aim of intimidating correspondents critical of the Greek establishment and the specific aim of preventing this particular American correspondent named Polk from broadcasting a possibly sympathetic account of the Communist enemy in the mountains were the interview with Markos to see the light of day. And in America Polk himself was brought back from the dead to support a version of this alternative hypothesis. In two "Washington Merry-Go-Round" columns published shortly after Polk's body was discovered,[22] Drew Pearson argued, on the basis of letters he had received from Polk some time before the murder, that the CBS correspondent, who was taken to have been severely critical of the Greek "rightist regime," had been "bumped off" because "dead men tell no tales." Pearson, quoting from what he identifies as Polk's letters to him, offers his readers a "tale" from George Polk's "blue, dead lips"—a "tale which may shake the graft-ridden Greek government to its rotten core" and will certainly "tell the American taxpayers what they are entitled to know about the millions of dollars they have dumped into Greece."

The tale told by Polk is in fact less one-sided than Pearson's rhetoric suggests, though it has its ominous implications. In his report to Pearson Polk first establishes his broad view of the situation in Greece: America is fighting a tough battle there; it is his feeling that "we should get in or get out, all the way." The situation is too grave for half measures, the political attitudes are dangerously extreme, and at the extremities, whether Communist or right-wing Populist, they are identical, at least in their propaganda, which charges the United States with interference in Greek internal affairs and with a desire to use the Greek people for the creation of an American empire. The ominous note is sounded when Polk is quoted as saying that "this kind of report" brings foreign correspondents under attack by "royalist right-wingers who are squeezing the country for their own benefit—and sending dollars out in diplomatic pouches," crooks who "hope to get a number of American reporters now working in Greece discredited or moved."

In the other "Washington Merry-Go-Round" column, Pearson shows Polk offering specifics on the theme of intimidation: the Royalist group known as the Populist party is "implementing a carefully devised offensive" against correspondents for American news outlets, including Polk himself, though he reports that his own treatment has so far been rather mild compared with the attack being made against other outspoken reporters on the scene. The first of these, says Polk, is Kosta Hadjiargyris of the *Christian Science Monitor*, for whom he has the highest respect professionally and who has been falsely accused by the Ministry of Foreign Affairs of drunkenness and of using offensive language. Another is Ray Daniell of the *New York Times*, unaccompanied by his wife and therefore, says Polk, open to malicious slander when his articles proved "displeasing for right-wing politicians." And another is Homer Bigart of the *New York Herald Tribune*, denounced as a Communist and ridiculed for supposedly " 'looking at things upside down.' " Polk writes: "The pattern of the right-wing's attack on the other American correspondents here is clever—public denunciation plus official refusal to allow a reporter to visit the civil war areas. . . . In addition, now that so many correspondents are writing such critical stories on the dominant right-wing faction of the government, there are a number of vague hints that 'somebody is likely to get hurt.' "

That Polk aligned himself with correspondents considered critical of the Greek government is suggested by another source, the long (some 140 pages) draft report prepared in October 1950, at the request of General Donovan by a junior member of his law firm, Mary G. Jones. This report on the Polk affair (subsequently referred to here as the Draft Report), though not submitted by Donovan to the Lippmann Committee nor made public in its complete form, sometimes provides information of value for our purposes and especially for clarifying Donovan's role in the Polk affair, as we shall see in chapter 10 below, where its broader implications are discussed. In this specific context, the Draft Report quotes Polk as saying that on several occasions he "felt the displeasure of the Greek authorities as a result of his reporting," and that, "lacking guts to attack us [that is, American correspondents in Greece who had been critical of the Greek government] openly, the Greek officials are working behind the scenes to get certain American reporters transferred or fired."[23]

In a dispatch to the *Christian Science Monitor* at the time of the murder, Kosta Hadjiargyris makes Polk's personal situation appear to have been less mild than Polk himself suggests in his own commentaries.[24] Hadjiargyris, whose job it was to review Polk's letters and reports to Pearson, to CBS, and to other news outlets and who had free access to Polk's study for this work, disclosed in his report that Polk had received several telephone calls in Athens from an unknown person who labeled him "a Communist" and who threatened to murder him if he didn't leave Greece. Unfortunately for Hadjiargyris neither Rea Polk nor anybody else close to Polk was able to substantiate these alleged threats to the satisfaction of the investigators, and almost from the start, Hadjiargyris, who was described by the police and others as himself a Communist with a highly dubious past that included helping to organize a leftist mutiny on his Royal Hellenic Navy corvette during World War II, found that he was an early and prime suspect in the Polk murder investigation. This was so even though the suspicion proved immensely awkward for the police investigators, because Hadjiargyris was the stepson of Themistocles Sophoulis, the Liberal prime minister then heading the coalition government in Athens, who had publicly stated as soon as Polk's murder was reported to him from Salonika that his government would "make every effort to discover the perpetrators of this atrocious deed and punish them relentlessly."[25]

The glimpse of Polk that the Pearson correspondence gives us, along with some of the details in the Burdett-Secondari report, seem characteristic of the man as he emerges from other sources, Rea Polk in particular. Named George Washington Polk after his father, who came from an old Virginia family distantly related to President James K. Polk, the CBS correspondent apparently prided himself on his forthrightness, his daring, on going wherever he had to go to get the news and then reporting it as he saw it. The *New York Herald Tribune* story on the discovery of Polk's body quotes Rea Polk as saying that her husband of eight months "felt he had had every experience in life and there was no new goal to look forward to."[26]

Polk had surely traveled much and lived dangerously after he quit Virginia Military Institute (the "family school," according to Rea) in his junior year to become a newspaperman: city editor in Alaska, correspondent in Shanghai and Paris, instructor at New York University (after taking a degree at the University of Alaska), navy pilot in the South Pacific, White House reporter, finally overseas correspondent for CBS radio with a number of key assignments in the Near and Middle East. As Rea remembered it recently, her husband had gotten himself thrown out of place after place because of his passion for telling the truth: Alaska, Japan, West Germany, she couldn't recall where else. And through his commitment to dangerous adventure, whether in the line of duty or for professional advancement, he was always getting himself banged up and then somehow coming out of it more or less whole and with some glory. He was wounded twice during World War II and had stomach problems after that which made him eat slowly. The one time he got into real trouble, when the plane he was piloting crashed into one of the smaller Solomon Islands still under Japanese occupation, he was saved by head-hunters who led him from village to village until he reached a place patrolled by American planes where he was eventually picked up and returned to Guadalcanal. Then he caught malaria, shipped out to a hospital in the States, received a presidential citation. And Rea remembers another high moment, while he was a correspondent in Palestine: the plane he was in crashed into an olive tree in Jerusalem and he came out of that with a badly broken nose but also with "his best news interview ever," dictated from the operating table for a broadcast by CBS, with publicity photographs of him all bandaged up like a hero. She still thinks of him as something of a hero, certainly the most charming—if sometimes the most difficult—man she has known.

In other photographs from the time of his tour in the Middle East, Polk looks like a version of F. Scott Fitzgerald before drink made Fitzgerald pudgy—but with a distinctly broken nose, even after plastic surgery. "The George Polk I married was a physical wreck," Rea says, with a tiny smile, "only I didn't know it then" (she never called him "George" like everybody else in those days, she called him "Gee"—with a hard "G"—but now, forty years after his death, she often refers to him in conversation as "George Polk," almost as though he has become a character in somebody else's fiction). George Polk would have nightmares "every night." They usually involved a dialogue with dead friends. "See, I'm alive," George Polk would say to them. And the friends would answer: "No, we're alive and you're the one who's dead." He was very jumpy sometimes, very alert too, always on the lookout for the unexpected—or maybe the expected.

But if he never quite got used to living on the edge of danger, Rea thinks he also never stopped enjoying it. And he had a sense of the dramatic gesture, a taste for the unusual. Rea remembers the evening in 1947, following on their quick and hot summer romance, when he took her out to dinner and while the two of them were sitting there gazing into each other's eyes, he reached in his pocket and produced a single airplane ticket to the United States with his name on it, dated for the next day. Rea began to cry. George Polk said there was only one thing in the world that could keep him from using that ticket: Rea's saying yes to the idea of his marrying her. Rea studied him, then said yes to the idea, then stopped crying. And after the wedding, he took her to Cairo where he'd rented a floor in a 400-year-old Mamluk Palace in the Muslim district of Cairo ("a great slum area—and you know what that means in Cairo"), a place that had built-in furniture decorated in the traditional Muslim way and that she was sure cost him a pretty penny but that her friends thought implausible and that one lady visitor, an ambassadress of some kind, thought disgusting after she went into what was called the toilet and found only a hole in the floor.

George Polk came to Greece with more than the abiding problem of his war wounds and his broken nose ("He told me when we first met that he'd already known enough pain for two lifetimes," Rea said): there was his broken first marriage and his temper, a match for his daring—a "terrible temper," according to Rea. She actually told the *Baltimore Sun* at the time of the murder that she suspected this temper is what did Polk in.[27] She said her husband "may have got mad. He talked back to everybody," and this may have led him into "an argument with an underground guide" who then shot him. As she described her husband at the time for the *New York Herald Tribune*, that was a thing that would not have surprised him: he was a "fatalist who often said his time was coming to an end" and who actually had a premonition of his death just before leaving her in Athens for his fatal trip north.[28] In the same *Herald Tribune* interview Rea was quoted as saying that her husband had been threatened by Arabs and Jews in Palestine but never by Communists in Greece. That was a remark the police investigators clearly did not take to any more than they did to her claim that Polk had been threatened by one or another agency of the Greek government or to Kosta Hadjiargyris's claim that Polk had received a threatening phone call in Athens from someone unknown labeling him a Communist.

Rea did not tell the American newspapers about the "spat" with her husband that had led to her abandoning her vacation trip north with him, but the Greek newspapers somehow got hold of that detail and called it a quarrel, and then the local investigators picked up on the question and tried to use it to develop the possibility of a serious conflict in the Polk marriage. As Rea recalls the "spat," she simply felt that it was silly for the two of them to take a trip like that just two weeks before they were due to leave more or less permanently for a new life in the United States and when she still had much to do to get ready, having managed by that time to pack only half their effects, "such as my mother's silver and china." Then Polk had said to her that if she wasn't going, he wouldn't go either, but he had changed his mind at the last minute and had slipped out early on Friday morning after packing his own things and saying goodbye to her father, in whose Athens apartment they were then living. She feels now that his last-minute decision shows that the idea of a possible trip to Markos's headquarters was an afterthought. "He wouldn't have tried to get me to go north with him if that was what he'd had in mind all along. I was a young girl. He would have wanted to protect me from any danger."

For their part, the Salonika authorities appeared not so much interested in protecting Rea after the murder as in linking her in some way to the still undefined conspiracy that they saw lurking behind the event. Two days after Polk's body was brought up out of Salonika Bay, Rea was interrogated in Salonika by Attorney General Constantinidis in the Hotel Cosmopolite, where she had moved to be in the company of AP stringer Helen Mamas. During this interview, as it was reported home by the American consulate, Rea did not add much to what she had already told Condon and Gibson except to emphasize her curiosity about finding Polk's three-day alarm clock still "set to ring at 6:30–7:00 a.m." and working on Wednesday when she reached his hotel room.[29] She spoke again about their planned vacation trip, the telegrams he had sent her, the letters and other personal effects she had found in the hotel room, his belief—evidently shared by most foreign correspondents—that a meeting with Markos would result in a great news story. She also mentioned that her husband had asked her to bring along a package of clothing for a poor Greek family he had met in Salonika the previous August, but she had forgotten to do so. She concluded her brief deposition by saying that her husband was "a man of strong character, dynamic," and that he did not pay much attention to his meals, normally eating "very little" both at midday and at night.

This deposition seems innocuous enough after Condon's earlier memoranda and Rea's own personal recollections recorded then and years later, but at the time it apparently did not so appear either to Attorney General Constantinidis or to Consul General Gibson. Constantinidis told Gibson, during a conversation a few days after the Hotel Cosmopolite interview with Rea, that "there are many things being examined, and it is my personal opinion that the young lady has not been honest in her statements or in her depositions."[30] For example, she had quarreled with her husband just before his trip north but had provided no details regarding this quarrel. And Constantinidis had been "informed" that when news of her husband's death was given her, she first asked: "Was he killed?" and then asked: "Did he commit suicide?" Constantinidis clearly did not like the young widow's attitude. It seems likely that he also did not much like her speculation about government involvement in the murder, in particular her statement that the police had threatened her husband. The attorney general indicated that he preferred the attitude of Rea's father, who "had impressed him with his sincerity" and who had stated that he knew nothing of any threats against Mr. Polk. Besides, Constantinidis said, Mrs. Polk had told him that her statement about these presumed threats was based not on first-hand information but on something she'd been told by a friend in Athens.

State Department archives do not give us a clear image of Consul General Gibson's response to the attorney general on this occasion, but there are hints that Gibson did not remain diplomatically neutral regarding Rea Polk.[31] A day after the Constantinidis interview he sent the secretary of state a confidential cable that included the sentence: "Strong belief that Hadjiargyris has knowledge that would help out investigation, and same is felt regarding Mrs. Rea Polk." And two days later he sent another cable that quoted in full the views of the newspaper *Phos* (Light) to the effect that Polk had quarreled with his wife before his departure for Salonika, and his wife's evident attitude of "indifference" was still "unexplained."[32] According to the news story, Rea didn't worry when her husband disappeared, or even when his body was found, but "spoke without much sympathy" and said her husband had become " 'mad,' " explaining that his temper was due to neurasthenia resulting from a wound he had received in Palestine in a plane crash. And the news story went on to speak of Hadjiargyris and the free access he (and of course Rea) had to Polk's study, from which correspondence was now discovered to be missing. A cable from Gibson three days later shows us that the stage had now been set for the Athens phase of the investigation that was to follow, its principal concern the attempt to establish an Athenian connection to the murder: "As a result conference held by Attorney General, Chief of Security Police and three other officials flying to Athens Wednesday with all documents on Polk case. Chief Security Police will reexamine Mrs. Rea Polk and Hadjiargyris. He also will plan to contact leftist friends of Hadjiargyris."[33]

Given the aura of the times, the quick assumptions of the Salonika authorities, and the inbred predispositions of Mouskoundis and Constantinidis in particular, it can be taken as something other than mere perversity that within two weeks after Polk's body surfaced in Salonika Bay, his young wife of eight months and his closest Greek friend and colleague had become the principal suspects for an Athenian connection to his murder. Less explicable, though again perhaps a sign of imminent McCarthyism, is the apparent collaboration of American authorities— initially Gibson, Rankin, and Griswold—in the local effort to direct the investigation down the particular avenue it took from the start, maybe even during the week before the body was recovered. But what is perhaps the hardest to understand are those early signs of an easy collaboration between Polk's two CBS colleagues Burdett and Secondari and the local authorities in establishing the circumstances of the murder and the likeliest culprits, especially when there were ample grounds for regarding the official account of things with a large measure of skepticism. Of course neither the Greek authorities, their American and British advisers, nor the press representatives on the spot could be expected to have known all that was going on around them, let alone all that was going on behind the scenes. And they certainly could not have suspected that they were dealing with the kind of complicated case that would become a metaphor—in Greece almost a folk fable—for the miscarriage of justice that allies in a common cause can create when they are governed in their separate ways by some combination of excessive power, distorting prejudice, and aggressive self-promotion.

III The War and the Press

WHEN GEORGE POLK reached Salonika in the spring of 1948, those living in the city or near it had good reason to feel as edgy as they often showed themselves to be, the local authorities perhaps most of all since they could regard themselves as under sentence of death should the rebel forces prevail. The aura from the official point of view was that of a city besieged by hidden barbarian forces. There was a strict curfew after 6:00 P.M., which effectively prevented the young from going into the surrounding hills for more or less private romance or heading for the beaches that lined one long arc of the bay, and it prevented the rest of Salonika from entering the outlying regions for work or pleasure, anyway during the late hours. No one without official permission got beyond the checkpoint at the army barracks a mile or so beyond the "Depot" where the archaic tram lines turned around, and if you lived outside those limits, you stayed home after dark.

The curfew and the army cordon did not keep the guerrillas in the hills outside the city from penetrating its defenses. At one point artillery shells somehow reached the Hotel Cosmopolite on a central street in town, and at another point a bus transporting air force personnel was blown up well within the city limits. Outside the cordon, the war touched even those villages that in peacetime gradually became residential suburbs. There were regular accounts of action involving guerrilla bands and army units on the slopes of the mountain that shapes a high backdrop to the city, Mt. Hortiati—accounts of raids that were matched by raids and atrocities that were matched by atrocities. A severed head would suddenly appear on one of the outdoor tables in front of a village taverna, and the local inhabitants who were able to identify it as belonging to a supporter either of the Left or of the Right could count on finding another severed head belonging to someone of the opposite persuasion in the same place a few days later. When a photograph of the clustered heads of three guerrilla women hanging by their hair from a soldier's saddle as trophies appeared in the British press, the then prime minister in Athens, Tsaldaris, explained that "exposing severed heads" was an old Greek custom that he would do what he could to prevent in the future, at least in the case of female enemies.[1]

The village named after Mt. Hortiati seemed especially vulnerable—perhaps, some thought, because of its star-crossed history. During the German Occupation of World War II, the village had been the setting for a massacre occasioned when a German military "doctor" (as the local inhabitants called him) and his soldier companions were ambushed by resistance forces as the German soldiers were on their way to their weekly task of adding chlorine or some other purifying chemical to one of the main sources of water in the region.[2] "They were doing that for our benefit as well as theirs," one old-time rightist villager asserted when asked to recount the episode. "But who cares about that forgotten fact now?" One version of the story, told by a leftist resistance fighter who was at the scene, has the soldiers ambushed as the military vehicle they were in climbed toward the village, the attack a well-planned resistance operation by the leftist EAM guerrillas[3] camped above the village. In the rightist old-timer's version, there were only two German soldiers in the area, not a carload, and these were attacked by leftist guerrillas who came out of hiding on the mountain and caught the soldiers off guard while they were at their work of purifying water in a ravine where the water source was located. The "doctor" was killed, but his companion escaped to carry news of the ambush home to the German forces for reprisal.

Within hours the villagers watched truckloads of German soldiers wind up the road to the village and begin burning it down with help from the Greek Security Battalions that certain misguided Greeks had created with German support to fight Communism—"the worst kind of Greeks, collaborators, bums," said the rightist old-timer. Most of the villagers were already on their way to the surrounding hills. Some of those who hadn't gotten the word soon enough were slaughtered as they tried to escape—many by the Security Battalion forces, the old-timer said. "Those so-called Greeks would grab women, children, the elderly, anybody they could catch, then slit their throats, then let the German soldiers shoot them dead." The villagers who found themselves trapped or who chose to stay behind in the village for one reason or another were finally rounded up and crammed into the local bakery, and after some flammable powder was spread on the floor, were roasted to death—except for one woman who clawed her way out of a rear window and escaped to tell the tale. When the villagers in the hills returned to the village some two months later, after the German forces had withdrawn from Greece in defeat, they found only ashes and bones left to identify the dead. The old-timer didn't blame the Germans so much as the guerrilla "andartes" who had come down from the mountains to start the whole business. "They knew what to expect from the Occupation forces if they killed a German soldier in cold blood. Those Communist andartes had their own reasons for bringing destruction down on our heads."

And there were other harsh episodes on Hortiati later, during one or another round of the civil war. The local gendarmerie—"or was it an army unit?" the old-timer asked himself—caught three Communist guerrillas and cut off their heads for a display they set up in the village square. He himself had witnessed that, and he'd also witnessed the consequences of another episode: a band of guerrillas had slipped into the outskirts of the village and had gang-raped a village girl before murdering her and her sister, who had been nursing a baby nearby. At least the baby was saved, he said, though it grew up without being right in the head. And the old-timer knew of at least three villagers who had been abducted as children by the Communist guerrillas and taken off "to the north." One was reported to be in Bulgaria still, working in a factory. Another had come back, but few people ever saw him. One village Communist who didn't leave survived the civil war and remained loquaciously active in village politics until he lost his voice, which didn't really matter, according to the old-timer, because by then the Socialist government in Athens had given him a medal as a veteran of the "national struggle," and he could wear that loudly on his lapel as he walked stoop-shouldered through the village to the gibes of those who knew him for what he was.

The "national struggle" that left such a residue of bitterness in the village of Hortiati more than forty years after the fact had actually begun to move relentlessly toward a resolution by the time George Polk reached Salonika in May 1948, though the besieged residents of the city could not be sure of that then, especially since the arrival of American military aid in support of the Greek army had not yet changed the rhythm of the war in ways that showed clearly. The guerrilla forces under Markos—still well equipped by neighbors to the north, morale still reasonably high—continued to harass the Greek army with hit-and-run tactics wherever it could effectively do so. Much of Greece remained under threat of rebel attack, and not only Salonika but the capital itself had begun to feel vulnerable, the Communist forces having proven audacious enough to plant a band of guerrillas on Mt. Parnitha above the outskirts of Athens. To most Communist guerrillas it still seemed that their dream of taking over the country and bringing in a "revolutionary" regime was possible despite the increasing strength of government forces as a result of the new Truman Doctrine aid program. If clear-cut victories were sparse, the guerrillas nevertheless felt that, with their own continuing aid from Albania, Yugoslavia, and Bulgaria, and with Russia behind these, they were more than a match for the Greek army and its foreign advisers, new and old.

What the Greek Communists did not know at the time was that their fate had come not only under the influence of the American military mission, which had already brought in Helldiver aircraft to blast away at their mountain retreats with increasingly devastating results, but also under the influence of internecine conflicts within the Communist ranks. The first conflict was between Markos Vafiadis and Nikos Zachariadis, the chief leaders of the guerrilla forces, as to proper strategy, Markos defending standard guerrilla tactics by small units, Zachariadis calling for the creation of a more formally organized army and more centralized military operations. Zachariadis won the debate, and—as most historians now agree—thereby lost both the possibility of a military victory for the rebel forces and, because of his orthodox dogmatism, any chance of a negotiated political settlement, but there are also those historians who believe that Markos did not in fact object strongly to the "static warfare" concept introduced by Zachariadis and recorded his reservations only at a later date in order to shift blame for the Communist defeat onto his colleague.

The major cause of the defeat in any case appears to have been the product of a second internecine conflict that was outside the control of the Greek Communist Party: the Tito-Stalin confrontation that would serve, within less than a year, to seal the Greek-Yugoslav border at Tito's direction and effectively cut off both a major sanctuary and much of the aid the Greek rebels were receiving from other northern Communist neighbors. There is now some evidence that not only Tito but Stalin too had decided at an even earlier stage, in order to discourage a Balkan Communist federation under Tito's leadership and to protect his grip on Eastern Europe, that the Greek Communists had to carry on their struggle as best they could without direct Russian support—anyway without the kind of support that his Anglo-American allies of World War II might consider a Soviet invasion of the Anglo-American zone of influence, which, as the latest scholarship would have it, had included Greece in exchange for Russian dominance in Romania, Bulgaria, Hungary, and Yugoslavia.[4]

By the fall of 1948, the Greek guerrilla forces—whose leaders had chosen to side with Russia against Tito—were essentially on their own, and Markos Vafiadis, succeeded by Nikos Zachariadis, had long since retreated into Albania with a few loyal followers. By the late summer of 1949, after the costly Grammos-Vitsi battles that the American general Van Fleet helped to supervise and measurably influence with his Hell-

divers and 114 napalm strikes,[5] the Communist forces were in full retreat to whatever sanctuary they might find beyond the northern borders, Zachariadis leading three thousand of his remnant guerrilla army
into Albania.

But in the spring of 1948, the "national struggle" still appeared not the
struggle for survival by guerrilla forces that it soon became but one of the
guerrillas consolidating their dominance over many rural areas of Greece
while extending their threat to the towns and, at least psychologically,
to the major cities. The government was still on the defensive politically
and militarily, however much better its image under the Liberal party
Prime Minister Sophoulis and however much better its prospects for
defeating the enemy under the new American military aid program. In
late 1947 and early 1948 the sides were still sharply drawn, both convinced that the struggle was now one of life and death, neither side
permitting room for dissent. Their mood painted the political climate of
Salonika in primary colors; the sea might be as brilliant as ever on a clear
day and Olympus across the Gulf a high purple monument with a rose
halo worthy of the gods, but all thought relating to the civil war had
become black and white. With the city still threatened as it was, in
matters of politics, no shading could be allowed, even for foreigners: you
were either with us or against us—and so it was to remain to the bitter
end and into the years beyond.

This uncompromising mood in wartime Salonika and in Greece generally promoted an attitude of suspicion and sometimes of open hostility,
both in local officials and in the public, toward foreign correspondents,
in particular those American correspondents who chose to view the
Greek government critically, whether their criticism was directed at the
government's policies or at the practice of certain of its agencies. The
attitude of suspicion was often reflected by American officials in Greece
who were pledged to support the Greek government's war against the
Communist forces, however perceptive these officials may have been
regarding that government's limitations in furthering democratic principles and whatever the degree of their own commitment to those principles, contingencies that too often depended on the distorted vision of the
individual in question. As we shall see, relations between the American
embassy in Athens and American correspondents in Greece became increasingly hostile as the civil war progressed, and the growing tensions
between American diplomats (whether in Greece or in Washington) and
American press representatives assigned to cover the war unfortunately
helped to create the kind of dangerous climate for journalists, both
American and Greek, that George Polk outlined in his correspondence

with Drew Pearson. This climate very likely influenced George Polk's fate, as it clearly influenced the investigation that followed his murder, though the CBS correspondent himself was generally well-disposed, if sometimes ambivalent, toward both the Greek government that had recently taken shape in Athens and the new American aid program under the Truman Doctrine.

What George Polk felt about the political and economic context of the civil war and about the American aid program was more than hinted at in his quoted correspondence with Drew Pearson, but a broader state-ment of his views appears in an article he wrote for the December 1947 issue of *Harper's Magazine*, based largely on what he had gathered in Greece that fall. In the article he sees the Greek "problem," testing ground for current American foreign policy, as one of "prewar poverty compounded by appalling wartime destruction." He also sees the post-war complications of a rigged economy run by thirty-five families that serve 2 percent of the population and, until recently, a corrupt rightist government that blatantly favors the few and mismanages an economy already devastated by inflation, limited natural and agricultural re-sources, and a trade imbalance like no other in Europe. Given the civil war raging between a now bloated Greek army—"the single properly-functioning organ of the Greek government"—and a determined Com-munist guerrilla force amply supported by Greece's northern neighbors, and given the political and economic instability, Greece may well "in-vite the appearance of a Strong Man—from either the right or the left."

The Strong Man, Polk tells his readers, could turn out to be one of two leading figures with last names beginning with Z. The first is right-wing Napoleon Zervas, minister of order in a recent Royalist cabinet, who directed a ruthless campaign against the government's opponents and who has the backing of the "British-organized Greek gendarmerie force," which Polk says still includes many officers and men who "did police duty for the Germans during the occupation," presumably as part of the notorious Security Battalions that so enraged the old-timer from the village of Hortiati. The second Z is the Moscow-trained secretary general of the Communist party, Nikos Zachariadis, resident of prison camps under both the Greek dictator Metaxas and the Germans at Dachau. The one thing that might prevent either of these extreme possibilities, both of which "could undoubtedly start another war," is the aid program of the American Mission to Greece. In view of the ordinary Greek's distaste for politicians in Athens—"all the crooks in Greece are in the govern-ment," a villager told the CBS correspondent—Polk feels that American Mission officials have been right to insist bluntly on supervision of all expenditures and to install themselves, with executive authority, in Greek ministries. The Griswold Mission "has had to use dynamic methods," he tells his readers. Mission officials "have refused to mince words."

Among the things the Mission didn't mince words about, according to Polk, was the Greek government in power when America provided $3 million in military and economic aid under the Truman Doctrine. Loy Henderson was rushed to Athens by the State Department "to tell the Greeks that they had better clean up their government politically" or "a disgusted American public opinion" might force the withdrawal of the aid program. This served to bring down Tsaldaris's rightist government and to make way for the coalition government of Themistocles Sophoulis, an event that, in Polk's view, was "a triumph for the Griswold Mission's farsighted, practical thinking."

But even with Sophoulis's more liberal policies, which included an offer of amnesty to the guerrillas and the release of "most concentration camp prisoners" (that is, leftists of various kinds held for reindoctrination on the prison island of Makronisos and elsewhere), as well as needed economic measures such as a rationing program, an attack on the high cost of living, currency restrictions and import controls, will Sophoulis be able, Polk asks, to conquer the "ineptitude, inefficiency, and corruption" that have "permeated the Greek government" for years? Anyway, it is a beginning, Polk indicates. And to argue that the United States should not " 'interfere' " in Greece "is foolish." Once the commitment has been made, the only remaining question in his view is whether the program is what it ought to be. The current allocation is "a poor investment" because it is "either vastly too much or vastly too little." Polk concludes: "the United States is now learning both that the treadmill of Balkan affairs is easier to board than abandon and that the treadmill cannot be ridden half on and half off."

Polk's view of the Greek political situation apparently remained ambivalent until the time of his death, and his optimism regarding the new Greek government continued to be qualified. In his last dispatch from Greece, dated May 4, 1948, he wrote: "The Greek situation is neither all black nor all white. Certainly, in comparison with Soviet-dominated Balkan countries, Greece is wonderfully free. Yet, judged by United States standards, Greece is sadly lacking in some of democracy's better features. Perhaps the best descriptive color for Greece is grey. It is only fair to report, however, that for a country fighting a civil war, Greece enjoys remarkable freedom. Yet Greece is in the grip of politicians who are amazingly unwilling to serve anybody except themselves. Black market dealings constitute one of the biggest businesses in the country. . . ."[6] But in view of Polk's generally positive attitude toward the American Mission and his hope for a new beginning in the Sophoulis administration, there was little in the *Harper's* article that American officials on the scene might have taken exception to, certainly nothing in his commentary that might lead one to anticipate the harassment that he later felt himself and other correspondents subject to, as reported in his correspondence with Drew Pearson. From the text of Polk's *Harper's* article one would gather that in the fall of 1947 he was little concerned with the kind of local American deficiencies that some months later would lead him to speak to Pearson of "our poorly informed American Embassy." And we have on record one largely favorable response to the *Harper's* article from an American official then centrally involved with the aid program. The coordinator for aid to Greece and Turkey in Washington, George C. McGhee, received an advance copy of the text from John Fischer of Harper and Row late in November 1947. McGhee wrote Fischer to say that the piece was "very interesting" and that it both "represents a perfectly valid viewpoint" and "brings out considerable new information"[7]—so much so, it seems, that McGhee decided to send a copy to Governor Dwight Griswold, chief of the American Mission in Athens.

The only aspect of the article that McGhee questions is Polk's expressed fear "that the present army in Greece might, in the event of economic collapse, fall under the domination of either Communist or Rightist leadership" and might then "embark on some adventure of conquest in the Balkans." McGhee argues that supplies would be inadequate for such an adventure—and in any case what supplies there are come from U.S. Greek Aid funds, which would eventually dry up without the possibility of being easily replaced. McGhee does not think the Greek economy would ever support such an operation, and he adds the revealing comment that "Greek confidence is at a low ebb and such an undertaking would serve to turn world sympathies, on which they now live, against them." As it turned out, the Greek sensitivity to sympathies outside Greece that McGhee shrewdly perceives here was to become a dominant theme, and a distorting influence, in the investigation of Polk's murder.

But if McGhee's response to Polk's political analysis is largely uncritical, his letter to Polk's editor at Harper and Row shows another face that indeed anticipates the tension that was to develop—in fact, that was already well advanced in some quarters—between American officials in Athens and correspondents arriving to cover the civil war and to report on the new aid program, a tension that finally led to the characterization of Polk and other American newsmen as irresponsible troublemakers. In the body of his letter McGhee comments on an awkward episode that was the likely cause of McGhee's quick reply to Fischer and that, in any case, clearly did not serve to endear the CBS correspondent to Governor Dwight Griswold and other officials of the Athens diplomatic mission. It seems that Polk, on returning to Greece by plane in late October from a trip abroad (a little over a month after his marriage to Rea), found himself held in quarantine for five days on St. George's Island near the port of Piraeus along with some fellow passengers on his plane and a larger group from the SS *Saturnia*. During his days on the island Polk evidently initiated a formal protest about sanitary conditions there and, according to McGhee, "the alleged failure of the Embassy and of the Mission properly to have looked after the interests of those placed under quarantine." The protest petition, signed by "most, if not all," of the *Saturnia* passengers, was addressed to the secretary of state in Washington, the American embassy in Athens, and the chief of the American Mission. A copy was to have been sent to newspaper correspondents in Athens but was subsequently withdrawn "at the insistence of one of the Saturnia passengers."

Before leaving the island, Polk evidently told another *Saturnia* passenger that he was going to write a story for the December number of *Harper's* describing the conditions on the island and the "hardships sustained by those under quarantine." McGhee tells Fischer that he doesn't know if Polk still plans to carry out his intention and that McGhee personally has no desire "to discourage any publication of facts arising out of this incident," but he wants to share several enclosures with Fischer that outline the steps taken by the embassy and the Mission on behalf of the passengers involved—steps that Polk may not have been in a position to know and that resulted, according to Governor Griswold himself, in expressions of appreciation to the embassy and the Mission on the part of several *Saturnia* passengers.

Polk did not write his story of bad sanitation and other hardships suffered on St. George's Island, but the tension between him and American officials in Greece that we sense here and see clearly in the Pearson correspondence was not simply a product of his "terrible temper," as his young wife might have put it. It was symptomatic of a conflict that already had a substantial history and that some took to be the root cause of Polk's murder in that it gave those extremists he and other correspondents chose to view critically an excuse to think that newsmen of his stripe were personae non gratae not only to the Right in Greece but to the country's new American patrons. In any case, the conflict proved to have an alarming influence on the course of the Polk affair. Its history can be traced back at least to 1946–47 and the final months of Lincoln MacVeagh's second stint as American ambassador in Greece, during the third and increasingly bitter round of the civil war. MacVeagh, Harvard roommate of G. Hall Roosevelt (Eleanor Roosevelt's brother) and classical scholar, had served as American minister to Greece from 1933 to 1941—the embassy was then a legation—and had returned as ambassador to Greece and Yugoslavia in 1943, while the Greek government was in exile in Cairo. White-haired, sharp-nosed, elegant, he was a man of much learning and style, self-assured, conservative politically, old-school in most ways, which included the quality of his devotion to both America and Greece. He did not suffer the unlettered or the unkempt gladly, and he evidently thought most American reporters either illiterate boors or irresponsible sensation seekers—an extravagant view apparently apt in some instances.

MacVeagh's distress over the conduct of correspondents in Greece appears in several cables marked "SECRET" that he sent his secretary of state between October and the end of December 1946.[8] The ambassador focused on three targets in particular, Seymour Freidin of the *New York Herald Tribune*, Robert Conway of the *New York Daily News*, and John Phillips, a photographer for *Life* magazine. The first of these is said to have been described by "friends" as a man who was "personally unhappy for one reason or another, very ambitious, and with a grievance against society," characteristics that MacVeagh tells his secretary of state apply to "the majority of American correspondents," who move in and out of Greece as trouble threatens or fades and who never stay long enough to acquire a background knowledge of the country, "even if that were within their capabilities." Conway is presented as a more complicated case. On the one hand, he confronted certain members of the embassy staff (sent specifically to feel him out) with "a long diatribe" against rightist atrocities, the Greek army, the Department of State, and the Athens embassy in particular, which he called "stupid and incompetent." On the other hand, when asked by the embassy staff members what he thought was the basic issue at stake in Greece, he replied: "Communist infiltration in preparation for attack." His principal criticism of U.S. and British policy in Greece was that it lent support to Greek government terror and was serving to drive "centrists into the arms of the extreme left."

Those in authority at the time might well have taken Conway's remarks as reflecting a biased and oversimplified view of the then current situation in Greece, but it was hardly an eccentric view, even in 1946, and it has been shared by many other students of the situation then and now. In any case, it is insufficient evidence for what MacVeagh calls Conway's "bibulous truculence" and "leftist slant." One suspects that the source of the ambassador's rhetoric is more personal than political. He tells the secretary of state that though one military member of his staff thinks Conway a "sensation-seeker" who will always be leftist in a rightist country and rightist in a leftist country, he himself prefers to think of Conway as "a social misfit, obsessed with an unhealthy consciousness of class," and this on the basis of an episode that the ambassador narrates in some detail. Apparently Alexander "Shan" Sedgwick, Athens correspondent for the *New York Times*, reported to MacVeagh that he had recently found Mr. Conway "under the influence of liquor" in the press room of the Ministry of Foreign Affairs, where a group of newsmen and officials had gathered in an effort to find out exactly where King of the Hellenes George II, restored to his throne by a plebiscite and due back that day, had chosen to reenter the country. Sedgwick reported to the ambassador that on this occasion Conway "loudly declaimed against the King of Greece, charging him with being a 'coward' for landing at the Eleusis Airport secretly and hastening aboard a destroyer." When Sedgwick told Conway bluntly that he had "no manners," Conway practically "burst out crying," reports MacVeagh, and "accused Mr. Sedgwick of 'belonging to the same class as the Lowells and Cabots.'" Since he might well have accused Ambassador MacVeagh of belonging to the same class, one can see why Conway evidently made two enemies with a single discharge, not counting the king of Greece.

Ambassador MacVeagh concludes his cable to the secretary of state with his own blast against editors who employ agents such as Conway and Freidin, the type who can renege on an appointment with the American ambassador—as these two evidently had done—because "they think the hotel bar is a better source of information than the ambassador's office." And, as a coda, he offers the secretary of state an ounce of rather petulant faith: "While believing, as an American, in the freedom of the press, I also believe that, like every freedom, this carries with it certain obligations, and that befuddling opinion according to the ideological bias of individual reporters, or their desire to get their reports featured, is not one of these."

John Phillips, the *Life* photographer, got on the wrong side of Ambassador MacVeagh for reasons that, seen from MacVeagh's point of view, appear quite legitimate; but they also serve to underline the ambassador's prejudices regarding reporters and his increasing ideological rigidity. Phillips and the United Press correspondent Robert Vermillion—"a decided Leftist," says MacVeagh, "like other correspondents here"—evidently borrowed a Greek War Relief jeep that was painted white, presumably as though an ambulance, decorated it with an American flag, drove it into "bandit territory," and then abandoned it there to proceed on foot in order to photograph and interview the guerrilla leader Skoufas and his small band of andartes in their hideaway. The abandoned jeep caused one segment of the Greek press to announce erroneously that the two reporters had been killed or captured by the guerrillas and another segment, more to the right, to publish a squib claiming that the two Americans were "in reality travelling under Moscow direction." But it wasn't the escapade by itself that brought on the ambassador's ire so much as the potentially dangerous generalizations about the civil war that Phillips brought back with him on the basis of this single interview with a single guerrilla leader, generalizations that MacVeagh feared would accompany the correspondent's photo-story for *Life*. For example, Phillips saw the "bandits" as "merely simple peasants who have taken spontaneously to the hills to escape government persecution," an image that was the consequence of the man's "abysmal lack of background," in particular, his ignorance of the fact—according to MacVeagh—that banditry had been chronic in Greek history. The essential new element in the civil war, MacVeagh asserted, was not persecution by the rightist Tsaldaris government then in power but "Communist and foreign incitement."

This is a position that some revisionist historians would take to be both an oversimplified interpretation of the guerrilla movement and a downplaying of Tsaldaris's commitment to extremist right-wing measures in the name of "law and order." Moreover, one has to question whether it represents MacVeagh's true reading of the situation, because barely four months had passed since he reported to the secretary of state that under the new Tsaldaris government, measures for " 'law and order' " were now "largely in the hands of unscrupulous reactionaries" and that there was a growing official tendency, first, to consider all persons Communists unless Royalists, second, to protect former supporters of the dictator Metaxas and others who collaborated with the Germans, and third, to accept armed assistance from disreputable elements professing royalism—in short, a rightist program under Tsaldaris that "actually approximates Fascism."[9] Given MacVeagh's abundant background in Greek affairs, one also has to assume that he would be familiar with the so-called white terror that was initiated by the extreme Right after the Varkiza Agreement in early 1945, that had indeed driven peasants of the Left into the hills to escape persecution, and that still had its influence wherever the Right exercised "law and order."

But it was a time of war. MacVeagh's image of local history and his dissemination of it had to be limited by the increasingly dangerous context that he felt himself, and his adopted country, to be enveloped by at that moment. Though he was a man of scholarly instincts, it was not so much the whole truth he knew or might discover that most concerned him as what he considered the necessary truth for the times. The main point of these secret communications with the State Department was to suggest that the situation in Greece might call for a certain manipulation of the American press in order to get the right kind of knowledge before the American public. In this connection, the ambassador records a hope that the State Department will take steps to diminish the influence of what he perceives as biased (that is, "Leftist") reporting, and in the specific case of Phillips, he suggests that the State Department may want to let Henry Luce of Time-Life Publications know that it trusts the Phillips story will appear "in such a form as to enlist US public support for Greece, bastion of true democracy and of US security in east Europe and Mediterranean," a position supported by what MacVeagh sees as Luce's policy regarding peace, namely, that the "best way to avoid war is by patient and firm resistance to Russian expansion." MacVeagh adds that in no part of the world is such resistance more justified or more necessary than in Greece, "and from no other part has the US press reporting to date been less discerning as to facts or less attentive to the real requirements of our national interests." In this more general connection, the ambassador feels the State Department may want to exert its influence "to induce our better journals and press associations" to maintain, in critical regions such as Greece today, "foreign correspondents of proven background-knowledge and tested judgement" rather than leave "a most delicate, demanding and important task of interpretation," as they presently do, to "roving specialists in the spectacular" or " 'small-time' permanent reporters of the police-court type."

MacVeagh's rhetoric here points to the origins of the unhealthy climate of local press-embassy relations that George Polk entered when he reached Greece to report on the civil war as CBS correspondent for the Middle East. By the time of his article for *Harper's* in the fall of 1947, the climate had heated up substantially, as had the war itself. And there were more reporters of various stripes on the scene to cover a "situation" that was not merely dangerous but that still seemed highly inauspicious from the Greek government point of view, especially with the sudden complications of the changeover from British to American protection.

Also, Lincoln MacVeagh, the senior American diplomat, with a broad and particular range of experience in the country, was absent at that time and had been replaced in Athens by an even more conservative career officer with considerably less experience in the area, Karl Rankin, then acting as chargé. Rankin—stout, ruddy, firm-jawed, eyes heavy-lidded at times but always vigilant—had little of MacVeagh's rhetorical gift and neither his learning nor his common sense, but Rankin was as firm in his convictions, which carried much the same ideological bias, though Rankin's conservatism was thought by some to include promonarchist sympathies (presumably limited to those few countries in the region where royalty still had dominion).[10] The historical record shows that Rankin subscribed blatantly to the principle of necessary American "interference" in Greek affairs that Polk had also defended in his *Harper's* article, as had Dean Acheson in explaining to Congress that the United States would have to put Americans into the key Greek ministries to oversee its aid program in Greece as it took over from the British on a grander scale under the Truman Doctrine: "You have to have people in these places . . . [Greek ministries and administrative bureaus], who have the authority to say to Greece, 'Stop doing this! You are draining off your resources.' "[11] At the same time, Rankin's fanatic aversion to the Left and his tolerance of the Right clearly promoted a less subtle and balanced perception of the Greek political reality than did Polk's, and this distorted perception in turn led Rankin to be intolerant of those local correspondents—by that time a majority, which included Polk—who were critical of what Rankin called "the current regime," a term that evidently included all elements of the Greek political, military, and security structure.

One gathers from a long confidential cable to the secretary of state dated a month before Polk's fatal trip north that Karl Rankin's bête noire among American newsmen covering the Balkans was Homer Bigart, correspondent for the *New York Herald Tribune*. Bigart seems to have represented in Rankin's mind the most pernicious kind of American reporting in Greece during the days before George Polk was murdered, and this impression is reinforced by several cables from Rankin to the State Department some weeks after the murder, when it became clear that Bigart had actually succeeded in traveling to Markos's headquarters from Yugoslavia in late June to get the interview with the guerrilla leader that Polk had been trying to arrange at the time he disappeared in Salonika. Bigart was a man given both to colorful writing and to plain talk, talk too crude for some tastes, and he was openly critical of much that he saw in Greece during the civil war, but he was hardly an extremist. In fact he showed himself to be more generous toward the local American diplomatic "establishment" than George Polk finally did in his correspondence with Drew Pearson, and Bigart fully shared Polk's view that American aid, and the restraint exercised by American officials on Greek government excesses, were all that had so far kept civil war Greece from coming under a dictatorship of either the Left or the Right. Yet Rankin labeled Bigart's dispatches from Greece in the spring of 1948 as representative of the "biased, fragmentary and hostile reporting of certain American correspondents" that was having, in both Greece and the United States, an influence that he considered "prejudicial to American policy and interests."[12]

Rankin explains to the secretary of state in his long April 7 cable just why this is so. American correspondents are given great prominence in Greece, he says, and those who are critical of the current regime not only deeply offend local opinion and undermine the confidence of Greeks in their political and military leaders but also cast doubt on America's intentions toward Greece. They even "tend to restrain responsible Greek officials from taking necessary action" for fear of further alienating opinion in the United States as this opinion is created by "the misrepresentations of local correspondents of influential American newspapers."

Just what sort of "necessary action" is thus frustrated, Rankin does not say, but his remarks did not exaggerate the Greek fear of alienating public opinion in the United States. That fear became a major preoccupation of the investigators in the Polk affair, and it was played on, for their own purposes, by both American officials and representatives of the American press who became involved in the investigation. We can surmise that what Rankin had in mind specifically in this instance was the issue of how the Greek authorities were dealing with law and order. Bigart, the April cable tells us, had been reporting extensively and most unfavorably on "arrests, executions and other measures which appear to him repressive," and this came after the correspondent had expressed the opinion to some local Americans that "our activities in Greece represent 'Operation Rathole.'" Rankin feels that Bigart's dispatches are given to easy comparisons between Greece and police states the reporter has visited, for example, "The roundup of leftists continues with all [the] vigor generally ascribed to a behind-the-iron-curtain-police state," and "Mr. Griswold in his second AMAG report to the Greek people made no mention of the current wave of arrests, deportations and executions which rival what is going on in Prague." The chargé does not deny that there have been arrests, deportations, and executions, but whatever "abuses" have occurred, he tells the secretary of state, were "in connection with attempts to establish order."

History, long after the fact, is more ample and forthright about what was going on behind the scenes. We learn from a historian of the period, Lawrence S. Wittner, that Karl Rankin actually told Greek officials directly that he felt "such arrests were quite necessary and justifiable,"[13] a position that the State Department came to support fully, no doubt in part through Rankin's influence (along with that of Ambassador MacVeagh earlier and that of Ambassador Grady later). When there was an international uproar over mass executions in 1948, the secretary of state sent out a cable stating that the Department "fully understands necessity for firm policy toward communists" and suggested, tellingly, that the one modification in current policy should consist of furnishing the press adequate information, thereby implying that the rule in the past had been to furnish insufficient information.[14]

Along with Bigart's criticism of the government's law and order measures, what seems to inflame Rankin most about this correspondent is Bigart's presumably "biased and unfavorable reporting" with regard to the Greek National Army, Bigart's attitude evidenced by a "violence" of language, for example: "Since last spring the Greek Army has sat on its rump allowing the guerrillas to terrorize new areas and to increase their strength by forcible recruiting," and, from another Bigart dispatch: "Their job, that of the American advisers, is to shake the Greek field command free from the idea of static defense, to press the idea of close combat and offensive action. It is a discouraging job because the Greek is free, independent and excessively mulish. Besides nobody yet has discovered how to tell an army tactfully to get off its fanny and fight."

Harsh as this image of the Greek army may have seemed at the time, it is not inaccurate if we are to credit a second American source that Rankin could hardly have accused of a like political bias. Almost a year after these dispatches from Bigart, when the war had taken a substantial turn for the better from the government point of view, the head of the American military mission, General James Van Fleet, expressed much the same sentiments (in more standard English) when reporting on the performance of the Greek army to its new commander-in-chief, General Alexander Papagos: ". . . lack of aggressiveness and determination to close with the enemy, combined with failure to enforce and comply with orders, have influenced operations adversely more than any other factors. Too many commanders all too frequently fail to take decisive action imposed by the enemy situation and the mission."[15]

In view of this, it would seem that the charge of bias belongs more plausibly on Rankin's than on Bigart's desk, and Rankin's claim that Bigart "has been indirectly one of Markos' most effective exponents" could well have earned George Polk, given world enough and time, a like evaluation from the embassy's chargé. But Rankin's cable on Bigart raises Polk's ghost inauspiciously in another context, having to do with the safety of American correspondents in Greece. At one point the chargé illustrates what he sees as the generally hostile response to Bigart's reporting on the part of the Greeks (specifically those who talk to the embassy staff) and the strength of public feeling on the question by citing a "well substantiated report" that a group of Greek youths had apparently planned to assault Mr. Bigart at one point and were dissuaded from doing so only with difficulty. Bigart left for the north and Yugoslavia shortly after this reported threat, thereby avoiding the possibility of any such incident, and he managed some two months later to travel through guerrilla territory for two weeks and return to Athens safely to tell the tale.[16] There is some irony in the fact that George Polk's shorter trip north for what Rankin later perceived to be an equally outrageous adventure ended up imposing a burden on Karl Rankin that even his sour image of American correspondents could not have caused him to anticipate in all its harsh complexity.

Rankin closes his April cable to the secretary of state with a paragraph out of Ambassador MacVeagh's book, offering a dose of his own brand of rhetoric in support of possible State Department influence on the free American press: "In these critical times one wonders whether we can afford the luxury not only of our recognized yellow press but also of such serious examples of irresponsibility among the correspondents of our most respected newspapers and agencies." The U.S. government finally must see to it that the press and the American public are fully informed on foreign affairs. In this connection he expresses a rather startling and provocative confidence: "The Department undoubtedly is giving careful and continuous study to the most effective means of obtaining the cooperation of the best elements among the Fourth Estate in furthering our foreign policy."

So much for the role of the Fourth Estate as watchdog against the excesses of extremism in government, whatever the agency and however critical the times. But what remains especially damaging about Rankin's biased view of Bigart's role as correspondent in Greece is the way the chargé chose to ignore—at least in his official reports—whatever implications the Polk investigation might have drawn from Bigart's trip to interview Markos. Bigart's account of his trip appeared in four issues of the *New York Herald Tribune* published from July 25 to July 28, that is, more than a month after the event itself, the delay occasioned, according to Bigart, by the reluctance of conservative elements at the paper to make Bigart's account public.[17] As he tells his story of the trip—and he does so with engaging detail and a keen sense of drama—he was approached in his hotel room in Belgrade by an unnamed man who called him "comrade" and who told him: "You had planned to return to Athens via Rome. Instead you will go via Free Greece and interview General Markos. Is that agreeable?" After some hesitation, it became agreeable. "Any Balkan correspondent," writes Bigart, "would give his right arm to see Markos."

It proved to be a demanding enterprise. The trip had to be kept secret from the Yugoslavs, for reasons that Bigart couldn't entirely fathom except to indicate that "konspiratsia" (the Balkan term for secrecy) is commonplace in the region. His escort, another Greek-speaking "comrade," turned out to be a "devastatingly moral" young man named John, whose English was inadequate and whose "friendship" with Bigart began to wear thin in due course but who guided him the full way to Markos over a period of two weeks, the first day to Skoplje by train in a compartment reserved for invalids, then across the Vardar Valley to Djevdjelia concealed in the back of a truck under the command of two unnamed men, and, on the morning of June 17, after barely escaping several Yugoslav border patrols and now accompanied by three armed men who appeared out of the bushes, into the Greek mountains held by rebel forces.

Bigart's journey took him westward for a week along the "razor's edge" of the territory that the partisans held below the Yugoslav frontier, traveling on foot or mule or horse, mostly in daylight, with only occasional evidence of the Greek army by way of distant booming artillery and also little evidence of traffic in men or materiel from beyond the northern border. Bigart was startled to find that the partisans "were quite ordinary flesh and blood who shaved and bathed regularly and were kind to their horses," men convinced that their cause was right, that they would eventually win, and that "the regime in Athens was completely subservient to American interests." He also found that the equipment in the one military hospital he came across, under the command of a single woman doctor who had performed more than a thousand operations, was so primitive that "often amputations had to be done without anesthetic and with a kitchen knife." Meals consisted mostly of "bitter unsalted bread" and goat cheese. Cigarettes were fashioned out of ripe tobacco leaves and whatever paper was at hand. No liquor—except that after ten days of "intolerable thirst," a village commissar produced a bottle of ouzo. As for airplanes to meet what the Americans had brought in, an officer pointed at a hawk circling high overhead: "That's our air force." But morale appeared to remain high. Minitri Karkori, who had once worked in a Ford plant in Detroit, told Bigart: "We gonna fight to last man. American people very good people, but Truman no good."

When Bigart finally reached Markos after a second week of travel that brought him high into the Grammos mountains and "over the backbone of the Pindus," he found the guerrilla leader unlike his published photographs, the "spreading mustache" now closely cropped, solidly built rather than lean, his mouth broad and expressive and with the "gift of a quick and charming smile" that could "alter instantly a face which in repose seems hard, impatient, pitiless." He was a man who talked with supreme confidence. Athens had rejected his peace offers, they thought it evidence of weakness; well, they wanted a fight and now they were getting it. Much of the interview focused on his body count of enemy dead contrasted to the enemy's body count, his image of how much new territory he had brought under guerrilla control despite the American intervention and despite his admitted defeat at Konitsa, how impotent the Athens regime would be "without American dollars and munitions." He said he kept hearing that funds for food and medical supplies were being collected by "our northern neighbors," but so far none of it had reached him, and though he wanted all the help he could get, he felt that "we are doing pretty well with our present resources," which consisted of much materiel captured from the enemy. When Bigart asked him why his government remained unrecognized by the Soviet Union, Markos refused to speculate. "We must continue to fight for recognition—both by our friends and our enemies," he said. "We will have a capital in Greece very soon." He also told Bigart that he did not hate Americans. They were a democratic people who were being misled by Truman. All he wanted was free elections so that the Greek people could decide for themselves what kind of government they wanted. And he preferred American help in the peaceful reconstruction of his country, not bombs and bullets. But if the American aid program meant fighting the Greek army under American advisers, then his partisan tactics would continue to "turn upside down every new thing they attempt."

Markos's boast was soon ringing hollow in the Grammos mountains, and, within two months (by late August), he had been relieved of his command and was bearing his sublime arrogance and a remnant entourage across the border for resettlement in Albania. But the Bigart interview clearly demonstrates that in June of 1948 Markos and the guerrilla movement in general were still much concerned about their image in

Greece and abroad, and Bigart's trip to get the interview, with a safe return via Yannina, shows to what lengths Markos was willing to go to get his point of view across by way of an American correspondent. It would seem that the complicated yet tenacious hospitality that he arranged for Homer Bigart's trip might have led some to believe that he would have wanted to do the same for George Polk a month earlier had the opportunity arisen, and that it was therefore at least highly questionable that his comrades in arms, had they managed to get through to George Polk in Salonika, would have chosen instead to shoot him in the back of the head and cast his body into Salonika Bay. But nobody, either at the *New York Herald Tribune* or in official American circles, appears to have considered this implication of the Bigart trip.

The *Herald Tribune*'s editorial accompanying the first of Bigart's dispatches (July 25) makes no mention of the Polk case and focuses only on the virtue of publishing "realistic intelligence" such as Bigart offers about courageous and enduring antagonists fighting in a bad cause, the kind of intelligence "as necessary for victory in the ideological sphere as in the military." Karl Rankin's extended cable on the Bigart trip immediately makes the connection with the Polk case, but it considers that connection only from his particular bias. Reporting on an andarte broadcast of June 24 announcing that Bigart is in "Markos territory," Rankin tells the secretary of state that "if report true apparent he has been allowed reach Markos only because Communist anticipate he will, for whatever reasons, broadcast or publish material favorable to Communists, probably including Polk case."[18] Whether such publicity is "voluntary or otherwise," Rankin continues, the subsequent Communist advantage is likely to be found in either of two courses: Bigart will be allowed to return from behind the Iron Curtain "unmolested as living witness to assert innocense [sic] of Markos in Polk case, abduction of children, etc." or Bigart will be assassinated by the Communists while he is with Markos or shortly thereafter, and his body will be allowed to be found in territory controlled by the Greek government "under circumstances planting blame on Greek Govt." If the first course is followed, Rankin says, it would put both the U.S. and the Greek governments in an embarrassing position "not only as regards Polk case and general US and Greek policy, but also vis-a-vis US press." The second course would prove even more embarrassing, he reports, since the murder of an American correspondent "under circumstances publicly pointing even more directly to Greek Govt than in Polk case" would give the Communists "excellent propaganda material against Greek Govt. and US policy in Greece"—from Rankin's point of view evidently the only considerations relevant. He concludes his cable by suggesting that the situation be fully explained to the responsible authorities at the *Herald Tribune* and to the Lippmann Committee, which may explain why no reference to the Polk case appears in either the Bigart dispatches or the *Herald Tribune* editorial and why the dispatches did not appear until long after Bigart's safe arrival in Athens, not from behind the Iron Curtain but via guerrilla escort to the outskirts of Yannina.

Rankin's conjecture that Bigart might be murdered by the guerrillas was shared by the other senior American official in Athens who had to cope directly with both the Bigart case and the Polk case during the spring and summer of 1948—Dwight Griswold, head of the American aid mission, former governor of Nebraska, and once a newspaperman himself. Griswold, submitting his own commentary on the Bigart adventure to the secretary of state on June 28, offered a second conjecture as well, one that revealed the bias he shared with Rankin regarding Bigart's reporting: "Greek Army personnel" might kill Bigart, "as he is now thoroughly detested after dispatches describing Bulkes camp as rest resort," while "Greeks believe the Communist saboteurs and assassins who operate in Greece are trained and dispatched from there."[19] The Bulkes (or Buljkes) "camp"—actually a town just north of Belgrade—was a Communist center devoted to the care of refugees, to indoctrination, and no doubt to some kind of military training, but what emphasis commentators chose to place on these diverse elements depended on the commentator's political perspective or, in a few instances, on firsthand observation (Kenneth Matthews, for example, who visited the town with a group of UNSCOB observers, highlights the noise generated by slogan-shouting residents during his visit to the place, and he tells us that when the Yugoslavs "finally tired of the Greek rebellion, broke up the Buljkes community and repossessed the town, they uncovered, in the elected leaders' cellars, a prodigious hoard, not of guns or ammunition, but of sugar, chocolate, tobacco and other luxuries intended for general distribution but retained disgracefully for black-market trade").[20] There was insufficient consensus among both Greek and foreign observers to permit the Greek Communist community in Buljkes to have been described simply as a refuge for the dispatch of saboteurs and assassins.

Griswold's inference regarding Bigart in his June cable probably has its origins in an earlier contretemps, one that reveals a characteristic distortion of the truth of things on Griswold's part, perhaps exacerbated whenever he had to confront Bigart's image. Though Griswold appeared— perhaps as the result of having been a newspaperman himself—less eager than Rankin to suggest that the critical times in Greece were such as to call for a certain manipulation of the press by U.S. government action, he was not averse to letting Bigart's superiors at the *Herald Tribune* know his negative thoughts about that particular correspondent's view of the Greek situation. In a letter concerning Bigart's reporting before his departure for Yugoslavia, addressed to "Editor, The Herald Tribune" and dated just two weeks before Polk's fatal trip north (April 17), Griswold speaks of himself as one who appreciates the importance of freedom in reporting and interpreting the news but who nevertheless feels called on to take issue with some of Bigart's articles and the subsequent comment in the *Herald Tribune*'s editorial columns.[21] Griswold's letter gives us an insight into the uncomplicated perception of recent Greek political history, and that of the civil war in particular, that most American officials in Greece felt they had to propagate, sometimes in response to exaggerations and misrepresentations published by the free American press, but more often in response to their own political prejudices mixed with a sense of what they took to be their duty to American national interests.

Echoing Rankin, Griswold takes Bigart to task for a line from one of his recent dispatches that focuses on excesses in the Greek judicial system: "Meanwhile, the mass execution of leftists continued." Griswold feels that a "considerable amount of distortion" has been packed into those seven words, since the executions in question were not carried out "because the accused were leftists, but because they were murderers," duly tried and convicted under a judicial system that as far as Griswold knows has never been criticized either by the several foreign missions that have worked in Greece or by foreign correspondents. The crimes committed by those executed, says Griswold, were by Greeks against Greeks, not Greeks against Germans and Italians (as the *Herald Tribune* editorial had it), and they were so gross as to have been excluded from the amnesty of the Varkiza Agreement between the Communists and the government that concluded the so-called second round of the civil war in February 1945.

The truth, according to the latest historical scholarship, appears to be closer to Bigart's than to Griswold's perspective. The executions were of leftists, the crimes they had committed were often gross (as the Hortiati old-timer witnessed), and they were not merely against Germans and Italians. But Lawrence S. Wittner concludes that the Athens government, consistently dominated by the Right even under Sophoulis, "imprisoned tens of thousands of suspect persons without charges or trials; executed thousands of individuals after summary court-martial proceedings; closed down the left-wing press and took occasional legal action against the remainder; . . . winked at the terrorist practices of the far right; instituted a 'loyalty' purge in the civil service; and forcibly 'reeducated' thousands of Greeks in barren island concentration camps."[22] The interpreting and carrying out of the Varkiza Agreement was entirely under Greek government control, and the judicial system, as the Polk case was soon to illustrate, hardly conformed to what either an American correspondent or an American official would consider a sufficient system were he himself to go on trial in civil war Greece.

Griswold goes on to defend himself against Bigart's claim that in a recent broadcast to the Greek people, Griswold had pretended that war-torn Greece was a pure and model democracy. The chief of the American Mission feels that he has in fact been "rather outspoken" in pointing out many deficiencies in the Greek government directly to Greek officials. But as far as he is concerned, the deficiencies often stem from too much rather than too little democracy. Regarding Bigart's specific charge that Griswold did not tell "the whole story" when he failed to mention the 10,000–12,000 officers and soldiers suspected of leftist tendencies who were confined on the island of Makronisos, Griswold states that he is now glad to mention it. Those so held have either refused to take an oath to serve their country "or were found to have affiliations which cast grave doubt upon their loyalty to the state." The government allowed "such men" to remain at home for a while but finally felt they had to act to halt large-scale draft evasions. Mission observers have visited the island and have found that the men are being well treated. "They are receiving indoctrination courses and other training," and two battalions of them have already been formed and incorporated into the Greek army. Griswold concludes, without irony or self-consciousness: "The situation may be compared in large part to the attitude we took during our last two wars toward conscientious objectors, and our treatment of Japanese-Americans on the west coast during the past war."

Indeed so, though the circumstances of those held on the island of Makronisos, according to several graduates of the "program" there, probably included a larger measure of brutal treatment and a broader devotion to useless work, such as endlessly hauling stones down from the hills to a sandy beach and then hauling sand back to the hills.[23] It is likely that those Mission observers sent to explore the island were presented with a holiday rather than quotidian image of the place. Anyway, Griswold rests his case against Bigart and this correspondent's analogies to police-state tactics by emphasizing that when the present Sophoulis government came to power, the number of civilians suspected of disloyalty and then being detained on the islands or elsewhere was reduced from 18,000 to 6,000—which, he thinks the editor of the *Herald Tribune* will agree, "is not the way a 'police state' does business." Griswold is in fact surprised, given the strong forces "hacking away at the country," with people dying and homes going up in flames, given a chaos "fed by the careful calculations of deadly serious enemies both without and within the country," that "the excesses have not been greater." And he adds that some people in Greece, including some Americans, have felt that tighter controls should be clamped down, and in this connection, criticism in the *Herald Tribune* "has not made the lot of Greek officials any easier." Diplomat that he now is, the former newsman does not tell the *Herald Tribune*'s editor that "some people" includes officials from the king of Greece on down to George McGhee, the Washington coordinator for the aid program, who wrote Secretary of State Marshall some weeks before Griswold's letter (February 1948) to recommend that steps be taken toward "bringing about the creation of a more authoritarian government" than was in place at the time.[24]

With the advantage of hindsight, one might be tempted to see Griswold's review of the Greek situation as a product of the same abysmal ignorance of history that Ambassador MacVeagh found in the typical American correspondent in Greece—for a start, Griswold's apparent ignorance of the fact that the "post-Varkiza" governments in Greece had each failed to carry out the terms of an agreement that was meant to restore a version of democracy that would allow for the representation of all political persuasions and that would protect civil liberties—not to mention human life—which had been so thoroughly violated by both sides in the civil war. A more generous view might hold that Griswold's perception of executions, imprisonment, indoctrination, and too much democracy under the government that he and other American officials were then sponsoring could be credited to a typical mixture of expediency and naiveté. Though Wittner tells us that there were U.S. officials who opposed the Greek government's law and order measures or tried to restrain their severity, most U.S. officials arrived in Greece at this time with an arrogant capacity for cultivating—often in the name of efficiency—extremities in government that they would not conceivably have tolerated at home, and they also arrived with insufficient knowledge of Greece to understand what they were confronting there: a people cruelly at war with its own, exhausted in spirit from the harsh German Occupation, in need of help from outside sources but too proud to accept it easily, the country's political and security structure—government ministries of public order and justice, gendarmerie, security police, paramilitary police, army, foreign advisers of various kinds—complicated in ways that both the terms "police state" and "democracy" as understood by Americans could make for only oversimplified perceptions and descriptive clichés.

Yet these new officials on the scene, pledged to support the government in power and the military-police apparatus against a Communist uprising, hardly had time for an "appreciation of the roots of things" (as Ambassador MacVeagh said of reporters like Phillips).[25] Their need was to deal with an emergency they could not fully comprehend, dispense vast aid they could not entirely control, and work somehow diplomatically with a client they knew not and who seemed to them more devious at times than they could profitably admit. In view of this, partial truths and clichés usually had to suffice. And their predicament may explain why both George Polk and Homer Bigart could be as well-disposed as they both were toward the American presence in Greece, though both would surely have been less so had they known how much energy was being expended behind the scenes to counter their critical perspective on much that was happening around them.

American officials at the highest level who were presumably more knowledgeable about circumstances in Greece—Griswold, Rankin, McGhee—evidently felt that their mission was to protect the American aid program at all cost while also seeing to it that their client government did not permit access to leftist elements and took whatever "security" measures might be thought necessary to challenge the Communist threat. If this interest required a certain distortion of history or a bit of eyewash (Bigart's term for Griswold's address to the Greek people) as they defended what they or their client were up to, so be it. The threat was taken to be justification enough. And the threat also justified the large measure of hostility toward the press and the rather casual tolerance of excesses in the judicial system that some American officials manifested, both factors that were later seen to have diverted the course of justice in the Polk affair.

Again, George Polk himself appears to have been less critical of some aspects of this high-level American attitude than one might have expected. According to Gerald Drew, Polk's cocktail host on the last day of his life, with whom he discussed Griswold's letter to the editor of the *Herald Tribune*, Polk was generally sympathetic toward Griswold's position in the letter, supporting "the absolute right of the Greek government to carry out the decisions of the courts in reference to death sentences" (what Polk appears to have had in mind specifically were the executions of Communist prisoners that had followed almost immediately on the assassination of Minister of Justice Christos Ladas in

Athens on May 1, 1948—that is, the week before Polk's Salonika trip—executions that Polk is also said to have felt were unfortunately timed).[26] Drew is quoted as indicating that Polk's only stated reservation about the Griswold letter was its conclusion, where Griswold compares Bigart's reporting on Greece to that of Russian journalist Ilya Ehrenburg's reporting on the United States, specifically, Ehrenburg's having written about only what he had seen in the South: racial problems, sharecroppers, poverty—factual material but, Griswold says, "not the whole truth." Polk, defending his colleague Bigart, found Griswold's analogy simply "not true."

Whatever one's sentiments about the propriety of executions under a regime that was meant to be more liberal than its predecessor, it is clear that Griswold was prepared to join Lincoln MacVeagh and Karl Rankin in using his office to promulgate an image of the Greek reality that was a partial truth at best and on occasion to undermine the more complete and more accurate image offered by outspoken American correspondents. If high-level American officials with a sense of responsibility and professional expertise could perform in this way, there seems to be ample substance to George Polk's feeling—as expressed to Drew Pearson—that there were other less responsible and more sinister forces at work in Greece bent on discrediting and even harming American correspondents critical of the Greek government and its military-security apparatus.

There is no way of knowing if Polk was aware of the hostile climate in Salonika generated by what local sources took to be unjust criticism of Greece in the American press, a climate that Greek newspapers in the region had begun not only to reflect but to stimulate just before Polk's trip north, but if he was aware of it, surely the Greek press had to be among the sinister forces he had in mind. In any case, a colleague of his who later became what some considered a key witness in the investigation of his murder, Daniel L. Thrapp, correspondent for the United Press, had to cope with this development at its most noxious and ludicrous in late February 1948, experiencing a rhetorical violence that anticipated the physical violence that did Polk in.

"L'Affaire Dan L. Thrapp"—as Marvin Sorkin, information officer of the American consulate in Salonika called the episode—had the city "bubbling over with indignation."[27] The Liberal morning daily, *O Ellinikos Vorras* (The Greek North) "went on a rampage," publishing an open letter by one M. Karagatsis, member of the National Institute of Notable Writers of Greece, that flailed Thrapp with satire ("I am not a physician, but I cannot help worrying for the very acute form of Mr.

Thrapp's illness") and followed this with an editorial calling Thrapp "that liar news reporter." The Liberal *Nea Alithea* (New Truth) accused the "irresponsible" Thrapp of slander, while the rightist-Populist *To Phos* (The Light) called the United Press correspondent an "old school" journalist "whose sole aim is to offer their readers sensational reporting, ignoring the interests or policy of their country."

What was the complaint behind this indignation on the part of both the liberal and rightist press in Salonika? Thrapp was held to have slandered the Greek army, to have inaccurately reported the facts about a "parade" of captured guerrillas, and to have posed as a member of UN-SCOB. In connection with the parade of captured guerrillas, he was specifically accused of having indicated that the number of guerrilla prisoners displayed before the public was 15 when in reality it was 150 and to have reported seeing rotten eggs thrown at the prisoners when no such thing had happened. Notable Writer Karagatsis testified (as translated by the American consulate) that "I have also attended the parade of those human beasts, and I have admired the Greeks who have shown superior civilization and did not even throw rotten eggs," let alone follow the American " 'Law of Lynch' " and "execute these inhuman criminals who have worked to enslave our race under the Slav-Communist horrors, who have slain infants, who have gutted pregnant women, violated little girls of ten years of age, killed innocent citizens by the shelling of Salonika . . . who are the enemies of freedom and of civilization."

Some ten days after this attack, Thrapp issued a statement in his defense, distributed by the U.S. Information Service in Salonika.[28] In this he denied representing himself as an observer attached to UNSCOB or any other official representative of the United States: that allegation derived from a misunderstanding on the part of an employee of the Mediterranean Hotel. Regarding the parade of guerrilla prisoners, Thrapp said that he reported only what he saw and that the "criticism of my dispatches resulted, for the most part, from a faulty understanding of what I dispatched" (Thrapp had told Sorkin earlier that he had cabled in a story saying that 121 prisoners had been paraded, but the story cabled out from New York put the figure at 15). His statement concludes: "I never at any time disparaged the Greek Army, nor any officer or man in it. I have repeatedly filed stories extolling the courage and efficiency of the Greek soldiers, and intend to continue to file such stories in the future. Any interpretation of my stories as being derogatory to the Greek armed forces or any member of it, is a faulty interpretation." As we have seen, even General Van Fleet was hardly so charitable toward the army he served as chief adviser.

According to Kosta Hadjiargyris, Daniel Thrapp was among those foreign correspondents who had thought of attempting to visit guerrilla General Markos Vafiadis in his mountain hideout during the spring of 1948 but had been discouraged from doing so by Consul General Gibson and had in any case left Greece for Italy in April, before the trip could finally be arranged. Thrapp refused to return to Greece to testify before the investigators in the Polk case, but he apparently indicated to an official who approached him in Rome that during his visit to Salonika he had been in touch with "a Greek contact," whose name he did not remember, in planning his aborted trip to the mountains, and Hadjiargyris later wrote the public prosecutor in Salonika, Attorney General Constantinidis, that he had learned from CBS correspondent Winston Burdett of another of Thrapp's Salonika contacts, namely, British Information Officer Randall Coate, one of the last people to have seen Polk alive.[29] Hadjiargyris also reminded the public prosecutor that Thrapp's visit to the guerrilla leader Markos was to involve "a journey by caique to the Pieria region" on the far shore of the Thermaic Gulf near Mt. Olympus, presumably the route George Polk would have taken had he made it beyond Salonika Bay. Hadjiargyris concludes wryly: "Mr. Thrapp was very lucky when at the end of April, 1948, he decided not to travel to Pieria."

All too true. The climate surrounding such a trip was hardly propitious from whatever angle one might choose to look at it, though especially so, it would seem, if one's starting point was Salonika rather than Belgrade. The civil war had polarized the northern region so that most political persuasions had moved to one extreme or the other, and neither extreme had tolerance for any point of view in between. And whatever the region, reporters critical of the government or the army roused passions that often seemed ready to find liberation in violence. For their part, American officials in Greece, from Lincoln MacVeagh to Karl Rankin and Dwight Griswold, were themselves sometimes aggressively intolerant of American correspondents who chose not to see the complicated Greek situation as they saw it—and most correspondents, from Conway to Bigart to Polk himself, did not so see it.

During those days, an American correspondent could not always anticipate thorough, objective guidance and assistance from his local diplomatic representatives, and he might well find himself undercut by these representatives through secret exchanges calling for the exercise of State Department influence against his point of view or through a letter of complaint to his editor from a high diplomatic source. It may well have been this sort of conflict between the objectives of State Department officials and the exercise of free criticism by the Fourth Estate that led the Special Committee of Inquiry of the Overseas Writers, known as the Lippmann Committee, to go directly to Secretary of State George Marshall and solicit State Department cooperation at the very start of their effort to see that justice was done in the Polk case. That early move, which Marshall responded to generously, appears to have had disastrous consequences in the long run, as we shall see in due course; but it also appears to have been undercut in the short run by Karl Rankin as he deemed necessary, which serves to illustrate the large degree of autonomous authority granted diplomats in the field at the start of the Truman Doctrine and the self-assurance with which they used that authority in furthering their ideological prejudices.

Regarding an American correspondent's relation to Greek officials in 1948, were he to fathom the local government and its entourage of civil servants, gendarmes, security police, military personnel, British advisers, and plainclothesmen with official and unofficial responsibilities of one kind or another so as to end up knowing exactly with whom he was dealing, he might be able to count on a show of courtesy and respect, even of hospitality, but he could never be certain of what he might be up against behind the scenes. And, as Daniel Thrapp discovered, his colleagues in the Greek press could be even more intolerant, certainly more ready to misunderstand and misrepresent, than the most arrogant, opinionated, and ideologically biased embassy and Mission officials.

Given the mood of the press in Salonika and the war climate generally during the spring of 1948, one can see why it was possible for some who were intimately involved in the Polk affair—Rea Polk among these—to believe that the threat to the CBS correspondent came from the Right rather than the Left, and one can also see why others could argue, as Polk did himself, that the Right and the Left were comparable at the extremes. There was danger at both ends of the political spectrum, and if you were an American correspondent with a mind of your own and a way of speaking it come what may, the spring of 1948 was not a healthy time for a trip north to Salonika in search of the year's biggest political story. And, it seems, George Polk knew it.

IV The Athens Connection

DURING THE BRIEF PERIOD that it took for Rea Polk and Kosta Hadjiargyris to emerge as the main suspects for an Athenian connection to the Polk murder, four American agencies joined the Athens and Salonika police investigators and their British advisers in forwarding the investigation. One of these worked under the direction of Karl Rankin and consisted of two embassy officers, Oliver M. Marcy and George Edman, who had been assigned to follow the case on a daily basis and establish liaison with William O. Baxter, assistant chief of the State Department's Division of Greek, Turkish, and Iranian Affairs.[1] Curiously—in contrast to the Rankin dossier—little appears in the State Department archives about the efforts of these two more junior embassy officers, which may be the basis for the strong belief among Greek students of the case that the CIA was somehow involved in the investigation from the start but of course never showed its hand. There is much more ample documentation regarding the role of another American official who was brought into the case by the State Department, an Aid Mission security officer named Frederick Ayer, formerly an FBI agent, who had worked in Greece under Dwight Griswold for a year and who was assigned to the Polk case just as he was preparing to leave Athens on another assignment.[2] Ayer was granted full access to the investigation by the Greek authorities and a direct line to the State Department by the American embassy because of his presumed expertise as a professional investigator. According to the State Department, Ayer's knowledge of local Greek conditions—evidently gained during his service as Griswold's security officer—"appear to make him ideally suited for this special reporting assignment."[3] The other American agencies on the scene represented the American press, which had responded to the news of George Polk's murder with the kind of outrage and lingering suspicion that we have seen in Drew Pearson's commentary on the threatening pressures that Polk and correspondents in Greece had begun to feel in the spring of 1948 from local officials.

The contribution of these various American agencies to the investigation then in progress in Athens under the Ministries of Justice and Public Order and in Salonika under Attorney General Constantinidis, Major Mouskoundis, and British police adviser Colonel Martin, proved to be that of complicating, misinterpreting, and obscuring an already too complicated and surreptitious enterprise. The effect, in the end, was not so much to steer the investigation toward unexplored avenues as to ensure that the investigation would persist in the wrong avenue it had taken from the start, and, in the case of the American press representatives, to promote a cover-up of dubious justice by the very people who had been sent abroad to pursue the truth of things.

The first American press group consisted of the two CBS representatives whose initial report we have seen, Winston Burdett and John Secondari, and the second consisted of General William J. "Wild Bill" Donovan and his assistant for the moment, Lieutenant Colonel James Kellis of the U.S. Air Force, these two representing the Lippmann Committee set up by the Overseas Writers. The first pair appeared on the scene a few days after Polk's body was discovered; the second arrived a month later, during the second week of June.

Burdett and Secondari found themselves in trouble with the Greek authorities almost as soon as they stepped off the plane in Salonika, and this may have served to traumatize them into an excess of caution in scrutinizing what was going on in front of their eyes. A report from CBS out of New York claiming that only Communists had so far been investigated by the Greek police raised a new uproar in the Greek press and put the local investigators, particularly Attorney General Constantinidis, immediately on their guard.[4] Burdett denied having had anything to do with the CBS report, which was apparently based on information sent out by one of the wire services, and he managed to get Consul General Gibson to send a cable to CBS New York relating the embarrassment he and Secondari had suffered over an account that was so completely untrue.[5] It transpired that in fact *no* Communists had as yet been interrogated by the attorney general's office, a circumstance that should have struck Burdett and Secondari as equally strange in view of Constantinidis's almost immediate assumption that Communists were responsible for Polk's murder—though reporters with enough background and time to explore to the roots of things might have known that bona fide Communists were hard to find circulating openly in a city that felt itself besieged by Communist insurgents. In any case, Burdett asked his employers to exercise greater discretion in reviewing dispatches sent out by the wire services, and Gibson defended the two CBS correspondents before Attorney General Constantinidis when the latter complained, telling him that Burdett and Secondari had not sent out the report in question and were in fact "satisfied with the investigation," this though they had been in town less than a week.

Satisfied they apparently remained, earning the confidence not only of local American officials but of the Greek police investigators, so that they were soon allowed the same access to witnesses that Frederick Ayer had been given and were thus able to help the former FBI agent build the case against both Rea Polk and Kosta Hadjiargyris, to the point where, two weeks after the contretemps with the attorney general, Ayer could report to the secretary of state that Burdett and Secondari "have strongly urged" Minister of Public Order Rendis and Chief of Athens Police Evert to question Rea Polk and Kosta Hadjiargyris thoroughly, "under arrest if necessary."[6]

If Ayer's secret account of things can be trusted—and there are times when one doubts that it should be entirely—this is a peculiar, not to say unprincipled, stance for two American newsmen to have taken after a little over two weeks on the scene when Polk's widow and a fellow correspondent for an American newspaper who had evidently earned Polk's full confidence came under police suspicion before there was substantial evidence against them, especially so since, as Greek citizens, the two suspects had little access to protection from any other American source. Still, there is now reason to believe that Burdett and Secondari were not acting simply on some hasty insight of their own in supporting the police pursuit of these two, but were much under the influence of Frederick Ayer in this as in other aspects of the investigation. And it turned out anyway that Chief of Athens Police Angelos Evert did not need much persuasion from either the CBS representatives or their security specialist adviser in order to go after Hadjiargyris, especially while Karl Rankin had the chief's ear.

We learn this to have been so as early as May 22—less than a week after Polk's body was discovered—when Rankin sent a secret cable to Washington outlining Evert's evaluation of the *Christian Science Monitor* correspondent's role in the case, beginning with Evert's conviction that Hadjiargyris was implicated in the murder.[7] Evert's reasons were, according to Rankin: (a) Hadjiargyris's leftist record; (b) the probability that he arranged Polk's Communist contacts; (c) the fact that Hadjiargyris and his wife planned to accompany Polk and his wife to Salonika but backed out at the last moment and ostensibly dissuaded Polk's wife from taking the trip; (d) the presumption that Hadjiargyris, who knew Polk well, must have known about his habit of jotting down all appointments

in his notebook, which was missing by then, very likely because Hadjiargyris had passed along the word about its importance to his Communist
conspirators.

A few days before this interview with Evert, Chargé d'Affaires Rankin
had received an urgent cable from Secretary of State Marshall warning
him that, in view of the "unfounded suspicions raised by Polk killing"—
presumably in America—there could be disastrous repercussions in the
American press were Hadjiargyris to be arrested at the present time
without "overwhelming and incontrovertible evidence his complicity
with communists or [sic] murder."[8] Marshall indicates that he is aware
of Hadjiargyris's background and his "dubious relations" with U.S. correspondents in Greece, which he assumes is what has caused the Greek
police to suspect his serving as Polk's liaison with the "communist
underground"—this and the police resentment of Hadjiargyris's story
about Polk's allegedly receiving rightist threats; but, Marshall notes, an
honest appraisal of Hadjiargyris's dispatches from Athens during the past
few months shows them to be among the "fairest and most informed and
objective emanating from Greece." In fact, they show "intelligent and
sympathetic understanding problems Greek Govt. and are by no repeat
no conceivable interpretation pro-communist."

Such a celebration of Hadjiargyris's objectivity seems not to have
caused Karl Rankin a moment's anxiety; in fact, he managed to turn it
to the advantage of the official Greek view of Hadjiargyris by reporting
back Evert's response to George Marshall's perception of the *Christian
Science Monitor* correspondent. Rankin quotes Evert as saying that,
while the department was correct in observing that Hadjiargyris appeared invariably scrupulous and balanced in his reporting, in his contacts with other correspondents he just as invariably took a pro-leftist
line and, "intentionally or otherwise, serves Communist purposes more
effectively than he could were his reportings slanted."[9] Rankin then
assures the secretary that Evert is fully aware of the difficulties involved
in arresting Hadjiargyris—the first difficulty that of his being the prime
minister's stepson—but things are clearly moving in that direction,
though the police are exercising great care to keep the investigation of
Hadjiargyris strictly secret.

Despite all the secrecy, Kosta Hadjiargyris was keenly aware of the
threat that had come into his life so early in the investigation, though
he was not at all sure about its source. It seems it did not occur to him
that one major source was the Athens police chief and his American
advisers, because in his rapidly growing fear of being implicated in the
Polk murder or of becoming a second victim himself, it was to Police

Chief Evert that he turned for guidance. In a letter to his London colleague William Stringer dated May 24, 1948, Hadjiargyris reveals, without the slightest sign of suspicion or irony, that he requested and was
granted a meeting with the chief of police but that it had to be postponed
for a day because Evert "was called to the American Chargé D'Affairs
[sic], Karl L. Rankin."[10] He goes on to say that he told Evert during their
meeting the next day that he considered himself in grave danger from
both Communists and extreme rightists, and Evert evidently agreed
with him about the threat from these sources—in fact indicated that
he had wanted to be in touch with Hadjiargyris in this regard and
had already begun to take certain measures for the correspondent's protection.

Hadjiargyris tells his London colleague—still, it appears, in full innocence—that he and Evert came to a number of common conclusions,
among these that the Communists might attempt to kill Hadjiargyris
in order to further weaken the Greek right wing in American eyes and
thus frustrate American policy, a plot that would be especially easy in
Athens, where the Communists had a stronger organization than they
did in Salonika and where they would have the advantage of being able
to exploit what Hadjiargyris described as "a savage right wing press
attack" that has "now been launched on me," an attack that "one can
qualify at the very least as 'an involuntary incitement to murder.'"
Hadjiargyris then offered his reasons for right-wing fury against him: he
had dared to reveal Polk's having told him about the threatening phone
calls that the CBS correspondent had received from someone who had
labeled Polk a Communist and, less subjectively, there were indications
now that the Americans were getting sick of "the state of anarchy en-
gulfing this country," with consequences that could only be unfavorable
to the Right. Hadjiargyris finally expressed the view to Evert that if
anything were to happen to him it would be to the disadvantage of
Greece and of U.S. policy. Evert, he concludes, "seems fully to understand this."

Maybe so, but State Department archives reveal that Evert's mind at
that moment was not on saving Hadjiargyris from either a leftist or
rightist plot but on trying to link Hadjiargyris to whatever plot it was
that had done Polk in two weeks earlier. Given the fact that these archives did not come into the public domain until three decades later and
given the curtain of secrecy that had been lowered to hide Evert's charade, it is easy to understand why Kosta Hadjiargyris could not have
fathomed at that time all that he was up against as the main candidate
for an Athenian connection to the murder, nor could he do so twenty

years later, when he began to put his views on record in what finally appeared as a book in 1975.[11] But even though his knowledge remained partial, Hadjiargyris's research and intuition over the years led to a more complete grasp of the case than that of his contemporaries. His review of the Polk affair is subject to his own strong prejudices—revealed especially in his largely unsubstantiated conviction regarding British motives and his stereotypical image of secret intelligence activities by both the British and the Americans—yet his limited account of those days does help to characterize several of the key participants in the affair, and some of his intuitions are now confirmed by once-secret documents that have recently been made public.

Naive though he was about the roles played by both Police Chief Evert and Karl Rankin in creating his problems, Hadjiargyris is correct in identifying three of his principal foreign pursuers as Frederick Ayer, Winston Burdett, and John Secondari. His evidence comes in part from several interrogations he was put through with one or more of these gentlemen present but mostly from Frederick Ayer's own description of the part he played in the case as this is narrated in an autobiographical history of Ayer's public service called *Yankee G-Man*, published in 1957.[12] Hadjiargyris emerges as the chief villain in Ayer's image of the Polk case during the period he was connected with it, and Ayer emerges as a major villain in Hadjiargyris's image of how the Polk investigation managed to get on the wrong track more or less from the start. Both images have to be tested against the more complete record provided by sources that were not fully available to either at the time each offered his version of the investigation then underway in Athens and Salonika.

Frederick Ayer was an educated man, with both a B.A. and a law degree from Harvard, and a devout conservative, who declined appointment as assistant counsel to the subcommittee investigating Senator Joseph R. McCarthy's charges of Communist infiltration in the State Department because the subcommittee chairman, Democratic Senator Millard E. Tydings, held up the appointment on the grounds that Ayer was then Republican candidate for attorney general of Massachusetts.[13] Ayer was defeated in the election (1950) and went on to become special assistant for intelligence to the secretary of the air force and the author of several books ranging from a biography of his uncle, General George S. Patton, to a spy novel called *Where No Flags Fly*, which carries an "Author's Note" telling the reader that "if I succeed in offending certain Americans a little—and certain Communist leaders a great deal—I shall have been successful in my purpose." At the time of the Polk murder, he was training his successor as chief of Dwight Griswold's security division and was asked by Secretary of State George Marshall to stay on and take part in the Polk investigation, reporting back regularly to the State Department, via the American embassy, on developments in the case. For the two months that Ayer was assigned to the investigation (he left it in late July), he was clearly the most influential American presence on the scene, at least when General "Wild Bill" Donovan was not in town.

Either through faulty memory, carelessness, or other cause, Ayer gets some of his facts about the Polk case quite wrong in his autobiographical account—dates, times, who did what when—but arrogance rather than inaccuracy is the major weakness he manifests, along with a deficient concern for the rights of others and a simplistic interpretation of Greek politics, not much different from what was demonstrated by other American officials assigned to Greece at the time, though in Ayer's case sometimes more crudely displayed. The former FBI agent tells his readers that he had serious reservations about taking on Secretary Marshall's cabled charge that he coordinate the Polk investigation and report to the secretary daily. Given the many Greek and foreign agencies involved in the investigation, with most of the local agencies "engaged in undeclared war" and everybody questioning everybody else's witnesses, Secretary Marshall's charge "was like ordering a man to coordinate a little league baseball team on which each of the nine boys has brought his own ball, and has been promised by his father that he can pitch." Then there was Ayer's lack of popularity with the American embassy because he insisted that he rather than the embassy should take command of the investigation—bad form, he assumed, for somebody who wasn't a member of the Foreign Service, but, fortunately for him, "it proved impossible" for the embassy "to argue with the plainly written word" of Secretary Marshall's cabled orders to him.

So Ayer took command, and in order to "prevent the various Greek organizations from cutting each other's throats," he got the minister of justice and the minister of public order jointly to sign a paper stating that Major Mouskoundis of the Salonika Security Police would be "in sole and exclusive charge of the investigation," that no one was to obstruct him, and that the forces of all other organizations would be put at Mouskoundis's disposal. Then Ayer had this signed document printed in the daily press and read over the radio to make sure it took hold. With this act of centralizing authority on the Greek side of things, Ayer saw to it that Mouskoundis had the greatest power for exercising good or evil in the early stages of the investigation, and since Ayer had as much access to witnesses as he wanted—though probably not all that Mouskoundis might have given him—he too was in a position to participate hour by hour in what occurred.

In his chapter on the Polk case, Ayer tells us that he was on to Rea and "Costa" (his barely disguised pseudonym for Kosta Hadjiargyris) pretty much from the start: "early in the case it appeared that there were at least two people who knew more than they were telling," which made them both suspect, though to different degrees, and "unfortunately," one was the victim's young widow and the other the victim's closest confidant. Rea, the less culpable of the two, is exonerated of what appear to have been contradictions in her testimony on the grounds that she was "probably attempting to shield Costa" and, as Major Mouskoundis suggested to him, was simply "one of those unfortunates who by some quirk at times cannot tell the whole truth and is unable to recite a story twice in the same way." Ayer apparently felt that Mouskoundis's "quirk" theory was confirmed when a report came in from Egypt to the effect that Rea had a few years previously been under the care of a psychiatrist who discovered the "same strange trait of mind" in her, and the former FBI agent adds that of course a good policeman has to be "a pretty fair psychiatrist," which presumably explains not only Mouskoundis's having anticipated the Egyptian psychiatrist's prognosis but also why both the major and Ayer himself ended up convinced that Rea was innocent of any crime—if not exactly innocent otherwise.

Ayer's broader image of Rea was evidently strongly influenced by a report that she was seen "on at least two occasions" dancing in Athenian nightclubs "a scant three weeks after her husband's tragic death" and, perhaps even more so, by a visit that Rea paid him at her request in his "so-called apartment," Ayer and his Greek assistant Papadopoulos dressed for the beach on this occasion and his attendant secretary Kay Geiger a bit more dignified, while Rea arrived "dressed to conquer," in black of course—"but there are blacks and blacks"—the dress "gauzy and not overly opaque," the black hat "broad and flattering," the gloves "black kid and elbow length," the perfume "less than subtle," the smile "practiced and lovely." We are told that Rea seemed disappointed that Ayer was not alone for their meeting; she said she didn't like discussing all her troubles in front of strangers. Ayer didn't point out that he himself was a stranger to her. He simply told her that if she wanted to leave Greece and settle in the United States as she apparently hoped to do (Ayer pointed out to her that he had been the one who had "arranged the orders that she should not leave"), she would have to go to Salonika, submit to interrogation by Major Mouskoundis, and "satisfy that astute man that she was telling the truth, and all that she knew." Rea promised that she would do so and "made her graceful departure, leaving in her wake a tantalizing scent."

But the confrontation with "Costa" was not so scented and graceful. Ayer approached him with ardent preconceptions: since Hadjiargyris was "strongly believed to be a secret Communist" and therefore certainly had leads into the Markos organization, it "seemed more than logical that he had furnished George with the identity of a Communist agent in Salonika who had led him, intentionally or inadvertently, to his death." Ayer cites no hard evidence at any point in support of this theory or of Hadjiargyris's involvement in any phase of the crime, so his conviction regarding "Costa's" guilt appears to have emerged solely from his policeman's psychiatric insight, though he was far from alone in believing Hadjiargyris a Communist, a belief shared by Polk's widow, some Greek journalists, and a number of American officials. (Hadjiargyris apparently never acknowledged being a Communist during the years after his conviction as a leftist naval mutineer in World War II, but some took his later association with left-wing journalism to be sufficient evidence of a continuing commitment to the Left.)[14] In any case, Ayer's insight about "Costa" was evidently based in large measure on a strong personal antipathy to the *Christian Science Monitor* correspondent. During Ayer's interrogation of "Costa," the former FBI agent felt that he had never before "tried to handle a man who was so quick mentally and so utterly aggravating." "Costa" made Ayer uncomfortable because "Costa" was "more devious than I and more than a match for me in any game of question and answer." Yet Ayer became certain that "Costa" was lying when he said that he had no idea whom Polk was planning to meet in Salonika. Nor did he believe "Costa" when he said he didn't know any officials of the Communist party personally, though as a correspondent he of course had to talk to all kinds of people. Ayer also didn't appreciate Hadjiargyris's complaint that a representative of the press should not be "continually persecuted like this by the police." "Costa" was certain his newspaper wouldn't approve of such persecution. But he said he wanted to be helpful, and with "a very condescending smile," he told Ayer that if he himself were conducting this investigation, he would look for the true story from a man who represented a trusted paper, surely a Greek if he were to have the necessary contacts, but one who spoke English because that was the only language George Polk understood well, in short—and here the deviousness in "Costa" presumably appeared blatantly—a man such as "Costa" himself.

This supposedly satanic self-description drove Ayer to feel rather savage instincts, the same kind of instincts, he tells us, that Burdett's CBS companion, John "Jack" Secondari, had expressed regarding "Costa" after a previous interrogation. Secondari, a professional journalist who ended up a novelist, is described by Ayer as having been short in stature but long on animal energy, coal-black hair, fierce mustache, snapping dark eyes, a man constantly in motion and an advocate of direct, even violent, action in the pursuit of what he felt to be justice. Secondari's vision, as quoted by Ayer: "I still think that S.O.B. Costa is in on it somewhere. I'm sure that he hasn't been telling the truth. He's too damn smug. He knows that nobody dares throw him in jail or rough him up because he's Old So-and-So's step-son and represents the majesty of the American Press. You know what I'd like to do? I'd like to take a few shots at him in the street at night, just close enough to knock his hat off. Then, when he was damned good and scared, I'd like to kidnap him for just a little while and have a heart to heart talk. I bet I'd find out what I wanted to know." Ayer says that "regrettably enough," he himself felt that he "could not approve such a course of action," though he fully agreed with Jack and knew Jack well enough to believe the man was not bluffing about what he would like to do to his Greek colleague. In the end Ayer seems to have come to terms with his frustration over Hadjiargyris by finally agreeing with Mouskoundis "that there was not much that could be done about Costa, other than hope that he might someday hang himself." In point of fact, Hadjiargyris outlived Ayer by ten years and Mouskoundis by thirty, dying of natural causes in December 1986, just as a Greek film on the Polk case, in which Hadjiargyris emerged as a kind of hero, was near completion.

Frederick Ayer appears to have been generally frustrated by what he saw as the restrictions imposed on him by circumstances in the Greece of 1948. He found that it was "regarded as bad police form to harass widows or members of the press." And there were too many observers following his every move and a glare of publicity, also commentators and writers, including Walter Lippmann and Edward R. Murrow, who had "a quite legitimate interest" in seeing that there was no cover–up of the Polk case in Greece and that the American press received the full story but who evidently contributed, along with all the rest, to Ayer's feeling "like a man who was not only a victim of back-seat driving but was, at the same time, being pursued by the Highway Patrol." It seemed to him that "it was almost necessary to invite the press into the actual interrogations" so that "we would not be accused of third degree methods or of fabricating testimony."

Given the instincts of the two press representatives from CBS, such an invitation in their case would have likely promoted an absurd redundancy. It appears that Winston Burdett joined John "Jack" Secondari in advocating a "third degree" approach to the interrogation of Kosta

Hadjiargyris. In a confidential memorandum of a conversation that the two CBS representatives had with Athens embassy officials just three weeks into the investigation, Karl Rankin reports to the State Department that "they [Burdett and Secondari] are definitely of the opinion that Hadjiargyris knows a 'great deal more' about the murder than he is willing to admit," and they added that "the only way to get out of Hadjiargyris further information on the case was to put him through an old-fashioned 'third degree.' "[15] Hadjiargyris was lucky enough to escape the treatment by police investigators that Burdett and Secondari recommended, saved, no doubt, because of his political connections at the highest level, but Gregory Staktopoulos, arrested after Ayer, Burdett, and Secondari were all out of the case, was not so lucky. Major Mouskoundis's particular version of the third degree was evidently beyond observation by anyone other than his own officers, yet one can't help wondering if the major didn't take courage from the expressed proclivities of his American advisers in dealing with Staktopoulos as he finally chose to do.

Frederick Ayer, apparently aware at some point in his research that the Security Police had been suspected of using violence to obtain information from witnesses, Staktopoulos in particular, declares in his book that "for my part I was entirely sure that no duress or physical brutality had been used in obtaining admissions from the contact man." Why, given his loose talk about the value of third-degree methods, he is so entirely sure he does not say, so the reader has to take what seems his naiveté regarding the Security Police treatment of Staktopoulos mostly on faith. At the same time, it is only fair to say that there is nothing in the official record to suggest that any of the Americans who participated in the early phase of the investigation were aware that Major Mouskoundis was given to the kind of third-degree methods that Staktopoulos came to know and that Frederick Ayer—if we grant him the benefit of the doubt—would presumably have been shocked to witness.

Kosta Hadjiargyris, perhaps understandably, does not grant him that benefit, claiming in his 1975 book, with his own measure of hyperbole and with no substantial evidence cited, that Ayer did not confine himself to advising the local officials, but, in keeping with the practice of "CIA 'advisers' in the various American-held countries who take an active part in tortures and executions," also took part in all the "interrogations and tortures for the extraction of 'confessions' in the Polk affair" (p. 319, my translation). And he did so, we are told, not only with Mouskoundis but also with Raleigh Gibson, the third member of a conspiratorial triumvirate, who, in his determination to pin the murder on the Communists, played a key role as the defender of Mouskoundis and as the sustainer of Ayer, supporting the latter's reports with his own and propagandizing those foreign correspondents who came to Salonika to follow the investigation at close quarters. As we shall see, there is much truth in Hadjiargyris's perception of Raleigh Gibson's interest in guiding the press along the path chosen by the official investigators, especially after the indictment of Gregory Staktopoulos, but the problem with Hajiargyris's image of a conspiring triumvirate is the fact that Frederick Ayer was off the case before it took the decisive turn that resulted in the apprehension of Staktopoulos on August 14 and the six-week-long isolated interrogation that led to his "confession" on October 1.

Ayer himself is probably responsible for Hadjiargyris's confusion on this point, because at the end of Ayer's account of his two months on the Polk case, the former FBI agent appears to want to share in the credit for the "Staktopoulos solution" that emerged from the official investigation some weeks later. He tells us in his *Yankee G-Man*: "I well remember that after the arrest of Gregory Staktopoulos, Raleigh Gibson, Winston Burdett, Jack Secondari and I had a not inconsiderable celebration at my rather seedy flat in Athens," where "we toasted the conclusion of the matter and each other in a mixture of one part Greek brandy, one part Triple Sec, and one part canned grapefruit juice." Ayer's memory in this instance leaves as much to be desired as his taste in celebrative cocktails: the State Department archives show a cable from Ambassador Grady that indicates Ayer had left the scene by July 30, 1948, and had taken "his entire file with him."[16] Winston Burdett, for his part, was in Rome by July 31, telling his CBS listeners that "unless a real and earnest effort is made to explore all sides, we cannot report to the American people that the Greek government has done everything it could to find and punish the murderers of George Polk."[17] John "Jack" Secondari was nowhere in evidence at this time, and Raleigh Gibson remained at his post in Salonika for the two additional months that it took to arrive at something that would pass for a "conclusion to the matter."

What we do find in the archives is a report from Ayer to the secretary of state, designated No. 15 and sent in three weeks before Ayer left the case, which includes the curious (and as it turned out, inaccurate) news that "Salonika police plan soon arrest one Gregory Stachtopoupos [*sic*], alleged Reuters stringer always under suspicion (see early Ayer reports). Exact grounds planned arrest not yet known Athens but believed because numerous contacts highly placed members KKE and possible espionage activities. On date for arrest Ayer or Kellis will go Salonika and report."[18] Neither in fact did so because both had left Greece by the time the arrest was made in mid-August, but perhaps this bit of inside foreknowledge is one aspect of the allusion to the Polk case in Ayer's 1974 *New York Times* obituary, which informs us that "Mr. Ayer was credited with laying the groundwork that led to the solution of the murder."[19]

Had Ayer brought his policeman's "psychiatric" insight to a review of the various public documents about the case that were available to him at the time he wrote *Yankee G-Man* (ca. 1957)—not to mention any secret files he may have had access to—he might not have been so eager to project himself as both a central figure in bringing about the "Staktopoulos solution" and an unequivocal advocate of Major Mouskoundis; but one has to assume that whatever he may or may not have known before leaving the case in late July, much was kept from him about the activities of the Security Police in Salonika after that date. And one would want to assume that much was kept from Raleigh Gibson as well—enough, anyway, to permit his continued ardent support of Major Mouskoundis to the very end of the trial, eight months after Staktopoulos was arrested, when Gibson issued a statement to the press in which he indicated that the "name of Major Mouskoundis must be especially mentioned and he must be complimented for intelligence, diligence, patience and brilliant work."[20]

Whether or not such support is evidence of conspiracy, as Kosta Hadjiargyris would have it, depends on how much Gibson knew about what was going on at Security Police headquarters. The record suggests that he did not know enough, and though he often appeared sympathetic to the Ayer-Mouskoundis anti-Communist line of inquiry, that speaks more to shared prejudice than to conspiratorial strategy. The image of Gibson that one emerges with from State Department files is that of a hard-working, articulate if sometimes unsubtle bureaucrat, a rather unimaginative Foreign Service officer at the end of his career trying, before he retired, to get through a difficult assignment with some cunning and grace, but who revealed too little insight about what was going on and too much tolerance of excess in others to pull off his assignment cleanly.

Winston Burdett and John Secondari do not appear to have been conspirators in the ordinary sense either, but they seem to have been easily swayed by Frederick Ayer so as to turn early and strong suspicion on both Rea Polk and Kosta Hadjiargyris and to prefer the "Communist angle" to the point not only of dangerously distorting their own vision but of influencing a like distortion in others, especially that of other American newsmen who relied on their initial explorations, the Lippmann Committee–Donovan group among these. Ayer tells us that the two CBS correspondents arrived in Athens with a preconceived notion that George Polk had been murdered by right-wing agents of the Greek government and descended on Ayer's office to tell him so. Ayer responded that he could not agree with that theory, told them the story of the recent murder of Minister of Justice Ladas by "an admitted Communist" and about reports he had been receiving that the Communists would commit another murder, which, instead of acknowledging it to be their act as they had in the Ladas case, they would try to blame on rightist elements in the government, who in turn would blame it on the Communists.

According to Ayer's account of this meeting, the three of them sat there trying to find a motive in the Polk killing: who might make capital out of the thing. "It soon became clear to the three of us that the only people who could profit were the Communists, that in fact they had already caused great trouble for everyone." The government, on the other hand, could only injure itself irreparably by "liquidating a critical, American reporter." If the police had committed the act with the intention of blaming the Communists, they would surely have seen to it that Polk's body disappeared forever in Communist-held territory and "would scarcely have arranged for his body to be found floating within sight of the American Consulate" after mailing Polk's identity cards (in fact, only one card) to themselves. Ayer does not stop to explain the paradox of making a body "disappear forever" if your intention is to have it discovered in incriminating territory, nor does he consider the possibility that somebody other than the culprits (whether police or Communists) may have found the incriminating documents and mailed them in to the Third Police Precinct. Nor, finally, does he acknowledge that the Right and Left were equally capable of attempting to create a charade if their intention was to blame the enemy for a murder they had committed. As though conscious of having loaded the argument too heavily on one side of the scale, the former FBI agent adds that it was of course possible that "some extremist right-wing organization, of which there was at least one in Greece called the 'X-ites' ['Chi-ites,' more accurately], might have done the murder," and, to the "everlasting credit" of Burdett and Secondari, the two CBS representatives "kept an open mind through the two months of investigation to follow."

Not so open, actually, if one is to judge from some remarks in the confidential report by Burdett and Secondari that included the itinerary we have seen, transmitted via Raleigh Gibson to Wells Church and Davidson Taylor of CBS on June 15, that is, one month into the investigation.[21] Along with the detailed account of George Polk's days in Salonika and of the activity that immediately followed on the discovery of the body—the most thorough and objectively narrated account we have— there is some subtle editorializing. Where the influence of Frederick Ayer shows most is in a comment that falls outside the narrative, and in a crucial assumption at the end of the report. After concluding that "so far, there is no evidence pointing with any degree of finality to one guilty party or another," the report adds that the police do have some leads, and "we ourselves have certain strong private suspicions." Since these "involve certain individuals," says the report, "there is no point in our setting them down on paper at this time." And then the report introduces a revealing clue to the derivative thinking of Burdett and Secondari: "Thus far, we have not been able to find the Greek in the story, . . . the Greek, that is, who was George's first contact. He must have been a man who spoke English. We can suppose that he was a man who had George's trust, perhaps even a man whom he had known for some time. He may not be a man of mystery at all; but one who was close to George and known also to his friends. Evidently, on this score too, we have our private suspicions."

One has to ask why the "first contact" would have to be Greek, and why would he necessarily have to be "a man who had George's trust" in the sense suggested, namely, someone he had known for a time, even someone close to him and therefore presumably living in Athens. In their own report, Burdett and Secondari show Polk approaching at least four non-Greeks, all in Salonika, and asking each of these if he or she knows of any way he could be put in touch with the Communists: one Colonel Miller at the consulate; Helen Mamas, AP stringer; Gerald Drew, UNSCOB delegate; and Randall Coate, British information officer. At least two of these possible "first contacts" in Salonika were people Polk was meeting for the first time (Drew and Coate), and the others he barely knew.

The source for the Burdett-Secondari assumption about "the Greek in the story" is not their own detective work but Major Mouskoundis, at least so one has to assume from Ayer's account of things. Ayer quotes Mouskoundis as saying: "The whole picture which suggests itself to me is that the contact man must have spoken fairly good English, as you have told me that Mr. Polk spoke no Greek. . . . It also suggests to me that he must have been in some way in the newspaper business, as I cannot see even so rash a young man as your friend going off into the night with just any stranger who promised him that he could lead him up into the hills to join that dog Markos. It finally makes me think that Mr. Polk might well have been sent to this contact by some friend of his in Athens, perhaps someone also in the newspaper business." Again, it is the Burdett-Secondari report itself that shows us that Polk was at least "rash" enough to consult a number of virtual strangers for possible help in getting access to guerrilla territory, most of these neither Greek citizens nor in the newspaper business. And Kosta Hadjiargyris was among those who remained convinced that Polk had in fact gone off into the night with one of these non-Greek "strangers," specifically, British Information Officer Randall Coate. In any case, whoever the hypothetical Salonika "Greek in the story," Major Mouskoundis clearly has Kosta Hadjiargyris himself in mind for Polk's hypothetical Athens friend in the newspaper business—though again, exactly why the so-called Athens connection had to be in the newspaper business does not emerge from the text.

Hadjiargyris is also undoubtedly among those "certain individuals" who aroused the "strong private suspicions" that Burdett and Secondari admit to in their report, because the *Christian Science Monitor* correspondent appears as a major suspect in several of their less reticent communications. We have already seen that, at an early point in the investigation, the two CBS representatives strongly urged the minister of public order and the Athens police chief to question Hadjiargyris under arrest if necessary.[22] In an urgent and confidential cable to their CBS colleagues sent via Karl Rankin a week later, they say, rather apologetically, that "it may have surprised you to learn that George's widow and his best Greek friend and closest collaborator in Athens were questioned on our specific insistence," and they wish to explain "our special reasons" for so insisting.[23] They report that during three weeks of private conversation with Rea and Hadjiargyris, they formed the definite impression that the two were withholding information, and their talks with these two failed to produce the name of a single Greek whom George knew either socially or professionally outside the circle of his wife's family and a few government officials.

Why Burdett and Secondari considered this restricted circle of acquaintances so unusual given George Polk's limited time in Greece is not explained by his CBS colleagues. Rea Polk, remembering those days forty years after the fact, confirmed that, as newlyweds, she and her husband had kept much to themselves in Athens during the short period they lived there, especially since George knew no Greek and was often on the move.[24] Had Burdett and Secondari accepted Rea at her word during their early interviews with her and had they been more familiar with the reality of Polk's life in Athens—or that of any recently arrived foreign correspondent—they might have led other investigators to conclude that the search for a "Greek contact" in Athens was misdirected.

But even by the time of this early cable, an Athens connection had become basic to the Mouskoundis-Ayer construction of the Polk case—as was, it seems, the nationality and profession of the victim's presumed Athenian contact.

In their cable, Burdett and Secondari elaborate further on their "special reasons" for holding Rea and Hadjiargyris suspect. They find that the behavior of Rea since George Polk's death "has shown callousness and spirit of opportunism hardly befitting a bereaved widow," though they cite no instances of such behavior. Again, one sees Ayer's image of a woman "dressed to conquer" lurking behind this news, totally inconsistent with Rea's recollection of herself as a frightened eighteen-year-old girl [actually twenty, according to the official transcript of her sworn testimony] who spent her time mostly in bed crying after she returned from Salonika to her Athens apartment as a widow, with her mother there to protect her from newsmen, showing them into her room and saying: "See this little girl? This is George Polk's widow. Now will you go away and leave her alone?"—and they, seeing how young and distraught she was, would go away ashamed.[25] And if by "spirit of opportunism" Burdett and Secondari have in mind Rea's efforts to get out of Greece and emigrate to America, Rea would now answer that by saying that she was advised to do so as soon as she possibly could by a young consular officer at the American embassy, warned by him without solicitation that her visa as Polk's spouse would expire at the end of June under the law then current and that she should get out of Greece by that time at all cost if she wanted to avoid the years of delay that a regular quota visa would occasion. Rea says that she took the young man's advice gratefully and acted on it as best she could under the constant pressures of police interrogation and newspaper publicity—and, as we learn from Ayer's book, against the efforts of the former FBI agent to prevent her timely departure.

In their cable Burdett and Secondari also claim to "know" that Rea tried to assist her husband George in developing Communist contacts, but they do not say how they know, only that her "testimony to us on this point has been wholly unsatisfactory," presumably because she denied any such attempts at assistance. They conclude that Rea has shown little cooperation with us in "our work" and has been consistently antagonistic toward the police. In view of the continuing police suspicion of the young widow that Burdett and Secondari not only confirmed, but shared, Rea's attitude at that time does not seem unreasonable. Hadjiargyris offers further evidence to support the logic of her response to the police, this from an interview that Rea gave out for the December 21,

1952, issue of *American Weekly*, where she speaks of having gone through a terrible trial at the hands of police interrogators.[26] Isn't it true, she quotes the police as asking, that you had a lover who swore to kill your husband—or maybe you yourself organized the murder out of jealousy of another woman? And Rea recalled recently that one of the investigators tried to create a story about her husband and some blond woman that she knew to be a complete fabrication meant to trap her into saying things she didn't want to say. These humiliating questions and constructions were, according to Rea, all part of an early effort by the police to push the investigation toward a quick and easy "erotic" motivation for the murder that would avoid or hide the kind of political motivation which might "prove to be dynamite."

But politics soon prevailed, and it was Hadjiargyris who became the focus of the political angle, especially since that route quickly turned into the "Communist angle." In their "apologetic" cable, Burdett and Secondari indicate that they have "definite facts to record" in the case of Hadjiargyris.[27] These are an elaboration of what we have seen in Karl Rankin's secret cable to George Marshall and what Frederick Ayer echoes in his book: Hadjiargyris occupies an extraordinary position in the colony of foreign correspondents, having succeeded, through diligence, ability, and a wealth of ready information, in making himself a unique, almost indispensable source of news and opinion for American correspondents. His own reporting for the *Christian Science Monitor* earns him high grades for balance and reliability, but the "news picture which he disseminates among his American friends bears all earmarks of deliberate political agitation against Greek Government and American effort here." One senses the shadow of Karl Rankin in particular crossing this portion of the cable, because presumably among the "friends," and surely among those that the "expert" Hadjiargyris "has made Greek experts of," we find the name of Homer Bigart, along with those of Drew Pearson, Raymond Daniell, Marquis Childs, and "at least over a certain period, George himself." Hadjiargyris has been able to operate with special immunity, the cable reports, because of his "favored position as the step-son of Prime Minister and of course member of American working press."

But what did this "operating" amount to in the view of Burdett and Secondari? As an "engaging and extremely intelligent person," Hadjiargyris first gained the respect of people like Howard Smith and Don Pryor, then, by "smuggling out" a series of letters (such as that to William Stringer already quoted), he laid the groundwork for his eventual defense in the American press should he become seriously implicated in the murder or actions leading to it, then he demonstrated himself to be a "man of great resourcefulness and cunning" in parrying the questions of interrogators, and finally he claimed that, when asked by George Polk to help him get in touch with top Communists, he declined to do so for fear of compromising himself should Polk's enterprise at a later date get the CBS correspondent in trouble of one kind or another. This sort of "operating" for his own protection can be seen in retrospect as an aspect more of Hadjiargyris's intelligence than of his cunning, especially given the pressures and suspicion he had to face almost from the first day he offered his services to the investigators.

The clue to Hadjiargyris's treatment by the Greek police and their American advisers is of course his evil past, as it was for so many in Greece who came out of World War II with a leftist history of one kind or another—and not only in Greece. Burdett and Secondari outline the "attested facts" of this past "solely for [the] information" of their CBS colleagues. The source of the attestation is not identified in all instances, but the "facts" recorded are the following. During the war Hadjiargyris was discharged by the BBC for "injecting Communist line into their Greek language broadcasts." He was subsequently arrested as the "ringleader in Communist inspired mutiny" on his Royal Hellenic Navy ship, the Corvette *Tombazis*, and there is "sworn testimony of six officers of Greek Navy" in this connection. Hadjiargyris was then interned for two years, first in Chatham, England, and later in the Middle East. He was released "not (as he claims) after getting a clean bill of health" but on a pardon granted by Admiral Voulgaris after the intercession of the Queen of Greece, "who had been interested in matter by Hadji Argyris' [sic] mother, wife of [Prime Minister] Sophoulis." The factual report concludes with this bit of information: "Athens Chief of Police, Evart [sic] states that Hadji Argyris is one of top propaganda and espionage agents of KKE (Greek Communist Party) in Athens."

Though never privy to this confidential description of himself transmitted via the American secretary of state, Hadjiargyris must have gotten wind of what his fellow journalists representing CBS felt about him, because he takes a broad swipe at Winston Burdett in his 1975 book. He finds it especially disgraceful that Burdett should have been among those who thought that Hadjiargyris should be given "the third degree" when Burdett had himself been a self-described fanatical and dogmatic member of the Communist party who had spied for the Soviet Union before rejecting Communism, turning double agent, and some years after the Polk murder (1955), providing the names of other journalists whom he identified as Communists for the Senate Internal Security Committee.[28]

According to Frederick Ayer, it was not at all surprising that Burdett turned anti-Communist the way he had. This "soft-spoken, quiet, almost whimsical" Harvard graduate—as Ayer describes him—whose photos of that period reveal a certain physical resemblance to Alger Hiss, had revealed in his testimony to the Senate committee that the Communist party had murdered his first wife, an Italian journalist, in Iran in 1942, a thing that evidently caused him to turn double agent and—in the McCarthyite fashion of the times—Senate informer.

It seems likely that what led Hadjiargyris to charge Burdett with favoring third-degree methods was a supposition based on Ayer's account of Secondari's violent instincts—a correct supposition, as it turned out—because Hadjiargyris did not have access to the confidential cable from Rankin to the State Department that links Burdett and Secondari in favoring this mode of interrogation for the *Christian Science Monitor*'s correspondent (the cable was declassified six months after Hadjiargyris's book went to press).[29] Since the comments attributed to the two CBS representatives are part of a "Memorandum of Conversation" recorded by a second secretary at the Athens embassy (Whitman), they cannot be taken as verbatim, but the memorandum clearly brings Burdett and Secondari in line with the Rankin-Ayer view of American correspondents in Greece by indicating that these two thought a majority of such correspondents "were giving their newspapers a very distorted view of the situation in Greece," a thing they were "inclined to attribute"—not without "some perplexity"—to the "diabolically clever and reasonable-sounding persuasiveness" of Kosta Hadjiargyris, who succeeded insidiously in imprinting in the minds of most of these American correspondents an attitude of criticism and hostility, which included "a feeling that the Greek Government was not only corrupt and reactionary but was hiding the truth of the situation."

Even the "apologetic" cable from the two CBS representatives concludes with some pique about the judicial process in Greece, sentiments that appear to reflect those of Ayer.[30] After offering an assurance that the "judicial interrogations were conducted with the utmost propriety and fairness," the cable adds: "If anything, they were too fair to elicit any important information," especially when dealing with someone like Hadjiargyris, who, Burdett and Secondari report, had little trouble parrying the questions of his interrogators. The CBS representatives are therefore convinced that "the case will never be solved or even greatly advanced through formal interrogations of this kind."

They didn't know it at the time, but they had little need to worry about matters of technique, because shortly after they left the case some six weeks later, less formal methods of interrogation were introduced by

Major Mouskoundis, the man Burdett and Secondari eulogized in their report to CBS as the most hard-working and effective of local police officers, the one who had "the highest respect of American and British observers."[31] The case had presumably passed into the best of possible hands after Ayer's intervention on behalf of Mouskoundis, and Burdett and Secondari give Ayer full credit for helping things move along appropriately: "His work and presence are, we believe, guarantee that investigation will be earnest and unflagging."[32] The only substantial worry that Burdett and Secondari express in their communications home, besides that concerning the formal method of interrogation, is a fear that the police in Athens, rather less collaborative than the police in Salonika, may get caught up in an attempt "to frame a guilty party and pass off the case as solved."[33] That a frame-up might be attempted by Major Mouskoundis and the Salonika security police, with or without the collusion of others, appears to have been out of the question. And the fear of a possible Athens frame-up was in any case not great, because "we think our presence here and our work here is one of the real guarantees against this," a thought in which immodesty contends with, but does not defeat, naiveté. The fact is, neither they nor Frederick Ayer stayed around long enough to test their perspicacity against the cunning of Major Mouskoundis had they eventually chosen to do so, and the record of their unquestioning faith in the major makes that possibility appear unlikely.

Both Salonika and Athens police—sometimes working together, sometimes not—continued to devote their major effort in June and July to finding an Athenian "connection" in the Polk affair. How else, they reasoned, could a Communist plot have been effectively planned enough in advance to be carried out efficiently in Salonika in less than forty-eight hours? And this persistent effort finally focused on the issue of documents and correspondence found to be missing from Polk's study in his Athens apartment on Skoufa Street. The fact that documents were found to be missing confirmed, in their view, an Athenian connection, since the documents must have contained a clue to that connection, the link between Athens and Salonika, and were therefore removed by somebody wanting to hide the incriminating evidence, perhaps the very culprit they were looking for. Only two people had unrestricted access to Polk's study besides the CBS correspondent himself: Kosta Hadjiargyris and Rea Polk, the former assisting Polk in preparing material, the latter in order to type and mail whatever was to be sent out.

As Hadjiargyris tells the story of the missing documents in his book, Athenian police investigators first conducted a survey of Polk's study four days after his body was recovered from Salonika Bay, that is, on May

20. Since none of the investigators knew English, their review of the various files in Polk's study produced no information of value. The following evening (May 21), Burdett and Secondari, having just arrived in Greece, conducted their own survey of the study to see if that might turn up a clue to the murderer or murderers of their CBS colleague. They found that the file containing correspondence with CBS held nothing dated after February 5, 1948, which meant that letters and memoranda from the three-month period before Polk's disappearance were missing from the file.

Burdett and Secondari reported their discovery to Polk's mother, who had reached Athens that day, and the following day they put the matter before Chief of Athens Police Evert, in Hadjiargyris's presence. According to Hadjiargyris, Evert did not appear much impressed at that particular moment by the problem of material missing from a CBS file; he seemed not as interested in possibly incriminating details as in the diplomatic problems of the case, his first mission being that of keeping the Polk affair from reaching dangerous extremes and expanding beyond what he could reasonably control. Polk's mother, on the other hand, thought a second look at the study was called for. Hadjiargyris declined to help her with this, having determined from the day Polk's body was discovered in Salonika not to enter Polk's Athens home unaccompanied (he admitted entering it once with others on May 19). Rea Polk now looked through the study and confirmed that material was missing from the relevant CBS file. When she was interviewed by the local police for the second time some ten days later, she told them that she was certain no material had been missing from the file at the time she left for Salonika to meet her husband on May 12, and when asked who else had free access to the study besides herself, she said only Kosta Hadjiargyris. She also said on this occasion that she had no idea how material from the file came to be missing—and that is what she says today, forty years after the fact, though her memory of this particular episode is now quite vague.

Hadjiargyris tells us that suspicion fell heavily upon him after Rea's second deposition, despite the courageous insistence of the Polks' maid, Despina Vroutsi, in the face of repeated police interrogation, that she had not encountered Hadjiargyris in the apartment at the time of Polk's trip to Salonika or alone anytime thereafter; on the few occasions she had seen him there during the period the CBS material was presumed to have disappeared, he was always accompanied by others. According to Hadjiargyris, the Athens investigators nevertheless began to construct a theory regarding the incomplete file that was intended to implicate him in the planning of Polk's murder. The key to the theory was a sentence in Polk's posthumously published "report" that had appeared in Drew Pearson's "Washington Merry-Go-Round" column of May 20, a sentence that clearly rankled the police: "Now that so many correspondents are writing such critical stories on the dominant right-wing faction of the government, there are a number of vague hints that 'somebody is likely to get hurt.'" What if that nefarious, antigovernment insinuation about the likelihood of somebody getting hurt had been added to Polk's text by Hadjiargyris when the report to Drew Pearson passed through his hands for review just before it was mailed out some weeks before Polk's trip north? The copy in the study file would not have shown this presumably handwritten emendation and therefore had to be removed from the file by Hadjiargyris to prevent the discrepancy from coming to light after the murder. If the discrepancy were discovered, that would imply that Hadjiargyris, in having added the phrase "somebody is likely to get hurt," had known in advance that Polk was a marked man, and if he knew that in advance, he was clearly implicated in the Communist plot that resulted some weeks later in his friend's fatal attempt to reach Markos.

From the Athens police perspective, Hadjiargyris tells us, this theory received substantial support when Burdett and Secondari, on questioning Rea Polk, learned that she had actually sent a messenger to her home on May 19—the same day that she returned to Athens from Salonika as a widow in mourning—and, before the police got to it, had the CBS file brought to her at the apartment of the British journalists Stephen and Mary Barber, where Rea had decided to stay for the while in order to have the benefit of Mary Barber's company. Her messengers for transporting the file: Kosta Hadjiargyris and Don Matchen, the York, Pennsylvania, correspondent for the *Daily Gazette* who happened to be on Polk's flight to Salonika and was sometimes with him during his last days there. Under further persistent questioning by Burdett and Secondari, Rea is reported to have become less sure of her messengers for transporting the file: she couldn't remember whether it was Hadjiargyris or maybe Mary Barber. Two or three days later, according to Hadjiargyris's account of the Burdett and Secondari interviews, Rea Polk could no longer remember who the messenger was. But Burdett was reported to have said that he had reason to believe Hadjiargyris had spoken to Rea on the matter in the meanwhile, and she had therefore decided to clam up.

What had in fact happened in the meanwhile, Hadjiargyris tells us, was that he, on his own initiative and unaware at the time of what Rea had or had not said during her interviews with Burdett and Secondari, went to the Athens police to report that Mary Barber had told him that she, at Rea's request, had gone to Polk's study, had retrieved two files (one marked "File on Rea" and the other "File of letters COLUMBIA"), and had then delivered these files to Rea Polk, information that Hadjiargyris repeated to the investigators as part of his sworn testimony on June 8.[34] At this point, despite the Athens police preference for their theory implicating Hadjiargyris alone, the Salonika judicial authorities Moustakis and Komotouros, then reviewing the Athens phase of the investigation, sent out an order denying exit from Greece not only to Hadjiargyris but to the Barber couple and to Rea Polk as well. As a result, on the sixteenth of June, Mary Barber, presumably on a news assignment, was kept from boarding a plane for Rhodes at Athens airport.

Why had Rea Polk asked for the two files? According to Hadjiargyris, she was reported to have told Burdett and Secondari that she thought some letters might be missing from the two files, including the copy of the report to Drew Pearson that was the basis of the local police interest in Hadjiargyris, and had wanted to check on this. But Hadjiargyris insists that Rea must have known that the Drew Pearson report was not necessarily in that file, and she must also have known that in any case the same report had gone out to a number of other news outlets besides Pearson, Rea being the one responsible for mailing the final drafts of all correspondence between her husband and colleagues in the U.S. Why hadn't she told all this to the Athens police from the start? Burdett and Secondari were said to have thought that Rea was afraid the police, for some reason of their own, would regard the whole business of the files as grounds for suspecting that she was somehow implicated in the murder—and, as we have seen, her presumed fear in this connection would have been justified by some of the questions the police confronted her with during one or another interrogation.

Hadjiargyris reports that for her part, Mary Barber admitted to the Athens investigators that she had delivered the files Rea Polk requested her to deliver because Rea told her that she wanted to make sure that her papers for her pending trip to America were in order.[35] This appears to have settled the matter as far as the police were concerned. Hadjiargyris concludes that, since the missing material from the CBS file remained missing and since nothing more than a series of suspicions emerged from the review of the circumstances surrounding its disappearance, the attempt by both the Athens investigators and Burdett and Secondari to discover something incriminating from this aspect of the case foundered and finally sank—and with it any substantial basis for developing an Athens connection to the murder. But not before Rea Polk had been required to travel to Salonika and appear before Major Mouskoundis for further interrogation.

Hadjiargyris has his own explanation of what happened to the missing material from the CBS file: it was taken by the Barber couple in order to cover the role they played in introducing George Polk to their Salonika friend, British Information Officer Randall Coate. As this explanation has it, Rea Polk had decided to cover the British couple as best she could because the British authorities in Greece promised her, via Stephen Barber, to exercise their influence in getting her relieved of further humiliating interrogation (Colonel Martin, the police adviser, presumably useful in this connection) and in realizing her wish to settle in America once and for all. Besides, Hadjiargyris argues, Rea probably saw no reason not to give in to British persuasion regarding the Barber couple since, from her point of view, it was the extreme Right in Greece, not the British, who were the hidden villains in the murder of her husband.

But, in Hadjiargyris's opinion, the police should have been smarter. The Barber couple was known to have been in touch with Randall Coate to get information about the guerrillas in the north not long before Polk's trip to Salonika. And though the Polk couple had nothing in common with the Barber couple politically, they were often together in the weeks before Polk traveled north. It should have been obvious to the police investigators that Polk had this couple in mind when he told Edward R. Murrow in his Salonika letter that he'd like to "get in touch with persons who count" on the guerrilla side "with a contact through a contact,"[36] Coate surely the former contact, and the Barber couple just as surely the latter. This is the theory that best explained, according to Hadjiargyris, why the Barber couple "isolated" Rea Polk in their one-room apartment after she returned from Salonika as a widow in mourning and why they had reason to take material out of the CBS file: that file clearly demonstrated the Barber-Coate connection and the involvement of the British Intelligence Service in the events that led up to Polk's disappearance.

Hadjiargyris would no doubt have felt that his theory was on firm ground had he known of a confidential cable from Raleigh Gibson to the State Department recording a conversation that Randall Coate was said to have had with George Polk during their Salonika meeting, as reported several days later by Coate to the deputy Greek liaison officer to UNSCOB, George Drossos,[37] a conversation during which Coate supposedly told Polk, in answer to a request from him, that he could give him an introduction to a cousin of Markos and was rebuffed by Polk's response: "No, I am not interested. You gave that name to Steve Barber. I need a serious contact" (Coate is described as having made his offer of help "to determine whether Polk was joking or not").[38] But Drossos also reported that Coate had told him at the same encounter, a few days after Polk disappeared and just before Coate left Salonika for good, that Drossos need not worry about Polk because "he is with the bandits," a remark, if taken as true, that implies Coate may well have known about Polk's meeting with some contact to make final arrangements for a trip to Markos but did not know that he had been murdered. For his part, Stephen Barber is reported to have told a friend in Denmark some years before he died that British Intelligence in Salonika had invited him to go to the mountains to interview Markos shortly before Polk traveled north but that he had refused the invitation. Barber apparently thought that he had been set up by the British to get killed and that Polk, the next correspondent to come that way, just happened to fall into the trap. According to Barber, the British motive was to frighten Western correspondents and hurt the image of the Greek Communist Party by making it look as though the Communists had killed Polk.[39]

There is now no way of verifying Barber's story, but for some still unknown or unrevealed reason, the tantalizing information supplied by Drossos was evidently never pursued in any way by the Salonika authorities or by their foreign advisers (though they could not have easily checked out Drossos's July 24 deposition with the Barbers, because by then the British couple was well beyond Greece's borders). And whatever the merits of Hadjiargyris's still unproven theory about the role of British Intelligence, the fact is that the order keeping Mary Barber from traveling to Rhodes was explained away almost immediately by the Greek authorities as an "error." The Greek newspaper *Acropolis* reported the following day that the person responsible for the "error" had been punished and an apology delivered to the lady correspondent. The Barber couple was soon allowed to leave the country—after the intervention, says Hadjiargyris, of Sir Charles Wickham, the Scotland Yard investigator who was head of the British Police Mission then assisting the Greek police. As was true of Randall Coate, the Barber couple never returned to Greece to testify in the Polk case or to offer any assistance to those left behind once they themselves were outside Greek jurisdiction. It would appear from the record that the Greek authorities and their foreign advisers lost all interest in the British couple once they had left the scene, which may seem explicable in the case of the British advisers if one assumes that they were embarrassed by the presumption of Coate's possible involvement and felt it necessary to cover his tracks but is hardly explicable in the case of all the others intimately involved in the investigation, unless one sees them giving in to strong British pressure.

A confidential cable from Frederick Ayer to the secretary of state suggests that the Barber episode had created a certain awkwardness on all sides, anyway sufficient tension between Greek officials and their various foreign advisers to make the local authorities a bit gun shy thereafter in dealing with foreign witnesses. Ayer speaks of "Stupidity shown . . . method prevention leave country, Steve, Mary Barber, with police advised but no personal notification beforehand. . . . Some damage done and official explanations came late. Inefficiency, not ill-will, part Greek officials, to blame."[40] One result seems to have been the relatively gentle treatment of another foreign witness who might have expected less tolerance on the part of Ayer and company: Don Matchen, the York, Pennsylvania, correspondent. Given the official reports of Matchen's presumed leftist credentials (among these, his having "expressed admiration for Henry Wallace's present position"),[41] one would have thought him a prime candidate for some form of rough treatment by his interrogators, but Ayer's cable on the Barbers tells us that the questioning of Matchen not only added little information but that the gentleman was "smoothly handled, no interruption his itinerary"—in short, that he was allowed to leave Greece quickly and without incident.

Not so Rea Polk and Kosta Hadjiargyris, though the failure of the Athens investigation to turn suspicion into substantial evidence in either case forced the center of interest in them to move back to Salonika. In the Barber cable, Ayer informs the State Department that "interrogation Athens completed for time being," and the archives reveal that he had become diligent, after the first week of June, in an effort to get both Rea and Hadjiargyris to the security police headquarters in Salonika where Major Mouskoundis might have a chance to interrogate both witnesses properly, since, in Ayer's view, it had been a "great error" to assign the case not to the police but to the ministry of justice in Athens,[42] where the "method interrogation to date" is described by him as follows: "two men Attorney General's office ask questions numerical sequence from prepared list. Witness gives answer and interrogator dictates it to clerk who copies long hand. Then comes next question. Then all present sign paper and witness signs. Is laborious and almost fruitless process from reluctant or timorous witness."[43] The implication seems to be that Major Mouskoundis would be more "professional," less inhibited, perhaps even capable of the "third degree" method preferred by Burdett and Secondari, or some equivalent Greek version.

Ayer's problem, though, as he himself reported it, was that the Greek government feared an outcry in the American press if the "inquiries" were to be "conducted confidentially by police";[44] and the Greek authorities in Salonika, Major Mouskoundis included, appeared reluctant to bring either Rea Polk or Kosta Hadjiargyris under their jurisdiction without more incriminating evidence to justify that move, a thing

Mouskoundis still seemed certain he would dig up in due course.[45] For his part, the attorney general in Salonika, Constantinidis, explained to his American advisers that he himself couldn't legally hold Rea Polk under custody; only the police could do that, and if they did, the one thing he could do to help the progress of the case would be to "overlook it."[46] But that, he said, wouldn't solve the delicate problem of Hadjiargyris and his connection to at least one person at the highest political level, namely, the prime minister. And in an earlier interview the attorney general had confirmed that he was worried about American public opinion, as Ayer had suggested.[47] The attorney general was apparently ready to arrest Hadjiargyris if the evidence justified it, but how would the American press in Athens respond to that? A "scandal" might be caused by such action, because "the American Correspondents [sic] in Athens were all in favor of Hadjiargyris and did not believe that he was connected with the case."

Ayer nevertheless persisted in his hope that he could get Rea and Kosta arrested before the interest in these two key witnesses dissipated dangerously, or at least get them placed under "protective custody" so that he had more time to persuade the Salonika authorities to take them on, in any case before Rea was allowed to leave for the States. He asked that the State Department advise him "when and if atmosphere newspaper world propitious" for such a move, though he felt that already at that time a majority of the correspondents in his corner of the world "would apparently" support it.[48]

Ayer seemed to be running out of luck when a new factor appeared on the scene that offered every hope of providing him with the additional weapons he needed not only to carry the investigation back to Salonika, where it could be kept under what he felt was proper police control, but also to bring it under even more weighty American influence than local diplomacy and visiting press had so far exercised: General William J. "Wild Bill" Donovan and his assistant, Lieutenant Colonel James Kellis, arrived in Athens on behalf of the Overseas Writers Special Committee of Inquiry (that is, the Lippmann Committee), with the full blessing of the State Department. Donovan's first visits to Athens and Salonika were quick but seemingly crucial from Ayer's point of view. On June 14, only four days after Donovan and Kellis arrived in Greece, Ayer could report secretly to the secretary of state, with what must have been a sense of rejuvenation, that the visit "had good results putting pressure even Prime Minister to assure eventual police interrogation Hadji and Rea Polk."[49] The Salonika attorney general had also given his assurance that "this would be done under arrest warrant" whenever the proper authorities felt it advisable.

Evidently on a high with his new prospects, Ayer allows his cable to serve up spicy if warmed-over potage as he quotes someone identified simply as "highly placed Salonika Communist contact Ayer informant" to the effect that the Polk murder was not planned or committed by a Salonika organization on its own but probably "on orders and through agents Cominform," with Rea Polk "certainly" and Hadjiargyris "probably" playing a part in the crime, and with an Athens agent "undoubtedly . . . involved," which makes the need acute for the two principal Athenian suspects to be held under protective custody, since they are likely to be killed by the Communists if there is any indication that they are furnishing information to the police, especially since "Rea known belonged KKE [Greek Communist Party] and also active for party in Egypt"—in fact, "strong rumors exist she today highly placed agent."

The euphoria occasioned by Donovan's presence on the scene may have accounted, at least in part, for the supreme recklessness, not to say downright stupidity, of this "Report No. 8" from Frederick Ayer to the secretary of state. There is no evidence from any source at the time of this report or subsequently that Polk's teen-age bride, recently employed as an airline hostess, had any particular politics at the moment of his death—though, like many Greeks and like Polk himself, she was suspicious of some elements that were part of the government then in power—and her expressed opinions during the years since have suggested a certain political conservatism. One can venture that the young lady who graduated from Barnard with a B.A. degree four years after Ayer's report would have been amused by its blatant nonsense—as even Frederick Ayer himself might have been in retrospect. But during the critical days when the cable was sent out, it was pernicious nonsense. Fortunately for some of the suspects in the Polk affair—unfortunately not for all—the particular Athenian connection that the report reaffirms eventually vanished in the desert regions of the Vardar Valley to the north, as did most of Ayer's wilder insinuations.

Kosta Hadjiargyris is not likely to have been among those who could find amusement at any point in Frederick Ayer's outrageous perspective on the Polk case, though he admitted in an interview with the author some months before his death in late 1986 that his own perspective had softened over the years. At the time of the interview Hadjiargyris was in his mid-seventies, white-haired, ruddy-faced, taller than the average Greek of his generation but now with a potbelly, teeth heavily stained, thick glasses, his mind still sharp, with a touch of acid and a large portion of cynicism remaining, but the manner amiable, and more irony than bitterness in what his memory allowed him to see of those trying days in 1948–49. "I was obsessed with the Polk case for some years, as you can imagine," he told me. "But not anymore. Not since I wrote my book." When I asked him if he still thought the British were behind the murder, his eyes shifted to the window. "I lived with the British for thirteen years before and after the murder. They always cover themselves. You won't find any of those who were involved coming clean about it. Randall Coate least of all." What about the Barbers? "Steve Barber was irrelevant, a simpleminded man, really. But his wife Mary, she was the shrewd one. So who can now say how much she was involved? Of course she covered her tracks." And the Americans? Raleigh Gibson, for example? "Raleigh Gibson knew his business, what it was and how to perform it." "Meaning?" I asked. Kosta Hadjiargyris turned back from the window with a tiny wry smile for comment. And Mouskoundis? What was his impression of Mouskoundis? "The man always behaved toward me with absolute politeness, even friendliness," Hadjiargyris said. "Of course we know about Mouskoundis and his kind of sweet hypocritical mask. We have had much experience of that sort of theater in this country."

The interview ended with talk of the Greek film then in progress on the Polk affair. Hadjiargyris had not only been acting as an adviser to the producers, but found himself emerging in the script as one of the "heroes" of the story and finally taking part as a performer, interviewed at length on camera and generally celebrated in that film version of the Polk affair as one of those who ended up on the side of the angels. He told an anecdote about another participant who hadn't ended up that way, an official in the case who not only refused to be interviewed but was so frightened by the prospect that he bellowed hysterically at the producers when they called on him personally, threatening violence if they ever returned to bother him, then slammed his door in their faces. "Perfect," said Hadjiargyris. "Just what the producers wanted. They had managed to record the whole scene on film. Only of course in filming as in real life, one version is not enough. So the producers went back the next day and got another even stronger dose of hysteria from the same official for their second take." Hadjiargyris's tiny wry smile returned. "Perhaps my second take on the Polk affair was my book. And now my third take is this film. Who is to say?"

V The Salonika Contact

IN PHOTOGRAPHS from the period of the Polk affair, "Wild Bill" Donovan looks anything but wild: chubbily avuncular when smiling, silver-haired, eyes wide ("Oh, I remember those big blue innocent eyes of his," says Rea Polk, though not with what sounds like nostalgia),[1] senatorial when not smiling, but with a suggestion of toughness, even of cruelty, when the eyes appear narrower and the mouth a thin line. Kellis also comes out a bit pudgy in the photographs, broad-faced, wavy-haired, black-browed, showing his Greek origins in his coloring and his military background in the firm set of his mouth and jaw.[2] Donovan was a kind of national hero—The Last Hero, according to one of his biographers (Anthony Cave Brown): a Congressional Medal of Honor commander of the "Fighting Irish" in World War I who had gone on to become head of the Office of Strategic Services during World War II and in that capacity was regarded by some as America's master spy. Kellis had served under him while Donovan was specifically in charge of undercover operations behind enemy lines in a number of countries, including Greece, which was Kellis's specialty.[3] At the time of the Polk investigation, Donovan was a New York lawyer, generally acknowledged to be the "father" of the newly established Central Intelligence Agency. He was chosen by Lippmann's special committee as their counsel and chief investigator in Greece because he was thought to be "the person most eminently qualified."[4] He was also a friend of the Overseas Writers' president, Ernest K. Lindley, and he agreed to serve as counsel without fee.

The special committee that Donovan and Kellis represented was formed during the week after Polk's body was recovered, evidently out of a fear that the case would not be handled properly by the Greek government, a fear no doubt based on reports of local corruption, dictatorial policies, and mistreatment of American newsmen that had been coming in from sources in Athens, Polk himself among them. The special committee included, besides Lindley and Lippmann, such prominent American journalists of the postwar era as Morgan Beatty, Marquis Childs, Elmer Davis, Eugene Meyer, and James Reston. These and several other committee members (James Reston not among them) met with Secretary of State George Marshall as early as May 24 to obtain his cooperation as they proceeded with their immediate purpose, which Lippmann said was to learn as much as they could about the official investigation then under way.[5] Secretary Marshall told them that he saw no reason why the Department of State shouldn't make available to the committee any information possessed by any agency of the government on the activities of Polk in Greece and any other departmental communication bearing on the murder. He also named those American officials in Washington and Athens who had been charged with "the matter"— William O. Baxter at State, Karl Rankin in Athens, Raleigh Gibson in Salonika—and indicated that the committee not only "may work with" Mr. Baxter but "may from time to time submit questions and suggestions to Mr. Rankin through the Secretary."[6]

Donovan and Kellis could hardly have hoped for more backup than this; in fact, it demonstrated an unusual commitment to cooperative enterprise between the executive branch of the government and the Fourth Estate,[7] though, rather ironically, with one of the principal designated agents for this cooperation, Karl Rankin, the man who had suggested that the State Department use its influence to promote a more stringent control by the American press over its representatives abroad. Of course cooperative enterprise of this nature carries with it the danger of collusion at one extreme and, at the other extreme, the danger of manipulation by officials whose public integrity goes hand in hand with a power to operate secretly behind the scenes and beyond what the press can know.

Both these dangers finally came to dominate the relationship between government and press in the Polk case, but not before Donovan and Kellis were able to use their State Department connection for an exercise of executive privilege and authority in a foreign country such as few diplomats even of that era were capable of exercising. When they finally arrived in Athens on June 10, a month after the murder, they were met by Frederick Ayer and then, within three hours, they were introduced not only to those figures on the American side who, like Ayer, had well established views on the Polk case—Ambassador Griswold, Rankin, Burdett, and Secondari—but to two of the principal figures on the Greek side in Athens, Minister of Public Order Rendis and Prime Minister Sophoulis himself, this before moving on to Salonika the next day to interview the principal American and Greek figures there. A visiting congressional delegation could hardly have expected more prompt and thorough access to official Greece.

Rankin's cabled report to the secretary of state on Donovan's two-day tour of the investigation sites confirms that Frederick Ayer, and probably Rankin himself, scored amply from this first visit by the Overseas Writers' representatives.[8] The points that Donovan "developed" during his conferences with Greek authorities are so much in keeping with the already established official American line as to suggest that they emerged from on-the-spot briefing: the Lippmann Committee would fully support whatever steps the authorities deemed necessary to the interrogation of material witnesses, including arrest, detention, or protective custody as might be required to ensure that these witnesses be questioned thoroughly; specifically, nothing should be allowed to stand in the way of a thorough questioning of George Polk's widow Rea and *Christian Science Monitor* correspondent Kosta Hadjiargyris. Rankin adds that "Donovan told the Prime Minister that he spoke thus frankly to him of his own stepson because he knew the Prime Minister to be an honest man." Rankin does not describe the expression on the prime minister's face as he received this frankness, though he does tell us that Sophoulis agreed about his stepson being "a witness of prime importance" and gave his word that he would "personally follow the investigation and insure its vigorous continuence" [sic].

Donovan also told the prime minister that no political obstacles should be permitted to block or thwart an honest investigation, and he referred especially to the fact that the interrogation of the aforementioned witnesses had been taken out of the hands of the police and entrusted to the Ministry of Justice, which, he said, was not equipped or prepared to conduct a searching interrogation. He hoped that this transfer of authority had not been done in order to give Rea Polk and Kosta Hadjiargyris a form of political protection, to which Sophoulis is reported to have answered that he appreciated the criticism of the interrogations in question and attributed the problem to a rivalry between the Ministry of Public Order and the Ministry of Justice, "a vying for honors in this case." He then assured Donovan that there would be no political meddling in the investigation.

One has to wonder from this account—if Rankin is to be taken as reporting these exchanges faithfully—what Prime Minister Sophoulis and his attendant officials must have said under their breath about this American lawyer who had served as an intelligence expert and now represented the American press and who had been in Athens just a few hours but who seemed to be full of assumptions not only about the victim's widow and the prime minister's own stepson but about the possibility of politicized interrogations he had not attended under a system that even a master spy could not possibly have mastered in such a short time. These officials would have assumed, of course, that Donovan had been thoroughly briefed by his embassy associates and that he was speaking for them as much as for himself, or, if he was speaking for the press first of all, that one was meant to assume the American press and the American diplomatic establishment spoke with one voice, an assumption that the Lippmann Committee surely would not have professed even after having begun their independent inquiry by soliciting the cooperation of General Marshall and the State Department. In any case, Donovan's interviews in Athens on his first day there set the tone for his further relations with Greek officials involved in the Polk case. What he showed was mostly a mixture of diplomacy and arrogance, of cajolery and inquisition, his air of authority evidently never seriously muted by the ignorance of local circumstances that he carried with him initially and only sporadically found occasion to modify during his time in Greece.

When Donovan and Kellis moved on to Salonika the second day, they encountered somewhat less reassurance and a touch more defensiveness on the part of Greek officials there, even a diminished courtesy despite the constant presence of Raleigh Gibson, Winston Burdett, and John Secondari to back up the new arrivals. Again, the ambition of the Lippmann Committee representatives in the first instance appeared to be not so much that of learning what they could about the official investigation then in progress—what Lippmann had indicated would be the first order of business for his committee—as that of pressuring the local officials to bring Rea Polk and Kosta Hadjiargyris north to Salonika under arrest or protective custody for more intensive interrogation, in keeping with the persistent wishes of Ayer, who had escorted the new arrivals in Athens, and Burdett and Secondari, who now escorted them in Salonika.

The visitors approached Attorney General Constantinidis first of all. We learn from Gibson's report on this meeting that it began with the attorney general's expressed hope that the investigation then under way in Athens would "secure the names of the contacts that were needed in the case," that is, the presumably necessary connection between someone in Athens and the Communist party elements that had planned the murder there and then made further contact with someone in Salonika.[9] The solution to the case, said Constantinidis, was to be found "in the mountains," but in the meanwhile there were many difficulties in the pursuit of specifics. For one, foreign correspondents were not watched by the police, so their contacts were generally not known. And then there was the problem of obtaining warrants for the arrest of people who had been close to Polk, suspects and informers to be questioned. And even if one could get the warrants, persons arrested by the Greek authorities had a right to name a lawyer, and these lawyers had the right to study the details of the case as prepared by the authorities. Constantinidis seemed to imply that this could give cunning lawyers and witnesses an awkward advantage.

The attorney general's remarks evidently provided Donovan his first opening to ask whether the authorities had the right "to place people in protective custody." The issue was complicated; Constantinidis explained that regular procedure in Greece "did not permit a person being held as a suspect or as an informer." Protective custody "is not under Greek law." It is "work of the police." And even the police can hold a person only for a short time, "generally for two or three days," then have to turn the party over to the inquiry magistrate for questioning, and the only way the police could rearrest the party would be under "special permission . . . given them by the Attorney General."

The confused—and ultimately deleterious—quality of Donovan's interest in these legal matters is suggested by the Draft Report, where we are told that Donovan "pointed to the inherent difficulties which [the system of justice in Salonika] imposed on the investigation," namely, the fact that "the police can generally only detain a person for a few days and thereafter must release them or order a formal arrest," and once the arrest is made, "the defendant may name counsel who has an immediate right to inspect the 'dossier.' "[10] The Draft Report indicates that "under this system, it was almost impossible to provide adequate protection for witnesses," but it then indicates that the real difficulty is the way this system slowed the investigatory process, though there evidently were more positive results when, "at the time of the detention of Gregory Staktopoulos and his mother, the Greek authorities did in fact defer their formal arrest for several weeks [actually over six weeks] in order to give the police authorities sufficient opportunity to complete their interrogation and investigation of the pair without the necessity to observe the formal requirements of interrogation required after a formal arrest has been ordered."[11] The Draft Report concludes that "it is difficult to say whether in the long run the decision to place primary responsibility for the investigation in the hands of the police would have achieved any prompter solution to the crime"—at best a naive conclusion in view of the way the investigation was handled by Mouskoundis and Constantinidis.

In any event, speed appears to be the essential concern in this commentary from the Draft Report; the violation of the civil liberties of Gregory Staktopoulos and his mother is either unrecognized by this text or justified by the "opportunity" it provided the police to "complete their interrogation and investigation." And whatever Donovan's concern, had Raleigh Gibson taken due note of the implications of Attorney General Constantinidis's explication during this first interview with Donovan, he would have had ample reason, as the American observer continually in contact with the Salonika Greek authorities, to question the treatment of Gregory Staktopoulos just two months later, held by the police for forty-five days before he was turned over to the inquiry magistrate, and, according to Staktopoulos's account, in a condition so damaged that the inquiry magistrate had to help guide the pen with which the Reuters stringer signed his presumably incriminating confession.

Donovan's growing restlessness over Constantinidis's legal talk at this point in the interview is suggested by his now telling the attorney general that "the people of the United States would judge Greece from the manner that the Greek Government handled the Polk murder case," and there was "no profit in discussing [the] principles" involved. What he needed was an answer to the questions: "Is there a person or persons that you would like to have placed in custody?" and if so, "why has it not been done?" The attorney general replied that "he had no information that would permit him to order the arrest of any person in the case," but, he said, there were two people who must have known about the murder, Rea Polk and Kosta Hadjiargyris, neither of whom were "direct culprits" but both of whom were "collaborators." Indeed, Donovan responded, these were the two people he himself had in mind, and he asked: "If this was [sic] an ordinary case, what would be done about Mrs. Rea Polk?" The attorney general replied, "Not much." Winston Burdett now wanted to know why. Didn't the attorney general consider her an important witness? Donovan followed by reminding the attorney general that Greek law would in fact "allow the authorities to place Mrs. Rea Polk in custody." Not so, said Constantinidis, he had to face the provisions of the law, otherwise he would put her under custody. And then he made a comment that was telling in view of Staktopoulos's subsequent fate: the police, on the other hand, could hold Rea Polk, and he "would overlook it."

Donovan did not pick up specifically on this rather startling revelation. He wanted to make sure that the attorney general understood how concerned the American press was that "this case . . . [be] handled right," because Polk had become "a symbol representing all correspondents that will go to foreign lands." And Burdett added that "the examination of a witness like Hadjiargyris will meet with the approval of all American newspapermen." Even Gibson entered the debate at this point to remind Constantinidis that the attorney general himself had considered issuing a warrant for Hadjiargyris's arrest on June 7 and had desisted only because he thought the arrest would create a scandal among American correspondents in Athens. Both Burdett and Donovan again reassured the attorney general that American correspondents in Athens and elsewhere would be "all behind any action of this nature on the part of the authorities" because they realized that Rea Polk and Hadjiargyris were important witnesses in the case, and for this reason correspondents in Athens and the U.S. "would not criticize any action by the authorities."

The attorney general apparently became defensive. He replied to this implicit criticism of his reticence by asserting that "an inquiry is a collection of information." And he raised the question of Daniel Thrapp, who had so far not come forward with the name of the Salonika contact for his aborted trip to Markos's headquarters, the man mentioned in Thrapp's one communication from Rome. The unstated question for Burdett and Donovan was, presumably, if American correspondents were so ready to be as cooperative as the two gentlemen were suggesting, why hadn't Daniel Thrapp come forward with more information on this Salonika contact? Donovan now said he would recommend to the committee he represented that a request be made for the United Press to order Thrapp to return to Greece from Rome so that he could be examined by the Greek authorities. As the interview drew to a close, Donovan stated that he had informed his committee that "the full weight of the investigation of the crime is on the Greek Government," and he was in Salonika to tell the attorney general that "all possible would be done to aid the Greek Government in the case." The attorney general expressed his thanks. Then Donovan asked—rather bluntly, it seems—"Is the Attorney General going to obtain the proper examination of Hadjiargyris and Mrs. Polk in the place that he desires?" Gibson tells us that the answer was yes, and that Constantinidis added: "the method of doing this would be turned over to the Police," presumably the Security Police under Major Mouskoundis.

Though Donovan had professed his lack of interest in principles and his commitment to specifics during this first interview of the day, he saved his review of certain grubby details of the case for a conference with Salonika Chief of Police Colonel Xanthopoulos, followed by a luncheon with Commander Gordon and Colonel Martin of the British

Police Mission (Gibson reminded the secretary of state in his report that "Colonel Martin is taking an active part in directing the investigation of the crime"). What was said during the luncheon we are not told, but Gibson's report includes a memorandum of the conversation between the visiting group and the chief of police.[12] Among the items discussed were several apparent lapses and still open questions in the investigation up to that point: for example, the large number of phone calls made by AP stringer Helen Mamas in Rea Polk's name that still hadn't been checked out, the question of whether not only restaurants but also wholesalers had been interviewed regarding lobster sales in the Salonika area, the still unexplained fact that Polk's last meal of lobster and peas was not "a typical Greek dish" (though it had been determined that May was the season for fresh peas), then the failure of the Astoria Hotel staff to provide much useful evidence (the chief of police said that he had little confidence in their testimony "due to their mentality"), and finally, whether or not anybody in Salonika worked for Hadjiargyris (the chief knew of no one). At the conclusion of the conference, "it was explained" to the chief of police that "American Correspondents in the United States and in Athens would be in agreement to the arrest of Hadjiargyris and Mrs. Rea Polk, and that no adverse criticism was to be feared."

In his covering memorandum to the secretary of state, Gibson sees the day's activities as grounds for optimism. He is now convinced that the attorney general and other local officials have lost their fear of an unfavorable reaction on the part of American correspondents "in case Hadjiargyris and Mrs. Polk are arrested," and this means that the visit of General Donovan to Salonika "was of value to the future activities of the investigation." And he was pleased that Donovan, after his day of meetings, agreed with him "that the police authorities in Salonika had and were carrying on an honest and thorough investigation," even an efficient one "when it was realized that [they] did not have scientific material to work with." Gibson was also pleased that Donovan considered Major Mouskoundis "a good policeman . . . doing an excellent job." But the fact is that by the time General Donovan returned to Greece six weeks later, the Salonika authorities still had not found sufficient grounds for bringing Hadjiargyris north for further interrogation, even though Hadjiargyris himself had by that time challenged them either to do so or finally leave him in peace.

They did neither, actually, which meant that in the aftermath of Donovan's first visit, Ayer, Burdett, and company emerged with only a partial victory and had to settle for the limited and finally dubious success of what Ayer reported to Secretary Marshall as Rea Polk's "voluntary" submission, "at request Ministry," to interrogation by Major Mouskoundis in Salonika.[13] Ayer, Gibson, and Attorney General Constantinidis all agreed, according to Ayer, that "Rea be thoroughly questioned until determined whether innocent, lying or implicated crime," and that she not be allowed to leave Greece "except in case complete innocence." Ayer adds that she "could be dangerously exploited publicity-wise by Communists and others in US" and that he feels "more damage can perhaps be done Rea in US than Rea in Greece."

But it turned out that Ayer had to live with the larger danger. Rea Polk journeyed to Salonika on June 26, a few days before her American visa was due to expire, and was interrogated there by the public prosecutor and the Security Police under Mouskoundis, who, Ayer reveals in another secret cable, "states satisfied although [Rea] not telling whole truth does not feel she has guilty knowledge."[14] That must have been a bitter pill for Ayer to swallow after having reported to the secretary of state less than two weeks earlier that his Communist informant had indicated not only that Rea certainly played a part in the crime but that the young lady was known to be a member of the Greek Communist Party and rumored to be a highly placed agent. Yet Ayer shows himself to be wonderfully resilient when he adds to the latest news from Salonika: "Independent investigation Ayer's office tends confirm [Mouskoundis's] conclusion. Information she of KKE [Greek Communist Party] not definite enough to justify any action." Rea, for her part, is pictured as coming around in at least one respect. In her deposition before both the public prosecutor and Mouskoundis, she was reported to have given "as her opinion crime committed by Communists." Mouskoundis took this to be a "sincere change of opinion" that was not dictated by a desire to tell the authorities what they might want to hear.

Whatever the value of Mouskoundis's perception, the authorities allowed Rea to leave the country two days later. Winston Burdett reported to his CBS colleagues, via Rankin, that the police "have assured us that her proposed departure for America will not hinder investigation as they believe she probably has no vital information to offer."[15] So much for his earlier view of Rea Polk as a witness so important that an arrest was called for. Still, Rea's departure was authorized only on the condition that she undertake to return to Greece if she was ever wanted for further questioning, and she was made to execute two affidavits to that effect before the Greek authorities and the American embassy. Burdett adds a rather surly and disingenuous note: "In reaching decision on this matter we have had to weigh damage that Rea might do by possible irresponsible talk in America against adverse publicity that would probably follow her enforced detainment in Greece"—this despite his quite recent assurances to Greek authorities in Salonika that there would be no negative criticism from the American press were either Hadjiargyris or Rea Polk to be arrested or held in custody. Burdett recommends in any case that General Donovan be asked to make every effort to question Rea again before his next trip to Greece.

So Rea Polk left Athens for Montclair, New Jersey, via Detroit, on an entry visa as Polk's widow, thus avoiding what would have surely cost her some years of waiting for a regular quota visa. Rankin's unclassified cable announcing her departure in late June 1948 sounds almost celebrative, almost an expression of harmony in the fraternity house after harsh debate: "Satisfactory undertakings obtained by Greeks and Embassy and Rea Polk departing today with permission Ministers Justice and Public Order, and concurrence Ayer Burdett and Embassy. TWA flight 989 due Detroit early Tuesday."[16] And the day after Rea left, Rankin quotes a statement from Rea's mother on behalf of her daughter thanking the Press Ministry for the exceptional and sincere interest it showed from the very first moment and asking the minister to express Rea's gratitude to the Greek government, "which has shown its full sympathy on the occasion of the tragic event," in particular the judiciary and police authorities of Salonika and Athens, including, among others, Constantinidis, Mouskoundis, and Evert.[17] Rea's mother adds thanks from Rea's father, Mr. Kokkonis, the gentleman early admired by Constantinidis and trusted as his daughter never was from the moment Polk's body surfaced in Salonika Bay.

As it turned out, Rea Polk did not return to Greece in connection with the Polk affair, though strenuous efforts were made to get her to do so less than a year later, by which time she was an undergraduate at Barnard College and well into a new American life that eventually brought her a B.A. degree, an amiable and prosperous second husband (who died some years ago), and a son studying to be a physicist. She now lives in Greece and thinks of settling permanently on the shore opposite the island of Hydra, but she says that back in the harsh summer of 1948 and the anxious months that followed, she felt that no man-made force could get her to return to Greece for further questioning. And fortunately, with the help of two American doctors and the intervention of General Donovan ("I am really grateful to that man for the assistance he gave me then, whatever else may have happened"),[18] Rea Polk was declared to be under too much mental strain even in the spring of 1949 to permit her to travel back to Greece to testify again and so was allowed to go on more or less peacefully with her new life.

With Rea gone indefinitely and Mouskoundis apparently reluctant to interrogate Kosta Hadjiargyris until he had more evidence against him, the investigation seemed almost totally stalled, and it continued to seem so as the summer moved toward its dog days. Even as Rea was being cleared in Athens for her flight to the States, Raleigh Gibson sent the secretary of state an account of a recent meeting that he and Frederick Ayer had held with Attorney General Constantinidis during which it became evident that prospects had not appeared to be very auspicious even before Rea's Salonika interrogation and that Constantinidis had begun to show that he himself was worried about the slow progress of the investigation.[19] He felt that the inquiries in Athens had established that there was a "person" who had served as a contact with Polk for the trip to Markos—and the "person" was probably two people, one in Athens and one in Salonika—but who was this person or persons? Did Rea Polk know? Did Hadjiargyris? Did Daniel Thrapp, the UP correspondent then in Rome who could easily have assisted the case but refused to remember the name or address of the Greek in Salonika who had offered to help him reach Markos, though he admitted knowing something about the man's background (according to Burdett and Secondari, Thrapp wasn't talking because he didn't want to compromise a professional contact, one that might be useful to him in the future)? Contantinidis simply couldn't understand Thrapp's attitude. And then there was this Helen Mamas, the Greek-American AP stringer. The investigation showed that Miss Mamas and George Polk were acquainted with each other, but Miss Mamas had denied that she knew Polk well even though she was one of the first persons Polk called on in Salonika, and Miss Mamas would not admit to having had any sort of serious conversation with Polk. The attorney general simply didn't believe her story, nor did the chief of police.

The rest of the interview focused on the attorney general's "person" theory, with much discussion of whether the missing files in Athens were a red herring or—as Ayer and Constantinidis finally agreed—held the clue to Polk's contacts in Athens and Salonika, since they must have been removed to hide that fact by a person who knew what they contained, most likely Kosta Hadjiargyris, despite his denials. Constantinidis said his personal belief was that the murder had been planned in Athens and was then carried out by the Communist andartes, and Major Mouskoundis shared his belief. But there was a certain problem with the major. The attorney general had tried to secure more information from Mouskoundis but had not succeeded in doing so. Constantinidis felt that the major had some person in mind for Polk's contact but was keeping the information to himself. The interview ended inconclusively, though before the end Ayer affirmed that Major Mouskoundis had indicated to him that he did not want to question Hadjiargyris "until he knows the name of George Polk's contact in Salonika or Athens." The implication was that the major must indeed be on to something.

A month later, when General Donovan came to Athens and Salonika for a second exploration on behalf of the Lippmann Committee, the search for "the person" was still on, but if there had been any substantial progress by Greek officials in identifying the likeliest candidate or candidates, American authorities on the scene gave little evidence of it in their communications with the State Department. Major Mouskoundis submitted a report to Raleigh Gibson on July 19 that provided the consul general with few grounds for optimism. In his confidential preface to the report, Gibson describes it as revealing that local officials are indeed encountering difficulties in securing new leads and that "the investigation is only being carried on in routine manner."[20] He tells the secretary of state that the police, now hoping that the Greek national army will solve their problem by capturing the murderer or murderers in one of its operations against the guerrillas, "are not working too efficiently in endeavoring to secure evidence in Athens or in Salonika." Gibson agrees with the police interest in obtaining definite information as to Daniel Thrapp's contact in Salonika, but he is now of the opinion that "the failure to secure such information will be used as an alibi by local officials to explain their failure in breaking the case."

This is the first indication we have of a certain cynicism on Raleigh Gibson's part regarding the attitude of his Greek colleagues, and the report itself confirms his estimate of police enterprise. There Major Mouskoundis offers up an old story: "we maintain our original firm and solid conviction that the unfortunate Polk was murdered by an [sic] anarchists from the mountains who collaborated with agents of the city to influence him and to take him in a small sailing vessel or a boat to the opposite coast of Pierria [sic], and from there to lead him to a place where he could meet Markos or his 'Ministers.' "[21] Mouskoundis feels that "this satanic conspiracy cannot be attributed to Greek brains, that is, to Greek brains uninfluenced by the Communist Party": the murder "was planned in detail by the Party which, when plans were ready, issued the order for the culprits to carry out their execution." The major then goes into a familiar review of police activities so far—study of photographs, surveillance of persons and vessels, pursuit of lobster sales, etc.—and a fulsome appreciation of the assistance offered by Ayer, Burdett and Secondari, and Colonel Kellis, left behind by General Donovan to continue investigating on behalf of the Lippmann Committee. The "person" theory is now defined in terms of the general theory, but with a new assumption regarding the linguistic competence of the Salonika contact: "there is no doubt that an English-speaking person was used for Polk's contacts here with the Communist Party. This English-speaking person must have met Polk at his hotel and accompanied him to the place where the murder took place." Mouskoundis's report ends with a plea that correspondent Thrapp be forced to clarify that part of his Rome letter where he mentions "a certain person with whom Polk was in contact, and who might have sent him to Markos' headquarters" (Thrapp in fact merely speculated that Polk may have met his unnamed and now unnameable contact in Salonika).

Major Mouskoundis's report gave General Donovan much room to exercise renewed pressure on the Greek authorities in the name of justice for the American press in foreign places, and it appears that this in turn provided Mouskoundis with a plausible excuse to bring the "person" theory cruelly to life in the shape of Gregory Staktopoulos. What the pressure from Donovan crystalized into during his second visit was a demand for a formal arrest of a kind that would presumably satisfy those Donovan represented back home, however awkward the local consequences. What Mouskoundis had to satisfy was both the increasingly forceful American demand that a culprit be found of whatever political persuasion—even if most Americans on the scene preferred the "Communist angle"—and his own commitment and that of his Greek colleagues to a solution that would put the blame squarely on the Greek Communist Party.

Donovan traveled to Salonika on July 24 to interview Major Mouskoundis in the company of Gibson, Kellis, and Burdett. By that time John Secondari had apparently left the investigation, and so had Frederick Ayer.[22] It also turned out that Major Mouskoundis had recently been in an automobile accident, which had occasioned what the consulate's text calls "a temporary stoppage of the investigation."[23] But it was the more long-range stoppage that interested General Donovan. Gibson's July 27 report to the secretary of state on this second Salonika visit, as recorded in a "Memorandum of Conversation" that seems based in part on the sometimes thoroughly confusing notes of the consulate interpreter, tells us that the general, after expressing his sympathy regarding the major's accident, reminded Mouskoundis of his having told the Donovan group five weeks earlier that "within two weeks the name of the murderer would be known."[24] Could the major state frankly whether there had been Greek government pressure that had served to delay the investigation? No, said Mouskoundis, there had been no pressure, just his automobile accident. Well, said Donovan, the major's report to Gibson, which he had been given to read, was not very helpful since "it was not a police report, but a political argument." The general would prefer a "true, frank picture" of the investigation, because without that, he would find it necessary "to make a public statement regarding the way the investigation was going on."

This bit of dialogue clearly distressed the major. He wanted to know what aspect of the report "did the General dislike," and why there was now such a change of attitude on his part. The general said that even after a period of five weeks, "the situation was worse than before," and he asked the major the reasons for this. The major had reasons, but they seem not to have convinced the assembled group. He said that the Communists who would have taken Polk to the mountains "had all been changed" on the other side of the bay. Information had thus been lost. What information? Well, a Communist leader—presumably one Colonel Vasvanas—had entered Salonika from the mountains on May 4, allegedly to engage in sabotage, but there had been no sabotage reported, and the Communist leader had then disappeared on the night of the murder. Colonel Kellis entered the conversation at this point to remark that he did not agree with the major that this Communist leader had left by caique but believed he had left by land—which presumably implied that the leader could not have escorted Polk on a caique trip to the opposite shore and thus been involved in a murder that took place on the water. The major replied that the leader may have left by land, but "this would be known when the murderer was arrested." That gave General Donovan his big opening. He stated, bluntly it seems, that "an arrest was desired."

Mouskoundis now appeared more than distressed. He said with what sounds like equal bluntness that "he did not like the General's remark." And he expressed the hope that if the general followed through on making a public statement about the way the investigation was going, "nothing would be printed that would affect his [Mouskoundis's] position as a police officer of so many years standing." There is no recorded response to the major's anxiety on this score. As the consulate's account continues, what we find is that Burdett, Kellis, and Donovan all went after the major, questioning his facts, his failure to check things out, his use of instinct, his belief in a telegraphed order that Kellis was convinced had been planted. Burdett even had the audacity to say that it was his belief the police had a theory of the crime that was based on political intelligence rather than on facts. The major asked what was this theory not based on facts, and Burdett said "that the Communists committed the crime, and there is political intelligence to support this, but there are no facts so it is a theory." One can imagine the bewildered major asking, under his breath, where Burdett's mentor Frederick Ayer was now that Mouskoundis needed him. He settled for replying that "the facts will come as soon as an arrest is made." Donovan didn't pick up on this a second time; he now wanted to know who the person was who had phoned Polk on the night of the murder or had visited him, apparently causing Polk to return to the Hotel Astoria suddenly if only briefly. The major now had his own opening: indeed, this person had not yet been found (even if some present presumably knew that the "person" theory was now dominating the investigation) and the major felt this had something to do with the information in Thrapp's letter from Rome regarding his contacts in Salonika.

Donovan evidently let the Thrapp issue pass unnoticed, and well he might have. One of the last reports from Frederick Ayer in Athens to the secretary of state, dated July 8, shows us that Thrapp had not taken kindly to Donovan's attempt in late June to make Thrapp testify in the case by going over Thrapp's head and appealing to his boss at United Press, Hugh Bailey.[25] Ayer recorded that "Thrapp, in angry letter to Donovan, again refused identify Salonika contact and said would be returned to Greece only after long legal battle, not in a box."[26] Thrapp's contribution to identifying a possible Salonika contact for Polk ended there, though the still unanswered question of who it was that Thrapp had approached for help with his aborted trip to meet Markos remained on the table as far as the Greek authorities were concerned.

The meeting with Mouskoundis now became less tense. The Americans, having made their principal point that an arrest was desirable, seemed ready to move from pronouncement to recommendation and from criticism to assistance. General Donovan asked whether the major had ever heard of a French Communist in Markos's headquarters who came to Salonika from time to time, and when the major said no, Donovan recommended that the police investigate this. Then Burdett recommended that Colonel Kellis give the major a review of the facts that the colonel had gathered, and Donovan agreed, "as a help to the Major."

Colonel Kellis's review took up much of what remained for the consulate to report about the Mouskoundis meeting. Kellis covered Polk's trip from Athens to Salonika and the correspondent's movements in the city until the hour he disappeared. His review served to contradict—as Kellis himself pointed out—the still current police theory that Polk had already been in touch with certain Communists in Athens before proceeding to Salonika and that this alleged Athens connection had worked to introduce Polk to a Communist contact in Salonika who then arranged his fatal trip across the bay. Kellis demonstrated that Polk had planned to go to Kavalla as late as Thursday, May 6, and had changed his plans abruptly on the morning of Friday, May 7, when he told the co-pilot of the plane taking him north that he would stay over in Salonika. Kellis concluded that "if Polk had a definite contact in Athens to meet a Communist in Salonika, he would not have made arrangements to go to Kavalla." Then, once in Salonika, while approaching a range of people quite openly for help in reaching someone who might arrange a trip for him to interview Markos, Polk had shown much interest in another quite different story having to do with the so-called child-abduction question. He may well have delayed his trip to Kavalla—and so notified his wife Rea—because, as Kellis had discovered, Kavalla airport was rained out on the day Polk originally planned to go there and remained rained out until Wednesday, May 12, three days after he disappeared. And Kellis could uncover no evidence indicating that Polk had actually found a "contact" before 8:00 P.M. on Saturday, which meant that the murder must have been committed between that hour and 12:20 A.M., when Polk's watch stopped, with time out for a last meal during that four-and-a-half-hour period. This led Kellis to raise a large rhetorical question about a murder organized in such a short time span: "Which force can commit a crime like this in Salonika and keep it covered up?" The "facts" led him to an inevitable conclusion: "If Polk did not have a contact until 8:30 [P.M. on Saturday], the Communists would not have murdered him without orders." The implication is, presumably, that there was insufficient time for such orders to have been given.

To this Mouskoundis could answer only that "he thought the Communists knew about it," by which he supposedly meant that they knew about the murder plan in advance of the period during which it was committed. General Donovan again appears to have lost his patience at this point. He stated that there had been too much talk about either the Right or the Communists committing the crime and not enough attention paid to individuals, for example, the failure of the police to talk to George Drossos, the deputy Greek liaison officer to UNSCOB, who had been brought to the consulate earlier in the meeting to review the conversation he had with Randall Coate during which Coate reported on his encounter with George Polk in Salonika (as we saw in the previous chapter, pp. 95–96). Drossos had concluded his remarks by acknowledging that, given Polk's frequent and open inquiries in Salonika regarding his interest in finding a Communist contact, it did not seem, "from the standpoint of logic," that Polk had a Salonika contact already arranged in advance of his trip north. Drossos also revealed that while in Rome recently he had seen Daniel Thrapp, who had offered the opinion that the crime "had been prepared in Salonika."

The evocation of Drossos by Donovan again led to acrimony. Mouskoundis tried to reestablish his position by making out a rather incoherent case for Polk having been killed by Colonel Vasvanas, the Communist saboteur, on orders from Zachariadis, because "it was realized" that Polk, "having made a lot of contacts, . . . had to be done away with." Donovan stated that he couldn't follow this line of reasoning. He wanted to know, finally, if the major, on the evidence he had at that time, could go before a Greek court and prove his case. The major replied no, he could not. The general then accused the major of having a preconception of the crime. The major replied that he had studied all angles but that "in his heart he was sure of the Communist angle." Donovan now insisted that the major had "established his belief" and then tried to adjust the facts to it. Mouskoundis answered that it was from the facts that he derived his belief. Burdett, revising his own early belief, entered the debate to say that the disturbing thing was that the police had examined chiefly Communists and not others. Not so, said Mouskoundis; his files showed that "neutral cases" had been examined. The revisionist Burdett persisted: all Communist angles had been followed, what about following other possibilities since "we have no proof" of the one on which the police investigation is based? The major stated that this was not correct, and he believed "that the Communists did it."

Donovan now reverted to his policeman-to-policeman mode. He knew the police usually had an instinct about a case they were working on, and the major had such an instinct, but he was relying too much on it and not pursuing other possibilities, as his recent report had clearly indicated. The major replied that it was true he had an instinct, but even so he had been investigating all angles and would continue to follow all leads. Donovan went for the jugular. "The General stated that he could not return to the United States and mention the Major's instinct, and tell his people that reliance must be placed on this instinct until the case was solved." Mouskoundis had been pierced in his amour propre. He replied that "it was an honor to work with General Donovan, but that he, the Major, must carry on his work as his instinct pointed out" and the public must not be told either what facts have been uncovered or the supposition of the police.

The debate moved to more neutral ground as it drew to a close. Maybe the slow progress of the investigation was due to Greek government indifference, suggested the general. He had heard that certain government officials were not exerting much energy on the case and were allowing things to slide. Not so, said Mouskoundis; Minister of Public Order Rendis was after them all the time, and he could assure the general that his own endeavors would continue unabated: no one could stop his investigation. And what about the Greek army? Was the investigation "protected" by the fact that the Greek national army had given orders to the commanding officers to question political and other guerrilla leaders regarding the Polk case? No comment from the major, which brought the debate to a dead end. General Donovan said in conclusion— rather vaguely and implausibly—that he would "see the Secretary of War and have further orders given."

What orders? And in what capacity? The comment in any case illustrates the extended dimensions that the new patron-client relationship between America and Greece had assumed by this time and the extraordinary role that Donovan had personally taken on in Greece: a Washington lawyer representing an American press association in a foreign country who evidently assumed that he was in a position to arrange for new orders to be issued by that foreign country's secretary of war for the purpose of serving an American citizen's particular interest—and Donovan's assumption may well have been correct. Still, one feels compelled to ask what Donovan's response, and that of his American companions, would have been had a foreign lawyer pretended to take on a similar role in Washington, D.C. The consulate report does not record how Major Mouskoundis took Donovan's remark or the implications of their renewed encounter. We are told simply that the general finally thanked Mouskoundis and stated that "he knew no offense would be taken at the frank discussion, and that all faith was being placed in the Major."

Such courtesy could hardly have fooled either Mouskoundis or his American visitors. That same day the general was talking behind the major's back, complaining to Chief of Police Xanthopoulos about the lack of progress in the case, the "fixed belief" on the part of the Greek authorities that no one but the Communists could have committed the murder, the failure to gather anything like enough facts to "secure a conviction in either Greek or American courts."[27] He was worried about possible influence, possible pressure, being exerted on the investigators by the politicians in Athens. He had seen Major Mouskoundis, he had had a long talk with him, had "pointed out some facts," would be back in Salonika within a week "in order to see how things were going." In the meanwhile, Colonel Kellis would be returning to the United States to report on the case, and his report "might show that the murder had been caused by the right."

This last bit of news must have brought the chief of police up short, but he apparently stuck to his script, replying that he had only a few words to offer the general to show that "no influence had or would be imposed" on the investigation. He had been in the police force for some thirty-four years, Major Mouskoundis for some twenty-five, and their subordinates also had years of experience. As a police officer he did not "have to give explanations to Governments that come and go." He had gray hair, would retire in two years, couldn't be influenced by anybody, and had done his job without "care as to the Government's attitude." If anyone tried to steer the police in a certain direction, it simply would not be accepted. Major Mouskoundis and three other experienced investigators had studied the four angles originally outlined—Right, Left, love affair, professional jealousy—and all relevant persons, "even the British." All the information obtained pointed to the Communists, and though "there were no definite facts," someday one of the andarte guerrillas would fall into the hands of the police and presumably the truth would out. In just how many days might that be? asked Donovan. That question couldn't be answered, said the chief. And he asked a question of his own: did General Donovan, with his years of experience, think that "the people of the right wing would have organized a trip for Polk to Markos's headquarters?" The general replied that "this would not have kept a man of the right from murdering Polk."

He might also have replied that the assumption Polk was murdered in connection with an "organized" trip to Markos's headquarters was still no more than an assumption, along with a contrary assumption that Polk had been murdered exactly in order to prevent his arranging a trip to interview Markos, but Donovan was thinking along different lines: the need to find a specific culprit or culprits so that he wouldn't go home empty-handed again. He asked the chief what his attitude was toward Kosta Hadjiargyris. The chief replied that at the beginning of the investigation, he was 100 percent sure that Hadjiargyris "had full information on the case," but the more he thought about it, the less sure he became; there simply were no facts to back up his initial conviction. Had Hadjiargyris been thoroughly questioned? Donovan asked. No, the chief replied, but he planned to have Hadjiargyris brought to Salonika for questioning when he had more facts to work with. How about next week? Donovan said. The chief answered that he didn't yet have enough new evidence to question the man. But, Donovan explained, Hadjiargyris had requested a transfer out of Greece and Donovan had been asked to approve the transfer—by whom and on what authority, he did not say. The chief then asked that Hadjiargyris not be allowed to leave for some time, and, since he was "a very clever man," that he not be given the right to study the charges made against him, despite his "close ties with the Prime Minister," which Minister of Public Order Rendis had told the chief were in any case to be ignored.

The interviews with Major Mouskoundis and Colonel Xanthopoulos proved to be the turning point in the Polk investigation, but how many of those who were responsible for making it so knew what they were up to does not show in the documents of the period. We learn that before leaving for Athens, Donovan made a quick courtesy call on Christos Moustakis, identified here as inquiry magistrate—elsewhere as attorney general—of the Court of the First Instance, and that two bits of news came out of this meeting: one, that Helen Mamas, the AP stringer, was now considered a key witness, who, Moustakis said, should "be made to come to Salonika" (presumably by the Americans, since she was a U.S. citizen); the other, that Donovan now stated openly that "nothing was to be gained from Thrapp."[28] But the important news remained behind the scenes, nourished by a number of new developments: Donovan's pressure on Mouskoundis to come up with an arrest, the general's criticism of the local authorities for not having produced the kind of evidence that would stand up in a court of law, and, finally, his revelation that Colonel Kellis's report to the Lippmann Committee might show that Polk's murder had been caused by the Right.

These developments must have convinced the Salonika authorities that their American patrons would not be satisfied that justice had been done in the case until somebody had been arrested and finally convicted, and if the Americans were also to be satisfied that the Left rather than the Right had been responsible for the murder, the person or persons arrested had to have proper leftist credentials. Just two weeks after Donovan's departure from this second visit, the Greek authorities made their first move toward the arrest of a Salonika "contact" who met—or could be made to appear to meet—the requirements of the long-standing Mouskoundis-Ayer scenario involving an English-speaking journalist with Communist connections: they brought in Reuters stringer Gregory Staktopoulos for questioning.

On the American side during the same period, Colonel Kellis's presumed reservations about the Communist angle and his persistent exploration of other angles, the right wing included, apparently created distrust among certain Athens embassy officials. Karl Rankin sent a secret cable to the secretary of state informing him that two officers of the embassy who had been following the investigation had discussed the case with Kellis and had reported that Kellis's "belief" (meaning, one assumes, his questioning of the Communist angle and his feeling that other angles ought still to be pursued) was based on little more than personal prejudice, and, in view of this, "Embassy believes sooner Kellis removed from scene the better."[29] It turned out that Kellis was on his way home at the end of July not merely to submit a report to the Lippmann Committee but, evidently without Donovan's knowledge, to be given a new assignment elsewhere by the air force. Despite Donovan's cabled message to "Ernest Lindley c/o State Dept." on July 30 that he believed it "important to [Polk] case that Kellis return next week for one month"[30]—a belief reinforced by a letter from Walter Lippmann to the State Department a week later[31]—Kellis never made it back to Greece in connection with the Polk affair.

The documents that outline Kellis's role in the affair create an image in conflict with itself, one that merits more detailed attention when the evidence has been presented in its proper chronological sequence: the several reports he sent Donovan that were retained among the Donovan papers (at least one appears to be missing); what he was reported to have said in State Department cables submitted during his days in Greece; what he himself recorded in secret notes while he was working for the CIA four years after he left the Polk investigation; and what he said in interviews, affidavits, and published articles some thirty years after the murder, when the case became a matter of public controversy again. In the CIA notes Kellis pictures himself as requesting that he be "relieved from this investigation" and as subsequently leaving Greece on his own initiative, having informed Donovan of his desire to give up his assignment and having been allowed by Donovan to do so "upon his [Donovan's] return to Greece,"[32] one assumes in early August. A letter dated August 7, 1948, from William E. Colby addressed to Donovan at the King George Hotel, Athens, speaks of "Kellis' own reluctance" to return to Greece for several reasons that Kellis outlined in a letter dated August 5, of which a copy was sent to the general.[33] Among the reasons, "the attitude of certain of the American officials in Greece regarding his [Kellis's] presence there and the fact that he feels that his reputation may be injured if further of their comments appear," also Kellis's feeling "that he has been compromised in his work there and would be shadowed in any future activities."

But in a *New York Times* article that reviews his role thirty years after the fact, Kellis indicates that he was forced to abandon his assignment because he was collecting "information that contradicted the official investigation" and because he refused to be "party to a cover-up."[34] In an open letter to the Greek press in 1977 he also pictures himself as having been in favor of conducting "an honest, penetrating, and impar-

tial investigation," but unfortunately his "colleagues in this investigation had a different view and their position prevailed." [35] There appears
to be little doubt that Kellis did indeed run into opposition while he was
in Greece. The August 7 letter from Colby to Donovan points out that
Ernest Lindley of the Lippmann Committee "has done some checking
and has learned that certain officials in the United States Embassy definitely wanted Kellis sent home from Greece," though "the State Department denies this." But the fact is that Kellis's own testimony, both in
the once secret CIA notes recorded in 1952 and in a Greek consulate
affidavit prepared in 1977, depict him as having included the name of
Gregory Staktopoulos on a list of suspects that he presented Donovan in
a confidential report before Kellis departed from Greece. There is also
evidence in his 1952 CIA notes that he was ready at that time to claim
some of the credit—and to give Donovan some of the credit—for what
became the official solution of the case, resulting in a prison sentence for
Staktopoulos.

Donovan's role in the Kellis controversy is also ambivalent. He seems
unaware in late July that Kellis wished to leave the investigation; in fact,
as we have seen, he worked to have Kellis brought back for another
month of service within a matter of days after Kellis's departure from
Greece. Yet we learn (from the Lippmann Report) that not long after this
effort by Donovan, "plans for sending Colonel Kellis back to Greece
were abandoned,"[36] presumably because during his second Greek visit
Donovan "had taken occasion to impress on Greek officials the necessity of exploring fully the leads which pointed to the Right as well as
those pointing toward the Left" and now felt this would be done even
without Kellis there to pursue the matter. It now seems just as likely
that plans for having Colonel Kellis return were abandoned once the
Staktopoulos solution got under way—and, if we are to believe Kellis's
own CIA notes, this came about when "General Donovan reviewed very
carefully all of the ten suspects that I had submitted to him in my
confidential report, and asked the Chief Greek Investigator to concentrate on one, a Greek newspaperman" who, within sixty days, "confessed complicity in the crime."[37]

At some point during those sixty-five days (August 1 to October 1),
most likely during late September, General Donovan fell in line with the
Staktopoulos solution that Major Mouskoundis, evidently in collaboration with Attorney General Constantinidis, had been working on assidu-
ously at Security Police headquarters in Salonika, whether or not the
lead behind this work received the kind of early, overt endorsement from
Donovan that Kellis's notes suggest. Just how soon Donovan came

around to accepting the solution then in progress is still open to speculation. The public record shows that during the final week of July, Donovan was still going about his business of criticizing the Greek handling
of the Polk investigation as though his American contacts in the local
diplomatic community were all in sympathy with his impatience and
still in league with his departing aide, and also as though "the person"
theory was still a theory which had not yet assumed the particular focus
that it clearly had begun to assume behind the scenes in Salonika.

While in Athens just before departing for Rome, Donovan saw both
Minister of Public Order Rendis and Minister of Justice Melas to tell
them of his dissatisfaction with the way things were progressing. Ambassador Grady, in summarizing Donovan's criticisms for the secretary
of state, pointed to the "bad criminology" of an investigation which
operated on the single thesis that the Left had committed the crime,
though Donovan also found that both Rendis and Melas "hinted to him
they would not be displeased if [the] 'Right' were embarrassed" and this
made him feel that they therefore "have no reason to cover up."[38] Donovan also complained that the investigation had been sloppy in many
respects, especially in the failure to interrogate "all persons with whom
Polk talked . . . (e.g., George Drossos)."

In the same cable the ambassador reported on a conversation that
Donovan had with Rankin—not, it seems, about Kellis and Rankin's
own feelings regarding the specifics of what Greek officials were up to,
but about the "necessity conducting investigation in such manner as to
avoid public criticism of government particularly if case remains unsolved," a necessity that Donovan is now said to have recognized, no
doubt under Rankin's persuasion. But the fact is that some five weeks
later (September 9), we find Donovan prepared to take part in a CBS
broadcast ("Report Number Three on the Murder of George Polk")[39]
during which he reviewed his earlier criticism of the Greek government:
"We told the Greek authorities that they had failed to explore, earnestly
and carefully, *all* the possibilities. I said this to the Minister of Public
Order, the Minister of Justice, the Foreign Minister, the Prime Minister,
to King Paul and his court advisers, and, of course, to the police officials
immediately responsible for the investigation." And he goes on to make
"two points," namely, that "the Greek Minister of Public Order, Mr.
Rendis, agreed with our criticism of the investigation," and "as a result
of our insistence, the government of Greece has been compelled to take
over the direction of the police inquiry at the highest level," with Minister of Public Order Rendis assuming "personal responsibility for the
conduct of the investigation."

Donovan's public position at this early date in September, anyway as manifest in the text of this broadcast, is still that of applying what pressure he can to have the Greek government exercise its "power to conduct a thorough-going inquiry into this crime." He adds that if the government fails "to use this power within a reasonable time, it is my opinion that it will then devolve on the United States Government to make formal representations to the Government of Greece and see to it that a truly comprehensive inquiry be made." And his commentary on the case ends with his announcement that the Overseas Writers Association is prepared to pay a reward of $10,000 to the person or persons giving them information which leads to the arrest and conviction of the murderer or murderers. It appears that whatever reports Donovan may have been receiving from Greece about the progress of the Staktopoulos solution at Security Police headquarters in Salonika were not yet sufficient to counteract the disillusioning effects of his late July trip to that city.

The depth of the general's disillusionment immediately after the Salonika trip is indicated by his having told Rankin on his return to Athens that he was thinking of suggesting the appointment of a special commission to review the Polk case,[40] and he went so far as to outline his proposal in a memorandum for the American embassy (a copy was sent to Walter Lippmann on July 31).[41] Donovan's fear was that "the cold trail and unfavorable circumstances" might deny the Greek authorities the "discovery of the murderer of George Polk" and result in "the compulsory abandonment of the investigation with the resultant failure of the Greek and American people to be made aware of the facts collected by the authorities," a thing that could "breed misunderstanding and recrimination between the two countries." To avoid this danger "in the event that it should appear the investigation is bound to collapse," Donovan suggested that a Royal Commission be set up with the approval of Parliament "for the inquiry into the murder of George Polk," the commission to consist of three outstanding members of the judiciary, selected by "their colleagues on the highest court" on the basis of "their character, legal ability and public confidence" and with full authority to conduct hearings in camera, subpoena witnesses compelled to testify under oath, etc., and upon completion of their work, "to make a finding of the facts as produced by the evidence submitted" and to print their finding so that it would be available to the press and the public. We learn from Ambassador Grady's July 29 cable to the secretary of state that the ambassador believes Donovan's idea "merits consideration."[42] We also learn that Donovan has decided that he will now go off to Italy for a week or ten days and then return to Greece "to see if progress is apparent."

It seems that progress of the kind the general had in mind did not become fully apparent to him until the late September reports of the success that Major Mouskoundis was having in obtaining presumably incriminating information from Gregory Staktopoulos, at which time Donovan's idea of a special commission was taken to be irrelevant. Gibson's report to the secretary of state dated September 23 is particularly to the point here: "Stahtopoulos [sic] now giving information, and the Major expects him to reveal when meeting was organized, where, under whose orders, reason for plot, and name of murderer. . . . Officials realize that great deal more information needed for final solution of case, but are confident that this [sic] in near future. Under present conditions, appointment special judicial committee not considered necessary."[43]

As we shall see below in our review of the developing case against Staktopoulos and the "official solution" it served, Donovan's proposal for a special commission had already run into trouble a month earlier, and there is some evidence in the State Department archives that during August and early September he was no longer privy to some of the information that was being transmitted secretly between Athens and Washington.[44] Also, his "man in Greece" who replaced Kellis, Theodore Lambron,[45] reveals as late as September 7 that he has been "trying to get the details on the new arrests," but Minister of Public Order Rendis "is rather reluctant about letting me know any details because the evidence points vaguely to the left."[46] Rendis is reported to have said—and Lambron agrees with the minister—that "they should seek no publicity on these arrests because it is possible that this effort will lead no where [sic], in which case, it might appear to some that the Greek Government attempted to create an alibi." A week later Lambron sent a further report that provides Donovan with much of the same information about the investigation of Staktopoulos and his mother, Anna, that appears in the State Department archives of this period, however questionable some of this data proved to be (for example, that in the past Staktopoulos "had high communists [sic] connections [Markos and others]" and "his mother, Anna Staktopoulos, a shrewd old woman, has also been an active communist to this date").[47] Lambron also indicates that during his recent visit to Salonika following the September 7 report, "Mr. Gibson was very outspoken to me about details of the case," and Lambron found that on his return to Athens "the people at the Embassy are not holding back on me either as they did before." Whatever it was that local officials chose to share with General Donovan during August and September, it becomes clear from the record of his participation in the Polk case after October 1, when Staktopoulos was formally charged, that the general gave his full-hearted support from that date on to the official solution promulgated by the Greek authorities.

Despite the declared agreement in late July that restraint in the public disclosure of criticism was necessary, word of Donovan's displeasure got out. Responding on July 30 to a *New York Times* report that General Donovan had criticized the conduct of the Polk investigation, Minister of Public Order Rendis expressed "astonishment" at a news conference, and he went on to say that from the beginning his government had ordered that the investigation include "all sides."[48] And in Salonika the next day, Attorney General Constantinidis, calling on Raleigh Gibson at the consulate to tell him that he had read in the newspapers about General Donovan's "dissatisfaction with the investigation" and the failure of local officials "to investigate the right," stated—surely without intending to be prophetic—that he did not believe "justice had been served by the General's statements."[49] Constantinidis reaffirmed what he had been saying all along about his commitment to investigate "all angles." He was still exploring both the new and the old, not only "the triangle Polk-Hadjiargyris-Astoria Hotel" (whatever that triangle signified) but, after studying the testimony that Major Mouskoundis and Inquiry Magistrate Moustakis had brought back from Athens, what he now considered an essential new angle: the roles of AP stringer Helen Mamas and Salonika Reuters correspondent Gregory Staktopoulos. Both these witnesses needed to be examined further, he said.

The attorney general now revealed a curious plot he had in mind in this connection, one suggesting that the Staktopoulos solution was beginning to come into clear focus among the Salonika authorities. He reminded Gibson that Colonel Kellis had promised to arrange for Helen Mamas, an American citizen, to come back to Salonika for questioning; on her arrival, said Constantinidis, the Reuters stringer Staktopoulos would be arrested, and Miss Mamas would then be advised of this, in the belief that the two would end up making counterstatements against each other.

Helen Mamas's name had appeared in previous aspects of the investigation as one of those whom Polk had asked, on first reaching Salonika, about a possible contact for the trip to Markos's headquarters, and also as the companion of Rea Polk during her days in Salonika after Polk disappeared. The AP stringer had been interviewed on several occasions, formally and informally, and her name had appeared in several depositions and reports on the investigation, but the first indication that Helen

Mamas had assumed the role of a "key" Salonika witness appears in Inquiry Magistrate Moustakis's statement to Donovan on July 24 that he could not understand why "she had not been made" to come back to Salonika, since he had been told that arrangements to that effect were in progress, and General Donovan had then promised to look into the matter on his return to Athens.[50]

Besides a passing reference to Staktopoulos in Kellis's review of Polk's itinerary for Major Mouskoundis's benefit, there are only four references to Staktopoulos in the archives that are dated before this July 31 conversation between Gibson and Constantinidis (actually transmitted on August 10). The first reference is in Constantinidis's June 7 interview with Raleigh Gibson, where the attorney general indicates that he is "interested in one of the local correspondents, Gregory Stahtopoulos [sic] who covered for U.P. in Salonika," this interest having emerged after Constantinidis read Thrapp's statement about his Salonika contact, whose name he didn't remember and whose background he refused to elaborate upon.[51] Constantinidis told Gibson that "Stahtopoulos" had been questioned informally and had said that "he had met George Polk through Dr. Ahmed, Press delegate UNSCOB, and Mr. Limberopoulos, Press Officer, Government General of Northern Greece." Staktopoulos's name again appears in the detailed June 15 report on the murder by Burdett and Secondari, where we learn that "a Greek journalist of Salonika named Statopoulos [sic]" and two others were introduced to George Polk in the Hotel Mediterranean bar during the cocktail hour on Friday, May 7.[52] The report continues: "According to Mamas, George is supposed to have asked Statopoulos if he could place him in contact with the Communists. If this is so, then this is the only contact we know of between George and any Greek here in Salonika."

Reading this reference in isolation, one can see how those who subscribed to the theory that there was an essential "Greek in the story"— as Burdett and Secondari themselves did in this very report—might eventually return to Gregory Staktopoulos as a possible candidate, especially since he spoke English and was well known among the community of foreign correspondents in Salonika. But it seems likely that this candidate did not come up front seriously until it began to appear hopeless that the police could pin anything substantial on an English-speaking journalist in Athens who—in the words of the Burdett-Secondari report—"had George's trust, perhaps even a man whom he had known for some time," namely, Kosta Hadjiargyris, at that time the chief suspect in the case not only for Frederick Ayer but evidently for Burdett and Secondari as well.

The third mention of Staktopoulos would seem to support a shift of focus from Hadjiargyris to the Reuters stringer in Salonika. Prefacing a cabled letter from Kellis to Donovan on July 7, Raleigh Gibson tells the State Department that Constantinidis and Mouskoundis "had both planned to interrogate Hadjiargyris in Salonika, but through fear of criticism from the American correspondents in Athens, as well as from American columnists, they changed their plans."[53] Now Mouskoundis "is endeavoring to open new leads" by searching houses in Salonika that had been visited by the Communist leader and presumed saboteur Colonel Vasvanas, and he also "plans to arrest the Reuter correspondent, Stantopoulos [sic], in Salonika, since all indications point to the fact that he has some information on the case." And, we are told, Helen Mamas is also assumed to have some information that she hasn't so far revealed, something that the local officials apparently connect to Staktopoulos. All rather vague at this early date in July, before Donovan's return to the scene: an image of men under some pressure grasping for straws. But, as we have seen, the pressure soon became much more intense, and given the power behind it and the predisposition of those experiencing its effect, it now appears an inevitable consequence that American influence in the Polk affair would eventually force some kind of resolution, rigged or otherwise. Gregory Staktopoulos is the man who finally emerged to fill that need as Rea Polk and Kosta Hadjiargyris moved into the background.

Once the plot had thickened, Frederick Ayer was not one to miss out on the action. In the last of his cables to the secretary of state still on record in the archives (some documents have been removed for security or other reasons)—this one "Report No. 15" dated July 8—Ayer includes what must have struck the secretary at that moment as peculiar news, assuming he took it seriously: "Salonika police plan soon arrest one Gregory Stachtopoupos [sic], alleged Reuters stringer always under suspicion (see early Ayer reports). Exact grounds planned arrest not yet known Athens but believed because numerous contacts highly placed members KKE [Greek Communist Party] and possible espionage activities. On date for arrest Ayer or Kellis will go Salonika and report."[54]

Of course neither did any such thing, because both were already out of the country when, on July 31, Constantinidis told Raleigh Gibson of his plan to arrest Staktopoulos as soon as Helen Mamas returned to Salonika. However Frederick Ayer may have perceived his role in the Polk affair—and his book suggests that he thought his role somehow crucial despite the problem he had with his Foreign Service colleagues—

there is evidence that other Americans on the scene took him and his contribution to the case less seriously than he himself did or than his 1974 obituary suggested ("Mr. Ayer was credited with laying the groundwork that led to the solution of the murder").[55] We find a succinct evaluation of Ayer among the Donovan papers that supports the dissident view: Theodore Lambron, the man who replaced Kellis, was quoted as saying, in October 1950, for the benefit of the report Donovan was then preparing on the case, that "Ayer's contribution to the investigation had been nil."[56]

Along with Ayer and Kellis, Burdett and Secondari were also off the case by this time, though the former still had much to say about it that was rather double-faced and, in view of the solution now in progress, naive. As Constantinidis was meeting with Gibson on July 31, Burdett was broadcasting a revisionist "Report on Murder of George Polk" from Rome to CBS New York in which he revealed that the Greek police had failed to explore all the political possibilities with equal zeal, having devoted "90 percent of their time and effort to exploring the Communist angle and a rather unenthusiastic 10 percent to examining other possibilities," with the result that "underneath all the arguments and all the theories there is as yet no concrete evidence linking the crime with any party or parties," in short, the police were still working on suppositions and "have uncovered no direct evidence which would stand up in a court of law."[57] But, Burdett concluded, "the truth is that only the Greeks will ever be able to solve the mystery of George Polk's death. An outsider cannot do it. He does not have the skill, or the intimate knowledge. Nor does he have the legal right. . . . The Greeks must do it themselves."

Now, with Ayer, Burdett, Secondari, Kellis, and Donovan all out of the country (and even the British Colonel Martin temporarily away on leave),[58] the local authorities could presumably exercise their skill and intimate knowledge more or less freely to provide a solution to the case. Within two weeks of Donovan's departure for Italy, the avenue toward a solution had been confirmed, what must have seemed to local officials a way out that would surely meet with the approval of all resident and absent foreign advisers and finally satisfy them once and for all, especially since the chosen contact man for the murder was an English-speaking journalist with Communist connections in his past who was evidently on the list of suspects designated by the visiting investigators representing the American press. While waiting to catch the bus home at the Kalamaria-Aretsou bus stop in Salonika on August 14, Gregory Staktopoulos, thirty-eight-year-old reporter for the local paper *Make-*

donia and Reuters stringer, was approached by a friendly plainclothes-man who escorted him to the chief of Security Police, Major Mouskoundis, for what Staktopoulos says he was led to believe would be news regarding the robbery of a spread of laundry from his backyard that his mother, with whom he lived, had put out to dry several days earlier. Staktopoulos reached home twelve years later, at the age of fifty.

VI | The Accused

THE GREGORY STAKTOPOULOS of 1948 who emerges from documents of the time and the recollection of some who then knew him projects a split image. On the one hand he is pictured as an unpretentious, run-of-the-mill journalist, conscientious as a reporter but only modestly ambitious and not very imaginative, gentle to a fault, a bachelor much tied to his mother and sisters, for whom he was the principal means of support—in the eyes of one former colleague, "a softy, afraid of his own shadow."[1] The State Department archives initially suggest a man so average and indistinguishable that nothing precise enough can be found to shape an image of any kind, and when he is actually referred to by name rather than simply as a journalist or a Reuters stringer, the name is never gotten quite right in transliteration (Gibson is quoted as calling him either "Stahtopoulos," "Stantopoulos," or even "Stathoupolos," Burdett and Secondari call him "Statopoulos," and Frederick Ayer—most creative of all—"Stachtopoupos").

But, on the other hand, there are those who saw the man as somebody who much wanted to be in touch with whatever newsworthy action came to town, always on the go for the main chance or anyway the hot item, restless, egotistical at times, something of a show-off, who, in the words of another former colleague and classmate, "always pretended to know everybody and everything and was ready to tell you so, especially if you were a foreigner."[2] And once he moved to center stage in the Polk investigation, the documents of the time, including some in the State Department files, see room in him for cunning, shiftiness, false witness, treachery, even diabolic plotting.

The details of Staktopoulos's early biography also project a rather mixed image. As a graduate of Anatolia College in Salonika (a high school under American administration that in those days was considered the most elite in town available to Greek nationals) and therefore fluent in English, he was much in demand locally as a translator and interpreter, but he seems to have sacrificed his chance for higher education when he became the principal source of support for his family (besides his mother, a brother killed during World War II, and two younger sisters)—and this included providing what was necessary to send one sister to Salonika University. To ensure the family's sustenance he was apparently ready to work for almost anybody of whatever political persuasion who would use his special qualifications as an English-speaking newspaperman.

According to Staktopoulos's own account of his early career,[3] he began by working for a local newspaper called *Phos* (Light) before the war, then continued in the same job under the Germans when they took over the facilities of the newspaper during the Axis Occupation (though initially fired for being "Anglophile"), then joined the Communist-dominated EAM later in the Occupation and actually became a member of the Communist party so that he could translate BBC broadcasts and hand them over to the Party newspaper, *Laiki Foni* (Popular Voice), which, according to Staktopoulos, was one of the few news outlets at the time and one dependent on foreign sources of information because of the financial contingencies then prevailing. He joined the Party, he tells us, because he needed the job in order to provide for his family, then dropped the Party—or was dropped by it—because of what the Party designated as "lack of interest," and during this same period began working for the British Information Service, now as a translator of Reuters dispatches, which—he reports—were disseminated during those years by loudspeaker to towns and villages otherwise deprived of news. After the Liberation, he left *Laiki Foni* and went to work as a translator for the Salonika branch of the Athenian News Agency. In due course he joined the staff of the centrist Salonika newspaper, *Makedonia*. Also, according to a press colleague (Christos Lambrinos) who began by working for the British and then attached himself to the Americans, Staktopoulos had some connection with the British Information Service for a period after the war.

Educated in an American-sponsored secondary school, reporter for Greek newspapers from left to center and for an international press service with no local politics, employed on different occasions by both the Germans and the British, a member of the Greek resistance and of the Greek Communist Party for a time but considered by most of his professional colleagues to be without extreme political belief or bias, a man of changing resources and sponsors but apparently innocuous in his habits—no alcohol, a lover mostly by mail—his speech slurred at times due to a nervous condition caused by an automobile accident but ready on any pretext to break into relatively smooth English. He was lean at the time, short, almost delicate, dark hair slicked back flat, eyebrows a thin black bow split by a frown, nose prominent, a soft mouth with the upper lip projecting slightly, thick chin curled in and, in some photographs, raised a bit, so that one sees in that face a worried gentleness contending with superciliousness. He was a man evidently much in love with his family and with foreigners of the right stripe, on the scene whenever English translation was needed or somebody important was in town, an ordinary and yet not-so-ordinary Greek journalist who had the bad luck to run into George Polk at the wrong time, however briefly.

Exactly how briefly depends on which of two contradictory sources one chooses to believe: Staktopoulos's account of his one meeting with Polk in his 1984 book, and Staktopoulos's account of his various meetings with Polk in the confession he signed and then revised several times thirty-six years earlier, in October 1948, after some six weeks of interrogation by Major Mouskoundis and the Salonika Security Police. From the 1984 book one can piece together at least a fragmentary narrative of Staktopoulos's movements during the days before and after Polk's body was discovered, as he records his memory of those days more than three decades after the fact. He tells us that he met Polk for the first and last time on Friday, May 7, 1948, for a total of five minutes. This happened as Staktopoulos was on his way to meet the Indian Press Officer for UNSCOB, "Mr." Ahmed, at the Hotel Mediterranean. In the hotel lobby he ran into AP stringer Helen Mamas and asked her if there was any news. She replied that no news had yet emerged from the UNSCOB meeting, and she invited him into the bar to meet three American journalists who had just arrived in town (actually two newly arrived journalists and one local official). Mamas introduced Staktopoulos to the American newspapermen as her "competitor" (presumably because he represented a rival news service), and the visitors asked him to sit down and have a drink. He told them he was a teetotaler, had been for years; they smiled, then asked him what was up. Staktopoulos said nothing was up really, there didn't seem to be any interesting news on the horizon, and he excused himself because he was late for his meeting with the Indian Press Officer. He then went upstairs to find Ahmed. Later that evening, while at his office, he decided to include an item in his paper, the *Makedonia*, on the arrival in Salonika of the American correspondents, so he called Helen Mamas at her regular restaurant, the Olympus-Naoussa, and asked for their names again. She said she was having dinner with them at that moment and gave him the information he needed. At a later point in his book, Staktopoulos says that he couldn't even have described what Polk looked like on the basis of that single encounter in the Mediterranean Hotel bar, let alone get the American's name right; Staktopoulos's memory had to be stimulated by those with more precise knowledge, for example, his Security Police interrogators.

That single meeting wasn't the beginning and end of Staktopoulos's interest in George Polk during those days. He tells us that after his own paper reported Polk missing, he felt that as a conscientious journalist he had a responsibility to gather any news of the American that he could, even if the boys in the office all seemed to agree that Polk must have simply "gotten mixed up with gamblers or women." So he, at least, went about his business of finding out if there were any leads, and only much later, when it was too late, did he come to see how his early efforts might have been misinterpreted as an excessive interest on his part in the American correspondent's fate, compelled, some thought, by a guilty conscience. He recalls that he visited the Hotel Astoria several times during the period Polk was missing to see if there was any word of Polk's return to Salonika from wherever he'd been, and on one of these occasions he had a brief encounter with Rea Polk in the hotel doorway, having foolishly followed the advice of people at the desk that he ask her if she'd had any news of her husband. Of course she'd had no news, but he thinks his having asked her something so personal cost him the comment she was reported to have made (by Hadjiargyris, among others) to her interrogators in Athens, namely, that she had found Staktopoulos "unlikable" the one time they had met.

Rea Polk now has no recollection of meeting Staktopoulos at the Astoria Hotel.[4] The one time she remembers meeting him was by accident at the Hotel Mediterranean bar, where she and Helen Mamas had stopped in briefly while out shopping during her first days in Salonika. But there is a memorandum among the Donovan papers from William E. Colby to the general that indicates a more substantial contact between Rea and Staktopoulos in Salonika during the period before Polk's body was recovered (the first version of Colby's memorandum is dated September 28, 1948, an emended version is dated September 30, and a third version—a translation back into English of a Greek rendering of the September 30 memorandum—is attached to a January 4, 1949, cable from the American embassy in Athens to the Department of State).[5] At the time Colby submitted this memorandum to Donovan he was a young lawyer in the general's firm. He had met with Rea on several occasions during the summer of 1948 after Rea reached the United States as Polk's widow, once in the company of Donovan and Davidson Taylor of CBS and on several occasions informally with Colby's wife Barbara present.[6] The memorandum in question has to do specifically with three meetings that took place on September 27, 28, and 29.

We learn from this document that Rea told Colby that she first met Staktopoulos when she arrived in Salonika on Wednesday, May 12, introduced by Helen Mamas "at a 'UN Conference' which was taking place there" (presumably an UNSCOB meeting). Staktopoulos told Rea that he wanted to write a story on Polk's disappearance and to include an interview with her. In order to protect her husband's exclusive right to whatever might emerge from what she perceived as his latest adventure and to keep the story from breaking before his return, she told Staktopoulos that her husband was in Kavalla, which, Colby records, "she had heard reported and then denied" (the Greek retranslation renders this sentence with incriminating inaccuracy as "on hearing this being mentioned, he [i.e., Staktopoulos] denied it," as though Staktopoulos had more knowledge of Polk's whereabouts at this time than Rea did). Rea told Colby that Staktopoulos responded to her attempt to put him off by saying that "if his boss agreed, he would write the story." So Rea called his boss that night ("a man," Colby reports, "whose name she has forgotten, but whom she remembers as a man who always wore a blue beret and who was quite a well known character"). Staktopoulos's boss "agreed to skip the story." That evening Staktopoulos met Rea at the door of her hotel with "the direct statement that he was going to interview her." Rea "disliked his attitude"—and Colby adds that, "incidentally, [she] dislikes him considerably." Rea proceeded to inform Staktopoulos that his boss had agreed that there would be no story. "Stahtopoulous [sic] then left."

According to the Colby memorandum, that was the end of the episode and of the contact between Staktopoulos and Rea, but his memorandum reports—incorrectly, it would appear—that Staktopoulos "did write a story [possibly Friday] entitled 'Is It a Crime?' about Polk's disappearance," and he adds that "this title may or may not be significant regarding Stahtopoulous' knowledge of the crime." In fact, the speculative article on Polk in *Makedonia* appeared without a byline, and it was published on the Sunday morning that Polk's body was discovered. The title: "After one week/ The 'Polk Affair' remains ever mysterious/ He has probably gone to the guerrillas/ Will he play the intermediary?"[7]

In his book, Staktopoulos does not reveal whether the speculative article that appeared was his or—as seems more likely from the text—a collaborative effort. His 1984 account of these days moves on to another enterprise that brought him in touch with the official investigators: his having acted as interpreter for an unnamed American colleague who came to town from Athens as a stringer for the Associated Press and who felt that he too had better look into Polk's disappearance to see if there was any worthy news in that development. This voluntary assignment took Staktopoulos and his American colleague first to Major Mouskoundis's office at Security Police headquarters, where Staktopoulos found not only his future interrogator but an English colonel named, he believed, Martins, and where he was told curtly by Mouskoundis to take his American journalist "and get out of here." Then, later that day, he decided to arrange an interview with his friend, George Drossos, the deputy Greek representative at UNSCOB, who, it turned out, had been assigned by the Greek authorities to look into the question of Polk's disappearance among the foreign diplomatic community in Salonika (Randall Coate included, as we have seen). But Drossos had nothing to report, at least not to Staktopoulos. Nor did Attorney General Constantinidis, who received the two journalists politely but was cautious in his responses: an investigation was under way by the Security Police, and his own office knew nothing yet.

So much for Staktopoulos's effort as interpreter and guide for his American colleague. But, he tells us, there were other meetings with local officials involved in the early stages of the investigation, for example, with Christos Moustakis, the inquiry magistrate, and, after Polk's body was discovered, another meeting with Major Mouskoundis. This second meeting was at Mouskoundis's request, and Staktopoulos went to the Security Police headquarters with his friend Avyeris of the *Makedonia* staff, who was also interested in the Polk case. What Mouskoundis wanted was for Staktopoulos to look specifically into what his fellow correspondent Helen Mamas might know about Polk's movements in Salonika: whom he'd met, what he'd talked about, anything that might help the police investigation.

Staktopoulos ran to find Helen Mamas, leaving Avyeris behind. The Reuters stringer tells us that of course he didn't reveal to Mamas who it was who had sent him to make this inquiry, but in any case Mamas knew nothing useful about George Polk—or if she did, she wasn't prepared to enlighten Staktopoulos, except to remind him that Polk had been among the American correspondents that she'd introduced to him at the Hotel Mediterranean and that he'd called her about later the same evening in order to record their names correctly for his newspaper. The interview with Mamas over, Staktopoulos hurried back to Mouskoundis's office to report on his useless intelligence mission, but nobody was there to receive him. When he checked with his friend Avyeris the next day, Avyeris said that Mouskoundis had told him to go home and not bother waiting for Gregory because "Gregory won't be back for some time."

In his book, Staktopoulos sees this episode as part of a "satanic" design: a plot to put distance between him and his friend Avyeris so that the "terrible" things that Staktopoulos would eventually be forced to confess would seem credible to his colleagues on the *Makedonia* staff, no one of whom—as Hadjiargyris confirms in his account—came forward at any time to testify on behalf of their fellow newsman. Neither Staktopoulos nor Hadjiargyris could have known what State Department archives now reveal: that the Salonika authorities had another secret design in mind, namely, establishing a possibly incriminating link between Staktopoulos and Helen Mamas.

Staktopoulos also recalls a second meeting with Attorney General Constantinidis, one that the Reuters stringer felt should not have implicated him any more than the first did but that would appear in retrospect to have proven considerably more useful to the prosecution. Some time after Polk's body was recovered, an item appeared in an Athens newspaper to the effect that the last person to meet with Polk before his disappearance was the Greek journalist Gregory Staktopoulos. A colleague at the *Makedonia* had shown him this bit of news, and the following day, newspaper clipping in hand, Staktopoulos had gone to the attorney general and had declared that the report was a lie and a slander. Constantinidis had calmed him by assuring him that no such final meeting between him and Polk was assumed to have occurred and therefore wouldn't be taken into account by the police investigators. Staktopoulos, grateful for this understanding, told the attorney general on leaving that he wanted to assure him that if he might be needed in any way, he was always at the attorney general's disposal.

The bitter irony of this parting remark did not come into Staktopoulos's consciousness until some time later, well into his incarceration and long after his third encounter with Constantinidis (the final encounter was at the murder trial, where the attorney general acted as public prosecutor). This third meeting with Constantinidis was for the purpose of introducing the attorney general to the Greek journalist from Athens who was in town gathering the latest news. On this occasion the two journalists learned that the attorney general thought the Polk murder was one in a series of three that the Communists had planned, the first that of Minister of Justice Christos Ladas, assassinated in Athens on Easter Eve, 1948, the second that of George Polk, and the third yet to be revealed. This was a prediction that Staktopoulos took very seriously when it came back to him during his incarceration. He became convinced at one point that the original version of the satanic design plotted against him had included his being murdered eventually by agents of the police and the murder being blamed on the Communists, as in the case of Polk. And he points out in his book that Mouskoundis himself had later said to him that he'd been marked for murder. Killing Staktopoulos would presumably be the easy way for the authorities to get him out of the picture once his usefulness to them was over.

Another way—the one Staktopoulos says the authorities finally chose—was to bring him "to his knees" so effectively that he would never open his mouth again. He gives credit to Major Mouskoundis for saving his life by pushing for this second alternative, the only "extenuating circumstance" that Staktopoulos allows the man. According to the accused's account of things, the process of bringing him to his knees took some forty-five days, beginning with his isolation at the Security Police headquarters after he was picked up at the bus stop as he was heading home on August 14. The detention of Staktopoulos began just two days after Kosta Hadjiargyris published a still unanswered "open letter" in a leading Athens newspaper, *To Vima* (the Tribune), reminding the authorities in Salonika that a month and a half had already passed since they declared to Mr. Burdett and General Donovan that they hoped it would be possible for them to examine him within a fortnight, and though "words, of course, remain always words," Hadjiargyris reaffirmed that he was willing to be examined by anyone, wherever and under whatever conditions, in fact, invited and challenged any investigating authority to call him for examination, and if they did not want to do so, should so "declare" and no longer permit an innocent citizen to be defamed in the columns of the press and from "the tribune of the Parliament."[8]

Had Kosta Hadjiargyris known at that time under what conditions the most recent suspect for a Polk "contact" was about to be examined, his freewheeling challenge may have found a somewhat more subdued rhetoric. In Staktopoulos's account, his interrogation began with some fairly amicable questioning in Major Mouskoundis's office—coffee and cognac available as required—and ended with a variety of tortures that Staktopoulos wryly suggests make the 1967–74 torturers under the Colonels' dictatorship seem neophytes in technique, at least hardly worthy to be graduates of the Mouskoundis Institute, except in the case of those who successfully mangled the heroic Junta resister Colonel Moustaklis, who lived on as a cripple until his death in 1987.

The first phase of Staktopoulos's six-week-long "private" interrogation, as he records it in his book, was evidently intended to establish his ideology. Q: Did the prewar dictator Metaxas want to hand Greece over to the Italians? A: I don't think so. Q: And the king? A: I think he was a democratic king. Q: What is your view of the Slavo-Macedonian question? A: The Slavo-Macedonian question? You know perfectly well that there is no such question. Q: But the Bulgarians say that there are Macedonians. . . . A: I don't know what the Bulgarians say, but what I know is that there was an exchange of populations. . . . Q: Gregory, one thing you haven't told us: Did you work for a newspaper during the German Occupation?

Here Staktopoulos felt that an extended response was necessary. He told Mouskoundis and the others present the story of his working for a newspaper that was then taken over by the Germans, his being fired as an Anglophile and then rehired because his co-workers complained to those in charge on his behalf ("Hardly a year has gone by since Stakto-poulos lost his brother in the war and you take his job away from him?"). Mouskoundis heard him out, then suddenly confronted him with a deadly sober face and asked, apropos of nothing: "Look here, Gregory, are you by any chance a Communist?" Staktopoulos felt another extended response was called for, and he went into his history as a member of the EAM resistance during the Occupation, his joining the Party in order to translate BBC broadcasts for the Party newspaper, *Laiki Foni*, his subsequent dismissal from the Party for "lack of interest," and his shift to more regular journalism of various kinds as soon as he could afford to do so.

The last telling question that Mouskoundis asked him during the amicable phase of his interrogation evidently seemed innocent enough to Staktopoulos at the time: What cadre of the Communist party showed up at the offices of *Laiki Foni*? Staktopoulos said he didn't know about cadre. He thought maybe Stringos, Mouzenidis, Vasvanas, and he couldn't remember who else used to show up at the office of the editor, Panayoti Mavromati. What did these people do in the office of the editor? He imagined that they conversed there and exchanged ideas. He couldn't really say; he knew them to look at but wasn't acquainted with them personally and didn't come into contact with any of them. They did their work and he did his, Staktopoulos told his interrogator. This information, vague as it was and seemingly in passing, evidently proved crucial to the third phase of the Staktopoulos interrogation, the "confessional" phase, when the names Mouzenidis and Vasvanas (the old "saboteur") assumed major significance as those of the principal accomplices in the murder of George Polk—but there was still the long second phase for Staktopoulos to get through.

This phase began with a dramatic change in mood at the interrogation. No more coffee and cognac and whatever drug it was that Staktopoulos was certain they'd used to fortify the things they gave him to drink. No more sweet talk. No more rational questions. Instead, the most violent language, especially from Major Mouskoundis, who cursed his victim and the man's family in a style that Staktopoulos felt simply wouldn't be used "by anybody who had self-respect and breeding." The Reuters stringer began to realize that something sinister was happening. As he looks back in his memoir on these days of his incarceration, he sees that at this point the "satanic" design to frame him was already taking shape. The inquiry was no longer interested in finding evidence against him—there was no evidence to be had, as far as he was concerned, nor was any needed. But in retrospect he finds that things he said to his interrogators and things they knew he had done before and after Polk's body was discovered—the visits to the Astoria Hotel, to Mouskoundis, and to Constantinidis in particular—became part of their design; and, presumably, had he been less naive or less confused, he might have been more on guard against what was in progress at the time, might have tried somehow to protect himself.

According to Staktopoulos's account, the second phase of his interrogation took a serious turn for the worse—from violent language to violence pure and simple—shortly after the arrival at Security Police headquarters of an important visitor from Athens, Minister of Public Order Constantinos Rendis, who was now apparently keeping a close watch on the investigation, perhaps still smarting from General Donovan's criticism of the way things had stalled during July. Staktopoulos was called up from his cell around midnight and taken to Mouskoundis's office to face Rendis, with the principal Security Police officers surrounding him. Rendis gave a short lecture on the need for duty to the Fatherland in this time of supreme danger, when the Communist rebels were at the gates of Salonika. Something got into Staktopoulos. He interrupted the lecture to say that he didn't need to be reminded of his patriotic duty since his family had already sacrificed one member to the cause. "Who?" demanded Rendis. "My younger brother, a soldier killed during the war." According to Staktopoulos, Rendis continued to pontificate: "Duties to the Fatherland are endless and everlasting. . . ." Staktopoulos, suddenly conscious that he was being forced "to play some kind of role in the whole affair," answered back: "Why, Mr. Minister, don't you ask your son to play the role you're hymning?" Rendis moved his head in what Staktopoulos took to be a signal, and the officers surrounding Staktopoulos then went for him from every direction. All he remembers after that was waking up in his cell with his hands and feet tied.

The torture that followed took some days because it progressed in calculated stages: standing upright hours on end, then sitting in a chair with hands bound, day in day out, kept awake with a twist of his neck by those on duty in four-hour shifts. Then thirst, unbearable thirst that would lead him to plead first for water but then simply to have his lips dampened, though he couldn't be sure he had voice enough to be heard. And nothing to eat, even if he had no appetite anyway. Then a hiatus. He doesn't know how long it lasted. Maybe it was during this period that he heard his mother's voice. But it must have been before his hands were tied regularly, because he remembered beating his fists on the metal door of his cell and being told that the voice was just that of a woman thief they'd caught. And another time he heard his mother say: "Next time don't wake me up at midnight." He felt his mind drifting away, but all this wasn't a hallucination. As he learned later, the Security Police had picked up his mother and she was in a cell somewhere at the headquarters while he was nearby, and so too were his sisters at some point. He still had no desire to eat and he was now becoming skeletal. The interrogation continued, only there were no questions. At night he would be taken to the same old place, hands bound, and they would study him silently, then send him back to his cell. Finally one night the cursing began again, the insults to his mother and his sisters, words he can't bring himself to repeat. When he would protest, especially about his mother, they would invent new and more hideous crudities about her until they made him bellow.

The next stage was entirely physical: nightly beatings, his hands still tied, the Security policemen protecting their own hands with iron knuckles, striking here and there until the victim cried out from the pain, wept, fell down in the end and was carried off moaning to his cell where he was left to recover with his hands and feet tied. Some nights Mouskoundis himself would take over. The major didn't wear iron knuckles for protection, says the Reuters stringer; he had his own special technique. He would stand Staktopoulos up against the wall and begin by stepping on his victim's feet as hard as he could, then have another go as the pain died away. That was followed by his knee striking at the genitals, and when his victim howled, head falling forward, Mouskoundis, a wild bull now, would strike it back into place and go for the genitals again until Staktopoulos would finally collapse. Where, Staktopoulos asks, had the major learned that method? Not a thing, he says, to create honor for anyone who uses it on a man whose hands are bound.

The hanging in his cell followed, hanging upside down, but not for long—he doesn't know for how long—maybe just enough to allow his mother to pass by and see him like that, as his sisters later reported had happened. His sense of time and place was now confused. But when they moved on to the electric shock treatment—the traces still visible on his feet years later—he realized that they were trying to pretend that the treatment was happening someplace other than at the Security Police headquarters, because they would blindfold him and carry him outside to a car on the back of a giant policeman, then drive him around a bit, then return him to a room on the back of the same policeman and leave him there for this new way of bringing him to his knees. He remembers screaming with pain, then begging for water, then hearing someone call out for Thanasi, the name of the assistant cook and waiter in Security Police headquarters. The next time he was in that room, maybe only the second and last time, he heard a voice saying "Don't let them bring you here again. Please talk."

But he couldn't yet. Mouskoundis faced him in his office, repeated again and again that his boy Gregory had gotten himself badly involved, badly implicated, that he simply had to talk. Staktopoulos told him he hadn't got involved in anything, he really had nothing to say. Mouskoundis circled his chair, kept repeating that Gregory was deeply implicated now but that Mouskoundis could save him, though he also could have made him disappear when he came home at midnight, his mother having a son who was killed in the war was the only thing that had saved Gregory then, but if he didn't talk now neither he nor his family would get out of the thing alive, they were now in the hands of the Security Police who were not accountable, who didn't give out a receipt when they took people in, and Gregory had gotten himself badly involved, the Security Police saw Greece in front of them but Gregory had gotten himself badly implicated. Staktopoulos found that he couldn't talk, literally: his mouth wouldn't work. Maybe he was trembling now, maybe it was the paralysis that comes with pure fear, he doesn't know.

The final stage, what Staktopoulos calls the most painful, was the binding of his arms and legs with wire. It began gently. They undressed him except for his sleeveless undershirt, and one of the policemen almost playfully pulled hairs out of his chest and back, while the supervising officer, George Tsonos, made him "confess" that during his Communist affiliation he was known by the pseudonym "Gorilla" because he was so hairy. They blindfolded him, then wound the wire around his arms from the wrist to the elbow, then around his legs from the ankle to the knee—tight, but not painfully so. Then they laid him on the floor, turning him over every now and then, silently, and when the pain started coming to him stronger and stronger, they put something in his mouth so that his yelling wouldn't be heard. They no longer had to move him because he began to turn with the pain, flip this way and that like a landed fish, on the back, the belly, vibrant, wriggling. He could hear a door open and close occasionally. Was he being watched? Near his limit the gag fell out. Staktopoulos, quivering, called out to his dead brother, asked to be taken beside him. In his ultimate pain he heard "Ether, ether." It was over then.

They massaged him with alcohol immediately, but for some days he couldn't stand on his feet or raise his arms. Before returning him to his cell, they let him rest in a room. It was dark, and his eyes weren't right, so he couldn't see who was there, but he heard Major Mouskoundis's voice, quiet now: "I said you wouldn't stand ten minutes of it. You lasted two hours." Staktopoulos didn't know whether to believe him or not, they always lied about things at the Security Police headquarters, but it had been long enough. He was "kneeling" now, he had been made ready for the third stage of his interrogation, the confessional stage. A doctor looked him over, said something to the pharmacist on hand, gave him an injection, prescribed more. They stopped further injections because they couldn't find the veins they needed. Once evening they again took him to Mouskoundis's office, the place much simplified, almost bare of furniture, and they sat him down to do some translating. They were watching him. He didn't want to live any longer, and they made him translate. He had no idea what came out of his head. Five police officers looked him over. They decided he was now "ripe."

The next day at noon two policemen escorted him to an office to be checked out by the Salonika investigators representing the Court of the First Instance, Komotouros and Moustakis (the inquiry magistrate whom Donovan had interviewed in July). And soon after that—it must have been late September by then—he began his "confessions" under the guidance of the Security Police, repeating whatever answers he was given to repeat to whatever questions he was asked. He learned his text as they wrote it for him, revised it when that became necessary, recapitulated it when they brought him in to do so in front of the official investigators Komotouros and Moustakis, with his principal torturers, Mouskoundis and Tsonos, always present. At some point Helen Mamas was also escorted in to see him. Staktopoulos says that he fell at her feet and begged her to say anything she could to save him. "Look at what they've done to me," he told her. "I can't stand on my feet. I hurt everywhere." And he wept. He can't remember what Helen Mamas replied. All he remembers is being raised by two policemen, one under each arm, and being led back to his cell yet another time.

Thirty-five years after the fact, Staktopoulos allowed himself to comment on a few general questions raised by his interrogation. About torture and torturers: Is torture ever justified? No, Staktopoulos says, except just possibly as a last resort in the case of someone dangerous to the state—a spy, for example, who holds secrets he won't reveal whatever the gentler persuasion. But an ordinary citizen who is innocent and who in any case will be made out to confess things he hasn't done? No. And, he asks, how can a group of true men attack a single man whose hands are bound? Staktopoulos calls himself just an average Greek (physically, one assumes he means), not really a match for the above average. Still, why couldn't the Security policemen, if they were honorable men, face him one at a time while his hands were free? He admits that maybe they, being experienced in such matters, would give him ten blows to his five, but he would at least get in his five. So many strong men against a man with hands tied? Those Security policemen simply had no moral substance whatsoever, he concludes.

When it comes to those who serve justice, for example the official Salonika investigators Komotouros and Moustakis, both members of the Greek judiciary who were destined to become members of the Supreme Court, both men of experience not only in their field but in general psychology, couldn't they have seen that they had a physical wreck in front of them? Staktopoulos asks. Couldn't they have seen that what this wreck was made to confess was pure myth, a fabrication contradicting their own line of inquiry (which, Staktopoulos tells us at one point, seemed to be headed toward Randall Coate and the British)? No suspicion even when Inquiry Magistrate Moustakis was himself required to put the pen in the confessor's hand because the confessor was too weak to take it up and sign his fake confession? Or were they maybe following instructions from the Ministry of Justice in Athens, which they visited regularly? Staktopoulos concludes: it is undeniable that "incorruptible Greek Justice" had in this case become the blind servant of the deranged Athenians then governing the country.

The "deranged" Athenians in charge of Greek justice did not have an easy time of it during the six weeks of Staktopoulos's interrogation that preceded his formal arrest. From the start of those hot summer days in August and September, Minister of Justice Melas was on the defensive. In mid-August he held a press conference to state that neither he nor Minister of Public Order Rendis had impeded the interrogation of Kosta Hadjiargyris as was claimed by some, and he personally had done what he could to prevent the departure of Rea Polk. He said the final decision in any case was not his responsibility but that of a judge who granted permission for Rea to leave "only after personal insistence of Rankin and acquiescence of judicial authorities in Salonika."[9]

The scramble to pass the buck among authorities in Athens, authorities in Salonika, American diplomats, American press representatives, and British advisers continued on and off through the summer. Colonel Martin, the British police adviser now back from leave, got into the act a few days after Staktopoulos was picked up. The colonel evidently conducted a review of the investigation and recommended that certain phases be repeated with different investigators, though at the same time he gave passing support to Major Mouskoundis, who, in Martin's opinion, had done "effective work on investigating the caiques (small cargo vessels) that were in the bay during the period that Mr. Polk was in Salonika."[10]

There is no evidence that anybody paid the slightest attention to his recommendation and much evidence that the Staktopoulos lead was pursued with increasing vigor, though the new American ambassador in Athens, Henry Grady, cabled a secret report to the secretary of state two weeks later indicating that "new life" had come into the Polk investigation as a result of Minister Melas's mid-August visit to Salonika and the fact that the investigation was now being reviewed and certain phases of it being repeated.[11] This misreading of the substance of things was followed by a telling parenthetical comment: "in view indications that Donovan suspicious of British role, he should not be informed that British Colonel is conducting review."

This is our first evidence that Donovan's manifest interest in the role of Randall Coate during the general's recent interview with Mouskoundis had actually reached the level of a stated suspicion by the time he had returned to Athens from his trip north. It is also our first evidence that the American embassy in Athens had not only decided to support British influence in the investigation but was prepared to do so behind Donovan's back. In a further paragraph of his cable, Grady also reports that there has been no progress in the formation of the special judicial commission that Donovan had recommended, and Grady now doubts the feasibility of such a commission. He reports, "for Department's information only," that a commission would require considerable political pressure, special legislation "perhaps touching constitution," and most important of all, coping with the friction that Donovan's criticism and his alleged snubbing of Melas by "studiously" avoiding him in favor of Rendis had caused between the Ministries of Justice and Public Order, a thing that could bring the coalition government down, since Melas had threatened to resign if the Donovan proposal were pushed further.[12]

But this late August (twenty-sixth) report appears to have been already beside the point both regarding Donovan's concerns and the need for a review of the investigation: the Staktopoulos solution was already well under way at Security Police headquarters in Salonika, and in a second secret report a week later, Grady appears to know it. He tells the secretary of state that his earlier recommendation that Donovan and the Lippmann Committee not be informed about Melas's threat to resign was compelled not merely by political considerations but "also by a desire give Greeks maximum opportunity follow Stachtopoulos [*sic*] lead their own way, since it is probably most promising clues [*sic*] so far developed."[13] But as we have seen, James Kellis's CIA notes suggest that both he and Donovan were already familiar with the Staktopoulos lead by this time and may well have helped in promoting its emergence as the official solution. In any case, Grady's point of view here, and the various internecine conflicts within the Greek judicial structure, worked well to provide Mouskoundis full opportunity to pursue his "interrogation" of Staktopoulos in his own way, without substantial outside interference (despite Melas and Rendis having named, on August 12, three local officials "to supervise the work" of Major Mouskoundis),[14] and it also seems to have neutralized any continuing suspicion of a British role in Polk's murder.

That suspicion was actually not limited to what Donovan and Kellis may have expressed before the investigation focused in on Staktopoulos. A "top secret" memorandum from the British embassy in Athens to Ambassador Grady dated August 26 reveals that the "director of town police" in Rendis's Ministry of Public Order, one "Mr. Panopoulos," was "actively putting about allegation that British agents responsible for murder Polk,"[15] and Panopoulos was known to have shared his views with General Donovan at some point before Donovan left Greece in late July. According to the British embassy, Panopoulos was offering the following facts as evidence for his allegation: on May 6, three days before the murder, "Mr. Martin" of the British police mission attached to the Salonika police directorate informed Mr. Xanthopoulos, director of the Salonika town police, that he—Martin—had received information regarding the expected arrival of a prominent Communist who was "likely to be cause serious trouble in town." Panopoulos's inference was, according to the British embassy memorandum, that the British "deliberately put about this story in order it might be supposed prominent Communist in question murdered Polk," this presumably to cover British involvement in the murder. The memorandum reports that the facts quoted by Mr. Panopoulos are true, but the proper "explanation" of them is simply that the British have "certain useful sources information about Greek Communist Party," and whenever it is thought that information from these sources might be of assistance to the Greek security authorities, it is passed on to them as a routine matter, and "this Martin did in present case."

Colonel Martin's information, old hat news at this point, served the "Communist angle" that Mouskoundis had promoted all along, in particular the possible role of the Communist leader Colonel Vasvanas, who was reputed to have been in town either arranging sabotage or pretending to do so at the time of Polk's murder, but this detail in the case had already been questioned by Kellis in front of Donovan and others. The new element here is the apparent assumption by this Ministry of Public Order official that Colonel Martin's information was a British cover. In any case, the British embassy "explanation" of August 26 was evidently a sufficient one for American officials in Athens and Salonika, and it presumably worked at this time not only to isolate Mr. Panopoulos's suspicions but, now that the Staktopoulos solution was in progress—with or without Donovan's covert endorsement—also to kill any active exploration of the "British factor" in the case by any agency. A not entirely coherent comment by Theodore Lambron in his September 14 letter to Donovan suggests that whatever Donovan's own suspicions of the British may have been, he was no longer prepared to pursue that angle. Lambron reports that "one of Gibsons' [sic] subordinates, who dislikes him told me that Gibson has no use for the Greeks and that he is too pro-British to do justice to his position as American counsil [sic]. In the course of one of our conversations, Gibson showed interest in knowing to what extent you shared the views of those that considered the British possibly involved in the crime. Naturally, I told him that wouldn't [sic] even discuss the possibility. To this he said that he was very pleased as he feared that all this loose talk might have influenced you." The fact is, nothing in the record suggests that Donovan or his man in Greece chose to discuss the possibility again after mid-September of 1948.

The decision by the Athens embassy in late August and early September to be less than open with the Lippmann Committee appears to have had its origins in a perception by Karl Rankin, after Donovan's July visit, that those representing the Overseas Writers were prepared to play out the Polk affair in the American press whatever the political consequences for Greece. A few days after Staktopoulos was picked up in Salonika—too early in that route to a solution for substantial hope to have reached the American embassy—Ernest K. Lindley appeared in Athens, and, as an ex officio member of the Lippmann Committee, spoke at length with Karl Rankin regarding the Polk affair—this on

August 18.[16] Rankin tells us in his confidential report to the State Department that Lindley "expressed himself forcibly [sic] as to the necessity of solving the case," and when Rankin suggested that the case might in fact remain unsolved, as happened in many cases in the U.S. and elsewhere, Lindley responded that if this proved to be so, it would be "very serious for the Greek Government" and would bring about "drastic action" by the Lippmann Committee at home, especially in view of Donovan's imminent interim report, which, Lindley said, would offer the opinion that the Greek authorities "had not pressed the investigation sufficiently in the direction of the 'Right,' " a "most serious omission" in Lindley's view.

This gave Karl Rankin just the room he needed for what appears to have been a barely restrained diatribe—at least Lindley is quoted as entering the conversation only once more before its end. Rankin began by explaining what he called the difficulties of the Greek position. With Rendis as minister of public order, a man "who is as far to the Left as anyone in the Cabinet," and the Liberal Melas as minister of justice, one could be reasonably certain that the Right would be sufficiently investigated along with all other angles. But whether the Right, the Left, or " 'the British' " were found guilty, "additional embarrassment might result rather than any closing of the case." This, said Rankin, would be largely the fault of the press. If, for example, it turned out that some rightist group had committed the murder, the foreign press would almost certainly blame the Greek government, in particular the Populist party of Tsaldaris—representing the Right in the coalition—and this might bring about the downfall of what Rankin called the only parliamentary government that has any prospect of existing in Greece under present conditions. If, on the other hand, the Communists were found to be guilty, certain sections of the press abroad would insist that this was a "put-up job by the monarcho-fascist Greek Government." And evidence pointing to "any degree of British responsibility" would be "equally embarrassing to almost everyone concerned."

Rankin seems to have paused here to catch his breath, because Lindley is reported to have come in at this point to deny indignantly that the American press would handle the matter unfairly in case the Right or the Left were found guilty, and Rankin, having probed the visitor's most tender spot, now dropped the press issue and returned in a gentler mode to the case itself. He suggested that perhaps it had been a mistake for both Greeks and Americans to assume that the murder was a political one. Polk may have written material critical of the Greek government, but no more so than some correspondents and less so than others, and he had been generally sympathetic toward American aid to Greece and Greek independence. Why would either Right or Left organize "an elaborate plot" to murder him? And to "condemn" the Greek government on the assumption that the murder had been politically motivated was "entirely unfair."

Who, then, was likely to have been responsible for the murder? Well, Rankin remarked, "human life is cheap in Greece at the present time," with one of the highest homicide rates in Europe—although lower than that in the United States. And eight years of conflict hadn't helped the situation. Then there was Polk's "violent temper," and his not speaking Greek. He might easily have aroused the anger or suspicion of some "desperate characters with whom he came in contact." He was known to have been in touch with "alleged dope smugglers, presumably for the purpose of getting a story" (one can't help wondering what implication Rankin's listener may have gathered from the "presumably" in this hypothesis). These smugglers, said Rankin, or "any number of other persons" might have murdered Polk. And the murder need not have involved an organization of any size.

These comparatively low-key, nonpolitical hypotheses must have struck Lindley as rather surprising after the various communications that the State Department had been sharing with the Lippmann Committee over the past months—those of Ayer and Burdett and Kellis and even Rankin himself—all plugging or challenging one or another aspect of the Communist angle, with virtually no mention of anything as politically neutral and casual as murder by unnamed drug smugglers or simply one or more of any number of unnamed "other persons." But Lindley is pictured as entering the dialogue not to express surprise at this turn in the conversation but to defend Polk as a correspondent who had been simply " 'going about his business,' " a description, Lindley stated, with which "you diplomats don't agree." Rankin was quick not to agree that an American correspondent had a right to visit Markos. No? Lindley wanted to know why not. If Americans could go see Stalin, why couldn't they see Markos? Rankin replied that the cases were not parallel. A much closer analogy, he thought, would be that of an American correspondent seeing Hitler during the war. But, said Lindley, we are not at war with Markos Vafiadis. Well that's what it amounted to, said Rankin: our spending hundreds of millions of dollars and using the services of many high-ranking American officers to bring about Markos's defeat. In any case, concluded Lindley, a visit to Markos would not "justify the Greeks in 'bumping off' Polk"—and with that Rankin found he could fully agree.

What is curious about this phase of the conversation—aside from its hyperbole—is the abstraction of it, as though the two were discussing a theoretical possibility that the murder of George Polk had negated in his case and that was yet to be realized by anybody else. As we have seen, the fact was—and both Rankin and Lindley knew it—that less than two months previously the American correspondent Homer Bigart had been escorted by a Greek Communist andarte across the Yugoslav border into Greek guerrilla territory to an interview with Markos, had obtained valuable information that was subsequently published in the *New York Herald Tribune* (July 25–28), had then been guided safely to the outskirts of Yannina by andarte guards, and had flown on to Athens—as Karl Rankin himself reported laconically on July 4[17]—without cost to himself or anybody else. Was Homer Bigart's trip to Markos, acknowledged by the *Herald Tribune* in an editorial as a useful source of "realistic intelligence,"[18] to be regarded as the equivalent of a visit with Hitler during World War II? And was the fact that Bigart had been escorted safely through an arduous two-week journey, to be received by Markos for what the Communists obviously considered important propaganda purposes, a fact that had no bearing on the "Communist angle" in the Polk case, still ardently promulgated as the root of the murder by both American and Greek officials?

The Rankin-Lindley conversation ended more or less diplomatically. Rankin put in a final complaint about the lack of cooperation that the Greek government had received from various American correspondents—only Helen Mamas designated by name—and Lindley gave his endorsement to Donovan's dormant proposal for a special judicial commission to review the Polk case, a thing that Lindley hoped might take place before the Lippmann Committee's interim report was published. Rankin concluded his account of the meeting by indicating that Lindley's attitude was "dignified and friendly," showing "no evidence of sympathy for the Left as such," but Rankin did find it disquieting to note Lindley's apparent feeling that "the Polk case must be tried in the American press, whether or not Greece goes down the drain in the process."

Lindley had no need to feel any sense of urgency about the special judicial commission and the publication of Donovan's interim report: with the increasingly propitious detention of Gregory Staktopoulos, both the commission and the publication vanished into thin air—and so did Rankin's need to worry about either the Polk case being tried in the American press or Greece going down the drain. The documents of late August and early September show the Greek authorities ripe with optimism. Attorney General Constantinidis visited Raleigh Gibson on August 31 and not only stated outright that he was "very optimistic" but for the first time expressed his feeling that "Stahtopoulos [sic] would give the information needed to settle the case."[19] This feeling was based on the latest development: handwriting experts in Salonika had now "categorically declared" that the handwriting on the envelope that had been used to mail George Polk's identity card (and Pan Am advertisement) to the Third Police Station during the week before his body surfaced was that of Gregory Staktopoulos's mother, Anna. The police would show the experts' decision to Gregory Staktopoulos, and "they expect that this will force him to break." Staktopoulos had been questioned daily, Constantinidis reported, and he had already written out statements regarding his relations with both Daniel Thrapp and George Polk, great detail regarding Thrapp, but little or nothing regarding Polk (in fact, no statement from Staktopoulos about Thrapp ever appeared in the records of the case). From all indications, said the attorney general, Staktopoulos was the "contact" that Thrapp had mentioned in his Rome memorandum but had not identified. And the attorney general was still of the opinion that Helen Mamas "knew more of the Polk case than she had told." In any case, Gibson reported, Constantinidis repeated his belief that the case would be broken in the near future.

In his covering memorandum, Gibson reveals that he himself is not quite so optimistic. Though Staktopoulos has apparently admitted to Major Mouskoundis that he worked with andarte colonel Vasvanas when the latter was with the Communist Central Committee of Salonika, Gibson is "of the impression that the local authorities are placing too much faith in their belief that Stahtopoulos [sic] will confess, even when confronted with the handwriting evidence." Staktopoulos is "intelligent and clever," and, says Gibson, he "probably realizes that the Government would have a long drawn out trial before he could be convicted on the evidence" gathered so far. Still, at this point, only two weeks after Staktopoulos was picked up virtually out of nowhere, Gibson tells the secretary of state: "I am convinced that he is the key witness in the case, and that he is in a position to give the Government the information needed to complete the investigation."

But getting what was needed out of Staktopoulos proved more difficult than all this early optimism would have it, and one doubts that even Mouskoundis himself was so complacent at this stage of the accused's interrogation, though Mouskoundis was the one man who surely would have known that the prospects in the long run were excellent, given room enough and time for effective persuasion. But there was a certain question of propriety, even of legality, regarding the detention of the accused that seemed to be bothering Raleigh Gibson. The consul general indicates that he raised the issue of Gregory Staktopoulos being held at Security Police headquarters without formal charges, an issue that had evidently already brought on "pressure from Athens newspapers" and that Gibson thought might call for a statement of some kind.

Attorney General Constantinidis had an answer ready. After all, General Donovan had been the one who had asked whether there wasn't a provision in Greek law that would allow people to be detained without formal arrest "and had requested that some means be found to accomplish this." So the attorney general "had carried out the General's request to detain people," and that now included not only Gregory Staktopoulos and his mother but seven "new people," Staktopoulos's two sisters among these; and though this "seemed to be causing some trouble in certain quarters," the attorney general stated that no one of those being held would be formally arrested at that time.

Gibson's uncertainty about how easily Staktopoulos might break and his unease about these detentions without formal arrest continued through September. On the first of the month he cabled the State Department to say that Gregory Staktopoulos and his mother would be formally arrested within two or three days, and he added that though he was not as confident as local officials that Staktopoulos would confess as expected, the consulate would in any case be furnished information by the attorney general as soon as it is obtained, and Gibson requested that the news about mother Staktopoulos's handwriting not be released to the press at this time.[20] On September 4 Gibson reported that during the previous day Minister of Justice Melas had ordered the attorney general "to formally arrest Stahtopoulos [sic] and mother immediately," but a conference of Salonika judicial and police authorities had decided against such action as harmful to the investigation and had sent the attorney general and the chief of police to Athens to explain their position to the minister of justice.[21]

Gibson also reported at this time that while Mouskoundis remained optimistic and had stated that he was "securing facts" from Staktopoulos, Gibson felt that the investigation would be a "long drawn out affair from present indications" because Staktopoulos "does not appear to be type to break easily." Gibson thinks that both police and judicial authorities realize that the handwriting evidence alone is not sufficient (it proved in fact to be highly questionable, as even Frederick Ayer hints to his readers in his book).[22] Gibson is also not positive "that present method of questioning is effective with an intelligent and clever man" such as Staktopoulos. Though Gibson offers this view not much before Major Mouskoundis apparently took it on himself to change the method drastically, or perhaps had already begun to do so, Gibson appears too naive to recognize the full implications of what he is suggesting in the context of a judicial system that permitted a suspect to be held for weeks in isolation at Security Police headquarters. He concludes his report by indicating that unless there is a lucky break, he expects that the investigation will continue at its present pace, and he doubts the advisability of trying to speed it up since such action would be used as an alibi by both police and judicial authorities "in case of failure."

Another source, the Draft Report, tells us that "some members of the Greek Government" were evidently concerned about the propriety of the long detention of Gregory and Anna Staktopoulos at Security Police headquarters, but Minister of Justice Melas announced on August 31 that "he would permit no interference with the work of the investigating authorities."[23] Then, in September, "Melas too became concerned and urged Salonika police authorities to release the pair from the custody of national security and turn them over to the judicial authorities for formal arrest." But Constantinidis petitioned for further delay and won the argument, hence the six-week-long detention. The Draft Report goes on to say that "American officials were in agreement with the advisability of leaving a free hand to the police although they recognized that formal arrest would have certain advantages in that the press would then be able to criticize and comment on the case thus acting somewhat as a spur to the investigation." Again the text of the Draft Report suggests that the principal issue here was not one of civil liberties but of speed in arriving at a solution of the case.

On September 11, Attorney General Constantinidis again visited Gibson to explain the delay in making a formal arrest. Constantinidis had hoped to be in a position to do so by that time and surely could arrest both Staktopoulos and his mother "because of their Communist activities," but unfortunately they were having difficulty "in making Stahtopoulos [sic] talk."[24] The minister of justice in Athens had telephoned to say that he could not accept any more responsibility for the delay, and the attorney general had replied that he himself was the one who had the responsibility since he had given the order to detain the witnesses—and he, along with the other Salonika officials, would be blamed "if there was a failure." In any case, he remained very optimistic, information of value had been obtained, and, Gibson concludes, Constantinidis is "positive" not only that the case will be solved by the interrogation of Staktopoulos but that "Major Moushountis [sic] must not be interfered with."

And he wasn't, neither by officials in Salonika nor in Athens—maybe partly because Minister of Justice Melas had now become quite distracted by his feud with Rendis and Donovan. It seems the Athens press had offered a version of Donovan's contribution to the September 9 CBS "Report Number Three on the Murder of George Polk," with its account of what Donovan had said to whom about the deficiencies of the investigation and with its statement that Minister of Public Order Rendis had agreed with Donovan's criticism, a remark that Melas took to be a stab in his back. Melas held a press conference on September 12 during which he said that he "could hardly believe" that a responsible U.S. citizen would have publicly and "so superficially" criticized the Greek investigation and the Greek judicial system, and he simply "refused to believe" that his colleague Minister Rendis would publicly criticize Greek justice and a fellow minister, particularly to a foreigner.[25]

Donovan's offer during the same broadcast of a $10,000 reward on behalf of the Overseas Writers Association served merely to complicate the situation. This news, which had also been cabled to Rendis,[26] occasioned a second statement by Minister Melas on September 18 to the effect that General Donovan and his collaborators had fallen victims to a deception that did gross injustice to the Greek people.[27] Only those who do not know Greece sufficiently well, said Melas, could be led to believe that a monetary reward would make a Greek disclose knowledge which he would otherwise keep to himself. The honesty of the Greek people, the nation's sense of hospitality, and its love and gratitude toward its American friends were too deeply rooted "to stoop to such baseness." As for Donovan's criticism of the Polk case investigators, Melas could say that the investigation had in fact been thorough if slow, and there was evidence of "unimpeachable good faith and honesty of Greek authorities." Therefore, the idea that the American government should give the Greek government a definite time limit for the conclusion of the case "seems somewhat preposterous," especially since even in America, in spite of the "acknowledged perfection of means of investigation," murderers have been known to evade arrest for months.

Quite true, but the pressure on Melas, Rendis, and the Salonika authorities to exercise what Melas called his people's obligations of international honor must have been felt at the Salonika Security Police headquarters, especially after Rendis's visit there to confront Staktopoulos. Time now appeared to be running out for Major Mouskoundis. On September 21, Constantinidis again visited Gibson to say that the formal arrest of Staktopoulos and his mother was pending, and that action had not yet been taken because—besides the "envelope" information—there was hope that Major Mouskoundis "would now be able to secure the full story."[28] That he hadn't yet gotten what he wanted is suggested by Mouskoundis's request that he be given one or two more days before turning Staktopoulos over to the inquiry magistrate, and also by Constantinidis's setting up some of the same old straw men: Thrapp (he was now convinced that Staktopoulos was the unnamed contact that Thrapp had mentioned), Don Matchen, whose name, Constantinidis said, had been brought in "numerous times" by Helen Mamas, and of course Helen Mamas herself, who, we now learn, had been the object of Constantinidis's suspicion "from the start of the case." But no more definite evidence. Not even anything about Hadjiargyris from the witnesses under detention, though Constantinidis said that the name of the *Christian Science Monitor* correspondent would be brought before Staktopoulos in due course.

Two days later (September 23) Gibson notified the State Department that Major Mouskoundis was getting more and more information out of Staktopoulos, so a warrant for the witness's arrest would not be issued until September 27—a silent commentary on due process in Gibson's northern region that the consul general allowed to remain silent.[29] This is the cable in which we learn that by that time Mouskoundis expected Staktopoulos to have revealed "when meeting was organized, where, under whose orders, reason for plot, and name of murderer." And it is in this cable that Gibson tells the secretary of state that, in view of the expected progress and the confidence of local officials that there would be a final solution of the case in the near future, the appointment of Donovan's proposed special judicial committee was no longer considered necessary.

The same confidence was repeated five days later, on September 28, by which date the attorney general was reported to have granted Major Mouskoundis still more time before making a formal arrest,[30] and this delay was given further justification on September 29, when Gibson cabled the secretary of state to say that Staktopoulos "is breaking,"[31] and the solution of the case "will only be matter of days." In fact, Staktopoulos "broke" by the following day, and Gibson could report that though the authorities had favored holding the Reuters stringer a few more days before taking his formal testimony, "Major Mouskoundis is understood to have changed his mind, and will now request immediate arrest, with full publicity regarding the case."[32] Staktopoulos's first formal confession is dated October 1, 1948, and that is presumably the date of his formal arrest, forty-eight days after he was picked up by a plainclothesman at the Kalamaria-Aretsou bus stop on his way home.

Now, so many years after the fact, it is difficult to see how professional public servants of some goodwill and a degree of personal conscience—Consul General Gibson, Minister of Justice Melas, perhaps even Attorney General Constantinidis and Counselor of Embassy Rankin—would not have questioned how "final" this solution to the case could be after having emerged so very slowly, yet in the end so abruptly, from testimony by a witness held in isolation at the Security Police headquarters without formal charges for over six weeks and interviewed at no point by any one of these gentlemen before the witness's first sworn deposition. Yet the record reveals no such questioning that September, no strongly stated suspicion or skepticism, only signs of relief. And now, with all the evidence on record available to be reviewed—the once-secret archives, the full "confessional" depositions in the original, the trial record, the recapitulations of evidence and the personal papers and memoirs—it is difficult to find anyone then on the scene in the role of observer rather than participant in the Polk affair who believes that Staktopoulos was innocent of substantial involvement in the case, and it seems even fewer believe that he confessed as he did merely because he was forced to do so. An extreme instance is Shan Sedgwick, the former *New York Times* correspondent who now says bluntly what most other observers of the case in Greece seem to take for granted but choose only to imply in one way or another: that of course Staktopoulos would, like any good Communist, want to revise the part he played in the Polk affair so long ago and now change black to white.[33]

Some of those familiar with the case who have read Staktopoulos's book and are fully prepared to believe that he was tortured—Hadjiargyris, for example—wonder if Staktopoulos's account of who did the torturing can be swallowed in full measure ("Mouskoundis himself? I don't know," says Hadjiargyris).[34] And others who have no doubt that Staktopoulos's account of the tortures is literal also believe that his confessions, though dubious in some details and occasionally contradictory, are pretty much literal as well. Even Rea Polk, who admits to not having read Staktopoulos's memoir of those days, lives with a single image of him that she finds incriminating.[35] During what she remembers to have been their one meeting, in the bar of the Mediterranean Hotel a few days before George Polk's body was recovered, when Helen Mamas happened to introduce her to Staktopoulos as he sat among others she also did not know, the man turned to give her a look of such terrible sadness that she became convinced on the spot that this Staktopoulos not only knew her husband was dead but must have actually been there to see George Polk murdered.

Gregory Staktopoulos is now in his late seventies and lives as a retired journalist in Athens close by the statue of Harry Truman that was toppled not long ago by anti-American demonstrators.[36] He lives with Lola, the woman he married shortly after he came out of prison in 1960, and the two spend their summers—increasingly long summers since Gregory Staktopoulos began to have heart trouble—in an apartment overlooking the sea at the edge of the Corinth Canal. Staktopoulos's hair is gray and thin now, still slicked back, his eyeglasses thick so that they magnify his eyes, his mouth a bit downturned on one side as though from a mild stroke, his body still lean but slightly stooped, his hearing giving out, but when he shakes your hand you feel a strong will there, and he still smiles to himself whenever he brings irony into the dialogue.

Irony comes into the dialogue whenever Staktopoulos speaks about his countrymen in general. They are their own worst enemies, he says, and they don't know what's good for them, beginning with their sometimes hostile attitude toward Americans, a matter of disgrace, he thinks, in view of what America has done for Greece and what Greeks have gained from going to America. Those who choose to return to Greece catch on quickly, he says, for example, a young relative of his who came back to Salonika to teach medicine after being educated in America and barely managed to unpack his bags and settle in before the opposition he encountered made him decide: enough, it's hopeless—and back to the United States he went. Staktopoulos's own pro-Americanism compels him to speak English—a quaint English that gets the clichés wrong sometimes—even when Greek would serve him better, though his Greek becomes a bit rhetorical whenever he comes to basic issues such as honor and patriotism. And the rhetoric turns to vituperation when memory takes him back to the Security Police headquarters in Salonika. "I am a gentleman, so I will not speak the words I should speak when referring to those beasts who pretended to be policemen, but whenever one of them dies—and this Tsonos, one of my principal torturers, died just a few months ago—I always use the Greek term one uses when animals die, because any other term would be too dignified. Excuse me, I am a man of emotion and I show too much passion sometimes, but those men were not human beings." And to prove his point, he shows the barely visible marks left on his arm by burns from the rope that held him for beatings, and the clean thin scar on one wrist from his attempt to commit suicide with the sharpened metal from a shoelace after the beatings had made him confess to things he never did.

He is also a man of emotion when he speaks of the one person who came forward to defend his character in 1949, his American teacher at

Anatolia, Carl Compton, and whenever he speaks of his family: his brother who died at the front, his mother who lasted only a year after her Security Police ordeal, his sister who went mad some time after hers, and the younger sister he had sent to college who found a way finally to get him out of prison after twelve years. He speaks of these with his head lowered and his mouth disfigured from the attempt to keep his broken English from breaking down completely, and then, as though some mechanism of survival has been switched on in his brain, memory triggers new passion, and that finds language in a further denunciation of the men who not only tortured him but brought on his mother's death and a sister's madness and then mistreated the younger sister even after she was free. "Beasts, and dying like beasts, all of them, there is no other way to put it."

As though to protect this man against further heart strain, his wife now takes over the dialogue with a calming cynicism about why the Security Police kept her husband illegally at their headquarters not only for forty-five days before he was formally arrested but for more than four years after he was made to confess. "How else could they keep people on the outside from learning the truth? They watched him day and night. How else could they make their sham trial stick?" And Gregory, calmer now, stays silent, nodding his head, then suddenly asks in Greek: "How do you say 'sham trial' in good English?"

Salonika Bay at the White Tower.

From *The Polk File on Air*

George Polk broadcasting for CBS and, lower left, after his nose surgery. At right, the Astoria Hotel in Salonika.

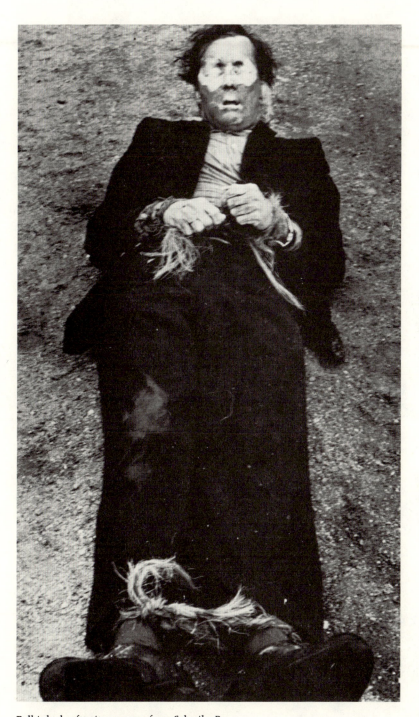

Polk's body after its recovery from Salonika Bay.

Rea Polk waiting for her husband's coffin and, below, the coffin being loaded on an RAF transport plane.

From *The Polk File on Air*

Major Mouskoundis, head of the Salonika Security Police. Greek caption describes him as "modest and inconspicuous."

At the top right, Winston Burdett of CBS; below him, Salonika Attorney General Constantinidis; and, lower left, Walter Lippmann, columnist and chairman of the Overseas Writers Committee.

"The American journalist Polk was victim of an odious crime":
headline in *Makedonia*, May 18, 1948. The inserts, a Pan
Am advertisement and Polk's identity card, were mailed to
the Third Police Precinct in the envelope shown opposite.

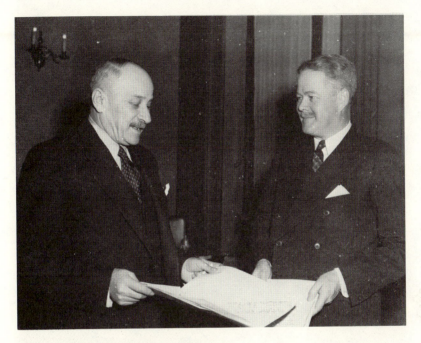

Minister of Public Order Rendis and American
embassy Chargé d'Affaires Karl Rankin.

At left, a 1949 newspaper reproduction of the
"incriminating envelope" and, on the right, a slightly
altered 1966 newspaper reproduction of the same
envelope.

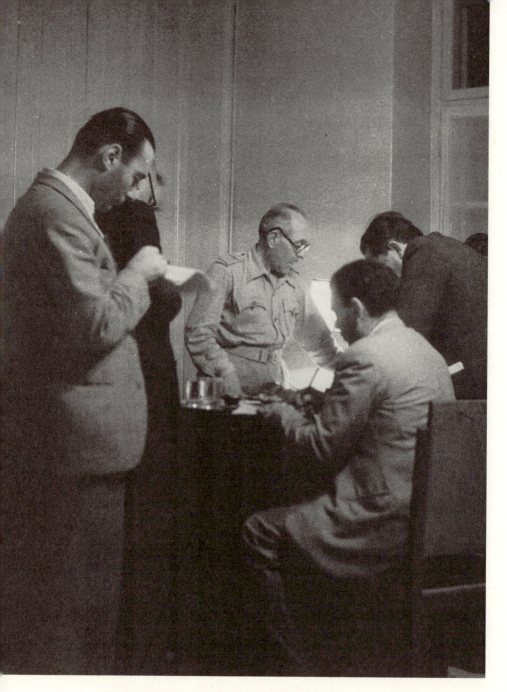

Reuters stringer Gregory Staktopoulos covering an army
press conference during the time before he became an official
suspect.

VII The Confessions

GREGORY STAKTOPOULOS'S confession of October 1, 1948, if taken at its word, supports those who still believe (and this includes George Polk's widow) that the Reuters stringer not only led Polk to his murderers but was present at the killing. In the course of the document Staktopoulos testifies that he was sitting beside Polk in a rowboat about a mile offshore in Salonika Bay when the CBS correspondent was shot in the back of the head at close quarters.[1] This first confession is not called that in the record but appears under the heading "Witness's Interrogation," and it is presented as a deposition under Articles 121 and 124 of the Penal Law covering testimony by witnesses who have been designated as not being in a position to appear before a court audience, in this instance because the witness was appearing before two judicial authorities, Christos Moustakis and Christos Komotouros, at Security Police headquarters in Salonika, where he had been held in isolation for more than six weeks. After being sworn in on the Holy Bible and "duly questioned" (though no questions are actually recorded), Staktopoulos offered an official narrative of his involvement in the murder of George Polk. The narrative may be summarized as follows.

A few days before Polk's arrival in Salonika, Staktopoulos received a phone call from someone he thought was an unemployed newsman named "Kissos" asking that he meet with Staktopoulos at a café frequented by local Greeks originating from the Pontus region of Turkey (the Reuters stringer was born in Trapezus, once called Trebizond). "Kissos" turned out to be someone else whose name Staktopoulos didn't remember but who used to show up often at the offices of the Communist paper, *Laiki Foni*, "burdened by the problems of the Workers' Center," during the period in which Staktopoulos translated dispatches for the paper. This man—"rather fat," wearing a gray suit and cap—told Staktopoulos that in a few days several American correspondents were expected to come to Salonika, and among them would be "one Polk," who would "go up to the mountains," presumably in the Pieria-Olympus region. The man requested that Staktopoulos act as Polk's interpreter "when he goes aboard the rowboat" (which we are to assume was to be Polk's mode of transportation), and he indicated that he would let Staktopoulos know when the trip was to take place. Staktopoulos was told that in the meanwhile absolute secrecy was called for, but were the Reuters stringer to agree to help, it "would be of service to a journalist colleague." As the two men parted, Staktopoulos said that he would try to be of assistance to the American correspondent in question.

Staktopoulos's first contact with Polk followed this encounter, after an UNSCOB meeting at the Mediterranean Hotel, where a journalist colleague named Stavridis told him that Helen Mamas wanted to see him in the hotel bar, and when he found Mamas there, she introduced him to some newly arrived American newsmen, including Polk. Staktopoulos describes this meeting in some detail: who was sitting where, Mamas being called to the phone (by prearranged signal, in his view); three people known to him who were seen passing by the hotel during this gathering, two of them—identified by the single names "Tassos" and "Ioannidis"—journalists who worked for the Communist newspaper *Eleftheria* and who were also presumably known to Helen Mamas because Staktopoulos saw them nod to her as they passed by the bar window; finally, the point of this meeting in the bar, which was Helen Mamas's passing the word to Staktopoulos that Polk wanted to meet Markos and "had come from Athens bearing letters of introduction." Mamas told the Reuters stringer that "we should help him [Polk] implement his plans," and when Staktopoulos asked, with his Pontus Café encounter in mind, how she thought he might help Polk, Mamas replied: "By acting as his interpreter at the right moment." Staktopoulos wanted to know from whom and to whom Polk had letters of introduction, but Mamas said that she didn't have that information at hand and therefore mentioned no names to him.

This first meeting was followed by a phone call from Staktopoulos to Mamas at the Olympus-Naoussa restaurant later that evening to get the names of the American correspondents straight, and at that time Mamas invited the Reuters stringer to have a beer with the group dining there. Staktopoulos says he didn't respond definitely at this point, but in the end did go to the restaurant and waited outside. When the group emerged, he kept his distance until the group broke up, and then he followed Polk into Carolou Diehl Street. Polk didn't recognize him in the darkness at first, but when they reached a lighted spot "greeted me and said, in English, 'Ah, it's you.' " Staktopoulos "asked him again" (the first occasion is not specifically indicated) about his planned trip to Markos and "he told me he had decided to take it without fail." And when Staktopoulos asked him about the names of those he had met or would meet in this connection, Polk said that he couldn't remember them but that Helen Mamas knew them. They now arrived at the Astoria Café, where Polk had a vermouth and Staktopoulos a coffee, and the two talked about the reconstruction of northern Greece, whether American aid for this purpose was substantial and criticism of the aid program justified, what damage had been caused by the guerrillas—and Staktopoulos provided Polk "with the necessary information." They agreed to meet at the Mediterranean before noon the next day.

They did so, in the street outside the hotel, after Staktopoulos had spent some time inside talking to Dr. Ahmed, at one point overhearing Polk's voice in an adjacent corridor. Staktopoulos now asked Polk about his arrangements regarding the Markos trip and Polk replied that these were progressing well and that he hoped to leave during the course of that day. They walked to Mitropoleos Street, where they separated, Polk remarking that he was going to his hotel and that he would be meeting Helen Mamas shortly thereafter. Staktopoulos went about his business the rest of the day, and at 7:30, now at the offices of the *Makedonia*, received a phone call from the person he had met at the Pontus Café. "Polk will leave tonight," the man said. "Between 8:00 and 8:30 P.M., you be at the Luxembourg Café and wait there to act as his interpreter and take him to the rowboat 'Aghios Nicolaos' when that arrives to pick him up." The man again requested absolute secrecy. Staktopoulos went back to his desk and thought about it, then put on his coat and left. He took the bus to the Luxembourg Café along the sea front several kilometers from the center of town and arrived there at 8:00 P.M., sat facing the café entrance, looked out occasionally toward the sea and the nearby pier for the rowboat, which had not yet shown up.

Polk arrived at the café by taxi at 9:00 P.M. He walked in, glancing at the few customers in the place, and when Staktopoulos stood up, came over to sit beside him, facing the sea. Polk told him that he'd been informed he was to leave that night and that Staktopoulos was to act as his interpreter and to guide him to the rowboat named "Aghios Nicolaos." Polk was in a good mood. He asked whether the rowboat had appeared. Staktopoulos looked out toward the sea: there was still no rowboat named "Aghios Nicolaos" among the several others out there. "It doesn't matter," Polk said. "It's bound to arrive." The waiter came up to the table and Polk ordered lobster and wine. Staktopoulos ordered mussels and a little retsina. The Reuters stringer again asked for the names of those Polk had been in contact with, but Polk avoided the question: he didn't know names, didn't remember names. During dinner Polk told Staktopoulos that this trip was the most important of his life as a journalist and that when it was over he would return to America to relax. Several times during the meal he asked whether the rowboat had arrived, and after they had finished eating, forty-five minutes to an hour from the time Polk had reached the restaurant, the rowboat showed up, joining the two or three others still at the pier. Polk got up from the table first, paid the bill, tipped the waiter, and headed outside. Staktopoulos now told his official interrogators that he had forgotten to mention that when Polk first arrived at the restaurant he had told him that he'd come from the Astoria Hotel, and he had brought with him a rolled package of something that looked softer than paper, something more than a foot long. Staktopoulos did not ask what the package contained.

The rowboat "Aghios Nicolaos" was not, in Staktopoulos's opinion, the normal length of a fishing boat but rather of an excursion boat, and it was painted red and blue, with its name on the inside rather than the outside, and with two plank seats between bow and stern. The boatman struck him as a man in need of sleep because his head was lowered to his chest. He was wearing a cap pulled down to his ears and a poncho covered with a camouflage design. As Staktopoulos and the American correspondent approached the pier, the rowboat came alongside and Polk jumped in. Staktopoulos could now see the face of the boatman, and that made him hesitate: the man was none other than the very well-known Communist leader Adam Mouzenidis. As Staktopoulos stood there, Polk called up to him: "Come on, jump in," and he did so, sitting down on the plank seat beside the American.

Here Staktopoulos explains to his official interrogators that this Mouzenidis is the brother of the Salonika dentist and that he used to appear at the offices of *Laiki Foni* when Staktopoulos was working there and, with head lowered, would go in to talk privately to the head editor. His "conspiratorial and shifty appearance"—as the confessional text puts it—had impressed Staktopoulos at the time and had led him to ask who the man was. A labor leader, he was told.

The rowboat now headed out toward the small nearby cape called Karabournaki, with Mouzenidis at the oars, then turned in opposite the Paparouna Café, Mouzenidis not saying a word during the trip there, and Staktopoulos not saying a word to him either, because Mouzenidis made him feel afraid. Polk, on the other hand, repeated to Staktopoulos that this was the most important trip of his life as a journalist and that he was very happy. But Polk didn't ask why they were heading toward shore now. Staktopoulos assumed they were going in so that he himself could be let off at the Paparouna Café, his task as interpreter presumably completed, but instead, when they landed they took on two more people who had been waiting on shore near a dimly lit shed not far from the café and headed out to sea again. One of the new arrivals was Colonel Vangelis Vasvanas, earlier identified by Major Mouskoundis as a "saboteur" and known to Staktopoulos from his days at the *Laiki Foni* newspaper, in fact—as he tells his official interrogators—a man who had challenged him in public on one occasion because Staktopoulos objected to the illegal use of violence against the police that Vasvanas had insisted was obligatory whenever one of "our men" was arrested.

The other new arrival was unknown to Staktopoulos: a man wearing dark clothes, unshaven but not actually growing a beard, thin and weak-looking, complexion dark, wearing a cap—as was Vasvanas—and no necktie. He sat in the bow, and Vasvanas took over the oars from Mouzenidis, who moved to the stern behind Polk and Staktopoulos. Vasvanas rowed on toward the point of the Karabournaki cape. No one spoke. Staktopoulos was worried now, thought he ought to be put ashore but didn't dare say so. When they came opposite the point of the cape, now well out to sea, Mouzenidis said to Staktopoulos: "Tell Polk that to keep him from seeing where we are headed, they will blindfold him." Staktopoulos told this to Polk and he replied "okay." Silently the unknown man in the bow reached below the gunwale and came up with a kerchief of the kind fishermen wear on their heads, handed it to Vasvanas, who passed it on to Mouzenidis, and he then used it to blindfold Polk. They continued on their way, and five minutes later, Mouzenidis asked Staktopoulos to tell Polk that for security reasons they would now tie his feet and hands. Polk didn't object, Staktopoulos reports, but on the contrary said: "As long as I get where I have to go, I don't mind getting there blind even," and "Now we are on our way to our destination." Without a word the unknown man in the bow silently produced the needed rope in two sections—thick boat line—and passed it to Vasvanas. Mouzenidis then came up in front of Polk and bound his feet and hands, leaving a play of rope between the bindings. Staktopoulos now reports that it was actually at this point that Polk said: "Now we are on the way to our destination."

As Vasvanas rowed on, Mouzenidis returned to his place in the stern, and Staktopoulos became increasingly alarmed. Why weren't they heading back to shore to let him off? His mission as interpreter was surely over now. But he didn't dare suggest at this point that they take him ashore, he was too afraid. Then, no more than ten minutes after Polk had been bound hand and foot, the rowboat now about a mile out to sea, Staktopoulos heard "a gunshot whistle beside me." He rose in his seat and saw Polk curl up and fall forward. Staktopoulos, almost paralyzed by what he had seen, fell back in his seat.

He was certain that Mouzenidis was the one who had fired the shot since he had been standing behind Polk, while Vasvanas and the unknown man in the bow had been facing him, and neither had moved as the shot was fired. That had occurred so suddenly that Staktopoulos hadn't actually seen Mouzenidis's movements, hadn't seen him draw a pistol or fire it. And he hadn't heard a sound out of Polk or seen him quiver. Then, as he overheard Vasvanas and Mouzenidis talking to each other hurriedly as though asking each other whether Polk was dead or not, he found he couldn't make out exactly what they were saying. He was in a state of shock, too afraid for his own fate.

Mouzenidis now bent over the prostrate Polk and went through his pockets, removing papers from his inside jacket pocket, then taking out his billfold and removing his identity card and a small Pan American "calendar," items that he handed to Staktopoulos, saying: "Hold these." Mouzenidis put the billfold back, then went through the trouser pockets, taking out some items that Staktopoulos couldn't recall because he'd been in a state of shock at the time and even more terrified after having been given the identity card and the calendar to hold. The body search over, Mouzenidis and Vasvanas changed places, but the unknown man in the bow remained where he was, still silent. Staktopoulos, in his shock and fear, didn't notice that the rowboat had turned toward shore until they actually landed again on the small cape below the Actaion Café. Vasvanas then told him: "You, dog, jump out, and you mail those things we gave you to the Third Police Station. Not a word about this, because the same fate is waiting for you."

Staktopoulos, short of breath, sweating, jumped out of the rowboat and scrambled up the bluff along the cape's point. At the top he turned to see the rowboat, now fifty meters offshore, heading toward the Axios and Gallikos rivers. He had heard no splashing sound to suggest that Polk's body had been thrown overboard. He moved on quickly now, more or less running, until he reached the streetcar terminal known as the "Depot" and eventually caught a bus that took him into town and to the offices of *Makedonia*, where he stayed until 5:00 A.M., working nervously, then went home, stopping on the way to pick up two blank envelopes from a kiosk.

Staktopoulos tells his official interrogators that he couldn't sleep when he got home, so around 10:30 A.M. he decided to go back to town, stopped to read some newspapers at the newspaper distribution agency, then sat for a while at the Astoria Café on the ground floor of Polk's hotel. Back home in the afternoon, while his mother was sitting out on the veranda of their house, he gave her one of the blank envelopes he'd been carrying and asked her, without explanation, to write out the address: "To the Third Police Station, City." But his mother asked: "Why do you want me to do that?" Staktopoulos said that "the American lady wanted it," meaning Helen Mamas, who had called his home several times. His mother then immediately addressed the envelope as he had indicated, using the pen and ink from his study. Staktopoulos himself inserted the number "3d" before the words "the Third," using the same pen and ink, and the next day he mailed the envelope, with Polk's identity card and the Pan Am calendar in it but with no postage stamp, from the mailbox outside the White Tower Branch Post Office. His first deposition, interrupted at this point because of the late hour, ends with his saying that he "cannot clearly explain exactly why he added the number '3d' on the envelope."

The second phase of Staktopoulos's official deposition, dated the following day, is called "Supplementary Witness's Interrogation," and it was again offered at the Security Police headquarters, but on this occasion Attorney General Constantinidis substituted for Moustakis as one of the two local authorities hearing the deposition, which may explain why this section of the "Witness's Interrogation"[2] actually includes some questions posed by the interrogators. This is, in any case, only the second recorded visit by Constantinidis to Security Police headquarters during the six weeks of Staktopoulos's formal and not-so-formal interrogation in that setting, the Attorney General's first visit having been a long one during the night of September 30—10:00 P.M. to 4:00 A.M., a Gibson cable tells us[3]—that is, just before Staktopoulos's first official deposition dated October 1 (the Gibson cable also tells us that Constantinidis advised Staktopoulos on this occasion "to be honest in his statements and to give a complete account of the crime").

The supplementary deposition of October 2 is concerned in large measure with a narration by Staktopoulos of his various encounters with Helen Mamas during the days following the murder and also with his commentary on her presumed involvement in the arrangements for Polk's trip to interview Markos. Neither the narration nor the commentary is fully coherent. Staktopoulos reports that he ran into Mamas at the Mediterranean Hotel the day after the murder. She didn't greet him, but he, after saying hello, asked her, out of what he says was curiosity and journalistic "duty," to tell him "with what persons Polk had come in contact in Salonika." Mamas answered ironically in English with the words "wise guy" and tried to avoid him, but Staktopoulos pursued her to the entrance with the same insistent question until she hurried off without answering and without asking him about the outcome of his mission as interpreter, though Staktopoulos says he is sure that she knew Polk had left on his trip to Markos the previous Saturday.

Staktopoulos here states that he has no doubt whatsoever that Helen Mamas was the person who acted as intermediary with those in Salonika whom Polk contacted regarding the Markos trip. Hadn't Polk met with her at noon on the Saturday before his departure according to Polk himself? She must have known at that meeting that he would be leaving the same night, as Staktopoulos himself had learned from Polk a bit earlier on Saturday. And since some days of advance planning were called for in making the necessary arrangements for the trip, that must have been Mamas's doing even before Polk reached Salonika, and this served to explain why she had been the person he had rushed to meet on arriving in the city. Besides, it was Mamas, in Staktopoulos's opinion, who at an earlier point had made the arrangements for Thrapp to go meet the guerrillas. And later in the week that Polk was murdered, on Friday night, after an UNSCOB meeting at the Mediterranean Hotel that the local press had covered, Staktopoulos ran into Mamas and thought she seemed uneasy. When he approached her to say: "What's going on here? My house has blown up"—by which he meant the murder of Polk—she answered: "Everything will turn out all right" and hurried off before he could tell her anything else. He was certain that she had learned about the murder by then from Polk's contacts, though when he couldn't be sure. The next day, Saturday, the news became public, but when he went to find her at the Cosmopolite Hotel at Mouskoundis's request (Staktopoulos here testifies that he told Mouskoundis that Mamas would "know things" about the Polk case) and asked her if she had any information about Polk, she answered that he had gone to the guerrillas and that there was "a battalion behind him"—presumably of those accompanying him.

Staktopoulos's interrogators interrupted him at this point to ask him why, if he'd approached Mamas the previous day with the remark about his house blowing up and if both he and she knew about the murder, why had he then asked her, a day later, if she had any information about Polk? Staktopoulos's response: "Mamas can give you the answer to that question." And as if to elaborate on that response—though not quite logically—the text has him tell his interrogators that he had found Mamas "upset" when he visited her at the Cosmopolite Hotel because she had just been reprimanded by her Athens bureau chief, Tsakalis, for not having immediately dispatched the news of Polk's disappearance as other correspondents had done.

Staktopoulos's deposition now begins to ramble even more. He tells his interrogators that he never told Mamas about his meeting with the "rather fat" person at the Pontus Café, nor about his appointment with Polk at the Luxembourg Café, nor about anything that followed on that. During Thrapp's visit to Salonika, Staktopoulos saw Mamas and Thrapp going out together often though they were professional competitors. Staktopoulos's chief at *Makedonia* had told him that Thrapp had visited the guerrillas and had returned; Mamas must have helped Thrapp do so because she knew Greek, while Thrapp didn't, and she also had a number of acquaintances in Salonika who could have brought Thrapp into contact with the guerrillas: Georgakopoulos, Georgiadis, Tassos, Ioannidis, Kissos, and a lame man whose name he couldn't remember, all of whom either worked for the Communist paper *Laiki Foni* or had connections with the Left. In fact, Staktopoulos records, Tassos and Ioannidis had walked past the Mediterranean Hotel while he and Mamas were with Polk in the bar the afternoon of their first meeting. Staktopoulos had run into the two Communists a few days later and, when they asked if he had any news, had mentioned to them that an American correspondent had disappeared. They had "laughed characteristically" at this, but Staktopoulos had gone on his way without asking them why they had laughed. And at one point the lame man had stopped him in the street and had asked him if Mamas was back in town from a trip to the provinces.

Staktopoulos's interrogators now posed several questions that he appeared unable to answer satisfactorily. Why, when Mamas invited him to join the group of American journalists eating at the Olympus-Naoussa restaurant, had he not done so, or at least joined the group when they came outside, but instead had followed them at a distance and had approached Polk only when he was alone in Carolou Diehl Street? Staktopoulos's answer: "I can't explain how that came about." The text then has him say, quite irrelevantly, that he had asked Polk three times about the names of those who had given him letters of introduction regarding the Markos trip and had been refused three times. The interrogators: "Since you had made an appointment to meet Polk at the Mediterranean between 11:00 and 12:00 on Saturday morning, why didn't you do so at the hotel after your meeting with Ahmed instead of leaving the hotel and then finding Polk by chance when he turned into Komninon Street? Staktopoulos (rather implausibly): "Because I didn't place much importance on that appointment." The text has him add, again without clear relevance, that in his opinion Helen Mamas passed on the word that

Polk should go to the Luxembourg Café since she was the one who "had the contact." The interrogators: "Why didn't you yourself address the envelope in which you mailed Polk's identity card and Pan American calendar to the Third Police Station instead of having your mother address it, and why didn't you put a stamp on the envelope?" Staktopoulos: "I can't explain why I did that."

The text of the deposition now has Staktopoulos adding certain details to the official record in fairly random fashion. Polk was wearing a blue necktie when he came into the Luxembourg Café. Staktopoulos doesn't remember whether he was wearing a hat. And he didn't notice any sort of heavy weight tied to Polk's body after the murder, or a stone of any kind in the boat. And since the murder he hasn't seen either Vasvanas or Mouzenidis or the silent stranger who sat in the bow of the boat. Then a shift to the past: he didn't notice anybody other than Helen Mamas coming into contact with Thrapp during his stay in Salonika and Thrapp's contacts with Staktopoulos himself were entirely professional. Then comes a detailed account of Staktopoulos's trip to Athens during "Catholic Easter" for personal reasons relating to a certain lady friend there and also in order to ask for a raise as correspondent for the newspaper *Eleftheria*. We learn that during this trip Staktopoulos met neither Mamas nor Polk nor Hadjiargyris (though why he tells us this, the text doesn't indicate), Hadjiargyris having been pointed out to him for the first and last time from a distance the previous winter during an UNSCOB meeting at the Mediterranean Hotel. But he met a long list of other people in Athens, including Mamas's bureau chief Tsakalis, who, Staktopoulos states, must have known from Polk about the American's plans to visit Markos, and Polk must have gotten Tsakalis to solicit Mamas's help with these plans. Staktopoulos also feels that Tsakalis must know Hadjiargyris, and he thinks that perhaps they collaborated professionally. He can't say what the connection between Hadjiargyris and Mamas might be or what Hadjiargyris's connections in Salonika might have been. Nor does he know whether or not Polk was acquainted with a poor family in Salonika.

As this supplementary deposition draws to a close, there are two more questions that Staktopoulos is shown having trouble answering. He can't explain to his interrogators why he didn't ask the fat man of the Pontus Café meeting whether he knew Polk and why the man was interested in having Staktopoulos be the one to help Polk. All Staktopoulos can say in this connection is that he believed he might be of friendly assistance to a foreigner, and all the fat man had told him was that he wanted Staktopoulos's help because the Reuters stringer could speak English. Then the interrogators wanted to know why, when Staktopoulos recognized Mouzenidis as the boatman outside the Luxembourg Café—a man he knew to be a conspirator from his days at *Laiki Foni* and a man who made him feel afraid—why didn't Staktopoulos suggest to Polk in English that he get out of the boat, which had not yet left shore, and in that way surely avoid the crime that was committed later? Staktopoulos said he couldn't provide an explanation (though he might well have responded by saying that this suggestion called for more prophecy than an ordinary man should be expected to exercise, including foreknowledge that Mouzenidis was carrying a gun he was ready to use). The deposition ends with a final question insufficiently answered. Why, the interrogators want to know, when Mamas asked Staktopoulos to serve as Polk's interpreter, didn't Staktopoulos tell her that the fat man of the Pontus Café had made the same request of him only a few hours earlier? Staktopoulos answers that it didn't occur to him at that time or, for that matter, later. And he adds, as though an exonerating afterthought, that he didn't tell his mother or his sisters about his role as interpreter or anything having to do with the murder of Polk.

Some—though far from all—the dubieties that are raised by Staktopoulos's depositions of October 1 and 2 can be dispelled if one chooses to treat them as fictional texts, in keeping with Staktopoulos's own view in his 1984 book. This approach seems at least the most rational starting point. In the case of the October 1 "interrogation," a fictional reading is aided by the fact that the original Greek text of the official transcript consists of a single "Answer" to unstated questions, the text in purist Greek—an artificial "literary" officialese that is now largely discredited—except for the occasional dialogue, which is offered in demotic, a mixed linguistic strategy that crudely imitates the great nineteenth-century short story writer, Papadiamantis. The typed transcript—no paragraphs, the punctuation casual—seems in turn a grotesque imitation of another nineteenth-century source, the wonderfully candid and down-to-earth *Memoirs* of the autodidact General Makriyannis. Yet it isn't merely the artificial (if in a sense also nineteenth-century-classic) style of the original Greek that suggests a "literary" text of some level. Even in translation one can't fail to see some of the clichés and oversimplifications of bad detective fiction that keep popping up in the deposition. The conspirators, Communists one and all, always seem to wear gray or dark clothes and inevitably a cap that sometimes helps to conceal their identity. Their names, except when they prove to be the actual murderers, are often unknown or only partially known, and they are identified with particularity as dark-haired, fat, thin, or lame. The accused murderers turn out to be high-level Communists, one a labor leader and—as we learn later—professor of literature, the other an instructor in the School for Party Leaders, but they are made to look and speak like low-level thugs. And the text creates an aura of melodrama around the meetings in cafés, bars, restaurants, or the streets outside them, and most of all around the murder itself.

The supplementary deposition of October 2, though in much the same style, highlights the bad aspects of the fictional view by adding inconsistency to the awkward plotting and an even more rambling presentation of seemingly unnecessary detail. There are a number of apparently irrelevant inserts, and at the end the narrative is broken rather arbitrarily by the intrusion of questions that the witness sometimes answers vaguely and sometimes cannot answer at all. The supplementary deposition suggests even more persuasively that the speaker was working from a memorized text only incompletely remembered or partially developed and in any case not developed merely by the witness himself. This does not preclude an uncomplicated reading of the text at times, nor does it preclude our seeing a factual basis for some of the witness's narrative (for example, we know from several sources other than Staktopoulos that he did in fact meet Polk and Mamas on at least one occasion at the Mediterranean Hotel), but some of the narrative seems too implausible for either life or fiction, and much of it seems planted for purposes other than a description of the way things actually were.

Along with the unanswered questions raised by the interrogators themselves, the texts of October 1 and 2 leave several large open questions in the reader's mind. For one, would a correspondent of Polk's intelligence and wariness, however great his ambition, really allow himself to be blindfolded and bound hand and foot without at all questioning the need for it? Why even the presumed murderers felt the need to bind a cooperating victim in advance of shooting him is a second aspect of the same question—though they might well have done the binding after the fact for purposes of show. And would Staktopoulos, also a man of some intelligence and certainly with an abiding concern for his family, really ask his mother to address a possibly incriminating envelope rather than address it himself?

Whether or not one believes that Staktopoulos was somehow involved in the murder of Polk, a number of the problems raised by Staktopoulos's first confession and its supplement can best be explained rationally if one sees the hand of Major Mouskoundis both prompting and editing the text as we now have it, a hand that is itself guided by the influence of those assumptions and prejudices that we have seen in progress since

Polk's body was discovered in Salonika Bay. It is also a hand that has to work with what little hard evidence was gathered during the investigation up to that point. The first influence consists almost entirely of theory: a belief that the murder was committed by Communists on the orders of the Party, a plot that was most likely organized in Athens well in advance and carried out, again with advance planning, by agents in Salonika who knew when Polk was expected to arrive there and who were charged by him to arrange a trip ostensibly to the guerrilla-held mountains of the Pieria-Olympus region but in fact to his death aboard a caique in Salonika Bay (now changed to a rowboat) after a meal of lobster and peas at the Luxembourg Café. The second influence, the hard evidence, consists of an identified body with a bullet hole in the head and the undigested remnants of a last meal in the stomach, two sections of rope that were found loosely binding the victim's hands and feet, a letter to Edward R. Murrow and other personal effects left behind in, or missing from, the victim's hotel room, an envelope addressed to the Third Police Station containing the victim's identity card and a Pan Am advertisement, the fact that some correspondence proved to be missing from a file in the victim's Athens study, and, finally, the testimony of presumably reliable witnesses as to Polk's movements in Salonika during the two days before he was murdered. What might be called the hardest evidence, because actually tangible, were the body, the rope, the letter, and the mailed envelope.

If one reviews Staktopoulos's first "confession" with the soft, hard, and hardest evidence in mind, one can see that an effort has been made to create a narrative that will accommodate this evidence in a way that will presumably be difficult for anyone to challenge. An unnamed and only vaguely described contact, with previous connections to a Communist newspaper and therefore doubtless a Communist himself, approaches Staktopoulos some days before Polk's arrival with the news that the American correspondent will be arriving in Salonika shortly, along with several other American correspondents, and will head for guerrilla territory in the mountains. This establishes the notion of a prearranged trip organized at least to some degree by the Party. The only questionable detail so far is that of the "several" other American correspondents accompanying Polk, which turns out in fact to be only one, Donald Matchen, who testified that he traveled north on the same plane with Polk by pure accident. The fat man of the Pontus Café also plants the idea that Polk will "go aboard a rowboat" for his trip to the guerrillas, an unlikely mode of transportation for the distance involved when larger caiques, plentiful in the area, are the usual mode. The problem that the text seems to be anticipating here is the failure of Mouskoundis and the Security Police to turn up a relevant caique after so thoroughly searching for one that even Colonel Martin, their critical British adviser, found it in his heart during his review of the investigation to pinpoint their "effective" work in this failed pursuit.

But before we come to that, the first deposition, having done its best to accommodate the theory of a Communist plot against Polk prepared in advance, still had to deal with what it could of the hard evidence. The body first of all. The action in the rowboat presumably illustrates how Polk could have been shot in the back of the head, Communist fashion, without a struggle and relatively relaxed, as the autopsy report suggested (the deposition actually has Polk declaring himself to be "very happy" just a few minutes before he is shot). And the scene in the sparsely populated Luxembourg Café—the Security Police's favorite theoretical setting for the last meal that Kellis, among others, brought into question but that is here restored to favor—presumably suffices for the hard evidence of only partially digested lobster, peas, brown bread, and wine that the autopsy report identified, as well as for the softer evidence of Polk's modest overnight luggage (consisting, one is meant to assume, of the pajamas that were said to be missing from Polk's Salonika luggage, here reappearing in a brown wrapper) and the CBS correspondent's supposedly relentless ambition to get the story of his career, only hinted at in the Murrow letter he left behind. A phrase from the same letter seems the likely source of the idea that Polk was blindfolded at one point and presumably said at the time that he didn't mind getting where he had to go "blind even," because there is no other evidence or clear rationale for these details in the narrative and also because Polk's phrase from the letter indicating that he is ready to reach the guerrillas "even if blindfolded" is picked out for quotation at a later stage in the official communiqué reporting the "final" solution.

The rowboat scene of the deposition also serves to accommodate the rather mysterious rope bindings that were found on the victim's body, however implausible the accommodation. The text might better have suggested that the rope was tied where it was found after the murder was committed, when Polk's presumably naive, even brainless, acceding to this phase of his own undoing could not become an issue. As it is, what we end up with here seems to be a case either of truth being stranger than even bad fiction or of fiction being manipulated awkwardly by those whose expertise resides elsewhere. And the unstamped envelope with its unwritten message, the last of the hardest evidence, is also brought into the rowboat scene, perhaps not quite as implausibly at this point (given a boat full of Communists that is supposedly about to head out to sea and not likely soon, if ever, to return to that particular shore, obviously the one person now allowed to set foot on land has to take care of getting the identity card and the Pan Am calendar to the police for whatever unexplained reasons), but surely more implausibly by the time the text has Staktopoulos asking his mother on their veranda to address the envelope with his own pen and ink.

The supplementary deposition of October 2 seems, at least in retrospect, a rather blatant effort by the interrogating authorities to create a Salonika connection in the image of Helen Mamas. Much of the deposition focuses on Staktopoulos's attempts either to find out from her the names of Polk's Salonika contacts after he failed three times to get them from Polk himself, or to offer his opinion that Mamas undoubtedly had inside information either from Polk (the evidence here merely Staktopoulos's own statement that Polk told him he was planning to meet Mamas at midday on Saturday) or from others. Staktopoulos's deposition emerges as the single source for the presumption regarding Helen Mamas's role in Salonika. And this too becomes the source for the idea that Mamas, through her Athens boss Tsakalis, is the likely link to an Athens connection, even if Staktopoulos tells us—here perhaps made to drop familiar names in order to keep a tired suspicion alive—that he met neither Polk nor Mamas nor Hadjiargyris in Athens and doesn't know if there is any connection between the latter two or between Tsakalis and Hadjiargyris (who outside of Security Police headquarters, one is tempted to ask, ever suggested there was?). And another red herring: Thrapp not only went to the guerrillas (Staktopoulos's boss at *Makedonia*, Ioannidis, is the single source given for this evident misinformation), but was helped on his way by Helen Mamas, who had many acquaintances in Salonika, some named, some nameless, some openly Communist, some merely suspect. Finally, several minor items that had come up during the course of the investigation are vaguely accounted for. The necktie that Rea Polk reported to be missing at one point now appears as a blue tie that Polk wears into the Luxembourg Café but that evidently disappears at sea. And, since no weight was found tied to the body, Staktopoulos here reports that he saw no weight in the boat nor a stone of the kind that might have "skinned" Polk, as his widow thought Communist captors were given to doing.

One of the mysteries of the supplementary deposition cannot be explained away as a possible construction of the Security Police imposed on Staktopoulos's memory: the several questions by the interrogators that Staktopoulos finds he cannot answer at all. If one takes the view that Staktopoulos's testimony is in large part an evocation of a dictated and memorized fiction, the only explanation for his failure to answer certain questions is that his ghost-writers failed to anticipate the questions and to give him proper answers in advance so that he wouldn't be stumped by his official interrogators. But since the final text was subject to revision by the authorities and did not include all the questions presumably posed by the interrogators, why allow these lapses in Staktopoulos's interrogation to appear as part of the published text? The only apparent answer is that there are authorities and authorities. The first deposition of October 1, which offers not a single question by the interrogators, was given in front of Moustakis and Komotouros, who, according to Staktopoulos's 1984 book, came to look him over some time before his deposition was recorded, perhaps even some days before (Staktopoulos's sense of time passing was understandably faulty after six weeks of isolation in Security Police headquarters). This suggests the possibility of at least some degree of collusion between these two judicial authorities and Mouskoundis's office. In the supplementary deposition, Attorney General Constantinidis appears among the two interrogators, and though he too saw Staktopoulos at some length during the night before the Reuters stringer's first deposition, he was maybe less fully briefed by Mouskoundis, maybe more eager to test Staktopoulos to see if his testimony would stand up in court—especially since Constantinidis was to act as public prosecutor—maybe even honestly interested in finding plausible answers to evident contradictions or inconsistencies in the testimony. Whatever the final mix of these possible motives, the attorney general may have been unwilling in the end to allow the embarrassing answers and nonanswers to be expurgated from the published text.

But if Constantinidis's presence on the scene may explain the intrusion into the narrative of awkward questioning by the interrogators, the State Department archives will not permit us to exonerate him entirely of at least the suspicion of collusion in some form, particularly regarding those aspects of the text having to do with Helen Mamas, since it was Constantinidis who had suggested to Raleigh Gibson two months earlier that he had in mind arresting Staktopoulos and then advising Helen Mamas of the arrest "in the belief that the two would make counter statements against each other" (see p. 126 above). The supplementary deposition seems intended in some measure to prepare the ground for a confrontation between these two witnesses, one that will presumably serve to put Helen Mamas on the spot by way of Staktopoulos's testimony about incriminating meetings between the two of them after the murder was committed (supplementing those already described in the first deposition). And there is further ground for embarrassing Mamas in Staktopoulos's "conviction" regarding meetings Mamas presumably had with both Polk and Thrapp while acting as their principal Salonika agent for contacting the guerrillas. Staktopoulos also seems to go out of his way to emphasize again that Polk refused to tell him "from and to what persons he had letters of introduction" but did tell him specifically that "Mamas knows them." Since the Security Police had failed to turn up any such persons after more than four months of investigation, it was now evidently up to Helen Mamas to supply the relevant names, fictional or otherwise.

The confrontation between Staktopoulos and Helen Mamas took place on October 3, the day after Staktopoulos's supplementary deposition, Mamas having arrived from Athens for the purpose. An American citizen born of Greek parents, she apparently felt that her Greek was inadequate, because she asked that an interpreter be present. Twenty-four years old and considered a clever, self-assured reporter, at moments feisty, she has been described by one of those on the scene as having had blond hair, sharp Garbo-like features (though with a more prominent nose), and wearing dark glasses for a touch of glamour and mystery, even if engaged at the time to a Greek gentleman named Zotos whom she eventually married for a while.[4] Rea Polk thought her strongly anti-Communist and, from Rea's point of view, generally trustworthy.[5]

Whether or not Attorney General Constantinidis was in on the preparation for the presumably crucial confrontation between Mamas and Staktopoulos, he chose not to attend either the first, second, or third sessions of Helen Mamas's testimony, replaced now by the original interrogator, Attorney General for the Court of the First Instance Christos Moustakis.[6] The testimony that emerged from these three sessions was, in any case, thoroughly unproductive of what Constantinidis must have hoped it would be, though highly illuminating in other ways. Mamas begins her deposition by telling her interrogators—without any recorded evidence of prompting—about an encounter she had with Kosta Hadjiargyris outside the Grande Bretagne Hotel in Athens following her last deposition in Salonika six weeks earlier, on August 15–16, and during a time when the Polk case was in the news because of Staktopoulos's detention. Hadjiargyris approached her and said: "May I ask you a possibly indiscreet question that you may or may not want to answer?" Mamas told him to go ahead and ask. Hadjiargyris: "Is it true that the journalist Staktopoulos has been detained as a result of your testimony during your recent interrogation by the Inquiry Magistrate in Salonika?"

Mamas replied: "Certainly not," and added that her information had it that Staktopoulos had been detained the day before her interrogation began (in fact true). Hadjiargyris then asked: "What do you think of Staktopoulos? What kind of man is he?" Mamas replied that she was not in a position to know about either his political inclinations or his character. Hadjiargyris: "Do you think Staktopoulos was capable of getting his mother to address the envelope enclosing Polk's identity card and then mail it to the police?" Mamas tells her interrogators that she had no answer to this and was surprised by the question because she didn't know at the time that handwriting experts had testified that the address on the envelope was written by Staktopoulos's mother. She didn't ask Hadjiargyris how he knew (though she might have surmised that his connections in high places were a likely source), nor could she "assure" her interrogators as to whether Hadjiargyris had approached her by chance or design.

After this curious prologue, the session quickly got down to its main business: Mamas's effort to repudiate almost every specific detail that either the interrogators or Staktopoulos himself proposed for the purpose of incriminating her, Mamas calling most of what came up lies, fabrications, or fantasies. The exchange, somewhat truncated, was recorded as follows:

Q: Is it true, in keeping with the deposition of Gregory Staktopoulos, that on Friday afternoon of May seventh, while you were in the bar of the local Mediterranean Hotel along with other foreign journalists among whom was George Polk, you sent a message to the above-mentioned Staktopoulos by way of the journalist Stavridis, asking Staktopoulos to come and see you in the bar?

A: No! That's a lie. I didn't send any message to Staktopoulos by way of Stavridis or anybody else at all to the effect that he should come and see me since there was no reason whatsoever for me to do so.

(Staktopoulos is here brought in, identified, and sworn in on the Holy Bible, in keeping with Articles 121, etc.)

Q to G. S.: Do you repeat that on Friday afternoon of May seventh you met Helen Mamas in the bar of the Mediterranean Hotel following an invitation from her conveyed by the journalist Stavridis?

A: Yes, I met her at her invitation, conveyed by Stavridis.

Q to H. M.: What do you say in reply to the foregoing?

A: I do not remember if, at the time indicated above, I asked Mr. Stavridis to request that Staktopoulos come and see me.

Q to G. S.: Do you reiterate that when you were with Helen Mamas, Polk, and three other foreign journalists [in the Mediterranean Hotel bar], the waiter approached Mamas and told her that somebody was asking for one of the foreigners on the telephone, and Mamas, at the suggestion of the journalist previously identified by you as Polk, went to the telephone and came back after three or four minutes, sat down in her chair, and when Polk asked her about the phone call, she replied, while adjusting her stocking, "Yes" in English?

A: Yes, the foregoing is true.

Q to H. M.: What is your response to this?

A: I am certain that at the time and place indicated, I did not move from my chair nor did I go to the phone.

Q to H. M.: Witness Gregory Staktopoulos has testified that at the encounter described earlier you told him that Polk wanted to take a trip to meet Markos, that Polk had letters of introduction from Athens, and that the two of you should help him realize his plans. And when Staktopoulos asked how he might help Polk, you told him: "By acting as interpreter at the right moment." Is the foregoing true?

A: The foregoing is a lie, and I am absolutely sure of it.

Q to G. S.: What is your response to Helen Mamas's denial?

A: I reaffirm categorically that all of the above exchange between Helen Mamas and me took place, our voices low, so that I can't be certain those around us heard, they being anyway engaged in a discussion of their own at the time.

Q to H. M.: Staktopoulos testified that when he took leave of Polk between 11:30 and 12:00 on Saturday noon of May eighth, Polk told him that he was going to his hotel and after that would meet you. Did this meeting materialize?

A: The foregoing is entirely untrue, since the last time I met Polk was the evening of the day before, that is, Friday, and I didn't see him again after that.

Q to G. S.: What is your response to the above?

A: I repeat most emphatically that Polk told me all the above.

(Photographs of Anastasios "Tassos" Voyadjis and Ioannis Ioannidis were now produced and identified by Staktopoulos as the "very same persons" who had strolled by the window outside the Mediterranean Hotel bar while the journalists were gathered there on Friday afternoon and who were greeted by Mamas with a nod.)

Q to H. M.: You have heard Staktopoulos's testimony. Do you know the men pictured in these photographs?

A: I've never in my life met either of those people in the photographs.

Q to H. M.: According to Staktopoulos's deposition, he met you on Monday, May tenth, in the Mediterranean Hotel bar and asked you to name the persons with whom Polk had come into contact in Salonika. Is this true or not?

A: That is a total lie. I did not meet Staktopoulos at the time indicated, nor did he at any point ask me any such thing. And he didn't ask me who the people were who gave Polk letters of introduction to assist him in reaching Markos.

Q to G. S.: What do you say to the foregoing?

A: Mamas is lying shamelessly in denying the above.

Q to H. M.: Staktopoulos testifies that you knew Polk was planning to set out to meet Markos on Saturday evening, May eighth, and that he has no doubt you were the person who acted as the intermediary for Polk's contacts with various people he met in Salonika in connection with his trip to Markos. Is all this true?

A: All that is untrue. I would have been mad to do a thing like that. Actually, my news agency directed me as far back as last December, through the Director Tsakalis, to try and see Markos, and since I didn't do it for my own agency, I would hardly help the representative of a competing agency do it.

(Mamas here explains that she didn't carry out Tsakalis's directive because a Greek general to whom she applied for help told her that Markos's government wasn't set up on Greek soil—more likely on Albanian soil—otherwise he would have taken her to Markos by plane. She reported this to Tsakalis and he told her that he himself should have carried out the directive rather than Mamas, a woman.)

A (cont.): Staktopoulos asked me in your presence to put my hand on my heart and with compassion for his mother and sisters to tell the truth. The truth is that I also didn't serve as intermediary for Thrapp's aborted trip to Markos. Liberopoulos, Counsellor of the Press Bureau, can tell you that I was not in the know about Thrapp's plans, who, it should be noted, is also a correspondent for a competing agency.

Q to H. M.: Staktopoulos testifies that on Friday, May fourteenth, after an UNSCOB meeting at the Mediterranean Hotel, he said to you: "What is going on here? My house has blown up"—implying by this the murder of Polk and its aftermath—and you replied: "Everything will turn out all right" as you left. Is this true?

A: No, it is not true. I may have told Staktopoulos "everything will turn out all right" but not at that point, maybe a few days before that, when there were still grounds for optimism about Polk's fate. By Friday, Polk's wife had arrived and we were all worried about his fate.

Q to G. S.: What do you say to the above?

A: I reiterate that the exchange I indicated occurred between Mamas and me.

(Here Mamas is questioned about her meeting with Staktopoulos, at Mouskoundis's instigation, at the Cosmopolite Hotel. Mamas denies that she told Staktopoulos that Polk had "gone to the guerrillas" and that "a battalion was following behind him," though she acknowledges having told him that she'd been reprimanded by Tsakalis for not reporting Polk's disappearance, a thing she did not do because she wasn't sure that it was a case of disappearance and didn't want to put herself out on a limb, though she did write her fiancé, Zotos, to transmit the news to Tsakalis, only to learn that Zotos was out of town at the time. Staktopoulos again reaffirms his version of the meeting and adds that he now remembers having asked Mamas whether she herself or Polk had met local high-ranking Communists. She replied, laughing, with the word "Yes"—in English—and at the same moment went into the phone booth to talk to Tsakalis, thus preventing Staktopoulos from asking who these high-ranking Communists were with whom they'd come into contact.)

Q to H. M.: Is this testimony about high-ranking Communists true?

A: It is not true. Nor is it true that I went out regularly with Thrapp. I met him four or five times in all. I don't know whether Thrapp got together often with Greeks here or who they might have been.

(Mamas here mentioned the names of several Greek officers she knew in Salonika, said that she had not become acquainted with "private persons" in the city, and denied knowing any of the people Staktopoulos had listed as her acquaintances, including "Michael Voutyras, the lame," whose picture she was shown.)

The examination of Helen Mamas and Staktopoulos "in confrontation" (as the English translation of the official Greek transcript has it) concludes with a curious exchange. The interrogators ask Helen Mamas if she remembers precisely how Staktopoulos put the question he asked over the phone when he called her the evening she was dining at the Olympus-Naoussa with Polk and the other visiting "journalists."

A: I remember that he asked me as follows: "What are the names of the journalists who just arrived? One of them is Polk; I don't remember who the others are."

Q to G. S.: When you phoned Mamas, did you ask her the question she testifies to?

A: I did not mention the name of Polk to Mamas but asked her for the names of all the journalists.

Why, at this twelfth hour, does Staktopoulos choose to say that he didn'ᵗ mention Polk's name, as though that too was to be presumed among those he didn't remember, even though he has already testified that he knew the name Polk from the "fat man" in the Pontus Café, had met Polk by this time at the Mediterranean Hotel bar, had been asked by Mamas to serve as Polk's interpreter, and, shortly after his phone call to the Olympus-Naoussa, would follow Polk up a dimly lit street to speak to him privately? The only plausible answer is that this final question of the day was not part of Staktopoulos's memorized text and he therefore simply answered it by telling the truth as he remembered it: when he phoned Mamas, he didn't recall Polk's name. Why then does Mamas testify as she does in this instance? Is her memory faulty here? Or was she influenced by Staktopoulos's text to believe that he knew Polk all too well by this time? Or is she finally trying to do her bit for the interrogators after some prompting in order to show her good intentions? The text here doesn't give us more than what we've seen to work with, but it turns out that Helen Mamas sticks to her version of the telephone dialogue when it is brought up again at the trial some months later.

During the second day of Helen Mamas's October interrogation, she is not made to confront Staktopoulos but those "persons" Staktopoulos has brought into his scenario to implicate her. She is contradicted during the first of the day's confrontations but encounters no challenge in all the others. The first is with Eleftherios Stavridis, Salonika journalist, who testifies that while attending a meeting of UNSCOB at the Mediterranean Hotel on Friday afternoon, May 7, along with other journalists including Gregory Staktopoulos and Helen Mamas, he "remembers well" having asked Staktopoulos, as they sat in the section reserved for the press, who the journalist sitting on the right side of them was and learning from Staktopoulos that it was "Polk of Columbia." He and Staktopoulos stayed at the meeting after the other journalists left, and finally Stavridis himself headed down to the lobby. Going down the stairs he saw Helen Mamas just outside the door of the hotel bar, and she asked him: "Is Gregory still up there?" meaning Staktopoulos. And when he replied affirmatively, she added: "Tell him, please, to come on down. Polk wants him." Stavridis raised his head to see Staktopoulos approaching the top of the stairs and told him that he was wanted downstairs, though he didn't linger to say who actually wanted to see Staktopoulos.

Confronted with this testimony, Helen Mamas responded by saying that she didn't remember if there was a meeting of UNSCOB at the time indicated and in any case she had never seen Polk sitting in on an UNSCOB session. Nor had she ever asked, by way of a third person, for Staktopoulos to meet Polk. Besides, she never called Staktopoulos "Gregory" but invariably used his last name because she didn't know his Christian name. Her interrogators then asked her how she could explain Stavridis having clearly remembered her telling him that Staktopoulos was wanted by Polk. Mamas: "I repeat that the above testimony by Mr. Stavridis is untrue. I don't know why, or by what line of reasoning, Mr.

Stavridis testifies as he does. Maybe he's a friend of his colleague Stakto-poulos and wants to support him." That served to end this particular confrontation—and along with it, even the remotest suggestion of possible support for Staktopoulos from any quarter.

Three more witnesses were now brought before Helen Mamas in sequence: Ioannis Ioannidis, Anastasios "Tassos" Voyadjis, and Michael Voutyras (previously referred to as "the lame"). All three stated that they knew Staktopoulos, and all three stated that they were facing Helen Mamas for the first time in their lives. The two former, though often given to strolling by the Mediterranean Hotel after work, did not remember seeing Staktopoulos on the afternoon of May 7, and both denied having heard the news of Polk's disappearance from the Reuters stringer: that, they said, had come from reading the papers. Voutyras also denied having asked Staktopoulos about Mamas near the Ellinis open-air cinema as Staktopoulos had previously testified: besides not knowing Mamas, he never walked along the quay-side where the cinema is located because of his lameness, least of all in the evenings (presumably because the quay is then crowded with evening strollers). End of second round.

The third session of Helen Mamas's interrogation was brief. The witness reiterated that she did not know with whom Polk had lunch on Saturday, May 8, and Polk did not disclose to her on any occasion the aim of his trip to Salonika, nor those who may have introduced him to his contacts in Salonika, nor the contacts themselves. And she didn't hear about the above from any other sources or about Polk's movements and efforts to realize his aim. Had she known anything about his contacts or his aims, she would have testified about them from the start. She concluded: "Consequently, everything that Staktopoulos has to say about me in this connection is untrue and imaginary." And she left with her interrogators a three-page letter in English addressed to Gregory Staktopoulos that she thought the interrogators might want to read to him. Hadjiargyris quotes a portion of the letter (evidently preserved in some official record) in his book, here translated back into English from his Greek version: "Mr. Staktopoulos, if you are not an abnormal person, this lying on your part against me was maliciously premeditated and constructed in a satanic fashion to injure me. For what reason I do not know. Listen to my simple advice. You yourself tell the truth, bear your own burden, free your heart of distress, and maybe you will save not only your mother but yourself as well."

Helen Mamas returned to Athens that day, and Gregory Staktopoulos, with or without the benefit of her advice, returned to his cell at the Security Police headquarters, where he was apparently strongly encouraged to rework his story. At this point Raleigh Gibson cabled the secretary of state to say that while local officials still had reservations regarding Mamas's denial of all of Staktopoulos's charges, "they are convinced she had no connection with murder" and therefore were letting her go.[7] The attorney general was ready to request that the ministers of justice and public order come to Salonika in order to issue a statement "from her [sic]" that the Polk case "has been solved," perhaps on October 10 or earlier. But it seems that by October 10 local officials still didn't have the whole story. Gibson had to send a second cable indicating that any statement about the case being solved would have to wait a bit because Staktopoulos "is giving more information which it is believed will result in securing details of Communist Party of Northern Greece," of which Staktopoulos is now considered to be "one of the key men."[8]

By October 14, officials in Salonika had a new deposition from Staktopoulos to work with.[9] The depositions of October 1 and 2 had obviously created certain problems that had to be dealt with, and so had the strong challenge to Staktopoulos's testimony by Helen Mamas. The first problem was that of establishing a credible Athens connection that would allow for a well-planned Communist plot to get Polk to Salonika for his trip to Markos and then have him done in at sea on his way there. Neither Mamas nor Hadjiargyris nor even Tsakalis had yet turned out to serve plausibly for an Athenian connection, and it seems that Mamas had also convinced the authorities that she was neither the Salonika contact they had been looking for nor a substantial link between Salonika and Athens. The investigating authorities were thus left with only a single possible candidate for the role of intermediary between the two cities: Staktopoulos himself—especially useful in this new role because his old role of the October 1 and 2 depositions by itself must still have seemed a bit thin for a major participant. After all, according to the text of Staktopoulos's testimony, he tried but consistently failed to find out who Polk's Communist patrons were, and though he was originally meant to serve as interpreter for a single moment only, as Polk approached the rowboat named "Aghios Nicolaos," he was cheated of even that duty when Polk jumped into the rowboat ahead of him without a word and called up to him to follow. Though Staktopoulos did end up translating Mouzenidis's request that the victim be blindfolded and bound, this was gratuitous service, since Staktopoulos presumably was not meant to be in the rowboat at all at that point, and, as has been suggested, the binding of a cooperative victim before rather than after the crime in any case remained—or should have remained—problematical.

The October 14 deposition—again a narrative uninterrupted by questions—has Staktopoulos much more at the center of things, along with Vangelis Vasvanas, the Communist colonel and Party instructor. The tale Staktopoulos now tells his interrogators has him receiving a phone call from one "Vangelis" as early as March 23, and when he meets this Vangelis the following day, to his surprise it turns out to be Vasvanas, who Staktopoulos thought had long since "left for the mountains." The colonel, a former acquaintance, proves to be as rude here as he was depicted to be earlier, when his role was more directly threatening. As they meet, Staktopoulos asks when was it that Vasvanas returned to the city from the "mountains," and Vasvanas replies that this is none of Staktopoulos's business, what should interest him is what Vasvanas is about to tell him, namely that "in keeping with an order from the Party, you have to leave this week for Athens, where you will deliver a letter and become acquainted with an American who is to come to Salonika for a trip to Markos." Staktopoulos tells Vasvanas that he can't leave before the coming Saturday, Vasvanas agrees to that, gives him 400,000 drachmas for the journey, meets him again on Friday evening to hand him a thick white unaddressed envelope. His contact in Athens is to be one Yannis, a thirty-year-old with blond, curly hair, who will be leaning against a telephone booth near Constitution Square reading the newspaper *To Vima*. Staktopoulos is to say: "Hello, Athens," and Yannis will reply: "Hello, Salonika." Yannis is then to introduce him to the American journalist, and Staktopoulos is to tell the journalist that he is authorized to inform him "that the whole mechanism of the Communist Party is at his disposal" for his mission, which, Vasvanas explains, will result in "a news sensation in favor of the Government of Free Greece and against the Monarcho-fascist Government in Athens" and will also result in a report on "the achievements of the Democratic Army" (here the new deposition appears to be drawing on what the authorities learned from Markos's comments to Homer Bigart during his interview with the guerrilla leader in June).

The Athens connection is made. Staktopoulos meets Yannis with all the right signals, and then, at noon, after the two have spent an hour discussing "the 'Democratic struggle' " over cakes at Zavoritis Confectionery Shop, in walks a tall stranger. "That is Polk, the American," Yannis tells Staktopoulos. "Speak to him." Polk greets Yannis in English with the words "Hello, John" (the English for "Yannis") and sits down. He orders a cup of coffee "à la Viennois [sic]," and pastries are brought to the table. Staktopoulos now introduces himself to "Mister Polk" in English and informs him in English as he'd been instructed by Vasvanas.

Polk replies that he has been planning to go to Markos for some time and will send word when he is ready to carry out his plan. They eat their pastries and then Staktopoulos says goodbye and leaves the two others sitting there because, he tells his interrogators, he wanted to be prompt for a rendezvous with his previously mentioned lady friend in Athens.

Back in Salonika, Staktopoulos again met Vasvanas and reported on his trip. Vasvanas then said that he would use the code name "Mitsos" from that point on and that in any case Staktopoulos's contact in the future would be "Nikos," who used to show up at the offices of the Communist *Laiki Foni*. Staktopoulos doesn't actually meet "Nikos" until more than a month later, on May 5, when Nikos turns out to be the fat man of the Pontus Café, now described as not only fat but fairly tall, with thick black hair, a cap, "gray working clothes." Nikos gives Staktopoulos the same message that we heard in the previous deposition: Staktopoulos is to act as Polk's interpreter. The next day Nikos again meets Staktopoulos "behind the Paradise Baths" and reports that Polk is due in the following day, then adds: "Make sure to meet him without fail and tell him that all the preparations have been made."

Staktopoulos now tells his interrogators that he tracked Polk down on Friday at the Astoria Hotel after calling the American consulate, without revealing his name, to verify Polk's arrival and after failing to turn him up at three other hotels. He was told by the Astoria desk clerk to go up and wait for Polk in the sitting room on the third floor, which he did, and after a short time Polk came out of his room. Staktopoulos said hello in English and told Polk his name. Polk took his billfold out and looked at some notes he had there, then asked Staktopoulos what his first name was. "Gregory," Staktopoulos said, and Polk replied: "Oh, you're the one I met in Athens." They had a five-minute conversation during which Staktopoulos told Polk that his coming to Salonika must mean that he was planning to go ahead with his trip to Markos and that indeed the preparations had been made. Polk confirmed that he had come to Salonika for the purpose of making the trip and added (rather out of context) that he would see Staktopoulos later at the Mediterranean Hotel.

And so he did, in keeping with the previous deposition—except that Stavridis is now shown to be standing in a hallway on the ground floor when he calls up to tell Staktopoulos that Mamas wants to see him, and once in the bar, Staktopoulos pretends to be meeting Polk for the first time. And at this point in his new deposition Staktopoulos tells his interrogators that his earlier testimony about the meeting in the bar and Helen Mamas's role there is untrue. Mamas did not say that Polk wanted to see him. Nor did she tell Staktopoulos that Polk wanted to take a trip

to meet Markos. In fact, the whole dialogue about Polk's letters of introduction and Mamas's asking Staktopoulos to act as Polk's interpreter at
the right moment, was, along with the rest, "untrue and false." And
Staktopoulos states that he testified falsely as he had in his previous
deposition because he wanted in this way to force Mamas to testify
about everything she knew concerning the Polk affair. He says that he
has no basis for judging what Mamas knows about the case, but after
much reflection he has come out thinking that she must know something. And he still insists that Mamas "returned the greeting" of the
Communists "Tassos" and Ioannidis as they passed outside the bar window, despite their testimony that they knew Mamas not at all.

The rest of Staktopoulos's deposition seems designed to put Vasvanas
in an even more prominent light and to cover certain details that were
either excessively exposed or awkwardly ignored in the earlier depositions, for example, why Polk went on his trip with a single package and
no camera, why there were no witnesses at the Luxembourg Café pier,
why Staktopoulos asked his mother to address the presumably incriminating envelope, why he didn't provide the police right away with testimony as to what he knew. It turns out now that the Friday night meeting
between Staktopoulos and Polk did not end at the Astoria Café at midnight but included a 1:00 A.M. rendezvous with Vasvanas, previously
arranged by "Nikos" of the Pontus Café. When Vasvanas's name is mentioned to Polk, the American repeats the name several times as though
it is vaguely familiar to him (this perhaps meant to suggest a remembrance from some earlier connection to the Party's grand design). When
the two meet, Vasvanas tells Polk about the rowboat trip scheduled for
the following night, and when Polk asks the time and place, Vasvanas
answers: "We will talk about that tomorrow." Polk then asks what he
can take with him. "Your pajamas and whatever you absolutely need for
your work." A camera? asks Polk. Vasvanas: "They have cameras up
there, and they will be able to give you whatever else you need." And it
turns out to be Vasvanas who calls on Saturday afternoon to give Staktopoulos the information about the Luxembourg Café rendezvous that
Staktopoulos himself then passes on to Polk.

The Reuters stringer now testifies that in fact there were no other
boats at the pier outside the Luxembourg Café. Had there been, he would
have made a point of going out to see if there was one among them with
the name "Aghios Nicolaos." Besides, it was raining lightly, so no other
boats would have been there that evening. And he also remembers now
that when Mouzenidis fired the shot at Polk, the victim was not silent
but groaned, undoubtedly on the point of dying. And it turns out to be

Mouzenidis who not only instructs Staktopoulos to mail Polk's identity card to the Third Police Station but also "recommended that I have my mother write the address on the envelope," having previously asked if Staktopoulos's mother was still living and having been told that indeed she was.

Staktopoulos's narrative ends with an account of the terror that came into his life during the days after the crime was committed, first as he scampered up the bluff to get out of range of the rowboat full of his Communist comrades ("I was afraid they would fire at me and kill me, because that's the kind they are: when they commit one crime, they commit a second one to cover up the first"). Three or four days later, "a certain Byron" called him up at the *Makedonia* and told him that if he dared open his mouth, they would blow up his whole house into thin air, and the same threat was repeated a second and a third time, and again a few days after Polk's body was found. This, one is meant to assume, served to keep Staktopoulos's mouth sealed initially (though that is hardly consistent with what we have seen to be his aggressive efforts to get a story on Polk's disappearance during the week before the body was recovered).

The third deposition does not end with the witness's narrative but with a kind of postscript that records Staktopoulos's personal opinion regarding the murder. He tells his official interrogators that it was planned by the Cominform and was carried out by the Greek Communist Party with the intention of casting the blame for it on the Right so that Greece would in this way be defamed abroad and the implementation of both military aid and Marshall Plan aid would be suspended or canceled as the result of protests against Greece in the United States of the kind that in fact occurred (though with considerably less dramatic consequences).

Staktopoulos goes on to affirm that the Greek Communist Party cannot do anything, even breathe, without orders from the Cominform. In this case, he says, the Party had received word from various people about Polk's desire to interview Markos and, taking advantage of this desire, had led Polk to think that he could successfully effect his purpose through Staktopoulos and various people in Athens (the official English translation omits the reference to Athens that appears in the Greek text of the deposition), though Staktopoulos himself—he tells his interrogators—had not been informed of this purpose and had no knowledge of it. But, he now adds, his name was crossed off the Communist party list fictitiously after the war, for reasons of security, because the Party was about to enter a phase of illegal activity, and since his days on the staff of *Laiki Foni*, he has continued to be "just a simple member of the Communist Party," without holding any special office in it.

Three days after this third, amply revised, deposition was taken at Salonika Security Police headquarters, the official communiqué on the murder "solution" was released by the Ministries of Justice and Public Order in Athens.[10] The communiqué makes thorough use of Staktopoulos's latest narrative in presenting its image of the conspiracy, the murder, and its aftermath (the text we have is the English version offered by the American consulate). Notification is given that warrants for the arrest of Vasvanas and Mouzenidis have now been issued in addition to those already in force for Gregory Staktopoulos and his mother, Anna. We are told that the first police investigations were directed toward those Greeks and foreigners who had met Polk, and "the only result of the investigation was to learn of the acquaintance of Polk with the Greek journalist Gregorios Stahtopoulos [sic], who has a command of the English language." With this bit of news, all other suspects of the past five months—Rea Polk, Hadjiargyris, Coate, the Barbers, Don Matchen, and Helen Mamas—are evidently expunged from the record. The long search for evidence from people and places is catalogued, but what comes out of this that is essential remains, first of all, the envelope presumably addressed by Staktopoulos's mother—evidence of her complicity a result in the first instance of a thorough house search by the Security Police—and then, the letter to Murrow, with its revelation that Polk thought it would be "a great success to reach Markos [sic] headquarters," his desire to do this so compelling that, as he wrote in the letter, he was ready to reach it "even if blindfolded."

And the communiqué's narrative of the murder demonstrates that Polk was indeed blindfolded at one point, as though fulfilling prophesy, actually saying, "when Mouzenides [sic] was covering Polk's eyes, . . . 'Even blindfolded I would go where I must go.' " The narrative is concise, giving the basic details as we have seen them, here and there highlighting items that the third deposition has brought more clearly into prominence: Staktopoulos is identified as a Communist of long standing whose name was removed from the Party lists fictitiously when the Party turned to illegal activities; his principal contacts were "Nikos" and Vasvanas; he met Polk at the Astoria Hotel as early as the afternoon of Friday, May 7; Polk arrived at the Luxembourg Café to eat lobster, carrying a soft package "presumably pajamas, in view of the fact that these were missing from his room"; Polk's feet and hands were bound in the rowboat in the manner ascertained by the autopsy report; after being shot, he fell "with a dying groan"; Mouzenidis handed Staktopoulos the identity card and what is here called "the calendar card of Pan American Airways"—the only items taken out of Polk's billfold—and ordered Staktopoulos to mail them and keep silent "against death threat"; Staktopoulos is reported to have feared being fired at as he left the rowboat because "such are the ways of Communists, when they commit a crime, they do a second one to cover the first"; and the final "real fact": Staktopoulos testified that he added the number "3d" on the incriminating envelope in front of his mother's "To the Third Police Station, City" in order "to make it more conspicuous," an admission that "agrees exactly with the report of the expert graphologists," who find that the figure "3d" was written by someone other than Anna Staktopoulos. The communiqué ends with a full quotation of Staktopoulos's personal opinion regarding the role of the Cominform and the Communist party in Polk's murder.

With three confessional depositions to back up this account of the murder—however inconsistent the depositions in certain details and however much revised—the authorities now appeared ready to prepare for the trial of Gregory and Anna Staktopoulos and, when captured, Evangelos Vasvanas and Adam Mouzenidis, perhaps as early as a month or forty days after the legal charge was filed.[11] There was no evident concern on anybody's part when the guerrilla radio reported on October 19 that Adam Mouzenidis had been killed in battle a month before Polk's murder.[12] Ambassador Grady transmitted the relevant broadcast without comment, though his translator spared little of the irony that must have heavily coated the original:

... So until October 4 nothing had been revealed. And yet Stachtopoulos [sic] had been detained in General Security since August. From that date [Ministers] Rendis and Melas, under pressure of events, decided concoct some sort of findings to cover themselves—considering also that [Secretary of State] Marshall was coming to Greece.... According these findings Adam Mouzenidis, a KKE official, who was killed before May 5, executed Polk on May 9, assisted by Vasvana [sic], Colonel-Political Commissar of Democratic Army, who has been fighting far from Salonika for two years now! These two KKE officials suddenly happened to be in Salonika, made arrangements very quickly on the spot with an editor of the Monarcho-Fascist newspaper MACEDONIA, who was at the same time a Reuters correspondent, say the findings. These men then put Polk, who agreed with pleasure to have his hands and feet tied and his eyes covered, in a boat. Then Mouzenidis (who was killed month before that day) killed Polk with his pistol. After that, dead Mouzenidis stepped quietly into his tomb and Vasvanas, undisturbed, got out of encircled Salonika in order to go ... no one knows where.... Stachtopoulos remained, of course, in order take Rendis out of impasse and save his personal prestige as well as prestige of Monarcho-Fascists in eyes of international opinion. There is only one truth, however. Now, these findings do not leave slightest doubt that Polk's murderers are in Athens Ministry of Public Order itself, in the Athens and Salonika securities and among the American secret agents in Greece, who killed Polk to prevent his coming to free Greece and writing the truth about the Democratic Army.

But if this response might have been easily dismissed, given the times, as a typical piece of Communist rhetoric meant to camouflage the truth, what could not be so easily dismissed was a bit of evidence that apparently turned up shortly after Staktopoulos's revised deposition of October 14: immigration records in Athens revealed that Polk was out of the country on assignment at the time that Staktopoulos was supposed to have been meeting him in Athens to make preliminary contact with him. This called for a further revised deposition, the fourth testimonial, though it does not appear as such in the State Department archives but as an enclosure with the officially recorded statements of Gregory and Anna Staktopoulos "in defense of the charges against them" (nor is it included with the three other depositions published by the Lippmann Committee as part of its final report).[13] On October 24, Staktopoulos appeared before Moustakis, Komotouros, and his recently appointed lawyers Vassilikos and Vafiadis, to testify that while he was with "Yanni" at the Zavoritis Confectionery Shop in Athens, "neither Polk nor any other person met us at this confectionery shop," "Yanni" already having made a phone call from which he learned that "the American was not then in Athens." Staktopoulos finds that he "is not able to give any explanation" of why he previously testified that he had met Polk there.

With only "Yanni" of no last name to work with, this news ought to have served to kill further talk of a substantial Athens connection, but there is one last effort to bring Hadjiargyris back into the story. Staktopoulos now reports that at the confectionery shop, "Yanni," while conversing with him about Polk's planned trip to Markos, said that Hadjiargyris, "who was Polk's friend, was also interested in the trip." He adds that he did not ask, nor was he told, anything else about Hadjiargyris, in particular nothing "as to how Hadjiargyris expressed his interest in that trip or who he came in contact with to facilitate that trip." The only other new information provided by this deposition is the appearance of Mouzenidis at Staktopoulos's first March meeting with Vasvanas, followed by a second meeting with Mouzenidis the next day, thus bringing the other absent Communist conspirator into the planning at the earliest stage. "Byron" is brought in again to report to Staktopoulos after the murder that the two conspirators who came into the city in March were now about to leave the city for Chalkidiki. Staktopoulos ends this deposition by reaffirming the terror he was made to feel by his Communist conspirators, especially Byron, and it was this that prevented him from reporting the murder and the murderers to the police. He tells his official interrogators (and his official lawyers), as though a final plea for mercy, that his character and temperament would not have allowed him to take part in a crime against his colleague George Polk. Had he known a crime was planned, he not only would have refused to accompany Polk to the rowboat but would have found a pretext to keep Polk from getting into the boat and would have persuaded the American to give up his trip.

When Kosta Hadjiargyris asked Helen Mamas what kind of man she thought Staktopoulos was, she refused to offer an opinion. At the time of the murder and the subsequent trial, nobody seemed prepared to say what kind of man Staktopoulos was—except his old teacher at Anatolia College in Salonika, Carl Compton, who proved to be the single character witness willing to appear on the accused's behalf. During the trial Carl Compton testified that as a student Staktopoulos was "good, not brilliant, faithful in his duties . . . always quiet . . . liked by the teachers."[14] In a broader context: "All I know of him as a student and what I happened to learn later was favorable. He was a peaceful and reserved type, not secretive. When this case was brought to Court, I talked with friends and their opinion is the same as mine, that is that he was a calm person and wanted to be of help to others." And when one of Staktopoulos's lawyers, Vassilikos, asked if, in keeping with the indictment, Staktopoulos could have known about the crime and could have participated in it, Carl Compton replied: "Absolutely not. There is no doubt in my mind. His character was good, and he could not change so completely within such a short period." Vassilikos: "Did you hear that Stahtopoulos [sic] was said to have been among the top-ranking Greek Communist leaders?" Compton: "Well, I heard he was interested in EAM [the leftist-dominated resistance movement], but I did not hear he was a member of KKE [the Greek Communist Party]." Vassilikos: "Was he a fanatic Communist?" Compton: "No. What I heard is that EAM was patriotic and that all young men joined in it as Stahtopoulos did. Later some were slow, others quick to withdraw."[15]

The image of Staktopoulos created by his confessions is as out of line with the reality of some who knew him personally as the confessions themselves are with the plausible reality of a crime they are meant to illuminate. Since no representative of the American government or of the American press then on the scene in Greece (with the exception of Helen Mamas) had occasion—or sought occasion—to talk to Gregory

Staktopoulos in person either before or immediately after his various confessions were taken at Security Police headquarters, it may seem excusable that no serious questioning of his testimony appears in the public record of those days—but it is barely excusable. The text of his various confessions, with its melodramatic excesses, improbable reconstructions, revised details, shifting accusations and admissions, was there to be read and interpreted by those with a presumed concern for justice in the case, all of whom were professionally literate. The irony is that the very contradictions and implausibilities of Staktopoulos's testimony apparently came to be accepted as evidence not of his having been cruelly manipulated by others but of his lack of reliability and his satanic propensities, which were made out to be sufficient for the kind of culprit needed to serve the official purpose at hand.

VIII The Official Solution

ON OCTOBER 11, two days after Minister of Justice Melas told Raleigh Gibson that he could expect the Polk trial to begin within a month to forty days,[1] General Donovan returned to Salonika in order to be able to report personally to the Lippmann Committee on the soundness of the official solution to the crime that was soon to be announced in Greece. Donovan's estimate of the new developments was expected by the State Department to serve as the "deciding factor" in influencing the attitude of the Lippmann Committee and the American press generally.[2] Lippmann himself was depicted by the State Department as having certain reservations about what was in the air. He had called for caution on the part of American officials when it came to commenting on the solution that would be announced in Greece, lest such commentary be seen in the U.S. as an effort to protect the Greek government by endorsing the Greek explanation of the crime before all the pertinent evidence was in. And he let the State Department know that his committee's final report had to be based on a completed court case and on a careful study of all available corroborative evidence. Even signed confessions would not ipso facto be considered full proof unless accompanied by incontrovertible supporting evidence.

For his part, Donovan appeared reluctant to return to the scene of the investigation at that particular moment, apprehensive that his presence might be interpreted as an attempt by him to assume credit for the solution of the case when, he felt, that credit should go exclusively to the Greek officials who had been responsible for what had now emerged.[3] He was evidently persuaded by those he represented that such reticence was beside the point. And as we have seen, Colonel James Kellis's 1952 notes for the CIA file indicate that Gregory Staktopoulos was not only on the list of suspects that Kellis submitted to Donovan before leaving the case in July 1948, but—if we are to take the notes at their word—was the suspect that Donovan chose to promote above the others in front of Mouskoundis before Donovan himself returned to the States that summer.[4] The general's reticence must have been mixed with a measure of satisfaction that the suspect he and his assistant had apparently pinpointed in late July had proven so useful to the Greek authorities.

As it turned out, the general need not have worried much about who would assume what credit for the official solution. On reaching Salonika, when he, Winston Burdett (also suddenly back in town), Theodore Lambron, and Raleigh Gibson went in to pay a courtesy call on Chief of Police Xanthopoulos—this time indicating that they were not there to annoy the chief with questions—they heard from Xanthopoulos that though the crime had been well planned and well organized so that it had proven a difficult one to solve, "with hard work and the help of God it had been solved."[5] The case would go to trial in January or February, the chief said (that is, two and a half to three months hence, not a month to forty days). But everything was going along fine. And now that people in the U.S. were getting more and more interested in the Polk case, he was happy that soon something would be done about it.

Donovan couldn't resist one awkward question at this point: Was there any danger of a witness being killed? No, said the chief, there was no such danger, because he was holding all the witnesses under his auspices (presumably at Security Police headquarters) rather than holding them in jail, a procedure that "all Ministers" were cooperating with by "overlooking" it. This brought on a cautionary statement from Donovan on behalf of justice: "the case must not only be solved," he said, "but the trial must be a fair one." To this the chief replied, ending the interview, that the investigation had been going on for five months and "now was no time to spoil anything."

When Major Mouskoundis met with the group the following day, he demonstrated a like optimism but a touch less candor about the recent turn of events. Donovan was able to remark at the start of the meeting that the major appeared to be "a well satisfied man," and the major replied that this occasion was quite different from the last time they'd been together when he was "on the spot," to which Donovan in turn replied that he was glad to see the spot was different now.[6] In this celebrative aura, Major Mouskoundis could state boldly that "with the man that the police had under detention complete light had been brought to the case." And he proceeded to outline in detail what the light had revealed through the confession of Gregory Staktopoulos, including some of those revised items and emendations that Staktopoulos officially offered his interrogators on October 14, two days after this cheerful reunion between the Donovan group and Mouskoundis (for example, Vasvanas's March visit to Salonika in order to give Staktopoulos instructions about his meeting Polk in Athens—a meeting that had to be excised from this revised confession ten days later, as we have seen—and the addition of a 1:00 A.M. meeting on Friday, May 7, between Staktopoulos, Polk, and Vasvanas on the street corner outside the Astoria Café).

Unlike the tense review of the case during Donovan's previous visit at the height of the summer, the major's account here was interrupted only by a few questions, and these were not really pointed enough to be penetrating. Burdett asked about Staktopoulos's being put ashore after the murder near a closed restaurant on the Karabournaki cape, and Mouskoundis explained that Staktopoulos's home was near the place the boat had landed to let him off, as though courtesy in the designated murderers was a sufficient motive here. Burdett then wanted to know how George Polk "was . . . approached regarding being blindfolded and tied up." The major responded that he would rather such facts were given to General Donovan and his party by what he called "official sources," but since he knew that what he told his American visitors wouldn't be repeated in front of any source, he would explain the whole case—and he went on to narrate what the confessions had to say about Polk's fatal voyage in the rowboat. Donovan evidently wanted to know one thing only: Who were these men in the boat with Staktopoulos and Polk? "Communists," said Mouskoundis. And was the first man who did the rowing—that is, Adam Mouzenidis—a "real boatman"? asked Donovan. No, replied Mouskoundis, he was a professor of literature, a Communist member of Parliament in 1936 and a leader of the Communist group there who had been exiled, presumably for his political beliefs, as early as 1927, at one time the manager of two newspapers in Salonika, and a man with a "criminal record"—all of this information that Mouskoundis said was not to be repeated in Athens, "even to any of the Cabinet Ministers." The call for such secrecy, nowhere explained, suggests the tension between official Athens and official Salonika that was already beginning to gather as the authorities prepared to promote the Staktopoulos solution for public consumption.

The remainder of Mouskoundis's account stays close to the revised confession that was to be recorded officially two days later and revised ten days after that so as to eliminate Polk from Staktopoulos's Athens visit. The only new insight to emerge from Mouskoundis's commentary here was his opinion that the fatal bullet did not strike the boat at all and easily missed both the man rowing and the man seated in the front, this opinion presumably to help explain why no rowboat with a bullet in it had surfaced during the investigation. And Mouskoundis also offered his impression of how both Anna and Gregory Staktopoulos had reacted when shown the envelope that was supposedly addressed by Anna: she "became extremely nervous" at the sight, and he, "when asked, 'Is this the writing of anyone familiar to you,' cried, 'Don't mention my mother.' " Apparently none of the Americans hearing this bit of dialogue or that reported from the rowboat trip raised a question about matters of style and plausibility, nor did they ask for a chance to interview the accused or the lawyers for the accused to see if they might clarify some of the gross absurdities and inconsistencies in the confessions. In fact, Gibson's cable gives no indication at all of the group's response to Mouskoundis's scenario, so that the archives allow the impression that Donovan and Burdett left Salonika prepared to take Mouskoundis's account for a reasonable version of the truth, at least until the evidence was presented at the trial of the four conspirators officially accused of being accomplices in the murder.

This does not mean that Donovan left Greece entirely at ease about the way the new developments in the case were being handled. The State Department transmitted to Athens and Salonika a confidential memorandum of General Donovan's "preliminary observations" on the Polk case that he had telephoned in from New York on arriving back in the States by air from Greece.[7] Here he reveals that he had urged officials in Athens to offer a sober account of the facts in the investigation without specific reference to the Communist party, so as to strengthen the government's position. He was sorry this had not been done; he assumed that Minister of Justice Melas, "who was fanatical on the subject," had been "unable to restrain himself." Donovan also returned with the strong conviction that the trial should be by a civil court and not by a military court-martial, and he hoped the Department of State would, if necessary, use its influence with the Greek government to bring this about (the same dispatch indicated that no such action was necessary because the department had already been informed that the trial would be a civil one). Donovan also felt that the trial should be held in the fairly near future, that is, within two to three months—"allowing time, of course, for complete preparation of the case." He indicated that in answer to press questions about the latest developments he would merely say that the Greek government had now presented an indictment, not a solution of the case, and that this indictment had to be tested through regular legal processes. And so he told the press at a conference on October 18.[8] But of course there was no comment by him on the quality of the various confessions that were the basis for the indictment or on the curious legal processes that had permitted the Security Police to hold Staktopoulos for forty-five days without formal arrest until the confessions finally emerged.

It appears, in any case, that his statement to the American press served to raise doubt in some quarters about the resolution of the case that was offered by the Greek authorities in their official announcement in Athens on October 17. For example, the *New York Times* of October 19 interpreted Donovan's statement to the press of the previous day that there now must be a trial to see what the proof was as reflecting an attitude that "seemed somewhat skeptical of the Greek Government's indictment of four persons, including two known Communists, for the murder." And in its editorial the following day, the *Times* offered its belief that, until actual testimony had been presented, "most Americans will reserve judgment on the findings of the Greek investigators," even though to the Overseas Writers group conducting an independent investigation and to "many other Americans," it had seemed that the official investigation had not been very thorough and "its findings were delayed unduly for reasons not fully explained." A trial in open court might answer the unanswered questions, the editorial concluded, and if not, there would have to be "a frank admission by the Greek Government that it does not have conclusive evidence." Since the good faith of the Greek government had been questioned, said the editorial, the Polk case was one that should not be left unsolved.

The *New York Herald Tribune* of October 18 began its editorial by linking a quick visit to Athens by Secretary of State George Marshall on October 17 with both the official announcement of the Polk case solution and the "drab picture of the prospects of restoring peace to harried Greece" that had been presented to the press by Ambassador Grady in anticipation of Marshall's visit. The editorial held that the statement attributed to Staktopoulos claiming that the murder was planned by the Cominform and carried out by the Communist party of Greece in order to throw the blame for the murder on the Right and thereby defame Greece enough to influence aid under the Marshall plan "makes out a very plausible case," but its plausibility derives in large measure from the fact that "the weaknesses and errors of the Greek government have created a climate of opinion in the United States which made it possible for the murder of an American correspondent to be used against that government." They are, concludes the editorial, the same weaknesses and errors which colored Ambassador Grady's remarks to the press on the eve of Secretary Marshall's arrival in Athens.

Both the *Herald Tribune* and the *Times* also carried news from the opposition, specifically the response to the official announcement by one Miltiadis Porphyrogenis, minister of justice in the guerrilla government, who reported from Prague that Adam Mouzenidis had been killed by artillery fire on April 5,[9] a month before the murder of George Polk. And in the *Herald Tribune* report, Porphyrogenis went on to say that Mouzenidis's grave was on view at the site of his death "at Kroessia" (probably the mountain region of Kroussia). He also went on to say that Vasvanas was killed by Greek police while engaged in underground work—the first such claim on record, subsequently refuted—and he added that Gregory Staktopoulos and his mother, Anna, jointly charged with complicity in the murder, "either were tortured into telling an untrue story or were provocateurs used to 'save the face of Greek authorities.' " Both New York papers also quoted from a statement by William Polk, then a student at Harvard, to the effect that, if he wasn't ready to doubt the government's findings, he still thought the case needed an impartial investigation and " 'I don't think the Greek Government is impartial.' "

Minister of Public Order Rendis was quoted in the *Times* piece as responding to these comments from Polk's younger brother by indicating that the family of George Polk was welcome to come to Greece to participate in the trial of those charged with the murder.[10] Minister of Justice Melas was considerably less hospitable. He issued his own press statement proclaiming that Greek justice had done its duty, and if William Polk, due to his inexperience and immaturity, considered the findings incorrect, the minister could only express his regrets and remind him that from the very first every facility had been granted to responsible Americans in Greece to form their own conclusions as to whether "standard Greek justice is equal to that of all civilized countries."[11] Donovan, perhaps catching a barb in this as one of the responsible Americans whom Melas had in mind and also having to face his own measure of hostility from the American press (with the *Daily Worker* representatives proving to be "particularly articulate and provocative" when he was questioned at length by the press on October 25), telephoned the State Department to warn them about moves in progress "to cast doubt on the *bona fides* of the Greek Government."[12] Among these were likely agitation by "Communist-controlled groups" to pressure the Lippmann Committee to use its funds to defend Staktopoulos and also to mount a propaganda campaign that would include using "Bill Polk," who, Donovan is reported to have said, "seems to have sold out completely to the Commies."

The response of the Greek press to the official announcement of the government's case varied with the political bias of the press source. The guerrilla radio offered, in its October 19 broadcast, the mixture of irony and vituperative rhetoric that we have seen (pp. 188–89 above): Staktopoulos was held through August and September without consequence until Ministers Rendis and Melas decided to "concoct some sort of findings to cover themselves" in view of Marshall's visit to Greece, this resulting in the choice of one dead KKE official and another official distant from Salonika as the culprits, with Staktopoulos the only visible conspirator on hand to save Rendis's personal prestige "as well as prestige of Monarcho-Fascists in eyes of international public opinion." The rest of the Greek press was generally more tolerant of the local officials and their findings. Ambassador Grady reported on October 23 that editorial comment was uniformly laudatory of the authorities, and he added a parenthetical note that quoted *Kathimerini* as saying, specifically, "including, to be fair, the Ministers."[13] And the Athens press, though cautious concerning details of the case, was said to have supported the conclusion that "absolute proof [had] been presented as to which 'political faction' committed crime."

There was also a note of triumph over the perceived attitude of the American public, as this had presumably been stimulated by the American press. *Estia* indicated that the Greeks had every reason to complain of the superficiality of foreign correspondents, while *Kathimerini* spoke of a solution arrived at "in spite of slanders, suspicion, and scorn." And *Oi Kairoi* suggested that it was now Greece's turn to hit back—which is what much of the Greek press did in the days following, as reports came in about the U.S. reaction to what was now openly called the "official solution." *Kathimerini* "accused US press of 'hastening to accept Communist lies,' " and *Oi Kairoi* asserted that "centrist US press trying overthrow present government and pave way for compromise" with Markos and the guerrillas. Ambassador Grady recorded what he called a rare note of moderation in *Ethnikos Kyrix*, which charged the "Centrist Greek press" with misrepresenting the attitude of the U.S. press, the balance of which had in fact "counseled patience," while only the "Leftist" U.S. press had attacked the solution. And *To Vima* provided what Grady called a note of resignation by commenting that, though Americans could not distinguish between Greece and the Orient and had yet to discard the notion that Greece was dominated by a totalitarian Right, "American objections will, no doubt, be quieted after the trial."

There was a touch of prophecy in this, but its fulfillment was slow in arriving, as was the trial itself. Despite the early triumphal mood over the Staktopoulos solution, serious problems remained. Attorney General Constantinidis, apparently nervous even about the initial press coverage, had to remind newspapers in Greece on October 19 that the order issued a month earlier forbidding articles on the Polk case was still in force.[14] The order had been invoked by Minister of Justice Melas on October 15 to bring legal action against four newspapers that had jumped the gun on his official announcement of the murder solution,[15] which suggests the kind of climate, already politically overheated, that the local press had to work in while exercising what limited freedom it might hope for, beyond the political commitment of individual papers, in covering the Polk affair.

The major concerns troubling Constantinidis these days appear in an interview he had with Raleigh Gibson in mid-November.[16] He told the consul general that, although the Staktopoulos case was progressing, especially the exploration of the accused's activities from the time of the Occupation until he was arrested, and though Staktopoulos was beginning to take his attorneys more and more into his confidence with the expectation that further details would emerge at the trial, there were still certain awkward areas that had to be explored further. For one, while a strict search had been made to find the boat in which the murder was committed—Staktopoulos himself going along twice to point out what direction the boat had taken—they had had no luck recovering it, either above or below the surface. Also, the indictment against both Staktopoulos and his mother Anna accused them of murder, of illegal possession of firearms, and of illegal bearing of arms. That could result in a time-consuming appeal, even as far as the Supreme Court, because Staktopoulos was likely to contend that he had committed no crime but was merely fulfilling a request by Polk to be placed in contact with Markos's headquarters (the attorney general apparently did not go into the question of how any court at any level might handle the charge that aging Anna Staktopoulos had been bearing arms, let alone committing murder with them). Still, even with the anticipated appeal, the attorney general stated that the trial would be held by the end of January 1949.

In the meanwhile, there were a few other minor problems to contend with. Though Staktopoulos continued to insist that he and Polk had eaten at the Luxembourg Café on the night of the murder, the authorities had not been able to find any witnesses to corroborate his contention. The waiter Staktopoulos pointed out as having served them that evening could not remember doing so. And Staktopoulos had now changed his original testimony in order to indicate that he had not sat there waiting at the restaurant table for Polk to arrive on his own but had actually picked Polk up at the Astoria Hotel and had escorted him to the Luxembourg Café (this detail presumably suggesting a more believable way of handling a foreign visitor unfamiliar with the city, while at the same time broadening Staktopoulos's role in the affair). Finally, said Constantinidis, Staktopoulos's mother was "not giving the authorities any information regarding her son's activities in the Communist Party," and his sister, Efharis, still being held in jail as a material witness, had yet to provide anything of value for use at the trial.

Raleigh Gibson's covering memorandum on this meeting does not show any concern on his part about the nature of the charge against Anna Staktopoulos or about the continued detention of her daughter without any charge at all. His expressed concern is with the current emphasis in the investigation. It is "evident" to him that "the Judicial and Police officials" are not continuing the investigation of the murder in order to clear up the problems that Constantinidis had identified but rather "are placing all their endeavors toward securing information regarding the Communist Party." He thinks there is now a great possibility that the authorities will use the trial as a means of attacking Communism and relegate the murder to a secondary role, a strategy that would be considered "the logical method" in Greece but would have "an extremely bad effect" in the United States. It is his view that the trial has to be conducted "on the basis that Gregory Stahtopoulos [sic] and his mother are accused of murder, and not as members or leaders of the Communist party of Greece," and he wonders if, given more indications of this emphasis, it might not be advisable for the embassy to "point out informally" to the minister of justice the virtue of calling this matter to the attention of the local judicial authorities.

Gibson's concern, however incomplete when it came to the legal rights of the accused and the plausibility of the charges against them, was entirely to the point regarding the direction that the investigation had taken. Strong efforts were in progress to establish—or generate—credentials for Staktopoulos as a Communist leader. The first of these was to link the Reuters stringer to the publication of a phony interview with Stalin that had appeared in his paper, *Makedonia*, in March 1947, over a year before the murder. The interview, supposedly conducted by an American correspondent for United Press and broadcast from Moscow, portrayed Stalin as a relatively benign statesman who hoped to promote peace for a hundred years and who believed that the American people also wanted peace but were being directed elsewhere by their leaders.[17] The interview had received much attention in Greece, though quickly disavowed by the paper in which it first appeared, and it had evidently caused the recall of the Russian ambassador to Athens. It was determined at one point that the interview had been furnished the *Makedonia* by what Gibson calls "one of the radio men of the paper," and Constantinidis reported that Staktopoulos had now confessed to being responsible for recording the false broadcast, having taken it down from a radio set installed in his home, this, in the attorney general's opinion, "under direction from the same group of higher-ups that ordered the murder of George Polk."[18] Again, there is no comment from Gibson on the credibility of this new development.

Soon other more violent credentials for Staktopoulos, apparently unsubstantiated elsewhere, emerged from the testimony of one Nicolaos D. Kondomitros, "forty-three years old, a news reporter and Christian Orthodox," who described himself as "merely acquainted with the accused."[19] Out of this acquaintance came much news of Staktopoulos's Communist enterprise, beginning with his having ordered the execution of a major in the Greek army who carried a pistol with a single bullet in it, which he was saving to commit suicide with if the Communists should come to power following the German Occupation and which, Staktopoulos was said to have told Kondomitros, made the major "an enemy of the people." This was apparently the reason Staktopoulos ordered the major executed during the Occupation—by what authority is not indicated—the deed having been committed, according to Kondomitros, by three civilians in an alley behind the Mediterranean Hotel. And soon after the departure of the Germans from Salonika, Staktopoulos presented a proposal at the Union of Newspaper Writers that all newsmen sign a declaration that no one of them would work for a non-EAM [the resistance movement dominated by the Left] newspaper, then asked all those present to sign the declaration, "doing so in a threatening manner, and taking care that none left without doing so."

According to Kondomitros, other activities by Staktopoulos led the British Intelligence Service to conclude that he must be high in Communist circles, probably attached to Ioannides, the leader of the Macedonian Communist party, or to his three assistants. And Kondomitros felt that it was no coincidence that a few days after Staktopoulos took a trip to Kavalla, Markos's guerrilla radio reported that the Americans were building large airfields around Kavalla, as it was no coincidence that after a trip by Staktopoulos to Epirus, the guerrilla radio broadcast information about the position and plans of the Greek national army in that area. Finally, after Staktopoulos fell passionately in love with one Maria Miha, a Greek Red Cross nurse who later proved to be a spy for the Italians, Staktopoulos said, without giving a reason, "that he would kill that woman," though Kondomitros thought the reason for this threat was her having used Staktopoulos to get information for her spy activities.

Raleigh Gibson's covering memorandum on the Kondomitros testimony offers no comment on the text's credibility, but it does state bluntly that the straight investigation of the murder of George Polk had now stopped while local officials continued to pursue Staktopoulos's Communist background. The efforts by Gibson to bring on an early trial appear to have failed. Another meeting with the attorney general on December 31 reveals that Staktopoulos's lawyers indeed planned to appeal his indictment, which would preclude a trial before mid-February.[20] The attorney general reported that investigating officials had been unable to persuade the man who telephoned in the phony Stalin interview to name the person who had ordered the broadcast; in fact, the man now claimed that he himself had written the article and that "it was his idea."[21] So, Constantinidis tells Gibson, the authorities "have closed" their investigations of Gregory and Anna Staktopoulos. Their attention had now turned to "other parties connected with the crime," a cryptic reference to the relatives of Adam Mouzenidis, who would soon be brought to center stage in an effort to solve the still vexing question of whether or not Mouzenidis was dead or alive at the time he shot George Polk in the back of the head.

But as the authorities turned their focus in that direction, there were several developments recorded in Athens that apparently did not come into the dialogue between Gibson and officials in Salonika. On December 23, the embassy's "Chargé d'Affaires ad interim" (unnamed but presumably Karl Rankin) had the honor to transmit to the State Department an account of the December 8 "kidnapping" by guerrilla forces of an American engineer named Carl A. Graessner, employee of the Atkinson Drake Company, on assignment in Greece as part of the American Economic Mission.[22] The kidnapping occurred on the Larissa-Kozani road, and Graessner and his Greek interpreter "were taken into the high country of the Mount Olympus region," the region some thought George Polk had been planning to head for by way of the sea as he began his fatal trip into Salonika Bay. The engineer and his interpreter were released unharmed a week later, after reaching a permanent guerrilla camp somewhere south of Olympus. This kidnapping paralleled one in the Peloponnese some days earlier involving another American Economic Mission engineer named Francis L. McShane, who was also released unharmed, evidently on orders from higher authority, after a short stay in guerrilla hands. Both of the Americans were treated well, according to the separate accounts of their experience that they provided the American embassy, and both were impressed, much as Homer Bigart had been impressed some six months earlier, by the morale of the guerrilla fighters and their leaders (a number of whom appeared to be drawn from former Athenian lawyers).

As was true of Homer Bigart's dispatches from guerrilla territory in late June of 1948,[23] there are several aspects of the Graessner account that carried implications for the Polk affair, as it carried useful insight into the limited perception of guerrilla attitudes in most official circles of the time and also into the evident failure of most guerrillas to recognize how poor their fading military prospects in the civil war actually were. The "rebels" (as the embassy dispatch labels the "Andarte" forces) insisted that they were still fully in command of the territory that Graessner had dared to travel through, and they made every effort to show him that their spirit was much alive. He reported that "after marching through the night in the bitter wind and snow of a mountain winter, the Andartes would gather near the campfires in the early morning and sing 'democratic' songs with obvious enjoyment and gusto." Graessner would find himself barely able to crawl into a tent after that kind of hike, "yet the rebels, some of whom had walked through the snow for hours without shoes, showed no interest in sleep or rest, linking arms around the fire to sing their 'battle' songs," maybe, Graessner thought, just to impress him, but a thing that "still took a lot of morale and guts!" And even after long forced marches and short rest periods, the guerrillas would hold regular thirty-minute gymnastic exercises in the mornings, officers, soldiers, and women all taking part "with the most intense enthusiasm." Though there were a few exceptions, Graessner also found the guerrillas "enthusiastic as to their chances of success and eager to go forward with the battle," and they assured him that they had "every chance to win," while he, as an American, was backing "the losing side in the struggle."

One telling item that the embassy cable designates "a sidelight" is the news that Mr. Graessner's captors, who made little attempt to indoctrinate him beyond "the typical Communist lines" that included "the normal attack on Truman, Van Fleet, Marshall and Grady as monarchofascists responsible for Greeks fighting against Greeks," at the same time strongly objected to certain stories that had appeared in the Athens newspapers (surprisingly available already at the camp) which stated that Mr. McShane had "accused the Andartes in the Peloponnese of swearing at President Truman." The Olympus region andartes called this accusation "a dirty monarchofascist lie." The guerrillas holding Graessner told him that, "while all Andartes hated Truman, they would never swear at him." They were honorable men, they said, who did not swear at the head of a state. Graessner reported that they were so serious "in this stand" that they made him swear he would not repeat the same error in his own account of his captivity.

As a distinguished historian of the civil war period, John Iatrides, has suggested,[24] if George Polk was killed on orders from the Greek Communist party with the aim of embarrassing the Athens government or of striking back at the American government, why was the fate of these two engineers, who were much more involved in American policy than Polk was, so different from that of the CBS correspondent? And one could ask the same question with reference to Homer Bigart's trip to interview Markos, which was solicited by the guerrillas and carried out with much expense of energy a little over a month after Polk's demise, though forty years after the fact Bigart himself does not entirely preclude his having been invited to Markos's headquarters in order to "cover" some sort of mishandling by Communist agents of Polk's interest in accomplishing what Bigart was allowed to accomplish so soon after Polk's murder.[25] If one takes that to be an outside possibility at best, with no current evidence to support it, the image of guerrillas in both the northern mountains and the Olympus region making every effort to demonstrate their high morale and their assurance of ultimate victory—along with their credentials as gentlemen with a due respect for Harry Truman as a head of state—suggests that the same guerrillas and their KKE leaders would have been likely to welcome rather than misconstrue and finally snuff out such a grand opportunity to present their case to the world as that which would have been offered them by George Polk's planned CBS broadcast, whether that opportunity was by way of an interview with Markos or with other guerrillas in the region Polk was presumed to be heading for.

That the embassy itself now became quite conscious of the propaganda battle that guerrilla forces were waging at this time despite their increasingly vulnerable military circumstances is suggested by the rhetorical call for countermeasures that concludes the embassy's cable transmitting Graessner's report: "The need for wider diffusion of the American viewpoint in non-metropolitan areas of Greece is pressing! The morale of most Andartes is high. Since this is the case, it should be brought under attack." The cable goes on to point out that if the morale level is falling in some cases, that makes it all the more important that this new advantage should be driven home by swift and sharp propaganda attacks from government sources. The cable closes with a rather naive recommendation in view of the Greek army's military campaign, amply supported by American arms, planes, and advisers, that would successfully send the andarte forces into full retreat across the northern border within a period of months: "Whatever else their stories may do, the reports submitted by Mr. McShane and Mr. Graessner point to the imperative need of a psychological warfare campaign to bring the full American viewpoint to the Communist-dulled ears of the Andartes in the mountains of Greece."

About two weeks after Graessner's report was sent in to Washington, the embassy transmitted the document designated "Retranslation of Report on Interrogation of Mrs. Rhea [sic] Polk," which the covering memorandum (dated January 4, 1949) explains is a retranslation into English of the Greek translation of the report from William E. Colby to General Donovan covering points raised in the series of conversations that Colby had with Rea Polk in late September of 1948, now among the Donovan papers (see above, chapter 6, pp. 134–36).[26] The Greek transcript of the report was given to the embassy by a police official who was "not aware of the means by which a copy of the original report came into the possession of the Greek police." The covering memorandum suggests that General Donovan's "local agent," Theodore Lambron, probably gave it to the police, though Lambron never mentioned its existence to the embassy—nor, apparently, did General Donovan himself, though Donovan was in Greece some ten days after the report was submitted to him by Colby. In any case, concludes the memorandum, the report offers little more than "a restatement of already known facts." One thing that it finds "interesting to note," however, is "Mrs. Polk's preoccupation with the two unknown individuals who allegedly burst into her room on May 13 and questioned her concerning her husband's whereabouts"— interesting from the embassy's point of view, it seems, because in none of her previous testimony had Rea Polk "offered information to the effect that these unknown individuals wore 'bloodstained shirts, revolvers, et cetera,' " as in this report, nor, again as in this report, had she "ever claimed to have seen either of the men involved on any subsequent occasion" (Rea told Colby that she later saw one of the two men— "somewhat fat," standing with a group of soldiers "outside a coffee shop outside Salonika"—when on her way to the airport behind her husband's coffin).

These details are indeed interesting to note, but they are hardly the only details that should have interested the embassy in these crucial days before Gregory and Anna Staktopoulos were put on trial. The embassy's version of the report is not an immaculate rendering of the Colby original, but it is only occasionally off the mark, and the substance of it does give us a new perspective on certain important aspects of the case.[27] First, some minor implications emerge from the inaccuracies—not to say deliberate distortions—offered up in the embassy's version, perhaps grounded in what the Greek police provided as a text. We have already seen that one misreading of the Colby report presents Staktopoulos as possibly knowing more about Polk's whereabouts before his body was recovered than his wife knew. Another mistranslation renders Colby's note about Rea's having heard a story "that George had spent over an hour in close conversation with Stahtopoulous [sic] at a gathering on Friday before his death" as Rea's having "heard that George had a talk with Staktopoulos, which lasted for an hour, about a meeting that was to take place on the Friday before his death"—a misreading or mistranslation that appears to anticipate one of the implausible meetings between Staktopoulos and Polk that later comes into the trial proceedings. Then we find Rea's defense of Helen Mamas as displaying an attitude of extreme opposition to the Communists, unless she is "a phenomenal actress," rendered, with additional nuances, as "a phenomenon of histrionics." And Colby's line that one of the stories circulating about Polk "was that George had a breakdown (which Mrs. Polk concedes would be within the realm of possibility)" is rendered as "one of these stories was that George had stumbled and fallen (which Mrs. Polk thought probable)"—perhaps the most innocent of the distortions.

But what is more important than the possibility of a minor tampering with the text of Colby's report to Donovan on his conversations with Rea are certain implications of the report itself, which come over clearly however rendered. For a start, the report provides an image of Staktopoulos's encounter or encounters with Rea after her arrival in Salonika that is different from that which either party remembers years after the fact, though the Colby report is closer to Staktopoulos's recollection in his 1984 book in that it shows Staktopoulos asking Rea on two occasions for information regarding Polk's disappearance days before Polk's body was retrieved from Salonika Bay. And the significant implication here is that the Colby report's image of Staktopoulos as an aggressive reporter out to write a story about Polk's disappearance, when that disappearance was linked to a trip to Markos's headquarters or possibly to a crime, does not mesh at all with the image of Staktopoulos as a terrified witness to a Communist murder, as established by his official confessions.

It is hardly credible that someone who had been present at the murder, had been terrorized by it, and had been threatened with death if he didn't remain silent about it—details that were all part of the official solution—would publicly seek out Rea Polk for an interview and press her for a story on her husband's mysterious disappearance. It is not even credible that Staktopoulos would do so if he had seen Polk privately before his disappearance and had offered his help with whatever mission Polk had in mind. Yet Rea tells Colby of two meetings she had with Staktopoulos over the issue of a speculative story before Polk's body was recovered, and Staktopoulos himself writes of a single meeting with Rea during which they talked about her husband, though his account of that occasion has him less aggressive and less focused than Rea pictured him as being in her conversations with Colby.

In his 1984 book, the Reuters stringer suggests that he simply ran into Rea at the Hotel Astoria and approached her on the advice of the desk clerk not necessarily for a story but, as a conscientious reporter presumably would, for the latest news about her missing husband, and when none was forthcoming from Rea, left the scene without debate or discourtesy.[28] No mention of there having been a story on Polk's disappearance in the Sunday issue of *Makedonia* or any indication of whether or not he had a part in writing it. As we have seen, the Colby report, on the other hand, has Staktopoulos definitely writing a story for his paper, probably on Friday of that week, under a title rendered very specifically as "Is It a Crime?" and this title underlined by Colby's remark that it "may or may not be significant regarding Stahtopoulous' [*sic*] knowledge of the crime." No source for this information is indicated in the Colby report.

The story that actually appeared in *Makedonia* on Sunday not only carried a very different title (see above, p. 135) but gave little emphasis to the crime mystery aspect of Polk's disappearance. Though there is a passing mention of the possibility that Polk was the victim of a chance crime, the likelihood of this is said to be so weak that it is hardly being considered by the investigators. What the story focuses on is the speculation that Polk left Salonika on a mission to visit Markos, that the CBS correspondent knew where he was going from contacts made with the Communists in Athens, and that his approach to one English and one American official in Salonika for help in finding a contact was simply to ensure that his absence on this mission would be understood once he undertook his journey. Further evidence in support of the mission theory is Polk's having left his typewriter behind—an unnecessarily heavy burden—and his having taken pajamas with him, presumably for more comfortable sleeping in awkward circumstances. And his having left his camera behind—"most uncharacteristic for an American"—could be explained, the news story tells us, by the guerrillas having made that a precondition. The piece concludes with the further speculation that, in view of the reverses suffered recently by the guerrillas, Polk may try to contact Markos in person in order to elicit from him proposals for reaching an agreement with the government.

The one clue we have that Staktopoulos may indeed have contributed to this story for his newspaper is a passing mention, early in the piece, of Polk's having reached Salonika with "his colleagues Cosby [sic], Manson [sic], and Pron [sic]," news which both Helen Mamas and Staktopoulos himself testified that he had gathered for his paper and that he ended up getting wrong in a related way years later in his book when he identified Polk and two of his companions—actually Crosby, Matchen, and Prohme—as "American journalists" who had just arrived in Salonika (Crosby was an Athens consular official and Prohme a USIS officer in Salonika). If Staktopoulos did in fact contribute to the speculative *Makedonia* story, it again seems rather incredible that he could have coolly done so in the particular terms that the story promotes had he been witness to Polk's murder in a rowboat off the Karabournaki Cape less than a week previously, as his official confession has it.

Rea Polk's recollection of the days before her husband's body was discovered now includes no encounter with Staktopoulos at the Hotel Astoria and no discussion with him of a possible story or news item about her husband's disappearance, simply an accidental and casual encounter with Staktopoulos at the Mediterranean Hotel after a shopping trip with Helen Mamas and the memory of a hauntingly sad look that Staktopoulos gave her on that occasion, suggesting to her that he had indeed witnessed her husband's murder. The one additional bit of evidence we have that her memory may be faulty in this connection is Kosta Hadjiargyris's reference in his book to Rea's testimony on June 24 in Salonika, during which she evidently indicated that she had found Staktopoulos "unlikable" and thought Hadjiargyris also shared the same sentiments—a "totally untrue" impression on her part, says Hadjiargyris.[29]

If Rea indeed found Staktopoulos "unlikable," she must certainly have met him on some occasion besides that following her shopping trip with Helen Mamas, and it seems plausible that her dislike was the consequence of some sort of confrontation akin to that described by the Colby memorandum—where Rea's negative view of the Reuters stringer is underlined by Colby's way of putting it: "She disliked his attitude (and incidentally, dislikes him considerably)"—or the less inflammatory account offered by Staktopoulos himself in his book. If so, the Colby report of Rea's recollection in September of 1948 has to be seen as more accurate than what her recent memory provides us, and this conclusion again

invokes a picture of Staktopoulos's movements following the disappearance of Polk that seems entirely out of line with the image of a terrified
if only partially implicated "conspirator" in a murder plotted by "fellow
Communists." The more believable picture is that of a reporter out to
get the hot news without benefit of privileged advance knowledge, certainly none that would be as incriminating as that of his official testimony at Security Police headquarters.

Whether or not Staktopoulos finally helped to write the *Makedonia*
story on Polk's disappearance, the implications of the Colby report on
this issue hardly justify the embassy's prefatory comment that "the
report itself is little more than a restatement of already known facts."
Since the retranslated report, in keeping with the Donovan papers
memorandum, is dated September 30 and indicates that it covered conversations that took place on the previous three days, it was made at a
time when the police were fully aware that it offered "facts" which
brought into question crucial aspects of what Staktopoulos would be
offering as his official account of the murder on the following day, that
is, October 1. For his part, Donovan surely must have been aware
of some of the memorandum's implications after his visit to Salonika
on October 11. And the embassy, submitting the Colby report to Washington three months later, should also have been fully aware that the
report served to undermine aspects not only of Staktopoulos's first confession but of the various revisions that followed it during the month of
October.

The embassy was not much more astute in its handling of the one
phase of the report that it recognized as a supplement to "known facts":
Rea's "preoccupation with two unknown individuals" whom she described (in the embassy version) as "cutthroats with blood-stained shirts,
revolvers, etc." ("ruffians, with bloody and torn shirts, revolvers, etc."
in the original), who had come into her room at the Hotel Astoria on
Thursday night and, as Colby has it, "requested and insisted that she had
news of George's whereabouts through some message left with her or
sent to her." Rea is reported to have thought that these intruders "were
either police or Military Police," further support, it would seem, for her
"intuition" that "the far right committed the crime," her suspicion falling most of all on "the Military Police organization, which she states is
made up largely of former Communists." The embassy apparently felt
that Rea's intuition and suspicion here were not to be taken any more
seriously than her account of her several meetings with Staktopoulos. In
fact, the embassy's commentary implies that this is "information" she
is offering for the first time late in the game, unsupported by any of her

previous testimony, though the embassy had every reason to know that much else in Rea's conversations with Colby had proven to be unassailably accurate by this point in the investigation, in particular her extended image of Helen Mamas as not only innocent of any conspiracy but, in Rea's view, actually an anti-Communist who had shown no signs of being anything other than sincere in her efforts to help Rea during those difficult days in Salonika and who did not appear to be "hiding anything whatsoever."

So much for one late opportunity on the part of American officials in Greece to raise what might have been crucial questions about the official "Staktopoulos" solution at a point before the investigation was finally closed and the trial set in the calendar. It is clear that long before that point, General Donovan, for whom the Colby report was prepared in the first instance, had decided not to do anything about its implications, certainly nothing that would "spoil things" once the official solution was announced in Greece in mid-October. And the Greek police official who finally handed the Greek text of the report to the embassy and who claimed not to know how the original came into police possession must have assumed that it would not be considered new evidence worthy of further review so long after the official solution had been made public— unless he wanted whatever protection there might be in having the document on record with the local Americans. In any case, we hear no more about the Colby report from any source, and this includes Raleigh Gibson, who received a copy on January 4, at the same time that it was transmitted to the State Department by the Athens embassy.[30]

Gibson, it seems, had other issues on his mind at this time. The investigators were now much preoccupied with the problem of trying to answer the andarte radio charge that one of the accused murderers, Adam Mouzenidis, had been killed in guerrilla combat at some point before the murder. And there were new problems of failing cooperation between authorities in Salonika and Athens that seemed certain to delay further the trial of Gregory and Anna Staktopoulos.

During the second week of January the Athens embassy reported that several relatives of Adam Mouzenidis had been arrested and were now under interrogation, first one Eudoxia Mouzenidis, wife of Adam, who was discovered in Piraeus, then her brother Anastassios Molyvdas,[31] and as an "outgrowth" of their interrogation, Adam's brother Stylianos Mouzenidis, his wife (unnamed), and Eudoxia's sister, Anna Molyvda, all residents of Salonika who had been brought to Athens to testify.[32] At that time none of these was said to be directly involved in murder, but the police expected to obtain "confirmatory evidence" that Adam

Mouzenidis was in Salonika when the murder was committed and that he had informed some of those being held that he was about to undertake a "dangerous assignment." A cable from Gibson dated January 17 that reviews a conversation with Attorney General Constantinidis fills in further details regarding these arrests.[33] The police now hoped to prove through these new witnesses that Adam Mouzenidis was in Athens after the murder of George Polk, thus discrediting the statements about his death in March promulgated by the andarte radio. The authorities already had testimony from an unnamed druggist who claimed to have seen Adam Mouzenidis in Athens, and Adam's brother Stylianos had visited Athens on May 3 for the purpose, the authorities thought, of contacting persons in Athens connected with the Polk murder. For her part, Adam's wife Eudoxia had now testified that she did not believe that her husband had been killed, nor did she expect to hear that he had been, since "correspondence of Communist leaders with their families was prohibited." As far as she was concerned, Adam was still in the mountains. She also testified that she did not believe her husband had killed George Polk.

So the issue of Adam Mouzenidis's role was still alive, more testimony had to be taken from the new witnesses—under Major Mouskoundis's supervision, as it turned out—but Constantinidis did not expect the current phase of the investigation to cause much delay in getting the case to trial, now set for the middle of February. The more pressing problem was that of a new attitude that had appeared among the authorities in Athens. It seemed, said Constantinidis, that there was a campaign in progress to discredit the government's case against Gregory Staktopoulos and his mother. In fact, the attorney general of Athens (unnamed) had told Salonika Inquiry Magistrate Moustakis "that in his opinion the case was very weak," and a similar attitude had been expressed by the president of the Supreme Court. Constantinidis was therefore going to Athens "to endeavor to stop such statements."

Evidently with Raleigh Gibson's blessing. We learn from his covering memorandum that the intrigue was more complicated than Constantinidis himself knew. Mouskoundis (who, Gibson tells the secretary of state with no apparent cunning, "was mainly responsible for the solution of the case") reported to Gibson confidentially that he was encountering a certair lack of cooperation from the authorities in Athens and that "personal jealousies" of the Salonika authorities—and presumably of their success so far—"were being built up." Gibson felt that the tone of the conversation with Constantinidis also made it evident that the Salonika authorities thought Minister of Justice Melas was trying to enter into the case for personal glorification now that it was due to be tried. And Gibson himself had learned from a personal conversation with Minister of Justice Melas that the minister did not have a high regard for Mr. Constantinidis, in fact thought that Constantinidis, who was designated to prosecute the case, did not have the ability that the attorney general of Athens possessed, and Melas was therefore not at all pleased with the situation.

Despite these developments, Gibson concludes his commentary with a typically optimistic, unpenetrating opinion that "the trial will convince the press and the public of the United States that the correct solution has been obtained." At the same time, he feels that a delay in bringing Staktopoulos and his mother into court will weaken the Greek government's position before public opinion, and an even greater danger is the possibility that the minister of justice and other Athenian officials will allow petty jealousies to affect cooperation between various authorities, a thing that, if the press gets hold of it, will damage the government's position at the time of the trial. No questioning here about what else besides jealousy might have been behind the perception in Athens that the case was weak, and no evidence of any effort on Gibson's part to test Constantinidis and Mouskoundis regarding the increasing evidence of inconsistency and implausibility in the case against Gregory and Anna Staktopoulos, quite aside from that against the two missing Communist conspirators. Gibson's effort seems to be focused entirely on getting a trial before the public as quickly as possible, whatever the new and old ambiguities in the case.

Almost one month later (February 14), Constantinidis offered a further report on the progress he had made in this regard, and that turned out to be virtually no progress at all.[34] The latest phase of the investigation—the interrogation of Mouzenidis's relatives—had produced the news that the accused murderer Adam was in Salonika from August 1947 to February 1948, and in February had taken a trip to Prespa, where guerrilla headquarters were then located, in order to receive his orders "to arrange for the murder of George Polk"—though who reported this news is not specified. And we learn that Adam's brother Stylianos testified that Adam was in Salonika in April 1948 and had talked to him over the phone, in particular about his family's health. Finally, we learn that the unnamed druggist had testified that he had seen Adam Mouzenidis two days prior to the official statement issued in Salonika by the ministers of justice and public order regarding the solution of the Polk murder case. That is all. The gist of Constantinidis's interview had to do with the problem of how the trial should proceed: whether Mouzenidis and

Vasvanas, still absent, should be tried separately or whether all four of the accused conspirators should be tried together. If the latter, the activities of the Comintern [sic] would have to be brought out. If the former, people would ask why the two absent conspirators had not been placed on trial as well.

Gibson here showed signs of finally losing his patience, but not for the most important of reasons. The trial they were talking about, Gibson told the attorney general, was essentially a murder trial, and while the relation of the defendants with Communism would be brought up, the trial "is not against Communism." Still, replied Constantinidis, more facts were needed. The only evidence against Mouzenidis and Vasvanas was Staktopoulos's confession, and there was the nagging issue of Mouzenidis's reported death. Also, according to Greek law, if defendants were absent, a three-month period had to elapse before a trial could be held. Of course, said Constantinidis, it might be possible to change the law so that only a month's notice was required. Gibson here revealed his hand openly: "I stated that the recent investigations, while of great value, only corroborated the confession of Gregory Stahtopoulos [sic], and that further investigation was not of such importance that the trial should be delayed for that purpose."

This message evidently gave Constantinidis pause. He returned to the dialogue the following day in an apologetic mood.[35] He wanted to explain to the consul general in more detail why the trial had been delayed. For one, Minister of Justice Melas had wanted to violate judicial procedure by holding a conference with the Athens and Piraeus chiefs of police to see if the case could be strengthened, and Constantinidis had not been willing to go along with that. Then there had been a governmental crisis in Athens and the government, including Melas, had resigned. And at one and the same time, the Piraeus police were arresting Adam Mouzenidis's wife while the Athens police were declaring that a satisfactory trial could not be held on the basis of the evidence in hand. Finally, when the government was formed again and Melas was returned to his post, Constantinidis had taken a trip to Athens, had succeeded in convincing the skeptical authorities there that he had enough evidence to win the case in court, and had consequently been allowed to handle things as he saw fit.

That effectively sealed the doom of Gregory Staktopoulos. Raleigh Gibson clearly was not worried at this point about the quality of the evidence. Still showing some pique, his concern again was that there be a trial and that it take place as soon as possible. When Constantinidis returned to the question of a trial date, he reported that March now seemed unlikely because he thought a better jury, made up of men "of some educational background," might be picked in April, a jury that would be selected from all walks of life, though care would be taken to have "men who could understand logic and the presentation of the case." Gibson objected to a delay for that reason: a picked jury was "a very dangerous act," he said, one that the American press would surely uncover and that would result in a complete lack of confidence in the trial. Well, said Constantinidis, a March date would not allow enough time for all the preparations that were necessary, such as finding a large courtroom, giving the American newspapermen an opportunity to arrive in Greece, and so forth. Then there was the problem of the three months required by law for trying men in absentia. Finally, he simply didn't have sufficient evidence at the present time against Adam Mouzenidis, and though he did against the other three, he couldn't split up the trial into two parts without drawing heavy criticism from Greek circles.

Gibson evidently lost his patience again to the point of becoming undiplomatically blunt: there would be heavy criticism in the United States if the trial were delayed until May, three months hence. Not holding the trial in February had been a mistake; further postponement as now planned would be interpreted in the United States as a lack of desire on the part of the Greek government to bring the case to trial due to lack of evidence, a thing that would cause loss of confidence in the government's October 17 statement outlining the official solution. So Gibson couldn't agree with the attorney general's postponement plan; it was "a serious mistake." The "four-hour conversation" ended with the attorney general agreeing to reconsider his position. The following day he sent the consulate a "statement" declaring that the investigation of Staktopoulos and his mother had been brought to a close and these two would be tried most certainly by the end of March or the first days of April, dates that could have been earlier were it not for the necessity of providing the accused with "all means for their defense," including "appeals for a stay of the findings" to be issued by the relevant Salonika court.[36]

This statement, however accommodating, did not entirely pacify Gibson or serve to restore his full trust in Constantinidis, as we learn from a confidential letter the consul general sent William O. Baxter at the State Department the following day.[37] The letter was apparently occasioned in the first instance by Walter Lippmann's having suggested at one point the possibility of Staktopoulos's being a double agent. Gibson tells Baxter that it is rather difficult for him "to follow Mr. Lippmann's imagination" on the subject, because, from the evidence that has been secured regarding Staktopoulos's activities, Gibson is of the opinion that Staktopoulos "rates high in the Communist Party, and may even be one of the fairly high officials of the Party"—an opinion that speaks at best to Raleigh Gibson's enlarged capacity for suspending disbelief. The consul general does, however, add a caveat: after Baxter's having read the recent consulate dispatches concerning the dialogue with Constantinidis, "you will probably agree with me that it is difficult to know what the Greeks do or think."

The substance of the letter is given over to Gibson's recent dialogue with Constantinidis. We learn that after one of the attorney general's reasons for postponing the trial "would be argued away," he would come up with a new idea, and this, along with his plan to pick "a special jury to try the case," had led Gibson to state that the attorney general apparently did not have confidence in the evidence and in his capacity to secure a conviction. The recent trip to Athens had clearly influenced Constantinidis to think of further postponement, and he would likely want to do that still if means weren't employed to bolster up his courage, for example, by showing him clippings from American newspapers that would appear when the trial date was officially declared. These might also be used "as a weapon" to stop any attempt to postpone the date yet again. Gibson adds that he might need a statement of support from the State Department in order to help force the issue, but he hoped to be able to control the situation (while also hoping that "this does not turn out to be a conceited statement") even though the attorney general was in a position to have the Court of Appeals, as well as the Supreme Court, hold up its decision on Staktopoulos's appeal in order to gain time. That, says Gibson, is a matter that "can be handled by the Embassy through the Minister of Justice, if such an indication appears."

The pressure from American officials to get Staktopoulos into court and the pressure from Salonika authorities to delay the trial until further evidence had been gathered did not conceal a shared assumption that remained unstated: the conviction of Staktopoulos was essential to a resolution of the case. An aspect of Constantinidis's predicament was that this resolution had to be promoted within certain obvious legal requirements, in particular, the defendants' right to legal counsel. The State Department archives are so thin on this subject as to suggest that American officials in Greece considered Staktopoulos's legal defense entirely beyond their sphere of interest or influence. The one early reference we have to Staktopoulos's lawyers again points to a degree of ignorance or naiveté on the part of the Salonika consulate: in a late October cable, Gibson reports that two lawyers "have been engaged" by Staktopoulos, "both well known in Salonika for honesty and experience," one a "cousin" of the accused and the other a former deputy of the Liberal party and 1946 candidate of the Social Democratic party.[38] Beyond this, there is no comment at any point in the files on how these lawyers came to be chosen some months after Staktopoulos had been held incommunicado at Security Police headquarters or on how they performed in Staktopoulos's behalf during the six months before he and his mother were brought to trial. Our principal source for the progress of Staktopoulos's legal defense comes from his own recollection of the goings on at Security Police headquarters during these many months of his pretrial detention, the accused in virtual isolation the whole of the time.

According to Staktopoulos's account of these days in his book, he was given a brief respite after his confession of October 14. While Mouskoundis was on a trip to Athens, his chief torturer, Tsonos, offered Gregory ouzo, told him repeatedly not to worry because the Security Police were now behind him and only if something happened to nine million Greeks would something happen to him, and besides, the plan after the trial was to send him to Argentina where he would live a blessed life. When Mouskoundis returned from Athens, he called Gregory up from his cell to tell him that all was well, he had no need to be afraid of the court-martial he would have to face in due course, nor should he worry about what Mouskoundis might testify to in open court because a court-martial was a controlled affair, directed toward a specific purpose, and it was what Mouskoundis would say personally to the judges that really mattered. As for lawyers, Gregory need not worry about that aspect either. The Security Police would find him a lawyer. And one would be enough: What was the point of two or three lawyers anyway?

The first lawyer to show up at Security Police headquarters was the Staktopoulos "cousin," Iordanis Vafiadis, actually husband of his mother's cousin. Staktopoulos tells us that Vafiadis had been solicited to offer help by other worried relatives of Staktopoulos but was not allowed to visit the accused until after the official solution had been announced, and it was not until the third meeting—according to Staktopoulos's account—that he was allowed to see his client alone. At this meeting, Staktopoulos broke down and wept, then told all: his confessions were myths, fabrications, all lies, the result of horrible tortures, and he began naming the torturers. Vafiadis cut him short: "Don't start giving me names." Vafiadis refused to believe that the Security Police could be involved in rigging a case like that; the man was an extreme conservative, says Staktopoulos, a committed nationalist. The lawyer left abruptly.

After this scene, Mouskoundis warned Staktopoulos that he'd better be careful what he said inside Security Police headquarters, the walls had ears. When Vafiadis returned some days later, he had a second lawyer with him, one Nicolaos ("Nikos") Vassilikos, the former Liberal party deputy, described by Staktopoulos as an "agent" of the Security Police who had worked his way into the case by getting a rich Staktopoulos relative to designate him as the family's lawyer. During this visit, Staktopoulos, speaking in a whisper, repeated the torture charges and was greeted by heavy skepticism. The two lawyers returned together several times, but Vassilikos came a number of times alone. Staktopoulos says that he thinks he finally convinced these two that the confessions were a charade which had been played out after torture (he showed them the marks left on his body), but he also says that at one point the first lawyer, Vafiadis, warned him that the second, Vassilikos, was not to be trusted, and that a third lawyer would be brought into the case.

The third lawyer, Theodore Economou, president of the Salonika Lawyers Association (in effect, the Salonika bar), also proved to be a "committed nationalist" who was shocked when Staktopoulos suggested, again in a whisper, that he was not only innocent of any involvement in the Polk murder but considered the Security Police responsible for it. On this occasion Staktopoulos also denied that his mother had addressed the incriminating envelope mailed to the Third Police Precinct, and when he did so, Vafiadis revealed that indeed his mother had made the same denial to him personally, indicating that her "confession" to the contrary had emerged only after Mouskoundis persuaded her that it was the only way her son might be saved. Theodore Economou still could not believe that the Security Police would behave as Staktopoulos was suggesting. "We don't have Praetors here in Greece," Economou said. But he nevertheless promised to review what case documents were available.

As a result of this review, Staktopoulos tells us, Economou returned some days later to confront Mouskoundis and accuse him of having orchestrated a charade on orders from higher up. The Reuters stringer learned about this confrontation only years later, after his release from prison, because he didn't see Economou again in Security Police headquarters. Apparently Economou elected to withdraw from the case when Vassilikos recommended that the three lawyers now assigned to defend Staktopoulos plan their defense on the assumption that Staktopoulos was guilty in the terms he had confessed. Vafiadis finally went along with the plan, though Staktopoulos felt that the man's heart remained in the right place: as a man, essentially good but something of a coward, and as a lawyer, capable of handling misdemeanors and the like but not a case of these dimensions, "international in interest." Vafiadis did not reappear on the scene until shortly before the trial, while Vassilikos now became a frequent visitor at Security Police headquarters, evidently taking on the role of chief counsel for the defense.

This arrangement allowed room for further charades under Mouskoundis's direction. Staktopoulos reports that in the weeks following, he was made to confess, after more unspecified torture, that he had killed a major in the Greek army during the Occupation and had later fabricated the interview with Stalin that appeared in his newspaper. Also, at some point before the trial he was called on to change his original deposition regarding the last supper he had shared with Polk at the Luxembourg Café on a night when it had apparently rained hard enough to make that partially open-air restaurant with a garden an unlikely setting for their rendezvous, especially when no one working in the place was ready to testify that he had seen the two men there on that particular evening. The supper was now shifted to Staktopoulos's own home, a meal of lobster and peas prepared by his mother and followed by the killing of Polk, presumably with the aid of his Communist guerrilla conspirators who were then lurking in the neighborhood.

This new version of the old story never emerged into open court not because it was blatantly in conflict with confessions already on record but, according to Staktopoulos, because the last meal and the murder would have had to take place on the eve of a memorial service for a deceased uncle of his, an impossible occasion for him to have invited a foreign guest into his home for dinner, with or without murderous intent. And apparently when Vafiadis was called in by Attorney General Constantinidis and presented with a written text of this new deposition, he interrupted Constantinidis's account of the last supper in Staktopoulos's home to say: "Please. Enough is enough." Constantinidis reportedly answered: "Since you, Mr. Vafiadis, can't accept this confession by Staktopoulos, we will not take it into consideration." Staktopoulos remembers Vafiadis coming to visit him to reprimand him for having confessed to the assassination of a Greek army officer and the fake Stalin interview, deeds against the nation that Vafiadis said would now make it impossible for anything to save either him or his family. Staktopoulos told him then that he couldn't have done otherwise, he simply couldn't stand any more torture, in fact had tried to commit suicide twice in recent days by cutting his wrist, once with the sharpened metal tip of his shoelace, once with a button he'd honed against the wall of his cell—and he showed his lawyer the raw slash marks of his failed efforts.

By the time of the trial Mouskoundis had apparently convinced Staktopoulos that the only way he could save his mother from a sentence for conspiracy was by going along with whatever case was made against him at the trial once his confession, however revised, was offered as evidence in court. Staktopoulos tells us that Mouskoundis also convinced Anna Staktopoulos that her acknowledging the address on the Third Police Precinct envelope to be in her handwriting was the one thing that might save her son from a death sentence.

For his part, Constantinidis appears to have gained immensely in confidence as the trial approached, his case evidently bolstered by certain confessions taken from relatives of Adam Mouzenidis that now began to emerge from Security Police headquarters and that were duly transmitted to the authorities in Athens. By early March, Raleigh Gibson was able to report to the secretary of state that during a consultation trip to Athens he had met with Minister of Justice Melas in the lobby of the Grande Bretagne Hotel and had been informed that Melas had changed his opinion of Attorney General Constantinidis and now felt that "he was a shrewd man and capable of prosecuting the murder trial."[39] And a week or so later (March 9), when Gibson spoke to Constantinidis himself, he not only found the attorney general demonstrating greater confidence in the government's case but evidently also found reason to expect that this confidence would increase (Gibson's account of the interview offers hints that the case against Vasvanas was now gaining strength from the testimony of a fellow saboteur and that against Mouzenidis from the testimony of Anna Molyvda, sister to Mouzenidis's wife, Eudoxia, and apparently Mouzenidis's occasional mistress).[40]

An official statement from Constantinidis on March 14 set the trial for April 12, with Staktopoulos, Vasvanas, and Mouzenidis charged with the murder of George Polk and the illegal possession of firearms, while Anna Staktopoulos was now charged merely with complicity in the murder.[41] Three weeks later (April 10), Gibson could cable the State Department that the attorney general "considers he has an airtight case."[42] Gibson reported that Staktopoulos had now confessed that Polk ate at his home on the night of the murder and that his mother had served the meal. She was told on Sunday morning that Polk had been murdered, but Staktopoulos still maintained that Polk was shot in a boat, presumably in keeping with his other confessions. And Anna Molyvda had now confessed to being the liaison between Mouzenidis, Vasvanas, and Staktopoulos and to having found refuge for Mouzenidis and Vasvanas near Staktopoulos's home on the day of the murder. Security Police headquarters in Salonika were evidently producing lively results.

There had been only one hitch in the effort to create a tight schedule for the trial after Constantinidis's confident March 14 announcement: Gregory and Anna Staktopoulos had decided to exercise their right of appeal to the Council of Judges against the Council's decision to charge them respectively with murder and complicity in murder. In the appeal, the petitioner argued, presumably through the lawyers for the defense, that he had offered a "sincere confession" of his activities aimed at simply facilitating the newsgathering mission "insistently planned and prepared long ago" by George Polk.[43] He never expected that the weight of a crime organized and committed by others would be placed on his shoulders. Nowhere, argued the petition, had the investigation uncovered proof that the petitioner was an accessory before the fact; nowhere was there evidence of a previous understanding regarding the crime of murder between him and the actual perpetrators of the crime. And his participation after the fact was "under the influence of threats against him." Also, the indictment had brought up unrelated matters that created "an unfavorable spirit of prejudice" against him, such as the murder of an army officer, Major Meligris, during the Occupation and the fake interview with Stalin. Then—the petition pointed out—there had been mistakes in the investigation itself, for example, the linking of the petitioner to arrangements in Athens for Polk's trip to Markos at a time when Polk was outside Greece and when the petitioner, far from spending his time making contacts with Communist leaders, had, according to the testimony of his lady friend Maria Miha, spent the day in question in her company, from 10:00 A.M. to 8:00 P.M. And the investigation had nowhere demonstrated that the petitioner's mother, Anna Staktopoulos, had any knowledge of the crime of murder before the fact or had come into any contact with the perpetrators of the crime; yet the Council's decree had referred her to trial as an accomplice in the murder of George Polk.

Though this appeal of March 17 affirmed the "sincerity" of Staktopoulos's confession—an incredible concession on the part of his defense lawyers—it was nevertheless rejected by the Council of Judges two days later, after the Council had sat in "the chamber of consultations" with Attorney General Constantinidis present.[44] It appears that Constantinidis's "written proposition" presented to the judges became the principal text invoked in the Council's notice of rejection. Here it is argued that the "complaints" of Gregory and Anna Staktopoulos are not "well-founded." Far from having a timid character that was incapable of participating in a crime, says the notice, Gregory Staktopoulos was the graduate of a school for high-ranking Communist leaders and had imposed on other journalists an agreement of "non-collaboration with noncommunist journalist" when EAM was in power (presumably during the Occupation). The notice claims that Staktopoulos's "evil personality" was amply demonstrated in other ways. The sole fact of his having known about the murder of Polk yet having failed to communicate his knowledge to the authorities condemned him in this regard. And his confession was—one assumes no mockery intended—"neither sincere nor spontaneous." While the inquiry had been facing hardships and difficulties, he had silently "followed with sullen cynicism its hard task," even after his own newspaper began running a front-page request for information from any source to help solve the mystery of Polk's undoing (the notice indicates that *Makedonia* ran its banner request from the first days of August, but the newspaper's archives reveal that it actually first appeared on August 10, just four days before Staktopoulos was picked up to be held in solitary confinement at Security Police headquarters, and that it ran until September 2).

The rejection notice goes on to tell us that Staktopoulos broke his silence only when he found himself "under the pressure of facts" (this phrase not yet as radiant with irony as it was to become), in particular, the report from the graphologists indicating that the address on the envelope containing Polk's "identity book" was in his mother's handwriting. The guerrilla radio had tried to claim that Major Mouskoundis replaced the original envelope with the one prepared by him and bearing the handwriting of Staktopoulos's mother, but "this assertion alone gives unquestionable proof" of the justness of the case against the two petitioners, since it is undeniable that the envelope in the hands of the inquiry was the one submitted to the experts and the one posted by Staktopoulos. In view of this and the rest exposed by the attorney general's "proposition" and the contacts and actions of Staktopoulos "as testified by the actual facts and the data contained in the lawsuit file," the Council concludes that Staktopoulos was "an actual party to the crime" and Anna Staktopoulos "a collaborator" in it.

The casual reasoning in this document, relying heavily on Staktopoulos's dubious credentials as a Communist leader and on the "facts" in his confession, anticipates that of the trial, as does some of the document's rhetoric, in particular, certain passages meant to ring loudly with appropriate political overtones. We are told at one point that (as translated by the consulate) "nobody could feel deeper sorrow for the criminal taking of the life of a distinguished and heroic son of the country towards which the thoughts of all of us are turned with gratitude, than the Greek soul, which felt the pain very deeply indeed, because in our country hospitality amounts to religion and our forefathers held strangers under the protection of their highest God." As it turns out, says the notice, the crime was planned and carried out "by people who are in serfdom to other nations" and who have exploited the traditional respect for every stranger in "an improper and unholy manner" that is "unfair to a people shedding lavishly their blood in order to keep burning, under the heavy dark clouds surrounding the Universe at large, the fire, which being reinforced, would set aside the powers of darkness and render freedom and peace to the world." But "happily, the responsible quarters of the friendly United States" recognized the "sincere efforts of the competent authorities to find the authors of this horrible crime," and this is "the best reward and justification" for those who had been assigned the task of seeing that justice was done. "Hellenic Justice, in carrying out its duty in conformity with the traditions which are sacred to it, kept open the doors of the inquiry, in all possible directions . . . etc."

The reasoning and the rhetoric of this document evidently worked to persuade Staktopoulos's lawyers that the assurance they had given Constantinidis in mid-March that Staktopoulos would not take the further step of appealing to the Supreme Court was a just assurance.[45] The stage was thus set for the final act in the courthouse, which brought most of the absent participants back to town—Kosta Hadjiargyris, Helen Mamas, Winston Burdett, "Wild Bill" Donovan—along with a number of foreign newcomers, including George Polk's brother, William. The only principal missing was Rea Polk, urged to return in the first and last instance by Attorney General Constantinidis, but also by Minister of Justice Melas, Ambassador Grady, and finally the director of Near Eastern and African Affairs in the State Department. Rea remained at Barnard College, protected by the college physician and General Donovan[46] from witnessing the bizarre trial that ended up acquitting Anna Staktopoulos of complicity in the crime, while at the same time condemning Gregory Staktopoulos, partly on the basis of his mother's testimony, to prison for life.

IX The Trial

THE TRIAL OF GREGORY and Anna Staktopoulos began on April 12 and ended on April 21, a date that now remains in the Greek consciousness not because of what happened to these two unfortunate defendants but because, eighteen years later, it marked the beginning of a seven-year dictatorship during which two of the principal judicial participants in the Polk affair, Komotouros and Moustakis, served on the Supreme Court at a time when Greek justice underwent a continually severe testing that it largely failed. Both men were clearly on their way up in 1948, and the outcome of the Polk affair was no doubt crucial to their advancement. Both had been present when Gregory Staktopoulos offered his official confession on October 1 and had sometimes been present during his subsequent revisions of that confession. And Moustakis, as attorney general of the Court of the First Instance in Salonika, signed the official indictment that became the basis of Attorney General Constantinidis's case in court.

The fifty-page translation of the indictment transmitted to the State Department by Raleigh Gibson on April 19[1] does not add much to our knowledge of facts in the case, or even to our assumptions, because it closely follows the official line that Constantinidis developed in presenting his long argument against the Staktopoulos appeal in late March. But through its misreading of certain documents in the affair and its hypothetical reconstructions of motive and action, the indictment adds nuances that should have roused the suspicions not only of Raleigh Gibson but of those presumably objective observers attending the trial, most of all the American press representatives (these included, along with Donovan and William Polk, Edgar Clark for United Press, A. C. Sedgwick for the *New York Times*, Barrett McGurn for the *New York Herald Tribune*, Winston Burdett and Alexander Kendrick for CBS, and Constantine Poulos for the Overseas News Agency).[2]

The letter from Polk to Murrow occasioned two instances of misreading on the part of the Greek officials, what could be passed off as simply a matter of bad translation were it not for the fact that Raleigh Gibson and other American officials were on hand to provide an accurate reading. Moustakis, in attempting to pin Hadjiargyris to the wall, tells us in the indictment that Hadjiargyris must have known well in advance about Polk's planned trip to Markos since Polk indicates in the Murrow letter that he had been thinking about the trip since 1946, two years before his fatal visit to Salonika. What Polk actually writes Murrow is that "since 1946 I've not had a contact with the Greek Communist Party that I believed was a real contact."[3] And later in the indictment, attempting to answer the claims of the guerrilla radio that Polk had spoken favorably about "Markos' rebellious movements," Moustakis asks how it was really possible for Polk to have done so when "we have a letter written, in his own handwriting [in fact typewritten], on the very day of his death, in which he calls Markos' government a 'gang of bandits.' " The terms that Polk actually uses are "the Markos government crowd" and "the Markos gang," the latter term offered in the context of Polk's interest in trying to get "really factual information" about the guerrilla government's objectives.

But there are more important distortions in the document if one sees it in the light of confessions forced out of the accused and revised in keeping with a changing police scenario of the crime, one that appears to have perplexed the prosecution at moments almost as much as it did the defense attorneys and a few cooler, more objective witnesses to Staktopoulos's account of things. The accused emerges from the document as a villain not merely sinister and cowardly but grotesque. He kept the secret of his participation in the crime for weeks, and when he was finally brought in by the police (we now learn that it became evident to the police that a certain "person" was Polk's Salonika contact but this person was not called in for even a routine inquiry "so that he would not suspect that there were certain suspicions against him"), Staktopoulos "pretended full ignorance of everything." His "impertinent and reckless attitude" was finally "smashed" when he was persuaded that his mother had disclosed that she, at his suggestion, had written the address on the envelope in which Polk's identity card was mailed to the police and when he "heard the news of the graphological survey and chemical examination of the ink" that demonstrated the ink to be the same as what the police found in his inkwell at home. Still, says the indictment, Staktopoulos continued to hide certain facts, and he presented other data different from the way events had actually taken place. This proved beyond doubt that he "had not played an unimportant and unconscious role" in the murder of Polk but, on the contrary, had participated "intentionally and deliberately in a skillfully organized plan" to commit the crime. Otherwise, why did he restrict himself to naming only Mouzenidis and Vasvanas as accomplices? His motive obviously was to protect himself at some point in the future before the Communist party, when he would be able to say that Mouzenidis and Vasvanas hadn't suffered from his revelations because they had safely returned to the mountains, while he had been careful not to betray any of the other still unidentified Communist conspirators involved in the murder. Staktopoulos clearly possessed "shrewd and devilish ways." Why else implicate Helen Mamas and then deny the implication? Why else initially conceal his preliminary contacts with Mouzenidis and Vasvanas? The man, says the indictment, played loose with the truth most perniciously, and this was the essential proof of his guilt.

The rest of the document outlines the evidence that confirms what the prosecution chooses to see as the partial truth that Staktopoulos has confessed, despite his shifty soul, including details that appeared to be confirmed by the autopsy, the graphology report, or the testimony of other witnesses—details that Staktopoulos tells us showed up in his confession when appropriate because they were fed him by his Security Police tormentors. We learn from the indictment, for example, that Staktopoulos confessed to Vasvanas's forbidding Polk to take his camera with him on the trip, and indeed, says the indictment, the camera was found in Polk's hotel room, while his pajamas were found to be missing from the hotel room, this in keeping with Vasvanas's instructions, as confessed by the Reuters stringer, that Polk take his pajamas along on the trip.

On the other hand, the document indicates, one cannot trust other parts of Staktopoulos's confession, for example, his having shared a last meal with Polk at the seaside Luxembourg Café on a night when it was raining. Staktopoulos was not so naive, the indictment suggests, as to have appeared in public with Polk just before the man was to be killed. Had he not consciously avoided eating with Polk, Helen Mamas, and the others at the Olympus-Naoussa restaurant on Friday evening and confessed to lurking outside instead, then followed Polk's steps from afar so as not to be seen, "exactly as a common murderer does in following his victim"? His only motive for proposing the "cunning idea" of the Luxembourg Café was so that he could use the very argument that spoke against the truth of this confession, namely, that had he known a murder was in the offing, he wouldn't have been naive enough to show himself with Polk in a place as public as that restaurant and then follow the victim into a rowboat. The Luxembourg Café business, we are told, was clearly a way of covering the true occasion for the meal he shared somewhere else with Polk and the other Communist conspirators besides the two he actually named.

But the indictment finds that the rest of Staktopoulos's confession is not only supported by independent evidence—for example, the autopsy confirms that Polk was shot from the back, in keeping with Staktopoulos's account of the murder—but it serves to explain certain unusual aspects of the hard evidence available to the police. The loose binding of the victim before the murder, for instance, makes sense only as the kind of "security" measure that the Reuters stringer said his co-conspirators requested, and the presence of money and certain identifying items on the body at the same time that some items were found to be missing—such as Polk's notebook and appointment calendar—coincides neatly with Staktopoulos's explanation of the search conducted by Mouzenidis after the murder. And Polk's willingness to be blindfolded is explained by his having told Edward R. Murrow that he "had decided to meet Markos even blindfolded": Why should he then refuse to be blindfolded "when he saw approaching the realization of his ardent desire," as Staktopoulos had described Polk's state of mind in the rowboat? And why would he be suspicious or worried? Hadn't Hadjiargyris testified that Polk "had confidence in newsmen"?—and here he was in a boat with a journalist colleague beside him.

The indictment establishes the envelope mailed to the Third Police Precinct as the central clue to the guilt of both Staktopoulos and his mother, Anna. The document poses the rhetorical question: Why hadn't Staktopoulos's newspaper *Makedonia* published a photograph of the incriminating envelope along with that of Polk's identity card, as other Salonika newspapers had when Polk's body was discovered? The answer: surely because Staktopoulos prevented that particular photo from appearing in his paper out of fear that his mother, who read *Makedonia* regularly, would see it and worry about being arrested. The indictment does not tell us how the Reuters stringer managed to keep the photo out of the paper, but it states that "not publishing the photo in 'Macedonia' was one of the first elements of suspicion against Stahtopoulos [*sic*]," as the analysis of the handwriting on the envelope became "one of the most interesting and unshakable elements not only of an indication but of a full proof of the participation of Stahtopoulos and his mother in the murder." In the case of Anna, the indictment does not accept the old lady's statement that she could not recall what explanation her son gave her for not writing the address himself. She is pictured as having agreed beforehand with the perpetrators of the crime to offer her help after the fact by way of addressing the envelope that would carry Polk's identity card to the Third Police Precinct and is therefore to be tried as an accomplice, though not on the charge of bearing firearms, there being insufficient evidence of that. At the same time, the prosecutor asks that the state not be required to pay any indemnity to Anna for having been imprisoned on that now annulled charge.

It appears from the Draft Report that those who were given the task of initially preparing General Donovan's response to the indictment that would presumably be included in the Lippmann Committee's final report on the case encountered some difficulty in accounting for the indictment's plausibility—and their failure to make a strong case for it as a coherent and convincing legal document may in part account for Donovan's decision in the end not to submit the Draft Report to the committee. The indictment is here described as "a strange mixture of solid realistic police reasoning on the one hand and an extraordinary naiveté and occasional factual and logical lapses on the other."[4] And after a long excerpt from the document, we find the line: "This type of reasoning, exhibiting a mixture of fact and fancy, logic and illogic, is apparent through the balance of the indictment." But this line is then crossed out, and in its place we are given: "The balance of the indictment consists of. . . ." Another line telling us that "the great bulk of the other corroborating evidence relied upon in showing conclusively the veracity of Staktopoulos's version of the crime would seem to be at least open to some question because of its essentially 'ex post facto' nature" has been altered to read: ". . . Staktopoulos' version of the crime concern [sic] facts which were known to the authorities prior to Staktopoulos' confession and which would have been deliberately included by Staktopoulos in his confession in order to enhance its credibility."

There is no expressed suspicion in the Draft Report of who besides Staktopoulos might have done the including or what motive might be impelling those who were feeding him ex post facto information. After offering some examples of ex post facto evidence, a line of thought that had vaguely begun to lead the drafters in the right direction is crossed out: "While none of these examples raises any inference that Staktopoulos was *not* telling the truth, it is strange that they should be given the weight attributed to them in the indictment without any indication on the part of the authorities of their awareness of the fact that even if Staktopoulos was not telling the truth, he would embellish his story with facts which would accord with information already available to the authorities and undoubtedly known to Staktopoulos at the time of his interrogation." The Draft Report finally does not consider the possibility that this embellishment is less strange if one assumes that it occurred under the persuasion of those very authorities who gave these ex post facto details such weight in the indictment.

Another clue in the Draft Report calls forth a marginal exclamation from Theodore G. Lambron. When the report indicates that "the indictment apparently ignores the fact that Bigart had actually the same intention [as Polk] to visit Markos and, unlike Polk, had succeeded in doing so," "TGL" comments in capital script: "BIGART WENT TO MARKOS VIA COMMUNIST YUGOSLAVIA AND NOT VIA GREECE." The report's handling of the indictment then concludes on a defensive note: "The argumentative and evidentiary nature of the indictment, while strange to American lawyers, is characteristic of such documents not only in Greece but in all civil law countries. Its political overtones, its lengthy justifications of Greek national honor and its vigorous defense of the conduct of the Greek investigatory authorities is perhaps not surprising in the light of the life and death struggle confronting Greece at the time. Similarly [sic] its attempt to make credible an incredible story and the absence of more substantial corroborative evidence must be evaluated in the same light."

The indictment does indeed conform to other documents in the case in allowing itself to indulge generously in editorializing, with ample argument as to why the Communists rather than the right wing were responsible for the murder, and it also adds a passing note of appreciation for the "objectivity and clearsightedness" of Raleigh Gibson, who "perceived the sincere and continuous efforts of all the competent authorities," even at times when no progress was being made in the investigation, and thus served to counter charges in the American press not only of bias on the part of the police but of their actually having participated in the murder through their agents. Raleigh Gibson returned this favorable notice from the judicial authorities in due course by telling the gathered press at the end of the trial that the "judicial part of [the] case was prepared with care and efficiency, and [the] trial was one that can be remembered with pride. All judicial officials are to be complimented."[5] His views were not fully shared by others who observed the event—seen from the perspective of normal American court procedure, some found the occasion a circus—but Gibson's image of the trial prevailed in the long run, becoming the basis for what quickly grew into a whitewash not only of the trial but of the Polk affair more generally. What the counter-image revealed was inadequate investigation, incomplete evidence, discrepancies in testimony, grossly deficient cross-examination, badgering of witnesses, leading questions from the judges, pervasive admission of hearsay, persistent solicitation of opinions—whether specific or general—by judges and jury and even defense lawyers, free expatiation on these by the same, intervention for questions at any moment by judges, jury members, prosecutor, lawyers for the defense, and defendants, total freedom for rhetoric of any kind from all but the spectators, though in particular from the defense lawyers, who drew on the full range of the three-thousand-year-old Greek tradition in presenting their woefully insufficient, prejudiced, sometimes incoherent and often boring defense pronouncements and summaries.

The trial took place in a courtroom described by Winston Burdett as "a bare, unattractive rectangle, without draperies or curtains."[6] The walls were freshly painted, but the only decoration, according to Burdett, was "a cheap Byzantine icon of Christ" that hung behind the president of the three-man bench of judges. The jury consisted of ten taxpayers selected from a group of twenty names placed in a box, with the prosecuting attorney and the accused (through his attorneys) each having the right to five peremptory challenges. The selection was made by lot, and "according to Greek law," from what Burdett described as "well-to-do citizens . . . from the higher levels of Salonika business and professional society," specifically—according to Gibson's account[7]—two lawyers, two doctors, a dentist, a merchant, a professor, a bank employee, a municipal employee, and a notary public, with a druggist and restaurant owner as alternates. There was disagreement among the trial observers regarding the jury selection, which apparently took only fifteen minutes. Gibson tells the State Department that there had been "some discussion" among American correspondents on the issue, and he seemed afraid that Constantine Poulos of the Overseas News Agency "may hint that the jury was hand-picked."[8] But "the defense lawyer [identified earlier as Vassilikos] appeared to be satisfied on this point,"[9] and fortunately for the local officials, General Donovan, speaking as the representative of one important segment of the American press, stated in an interview on opening day that the "case was well prepared" and informed Gibson that he was "satisfied with conduct of trial."[10]

The Draft Report suggests that Donovan was also satisfied with the jury selection. It describes the jury, quite inaccurately, as representing "a typical cross-section of the Greek citizenry," though in fact it did not include any representatives from the two largest categories of Greek citizenry, farmers and laborers, and it goes on to say that "some American correspondents raised the question of whether the jury had been hand picked because of the short time consumed in its selection," but after the customary practice under Greek civil law of jury selection by lot was explained to them, "they expressed themselves as satisfied with the fairness of its selection," as we assume Donovan was himself.[11]

Following the selection of the jury, the morning session of the first day was devoted to the reading of documents. All the witnesses in the case were called in to hear the indictment, the appeal by the two Staktopoulos defendants, and the rejection of their appeal. Burdett tells us that Staktopoulos—"a sharp-faced, stoop-shouldered" man of thirty-nine—and his mother ("an old woman, 68")[12] sat on a hard black bench in the well of the courtroom listening silently to the rhetoric we have seen from the attorneys for both the prosecution and the defense, the two sides sharing the assumption that the murder was committed by the Communists and that the only real issue was the degree of complicity on the part of the two defendants. When the name of Rea Polk was called as a witness and she did not appear, one of the two defense lawyers (Vassilikos) asked for a postponement of the trial on the grounds that she was an essential witness.[13] Attorney General Constantinidis, responding as prosecutor, stated that she would appear in due course, and though the president of the court then read a telegram from the Greek ambassador in Washington indicating that Rea would arrive in Salonika, Vassilikos didn't consider that sufficient: he wanted to know if she had actually left the States. She had not, but the judges voted in any case to refuse his request for postponement.

The absence of Rea Polk subsequently became a focal center of Vassilikos's defense argument, just as it had been a focal center of Attorney General Constantinidis's complaint in his pretrial dialogue with Raleigh Gibson, where it had appeared to be largely a defensive maneuver while the trial was still being delayed. What Rea Polk might have added to the ample testimony she had already given the authorities in Greece one cannot say, but the failure of both the Greek police and the American embassy to follow up on her September conversations with William E. Colby suggests that had her account of meeting with Staktopoulos over the issue of a story about her husband's disappearance somehow entered the court record, it would not have much diminished the progress of the official solution in the Polk affair. And in any case, by the time of the trial General Donovan had seen to it that Rea's wish to be released from her obligation to return to Greece had received the endorsement of the medical authorities at Barnard College, and that served to keep her where she was.

The afternoon session was given over to the trial of the two absent defendants, Adam Mouzenidis and Evangelos Vasvanas. Evidently it was determined that no jury was needed for this phase of the prosecution, because the jury was excused.[14] What emerged from this session that still remains a matter of controversy in the Polk affair is the apparently incriminating testimony of Anna Molyvda, sister-in-law to Adam Mouzenidis and his sometime mistress.[15] Before she took the stand, an Athens druggist was called in to testify that he had seen Mouzenidis in Athens on August 16, 1948, at Kaningos Square, and had called out to him, but Mouzenidis, who appeared to be growing a moustache, did not stop to acknowledge his greeting. A "Surrendered Bandit Leader" named Zafiriou then took the stand to report that he had seen Mouzenidis in March 1948 and that Mouzenidis had told him he was about to undertake a difficult and dangerous mission. Zafiriou expressed his opinion that the Communist party had planned the murder of Polk—"I am deeply convinced in my heart of it"—and that Mouzenidis was entrusted with the mission of carrying it out. George Drossos of UNSCOB then appeared in court to testify that he had received a message from Salonika Chief of Police Xanthopoulos a few days before Polk's murder to the effect that Vasvanas and other terrorists would "like to commit [a] crime against members of UNSCOB." He also remembered that at the time the guerrilla radio was urging Communists in the towns to be more active— this during the days when Minister of Justice Ladas was assassinated. Then a member of the Athens Security Police gave an account of the useful information that had been gathered from Adam Mouzenidis's relatives, Anna Molyvda and Adam's brother Stylianos in particular. These two then appeared to complete the afternoon session and the case against the two missing culprits.

Anna Molyvda took the stand to tell a curious tale, the curiosity of it in part its brevity for a deposition so crucial in condemning two of the suspects and in adding measurably to the case against a third. And the tone—at least in transcript—seemed almost laconic, as though the witness wanted to report as quickly as she could only what she had to before being allowed to go her way—which, given her testimony, could well have meant straight back to jail. She tells us that Adam was her brother-in-law and that since 1947 she had "stayed with him and accompanied him everywhere," though not, it appears, to the mountains, where Mouzenidis had another companion, Efstathiou, described by one unidentified questioner as "wife of Mouzenidis, when Mouzenidis was in hiding," presumably to distinguish her from Anna Molyvda's sister, who was Mouzenidis's wife when he was not in hiding and when he was not traveling with Anna.

The two lovers, Adam and Anna, evidently traveled together frequently: to Patras, to Salonika, to Athens, back to Salonika, back to

Athens, and so forth until certain conspiratorial meetings in Salonika during the spring of 1948, soon after one "Kosta," otherwise unidentified, was mentioned within Anna's hearing. A rendezvous took place during these days with "two persons" whom Anna observed but without overhearing anything they said—persons "unknown" to her, though "he" [presumably Adam] had met one of them before. At this time Adam was staying with a Molyvdas relative at the YMCA in Salonika.[16] Anna brought her lover food and clean clothes, then took him to his brother's house, where he stayed three days. "From there I accompanied him to a rendezvous where he met the first person mentioned above. This time I heard, 'The rowboat is OK,' and I saw Stahtopoulos [sic] and perhaps I saw Polk." Another rendezvous was fixed, and on Saturday, May 8, at 7:00 P.M., Anna tells us that she accompanied Mouzenidis "to meet the same two at Salonika." She "left them there"—the "there" never identified—and had not seen Adam since, though she saw his picture in the paper, along with "the other person's who was Vasvanas." End of her testimony.

The only recorded cross-examination has the attorney general asking Anna where Mouzenidis hid out in August 1947, that is, eight months before the murder. We learn from her that he hid out in Efstathiou's home, and at the YMCA, where he was not welcome in the beginning but later became so. Other testimony had already established that Efstathiou, Mouzenidis's "wife" while he was in hiding, had been executed by a military court in March 1948, presumably because she had harbored a Communist enemy of the state and had acted as liaison for him. Anna Molyvda was now in exactly the same position, and her testimony could well place others—including Mouzenidis's brother—in like jeopardy. This death threat held over Anna Molyvda by the authorities, and the assumption that she had been subject during her incarceration to much the same treatment that Staktopoulos had received during his, provide Hadjiargyris with the explanation he offers for what he takes to be Anna's perjury here, false witness that served to condemn two men to death in absentia and that hardened the case against the third alleged conspirator, Gregory Staktopoulos.

The second key witness of the afternoon session, Adam's brother Stylianos, a local dentist, did not provide any significant new facts, but he did offer several opinions that were hardly helpful to Adam's case, even with an acknowledgment that Adam had worked three years to provide for his brother's education (a debt that Stylianos had partially repaid while Adam was in hiding). Stylianos spoke of Adam's comings and goings in 1947 and 1948 and of warning his brother that his staying with relatives in Salonika exposed those relatives to danger. He became particularly worried after a phone call from Adam in April 1948 inquiring about Adam's children. Stylianos then decided to move on to Athens, where he visited Adam's wife and children and eventually heard about his brother's involvement in the Polk affair. When arrested by the police, he and other relatives "testified sincerely and clearly before the authorities all we knew."

But beyond what he knew, Stylianos offered some opinions. Though he acknowledged his brother to be a "dynamic" Communist leader, he could not believe that he was guilty of the odious crime he was accused of having committed. Stylianos allowed, on the other hand, that Adam had given his whole life to Communism and "could not ignore or disobey orders given him by the Party." Reminded by the president of the court of what Anna Molyvda had testified to, Stylianos replied that he did not have a "single doubt that the crime was committed and that his brother was a participant," but he still couldn't believe that his brother would use a firearm to kill "an innocent person, a friend of Greece." Yet again, since the conspiracy was ordered by the Communist party, "something inside [him]" told him that Adam "could not refuse to carry out even that order." And when the attorney general asked Stylianos if one could rely on the testimony of Anna Molyvda, Stylianos answered succinctly: "Yes, you may. Annoula would do whatever Adam would ask of her."

The translated transcript of this first day's work in court ends simply with Raleigh Gibson's signature, but in a cable transmitted on the day the session actually took place, Gibson tells the secretary of state that the afternoon trial "proved that Mouzenides [sic] and Vasvanas were in Salonika on May 8, day of the murder,"[17] a conclusion hardly justified by the text of the transcript that he submitted a day later. His one-line report on Anna Molyvda's testimony also creates a distorted image of the "proof" she provided: "Anna Molyvdash [sic], liaison of Adam Mouzenides, stated that Mouzenides said in her presence night before the murder 'We've got the rowboat.' " The transcript itself does not identify who made the remark, quoted there as "The rowboat is OK"; but more important, Anna's vague reference to Polk ("perhaps I saw Polk") is suspicious enough to have called for cross-examination, and one can say the same for other aspects of her laconic testimony. Raleigh Gibson either swallowed that testimony whole or felt obliged after the first day to begin painting a picture of the goings on in Salonika that would conform with his pretrial opinion, formed as early as January 17, that "the trial will convince the press and the public of the United States that the correct solution has been obtained."[18]

Helen Mamas, the principal witness during the morning session of the second day, was not prepared to swallow a thing, including some of the modes of trial behavior she was meant to accept. Her testimony, and her sometimes feisty response to badgering questions, began with an account of her relation to Staktopoulos, Polk, Rea Polk, Hadjiargyris, and others that conforms to what she said in her several depositions while the investigation was under way the previous summer.[19] She knew Staktopoulos as a "professional newsreporter representing the opposition," had never discussed politics with him, usually talked to him for only five or ten minutes. During her first meeting with Polk in Salonika on Friday, May 7, she asked the CBS correspondent to take a package with him "for my folks" when he returned to the States in late May, and during the same meeting he asked her if she had any friends who were Communist agents. She replied no, she worked only through official Greek channels—and she reaffirmed that Polk did not tell her that he was planning a trip to interview Markos.

During her second meeting with Polk for cocktails in the Mediterranean Hotel bar, when she introduced Staktopoulos to Polk and the others with him, "there was no indication proving that Stahtopoulos [sic] knew any of the party," a thing she remembered "very well." Staktopoulos sat with them for a few minutes, declined to take a drink, then called during the dinner at the Olympus-Naoussa that evening to check out the names of the visiting journalists, "except Polk." She herself did not see Polk again after the dinner group split up that evening. When Rea reached Salonika the following week, she and Don Matchen tried during the rest of the week "to calm her down, though ourselves were uneasy" about Polk's disappearance, and after the body was discovered, Raleigh Gibson asked Mamas to go with him to break the sad news to Rea, which she did, then took Rea to stay with her in her room, and during the days following tried to comfort Rea as best she could.

Mamas's testimony was interrupted at this point by a barrage of questions, reconstructed here from the consulate's rather awkward and sometime incoherent translation:

Attorney General Constantinidis: Did you ask Mr. Gibson whether the crime was perpetrated by anarchists?

Mamas: Mrs. Polk was hysterical, and she asked him who had committed the crime: "the Nationalists"? Mr. Gibson assured her to the contrary.

Constantinidis: Did Mrs. Polk tell you that George had told her he wanted to contact the Communists?

Mamas: No, she didn't. She told me Polk had presentiments about the future and sometimes told Rea he would not see California again. He handed her certain identity cards, then wept, cried like a baby, Rea said.

Constantinidis: When did this take place?

Mamas: A week before Polk left Athens, at the time she and Polk had a small quarrel.

Mamas then goes on to tell about Rea's being unable to sleep because of her own presentiments about her husband, then about Mamas's own tribulations as the result of Staktopoulos bringing her into the case and offering "fantastic information," including his claim that she was acquainted with some fifteen Communists she knew not at all, as was proven by those she was made to face before the authorities, all of whom denied knowing her. So she wrote Staktopoulos a letter that gave him "friendly advice to tell the truth."

Attorney for the Defense: Did Staktopoulos ask you why Polk came to Northern Greece?

Mamas: No.

Attorney for the Defense: Did you meet Staktopoulos the evening before Polk's body was discovered?

Mamas: I don't remember.

President of the Court: May I help you? Did you meet him on your way to the TAE airlines office?

Mamas: Yes, now I remember. I was waiting for my fiancé Zotos and I saw Staktopoulos on the other side of the street. He came over and said: hello, where are you going? I said jokingly: I'm going to meet George Polk.

President of the Court: Why did you write that letter [to Staktopoulos]?

Mamas: To clarify my position and, secondly, to appeal to Staktopoulos to tell the truth.

President of the Court: Did you meet Hadjiargyris in Athens?

Mamas: I have not seen him for the last six months. I met him on August 16, 1948, when I returned to Athens from my interrogation here. Hadjiargyris ran into me at the Grande Bretagne and asked me if it was true that Staktopoulos had been detained because of my deposition. He asked me: How did you find Staktopoulos, and can you imagine him being capable of making his mother address that envelope? I learned afterwards from the newspapers that Mother Staktopoulos addressed the envelope.

Judge: Did you seek information from Staktopoulos during the period of the investigation?

Mamas: No. He sought information from me.

Judge: Have you formed a definite opinion as to what side of the fence Staktopoulos is on?

Mamas: That is up to the court to decide. I heard the indictment and was surprised.

Judge: Since the court has indicted Staktopoulos for the crime, what is your opinion?

Mamas: I cannot answer.

Judge: Staktopoulos confessed to his presence during the murder. What is your opinion—especially in view of the fact that the next day Staktopoulos met you and asked you: What news do you have of Polk?

Mamas: I don't think it is fair to express an opinion. The jury has heard how Staktopoulos wanted to involve me. Even before my presence in this court I was of the opinion that Communists were the perpetrators.

Judge: If we take for granted that Staktopoulos escorted Polk to the place where he was murdered, was Staktopoulos's assistance necessary?

Mamas: That is up to the Court to decide.

Judge: Hadjiargyris questioned whether Staktopoulos ordered his mother to address the envelope. At that time it was known that the handwriting experts had offered their opinions.

Mamas: I didn't know about that. Nothing about it had appeared in the press.

Judge: Did Hadjiargyris ask to meet you?

Mamas: No. We met by chance in the lobby of the Grande Bretagne.

Juror: What is your opinion of and feeling toward your colleagues in the Greek press? Do you have confidence in them?

Mamas: I do not.

Attorney for the Defense: I admire you for avoiding the expression of an opinion that might commit somebody.

Juror: You said Staktopoulos represented the opposition. Do you mean the opposition of the Communists to the country?

Mamas: No. I mean a rival press association [Reuters].

Attorney for the Defense: Since you have been in Greece since 1947 as a journalist, you should know what the government is and what the opposition is and what banditry is. Where do you place Staktopoulos?

Mamas: I don't know. I can't offer an opinion.

Attorney for the Defense: Since public opinion in the United States is divided, isn't it the duty of a journalist to pronounce an opinion?

Mamas: Not in court.

Attorney for the Defense: The defense is of the opinion that the witness avoids expressing an opinion and it would like to ask the court that she be cross-examined before witness Stavridis.

Second Attorney for the Defense (Vassilikos): Ask Miss Mamas whether her relations with Polk were professional or friendly.

Mamas: Purely professional. We belong to rival press organizations. His subscribes to ours. They buy our news.

Vassilikos: How do you explain that two hours after Polk's arrival in Salonika, Polk approached you to ask if you had any contacts with the guerrilla circles.

Mamas: I don't know why, and I don't remember the time.

Vassilikos: Is it because you can't remember the time or for other reasons that you can't reply? Did he call on you maybe because when in Athens you told him that you would be glad to see him in Salonika? And is it true that five months ago, previous to meeting Polk, you received instructions from your employer to go interview Markos?

Mamas: Yes, I received a cable from my employer, Mr. Chakalis [previously spelled Tsakalis]. My going was a Christmas present on the occasion of the formation of Markos's government. I called on General Papageorgiou, Commander of the C Army Corps and asked him if I could have an airplane to take me there. He replied that Markos's government was not on Greek soil but perhaps in Albania.

Vassilikos: Did Polk know about this?

Mamas: I can't know that.

Vassilikos: So you can't explain why, two hours after his arrival in Salonika, Polk would call on you?

Mamas: It is natural, since I have been in Northern Greece for six months, that correspondents should call on me.

Vassilikos: Do you find it natural that, when there is an official government in Greece, foreign journalists should try to smuggle themselves into bandit territory?

Mamas: I don't see why not.

Vassilikos: Is that logical in view of your saying that all your work was done through official channels?

Mamas: That sort of thing is the basic work of an objective reporter. General Papageorgiou understood this.

Vassilikos: In his deposition Matchen says that Polk asked you about your contacts with Communists. He therefore contradicts you.

Mamas: I deny Matchen's statement. No one knew Polk's ideas.

Vassilikos: Besides Matchen, Mr. Coate of the British Information Service also mentions Staktopoulos as one of the persons Polk asked about Communist contacts. Do you think this contradicts your deposition about your being impartial, etc.?

Mamas: I don't know why Matchen says what he does, because Polk never told me about his idea of going to Markos.

Vassilikos: Did you ask that Staktopoulos meet you in the lobby of the Mediterranean Hotel?

Mamas: No.

Vassilikos: Well, the Greek journalist Stavridis says that you asked him: Is Gregory upstairs? You used his first name.

Mamas: No, I never called Staktopoulos by his first name.

Vassilikos: Can you tell us your opinion of Rea Polk's calmness [when she found her husband missing]. Was it because she knew her husband had gone to visit Markos and was safe or what?

Mamas: She was worried at first.

Vassilikos: How and why did she change?

Mamas: Friends calmed her down. And then because she found the Murrow letter.

There is more dialogue about Rea's presumed "calmness" and her presumed contact with Communists in Athens. Then:

Vassilikos: In her first outburst, in the presence of Mr. Gibson, Mrs. Polk's first question was: Did the Monarchofascists do it? Is this so?

Mamas: Ask Rea Polk. I have no opinion. I'm here to state what I know and what I heard.

Vassilikos: In your opinion, was there ample time from May 7 to May 15 for the preparation of the plot which led to the murder or was it organized before that date?

Mamas didn't reply. The attorney general interceded to read out the article of the law which indicated that witnesses may express an opinion but are not obliged to do so. Vafiadis then took over as attorney for the defense and proceeded to ask Mamas a series of questions concerning details about which she refused to have an opinion or couldn't remember precisely enough to respond: the missing file, a telephone call for her during the gathering in the Mediterranean bar, Staktopoulos's statement that "while pulling up your stockings Polk told you something and you replied simply 'yes.'" Vafiadis then reported that Prohme and Matchen had testified that Mamas went to the phone twice, presumably during the Olympus-Naoussa dinner.

Mamas: It may be that I went to the telephone. I don't remember.

Vafiadis: Did you or did you not receive a second telephone call? Prohme says that you were called twice, adding that each time you gave them an explanation about these [calls], and it sounded very peculiar to them that you should do so. Is Prohme honest or are you concealing the truth?

Mamas: I don't remember.

Mamas might well have asked why it was so peculiar that she should tell the visiting journalists, among other things, that their names were to appear in the paper the next day, but Vafiadis clearly felt he was in hot pursuit: Was she reprimanded for not having sent in a cable to her boss Chakalis in Athens about Polk's disappearance (her not having done so presumably implying some sort of guilty collusion in the Polk affair)? Mamas repeated her earlier testimony: she had counted on her fiancé Zotos to pass on a letter containing the full details of the disappearance and he had failed to do so. The transcript provides what appears to be further pursuit by Vafiadis, but it is not entirely clear where the line of questioning is meant to be leading. Then Staktopoulos himself suddenly takes up the questioning from the defendant's bench.

Staktopoulos: Could you tell me this: Were you the first to give Stephanakis the information that Polk had disappeared?

Mamas: I was.

Staktopoulos: When Mrs. Polk came [to Salonika] you met her in the Olympus-Naoussa [restaurant]—this was Wednesday. Do you remember when you wrote the letter to your fiancé for transmission to Chakalis?

Mamas: I don't remember—maybe Friday.

Staktopoulos: The news was very important—the authorities had already been called into the case. Did you cable your office?

Mamas: Mr. Staktopoulos asked me that once before. I did not send in a cable for the following reasons: one, I believed the letter I sent to my fiancé by airplane would be transmitted to Mr. Chakalis within two hours and I wanted him to report it to our headquarters; two, no official government authority told me about the disappearance; three, the American consulate wanted an official investigation but Mrs. Polk did not because she told me that Polk would be back by the end of the week.

Someone (presumably Staktopoulos): You knew about the disappearance Wednesday and did not cable in the news, yet when an American member of AMAG was killed we all moved immediately to report it.

No recorded response.

Someone (incoherently): You told me that Chakalis should not have reprimanded me because I have written him "long ago."

No recorded response.

Attorney for the Defense: In your letter to Staktopoulos you said "my mother taught me to tell the truth." Do you hate liars? The defendant tried to involve you in this case. If he is acquitted, the investigation will be continued and you might be seriously involved later.

The transcript records "End of Session."

The afternoon of the second day in court was somewhat less volatile, concerned mostly with questions to the harbormaster and the coroner. The main debate was over how long it takes for a body to float after it is cast into the sea and what position it normally assumes underwater (according to the coroner, "usually drowned men are found straight up, women flat, until air gets into the body").[20] At one point a juror asked Staktopoulos whether he agreed with the coroner's findings, and the defendant answered yes, except that he didn't believe the body was underwater for seven days, since the murder was committed "at night between Saturday and Sunday," timing that is considerably more vague than his official confession. Defense Attorney Vassilikos then congratulated the coroner on the excellence of his report, very professional, an honor for Greek scientists, in fact, "it is as if it was prepared after consultation with Staktopoulos"—this last remark apparently offered without the slightest irony, as is true of Vassilikos's subsequent pronouncement that "the report of the Coroner agrees with Staktopoulos's confession." Vassilikos's admiration for the coroner extended to his asking him in open court for his professional opinion regarding the mental condition of his client: Did he find that Staktopoulos was "in a position to think well" or was his thinking impeded by the automobile accident that Staktopoulos had been in at an unspecified earlier time in his life? The Coroner: "Perhaps. But his mannerisms denote nervousness, not a mental ailment."

Defense Attorney Vafiadis was not quite as taken by the coroner as was his colleague Vassilikos. Vafiadis introduced a bit of drama during the afternoon by questioning the timing of the death.

Vafiadis: You said Polk was killed ten to twelve hours after shaving?

Coroner: Yes, because after death, hair does not grow.

Vafiadis: I have read Napoleon's memoirs, and in many similar crimes I have read that the dead have been found growing beards. Medicine is behind [the times].

Coroner: We must have confidence in our experience.

The main drama of the afternoon came with the return of Helen Mamas to the stand to confront the journalist Stavridis, a former Communist deputy now evidently anti-Communist, generous with bad news about Staktopoulos ("He was always trying to collect information from UNSCOB members who were hostile to Greece"), full of ardent opinions (Question: "Do you believe Staktopoulos could have committed the crime?" Answer: "Yes. Even if the archbishop were a Communist, he would carry out his orders and become a criminal." Question: "If the crime was committed by the Greek Communist Party—a hypothesis that the defense accepts—would Staktopoulos have been selected to participate on the basis of his knowing English?" Answer: "Yes, and Staktopoulos would have accepted the mission on the expectation of reward from the Party").

The confrontation with Helen Mamas was prefaced by a statement from Vassilikos to the president declaring that the case was a serious one and "we have already been too kind to this lady this morning," then by a request that Mamas's interpreter Lessios translate accurately and not add his own words to the testimony, as was reported by other English-speaking newsmen. Mamas now took the stand to answer Stavridis's claim that she came up to him in the lobby of the Mediterranean Hotel after an UNSCOB meeting and asked him "to tell Gregory that Polk wants him." Mamas began by exhibiting a document "proving that UNSCOB's session on the seventh was a closed one, and that no correspondents were allowed to attend it." And Mamas indicated that Dr. Ahmed, the Hindustani press officer for UNSCOB, had "certified" that Polk never attended an UNSCOB meeting. Stavridis repeated his claim that Staktopoulos pointed out Polk to him at the UNSCOB meeting, a thing that Ahmed could not certify "because he sat with his back turned to the correspondents." And he repeated his claim that Mamas had asked him to tell Gregory that Polk wanted him.

Mamas: There was no open meeting. The meeting on May seventh was closed. Polk could not have attended it. The meeting on May fourteenth was an open session.

Stavridis: She should admit that many sessions started open and ended closed and vice versa.

Mamas: If I knew that Staktopoulos wanted Polk I would not have bothered to introduce the two of them.[21]

Stavridis: You knew Staktopoulos's first name. You ate with him and went for walks with him.

Mamas: I never went out with him. I never had a drink with him.

Attorney General Constantinidis: Why all this? Is it because the defense insists on what was originally said by Staktopoulos [presumably implicating Mamas] or because the defense believes Miss Mamas participated in the conspiracy which started in Athens?

The transcript does not provide an answer to the question. Before the session ends, Mamas asks Stavridis: Do you consider me a person who would take part in a crime if I knew about it?

Stavridis: I have already replied to that. I believe a devoted Communist would do it. I believe that once one is a devoted Communist, one is able, and obliged, to do it.

And the attorney general concludes his contribution to the afternoon in court with another question that is left dangling: Why is it necessary for a trip of that kind [i.e., Polk's trip for an interview] to be so much trouble: rendezvous, etcetera.

Gibson's summary of the session for the secretary of state, though more detailed and objective than his first-day summary, reveals a perhaps understandable confusion about what was being testified to (e.g., he interprets the issue of the "Gregory" dialogue between Mamas and Stavridis in the Mediterranean lobby as having to do with a phone call) and a perhaps less understandable implication that Mamas failed in some way to stand up adequately under cross-examination that was "sharp and intense," being unable "to remember number of telephone calls received during evening prior to Polk's disappearance" and "her failure to send news cable on Polk disappearance."[22] But he also reports an evident discontent on the part of American press observers regarding the mode of the trial: "Representatives U.S. press continue show obvious surprise inclusive hearsay and opinions in evidence, immorality of trial, questioning of witnesses by defendent [sic] and other peculiarities contrary American legal system."

The cable reveals that U.S. press representatives also commented on other matters: the sharpness of the attack on the credibility of "first and possibly only U.S. witness" and of the attempt by the defense attorneys to get her to voice opinions, and they "noted defense questioning of Mamas opinion as to right of correspondent accredited to government to seek contact with rebel government engaged in civil war." Gibson restates, without comment, the "strong" defense argument that correspondents seeking such contact were performing an illegal act—an argument that was no doubt the basis for the American consulate's attempt to dissuade George Polk from attempting a trip into guerrilla territory. Gibson concludes his cable by indicating that U.S. press coverage has now been reduced, "as Sedgwick TIMES and Clark United Press returned Athens cover government situation."

It was during the third day of the trial that the primary defense strategy became apparent enough to clarify some of the confusion about the defense's line of questioning since opening day: Vassilikos and Vafiades hoped to diminish the severity of the charges against Staktopoulos by implicating others in the conspiracy—Helen Mamas and Kosta Hadjiargyris in particular—presumably so that Staktopoulos would appear merely one of a number of culprits, no more guilty—if also not much less guilty—than others who had not yet been charged in the case, all agents of a plot planned well in advance by the Communist party of Greece on orders from the Cominform, as Staktopoulos himself had deposed.[23] Of course this line of defense also dramatized the fact that the defense attorneys not only fully agreed with the prosecution that Staktopoulos had taken part in a Communist conspiracy but that his confession (in some form) was to be taken as the whole truth, in fact, was to be represented, with their help, as a testimony that was generally supported by other evidence and the corroboration of other witnesses.

The defense thus did much of the work of the prosecution in establishing the presumed authenticity of Staktopoulos's confessions. And Staktopoulos himself was brought in often to assist their line of attack, evidently resting his hope upon appearing to be cooperative with the authorities and upon demonstrating that he was an honest man confessing honestly to participating in an action that he had understood to be other than it proved to be and was therefore innocent of complicity in the murder, while at the same time guilty only of attempting to help a journalist colleague travel to meet Markos on orders from the Party. Staktopoulos's own explanation of his conduct in court long after the event suggests that there had been no hope for him to rest upon: he was under threat of death after having been broken in body and spirit by severe torture and could not have done other than he was directed to do. The only room he had for maneuver in court was presumably to put the best face he could on what he had been forced to confess and to defend himself against excessive attacks on his character by certain witnesses out to serve their own interests.

The third day was focused on an attempt to implicate Kosta Hadjiargyris, as the second had been focused on a failed attempt to implicate Helen Mamas. The efforts of both the prosecution and the defense were no more successful in this instance, though Hadjiargyris's leftist background evidently created broader sympathy for their impulse. The day opened with the testimony of Rea Polk's father, Mathew ("Mathaios" in the transcript) Kokkonis, who told the court much of what was already on record.[24] The questioning was directed toward establishing Hadjiargyris's presumed role as a part of an Athens phase of the conspiracy, but Mr. Kokkonis was not very helpful in this. People may have thought Polk a Communist because he "went about with Hadjiargyris," but Polk in fact said that the Communists were barbarians; he "liked" the Greek army "very much," and he "loved Greece." In any case Mr. Kokkonis did not think Polk was influenced by Hadjiargyris. When Polk had sought Hadjiargyris's help in coming into contact with the Communists, Hadjiargyris "asked him not to mix him up in this matter." It was true, said Kokkonis, that Hadjiargyris was free to enter Polk's office, but he did not do so during Polk's absence, and the maid who had so testified was also trustworthy.

Mr. Kokkonis refused to give the court an opinion on who might have removed the material missing from Polk's files or whether the plans for Polk's trip to Markos were made in Athens or in Salonika or who might have murdered his son-in-law: "He had no enemies. I do not know the reason for the murder. [He] was murdered by either the Right or the Left." Mr Kokkonis had heard from his daughter that Polk had been threatened by phone, and he himself had an unexplainable premonition about the trip north which had caused him to warn his son-in-law to be careful, but he could not say who had made the threatening call. All he could say was that "when Hadjiargyris states that Polk told him that he had received threats, he means to say the phone call was made by the Right Wing." It was Staktopoulos who rose at one point to speak out for what appeared to be the general opinion in the court room: "There is no doubt that the Communists made the call."

The "trustworthy" maid, Despina Vroutsi (identified in the transcript as "Maria Voutsi"), took the witness stand to confirm that no one, Hadjiargyris included, had entered Polk's office during his absence. Judging from the English transcript of the court record, she appears to have stuck to her statement under cross-examination, as she had in her earlier deposition. Curiously, Raleigh Gibson's cable to the secretary of state summarizing that day includes the sentence: "Servant Vroutsi testified reply question who took missing Polk papers 'Hadjiargyris.' "[25] Gibson was either hearing things in court that others didn't hear or was working from a different transcript than the one he later sent in to the State Department for their files. Hadjiargyris implies in his book that it was the persistent testimony of Despina Vroutsi that best served his claim of innocence before the court, in particular, her insistence that she did not remember any "suspicious" visit by Hadjiargyris to Polk's apartment, the most effective challenge to the official hypothesis that the *Christian Science Monitor* correspondent had removed documents from Polk's office presumably in order to delete incriminating evidence from Polk's correspondence with Drew Pearson. Despina's testimony was corroborated by the witness who followed her, the doorman of Polk's apartment building, who also stated that he had not seen Hadjiargyris visit Polk's home during the victim's absence and saw him there only after the authorities had searched the premises, one time in the presence of Polk's mother and another in the presence of Stephen Barber (that time Hadjiargyris was carrying an envelope in his hands that became the cause of further inconclusive debate).

The trial record shows several more curious moments in court before Hadjiargyris took the stand himself for a long afternoon and evening session devoted to his self-defense. The manager of the Astoria Hotel could not recall having seen Staktopoulos at the hotel on Friday afternoon, when the Reuters stringer was supposed to have first visited Polk in connection with the Markos trip, and Staktopoulos then had to interrupt the proceedings to reconfirm his having testified to a 5:30 P.M. visit on Friday. The manager went on to say that Polk had told him at about 10:30 on Saturday morning that "someone would ask for him," but he didn't say if that meant "one or more persons, man or woman." Another hotel employee, one Nanos, testified that he saw Polk in the hotel at 8:00 P.M. on Saturday: "He went to his room, then out and back again, and stayed for ten minutes." He was carrying a small round parcel in dark-colored paper that "looked as if it contained clothing." Staktopoulos was then asked to verify that this was the parcel he had mentioned in his confession. Indeed it was, he told the courtroom, and it contained pajamas, in keeping with Vasvanas's instructions that Polk take pajamas with him—but no camera—on the trip to meet Markos.

A merchant named Angelakoudis now appeared in court to tell a tale that evidently much impressed Raleigh Gibson, because it is the one bit of morning testimony that he highlighted for the secretary of state along with that of Despina Vroutsi.[26] Angelakoudis told the court that he and a friend had gone to the Luxembourg Café on Saturday evening, "didn't like the place, so we went to Neraida [another café some distance away]."[27] It was raining a bit, the time about 10:00 P.M. He and his friend ordered a drink. "We saw a boat, which left from the Luxembourg, going towards the small Cape [Karabournaki]. Three or four persons were in it. We heard a shot. My friend, who is a police officer, asked if I had heard it. The light on the boat was out." Staktopoulos was asked by the president: "Is this correct?" Staktopoulos stood up to say that his group left the Luxembourg at 10:00 P.M and that Polk was killed between 10:30 and 11:00. He added: "The witness tells the truth." The president then asked Staktopoulos if it was raining that night, and the defendant answered yes. A juror now entered the dialogue.

Juror (to witness Angelakoudis): Staktopoulos says that there was no light on the boat. How did you manage to see that there were three or four persons in the boat?

Angelakoudis: I didn't say that it was Polk or Staktopoulos, but we could see because the coast was lighted.

Attorney for the Defense: You say that the boat was sailing towards the small cape and that you saw three or four persons?

Angelakoudis: Yes

Attorney for the Defense: After how long did you hear the sound of the shot?

Angelakoudis: Half an hour later.

Attorney for the Defense: Was there another rowboat near that area?

Angelakoudis: No. As for the light, I cannot say whether it was a lamp; it may have been a cigarette lighter. I can't describe it exactly.

End of testimony. End of cross-examination. End of the transcript covering the morning session. It is not clear from this portion of the transcript what "light" the witness is referring to at the end, though we learn from later court proceedings that the witness, contradicting Staktopoulos's testimony, finally acknowledged that there was light of some kind on the boat at some point in its travels. But there is no evidence of any further attempt to question this witness, or even more significantly, his companion the police officer—a surprising lapse in the case, since this is the only recorded instance of anybody sighting figures in a rowboat, however obscurely, on the rainy night in question. The fact that there was no follow-up in this connection makes the relevance of Mr. Angelakoudis's testimony rather suspect.

Raleigh Gibson's summary of Hadjiargyris's performance on the third day of the trial is not only essentially accurate—if highly truncated—but, for once, unweighted in any particular direction. He tells the secretary of state that in a lengthy afternoon and evening session, Hadjiargyris held the stand for more than four hours, and "despite heavy attacks by prosecutor, judges, members of the jury and defense attorneys, he maintained position taken in depositions as given in Stahtopoulos [sic] indictment with one major exception."[28] The exception, says Gibson, was his naming Rea Polk, Stephen Barber, and Mary Barber as those with the best opportunity for removing the documents that were discovered to be missing from George Polk's files. "When questioned closely on this point he stated many newsmen know this is true and Barber should have been cross-examined with me." The summary continues: "Despite intense examination, Hadjiargyris maintained Polk had not informed him of plans, that he was not responsible for removal of missing documents and that he knows no more about case than he has told."[29] And Gibson reports a crucial moment in the four-hour examination of the witness: "Stahtopoulos placed in evidence allegation he was told by John ["Yannis"] in Athens that Hadjiargyris is interested in Polk's trip to Markos. On request of judge for comment, Hadjiargyris replied 'he lies'; judge [:] 'why should he and John mix up your name [?]'; answer [:] 'it is in his interest to mix up as many names as possible.' "

What Gibson's succinct account fails to suggest is that Hadjiargyris's comment here provides the essential clue to the defense's strategy, in which Staktopoulos willingly collaborated, to the point of perjury. Had Gibson picked up the clue, he might not have been so ready to declare, the minute the trial was over, that it was an unequivocal triumph. But there are also other nuances in the record of Hadjiargyris's testimony that could have provided both American officials and American newsmen with a clearer perception both of what was going on in front of their eyes and what had taken place backstage before and during the official investigation. In countering the effort to establish an Athenian connection to the murder, Hadjiargyris made a strong case for the crime having been arranged in Salonika; and at the same time, though Staktopoulos attempted to implicate him, he was scrupulous in denying any knowledge of Staktopoulos's possible role as a contact. At one point the president of the court asked him whether Polk had told him about his interest in arranging a meeting with Markos, presumably at the time of Polk's trip north.[30]

Hadjiargyris: No. I didn't want him to.

President: Who could tell him of a person who could put him in contact? Did he know Staktopoulos?

Hadjiargyris: I don't know.

President: Did you know Staktopoulos?

Hadjiargyris: No. I heard about him from Modiano, Reuters' reporter.

President: You [said in your deposition] that only a reporter could have put him into contact.

Hadjiargyris: Yes, I did, and I support my statement because this is natural. He would have had confidence in a journalist. The only thing I heard about Salonika is that in 1947 when I made Polk's acquaintance, he was helping a poor refugee family [there]. Another thing I heard was that in December 1947, Bigart came to Salonika, met the head of the British Information Service, whom he told that he wanted to go to the andartes. When he returned to Athens Randall Coates [sic] received a note, said to have originated from bandit headquarters, inviting Bigart to go to Markos. In July, Mrs. Barber said, she came to Salonika, and after many difficulties managed to get a photo of Markos, later printed in *Time*.

President: Could Staktopoulos put him into contact and send him to Markos by a sailing boat?

Hadjiargyris: I heard about it later [*sic*] when Thrapp, Polk and others discussed the possibilities of going to Markos from Salonika to Pierria [*sic*] by boat. Werner told me that Thrapp and Polk discussed the above. I was also told that Thrapp had found the means to go to the bandits but was stopped by the British embassy.

One of the judges then asked Staktopoulos to repeat his testimony about guiding Polk to the waiting rowboat at the Luxembourg Cafe, and Staktopoulos did so.

President: Polk believed that the boat would leave from the Luxembourg to Pierria [?]

Staktopoulos: Yes.

No one rose at this point—or apparently at any other point—to suggest that traveling by rowboat from Salonika harbor to Pieria (as it is normally transliterated), some thirty nautical miles away, would be an arduous journey of some twelve to fifteen hours with strong rowers on a sea with no headwind and substantially more difficult on a rainy night, as Polk himself would surely have realized. That aspect of Staktopoulos's story clearly called for further revision, but this was evidently not the right moment. The president now asked Hadjiargyris, since it was clear that theft was not a motive, why Polk was murdered.

Hadjiargyris: The crime was political. It was in the interests of KKE [Greek Communist Party] to defame Greece.

The attorney general now interceded to appeal to Hadjiargyris—as a Greek and despite the past record of his having been accused of Communism—to tell the truth "for the sake of the bloodshed, the defamation, and the slander for which Greece has suffered and is still suffering." Hadjiargyris then denied being a Communist, though he told the court that he was a former member of the EAM resistance movement and had been sent to "a concentration camp as a Communist" from 1943 to 1945. He subsequently refused to "take charge of EAM in England," and though he admitted having made mistakes, "in the long run, my articles have done a lot of good to Greece." Still, in spite of his respect "for Drossos and other politicians," he declared that he "cannot be one of the Rightists." The president cut in to say that "we do not want political speeches" and that the witness should limit himself to the subject of the trial. The attorney general was more generous, recognizing that Hadjiargyris "wanted to justify [his] position." He returned in due course to the question of whether or not Hadjiargyris knew that Staktopoulos was Polk's Salonika contact.

Attorney General: From the start we believed that if you and Thrapp had talked, we could have learned earlier who wrote the envelope for Polk's identity card. For example, you say that only a newsman could have helped Polk go to Markos. Thrapp says approximately the same thing. You leave a gap. It is as if we have the clay but cannot make the statue.

Hadjiargyris: Even Polk would not have said who his contact was.

Pressed further, Hadjiargyris again stated that "he did not know anything about Stahtopoulos," and he successfully fought off both Vassilikos and Vafiades when the defense took up the cause of trying to establish Hadjiargyris as the Athens link to the Reuters stringer, Vassilikos providing grim comic relief by revealing further blatant prejudices (Vassilikos: "What about Mrs. Cazoulis' statement [that drops of perspiration fell from Hadjiargyris's forehead when she asked him about the missing files]?" Hadjiargyris: "She is a bit hysterical." Vassilikos: "All women are, a little . . ."). A juror came into the dialogue at one point to ask his opinion of what profit Staktopoulos might have gained from either concealing the murderers or going to the police "to tell everything." Hadjiargyris, taking his text from Helen Mamas, said "I do not know" to either contingency.

The day ended with a poignant if still controversial episode. The transcript shows us that Hadjiargyris was followed in the witness stand by a post office employee who described his having found the envelope with Polk's identity card in it, and Staktopoulos was then called on to testify that he had asked his mother to address the envelope after buying it at a kiosk on Sunday and then mailing it in on Monday morning. Anna Staktopoulos was then asked, "Did you address this envelope?" The transcript has her answering simply: "Yes, I did." But Raleigh Gibson's cable reports that, "in reply to question whether writing on envelope was hers, Anna Stahtopoulos after hesitation said 'yes, it is mine.' "[31] Gregory Staktopoulos tells us in his book that is was only after an imploring look from him that Anna gave up her outright denial and said "It looks like my writing."[32] And Gibson's "running summary" of the following day has the president of the court opening the morning session by showing Anna the presumably incriminating envelope and asking her again: "Is this your handwriting?"[33] Anna replied: "It doesn't resemble it very much, but it appears that I wrote the address on the envelope."

The president then consulted the court files and reported that Anna Staktopoulos admitted in her deposition that she had written the address. Vassilikos then objected to his reading Anna's deposition, and the issue was brought to a close for the moment with further humble uncertainty from a witness clearly trying to do her duty by her son, by the authorities, and by God's truth: "I do not remember if I wrote it, but if you say so, I did write it." Evidently the jury found Anna's hesitation and uncertainty closer to the truth of things than her official deposition. Gregory Staktopoulos was not so fortunate.

The trial was now given over for two days to witnesses offering their opinion of Staktopoulos's past and experts offering their opinion on handwriting and ink. As Raleigh Gibson reported,[34] the witnesses disagreed on whether Staktopoulos's removal from the Communist lists was real or faked, and they disagreed about the extent of his possible complicity in the murder, though none seemed to think he was capable of knowingly committing the crime itself. One witness found it "unnatural" that he would get in the rowboat with Polk if he knew the American was to be killed.[35] Another thought he might have simply agreed to act as interpreter and then failed to inform the police about the crime because "he was threatened or he had other reasons for not doing so."[36] When the same witness was asked if Staktopoulos could be an "Intelligence Service agent," he replied: "I cannot speak on that case openly. It might hurt Greece."[37] A third witness, Nikos Kondomitros, who had already deposed at length about Staktopoulos's dubious history during the Occupation, his having forced other journalists to sign a pro-leftist declaration, his having ordered the murder of Major Meligris, and his having been involved in vaguely defined intelligence activities, repeated these charges despite an attempt by the defense to have him disqualified as a prejudiced witness.[38] Staktopoulos rose several times to defend himself before the first two witnesses, once against the implication that the Communist party "sent him to work with the Germans" and once to deny that he altered information put out by the UNSCOB press office. "There are surprising things being told about me," he protested. In the case of Kondomitros, he settled for irony and was called out of order.[39]

Staktopoulos: I see that the witness is very serious and repeats what he said; that is, that I ordered the murder of an officer, I was a spy, I wanted to kill Miha [his lady friend in Athens], etc.

President: I shall give you a chance to defend yourself, Staktopoulos.

And chance he got, beyond anything an American courtroom would have thought warrantable.

But first the experts, who proved to be full of authority and pedantry, enough to bore even the court recorder, the ink expert in particular: after testifying that the blue-black ink on the incriminating envelope was the same as that on other documents that Anna Staktopoulos had been made to write in front of the police, the expert felt that he had to "point out that the analysis was easy because the writing was not very old," whereas had the text been written long ago, the job would have been more difficult because "ink evaporates with time"—and here the court recorder resorts to a succinct parenthesis "(He gives a full scientific analysis of the ink)."[40] Questioned by a judge, Anna apparently admits to having addressed the envelope with the ink they had at home and then to writing other documents at the police station "using the same ink, same inkpot, which were confiscated from our house." One of the jurors does not seem satisfied: Can similar ink be purchased in the market? he asks the expert. Expert: Yes. Juror: If Mrs. Staktopoulos had not confessed to using her own inkpot at the police station, could you prove that she had used the same ink for both the envelope address and the other documents she wrote? Expert: We cannot determine whether the ink used was from the same inkpot. A second expert was asked if other local firms manufactured a similar kind of ink. Second expert: Yes and no. Blue-black is a type of ink. It would depend on whether the formula were the same and the proportion of chemicals the same. Was the juror implying the possibility of police hanky-panky in all this ink business? Evidently no one rose to take on that issue, and there was no further comment on it by the press, foreign or domestic.

Then the handwriting expert called to the witness stand complicated the smooth progress of things immensely by revealing that, though "it was easy to declare that the person who wrote the envelope was Anna Staktopoulos," she had tried to alter her handwriting, and they had not been able to determine whether this was "because of a shock, fear or worry."[41] That raised the question of whether the envelope she had addressed was empty or contained the incriminating identity card, and if the latter, this presumably would indicate foreknowledge of the crime and would explain the old lady's fear or worry. Staktopoulos now announced that the envelope was empty when his mother addressed it. A juror then wanted to verify that there was a difference in the form of the letters on the mailed envelope and those on other envelopes that Anna addressed after the fact. Yes, said the expert, but the police were to be praised for their shrewd handling of that issue, because they had obtained a long written text from mother Staktopoulos, and the experts, reviewing this text, had "noticed that at first Mrs. Stahtopoulos wrote freely, but later, when she probably understood that the writing might be compared with the [incriminating] envelope, she made efforts to alter her writing." Juror: Had the experts compared the texts in question to samples of Mrs. Staktopoulos's handwriting before the crime? No, said the expert, there was no need for that. He was grateful that it had been "God's will to have the writer use small letters" in addressing the envelope, because had she used capital letters in a text so short, "it would then have been difficult to pronounce an undisputable conclusion." Attorney for the Defense Vassilikos suddenly entered the debate.

Vassilikos: You said that God made Mrs. Staktopoulos write the envelope as she did. You say, however, that the text of the original envelope proved that the writer wrote under stress of fear, worry, etc.

President of the Court: Your statement is nonsense.

Vassilikos protests. The president apologizes: he didn't mean to insult the attorney for the defense; he "made a slip"; and he was sorry. Vassilikos accepted his apology and made a little joke: now "in a temper," he too would alter his handwriting were he to write something at that moment. But his point appears to have been lost: if God made Anna write as she did, Anna could hardly have been under stress at the time she wrote the address on the incriminating envelope and therefore presumably did not know about the planned crime of murder in advance. The debate suddenly shifted to the supposedly altered handwriting in the text Anna wrote under the eyes of the police.

Vassilikos: The way things are presented [by the witness] would prove that Mrs. Staktopoulos knew of the crime and that she wanted to conceal it.

Expert: Yes. Perhaps when she was writing in the presence of the police she knew that her son had been arrested.

Vassilikos: If it was due to the police searches [of her house] that she was worried, would that alone have contributed to the alteration of her handwriting?

Expert: What do you mean?

Vassilikos: I mean that she will be indicted as a direct accomplice in the crime with her son.

Expert: That is up to the Court.

This rather incoherent exchange concludes with an opinion by the expert on the stand that the previously expressed opinion of his fellow handwriting expert is correct, namely that the incriminating envelope contained Polk's identity card at the time Anna Staktopoulos wrote the address on the envelope. Nobody at this time or any other time asked why the presumed murderers included a Pan Am advertisement (presumably in the form of a "calendar card") along with Polk's identity card in their instructions to Staktopoulos and why he himself bothered to put that innocent item in the envelope as well. The Pan Am advertisement mysteriously disappeared from the case, somehow considered an irrelevancy. A smart and conscientious lawyer or reporter might have seen that the presence of the innocuous Pan Am advertisement could well have suggested a more casual recovery of these two items and a more casual mailing than Staktopoulos's confession tried to promote, further cause for seeing his confession as grossly suspect both in this particular and in its account of how Polk's body ended up where it did.

Another disturbing aspect of the record at this point in the trial emerges from the Donovan papers, where one finds three pages of handwritten notes by Theodore Lambron (the script in capital letters) dated Sunday, April 17, 1949, and having to do with a visit by Lambron and General Donovan to Attorney General Constantinidis for an hour's talk during the morning of that day (since it was Orthodox Easter Day, the court was not in session). Lambron's notes record that General Donovan told Constantinidis that "he [Donovan] was impressed with the efficient and thorough manner in which the court has prepared its case and congratulated him." Donovan also "praised the judges, especially the President of the Court by saying that he was honest, just etc." And Donovan went on to say "that the jury was most intelligently conducting itself and that he had pointed out to the American journalists that the spontaneous active participation of the jury in the trial was in itself adequate proof that the trial was a fair and unbiased trial."

These remarks followed several days in court which were characterized, as we have seen, by much sniping between witnesses, the defendant, the president of the court, and the attorneys for the defense—as well as by some astute questioning from individual jurors, who brought up a few issues that the defense chose to ignore. But Donovan's enthusiasm about the trial at this stage, and his remarks to the American journalists present, seem especially inappropriate—not to say disingenuous—when we remember that he had on record a report which he had solicited from his own handwriting expert and which suggested that the script on the incriminating envelope was that of "a man not over the thirties," Greek educated but "not literate," with a basically strong constitution though in a nervous condition at the time he addressed the envelope—a description that hardly fits Anna Staktopoulos, a lady well over sixty who came to Greece as an adult from the Pontic region of Turkey.[42] The question is highlighted in Lambron's notes about this meeting when he reports that Constantinidis told Donovan that he thought Staktopoulos "a very strong individual" who "didn't confess but was forced to yield by circumstances" and who "first retreated when his mother confessed." These remarks by the attorney general, and his tenaciously expressed "doubt that Mamas didn't know something about Polk's plans" despite persistent evidence to the contrary, should have been grounds for raising serious suspicion in Donovan had he been at all inclined in that direction, which he clearly was not.

Staktopoulos took the stand on the morning of the sixth day, after the court completed the reading (begun during the previous session) of depositions by those not present at the trial—among others, Drew, Matchen, the Barbers, and, most important of all, Rea Polk—and also heard the testimony we have seen by the single character witness to appear in court on Staktopoulos's behalf, Carl Compton of Anatolia College.[43] Defendant Staktopoulos's statement in defense of himself took the form of a speech ("Mr. President, Mr. Attorney General, Members of the Jury, colleagues . . .") that lasted through the morning, and after a break for lunch, well into the afternoon session. The transcript shows two interruptions only, once when Vassilikos apparently apologized to the court for Staktopoulos's pace ("Due to his injury in an automobile accident he has some difficulty in speaking rapidly") and once when Vassilikos spoke up in protest over a news story in *Vorras* stating "Staktopoulos ordered the murder" of Major Meligris during the German Occupation, a "criticism" that the defense attorney thought "should have waited the Court's decision," in this way conceding that the Meligris murder charge was somehow plausible.

Staktopoulos opened his speech with the declaration: "Greece is innocent of Polk's blood. I accuse the KKE [Greek Communist Party], the Cominform and Moscow." He then proceeded to thank Carl Compton for his support and to tell him that "Anatolia College does not produce criminals."[44] He offered the story of his life as evidence: his school record, his hard work to support his family after becoming head of it at an early age, the assistance he provided toward the education of his siblings, his diligence and honesty as a copyreader, messenger, reporter, and translator during the progress of his journalistic career. He acknowledged having had, like other young men, certain hopes and plans in life which presumably led him into politics, but "I cannot say that I was a devoted Communist. I shall lie if I do. I was a leftist or was made a leftist." He defended his work during the Occupation—much of it was essentially patriotic—and his joining the resistance movement EAM in 1943. At the end of the Occupation, when he began working for the Anglo-Greek Information Service as a translator, he received a number of letters from his superiors congratulating him on his good work. Unfortunately "outsiders addressed letters to my Chiefs slandering me," but after being reprimanded for "allegedly taking away radio sets belonging to Greek citizens, commandeering houses, etc.," he requested an investigation, was exonerated, returned to work freely and with a salary increase. And after his automobile accident, many British officers came to the hospital to visit him.

Regarding the specific testimony against him by some witnesses, Staktopoulos declared that while working for *Laiki Foni* (People's Voice), he in fact never altered the text of what he heard over the radio as he had been accused of doing. And though it was true that he spoke at a meeting of the Union of Newsreporters about "our work for the urban newspapers," he did so not loudly or in a threatening tone as a witness had testified but actually in a tone lower than that of his current address to the court, and though indeed "we did sign a protocol" on that occasion, several attending the session chose not to sign, and he himself had neither the power nor "the criminal psychology" to hurt anyone at the meeting. As for the accusation by Kondomitros that he killed a Greek major and "wanted to do so to a woman" (Miha)—no, he was not a murderer; in fact, as his neighbor Mr. Vekiaris would testify, he could not even kill a chicken, literally, and he would ask Vekiaris's wife to take on that domestic chore whenever it was supposed to be his. Kondomitros had "made a novel out of my drama." That witness would repent some day, because he was "a good boy," and Staktopoulos felt sorry for him.

When he came to his relationship with Mouzenidis and Vasvanas, Staktopoulos told the court that he had met these two while working for *Laiki Foni*—both were conversing in the Pontus dialect of his own background—and on one occasion he had challenged Vasvanas by suggesting that it was not right for Communists to use illegal means to defend themselves against the police. As for the fake Stalin interview, Staktopoulos asked the court to please believe that he had nothing to do with that. Nor did he ever deliver speeches to workmen at Vardar square or serve as an EAM instructor, as witness Boudouris had claimed. Maybe someday witness Boudouris would be reminded of his lies by a colleague and feel ashamed. Still, Staktopoulos felt he had to tell the court that he himself would be lying if he were to say that he had abandoned the Greek Communist Party; his having been crossed off the party list was "fictitious," and he wanted the government and the police to be careful about fictions of that kind. At the same time, he could not agree that "all Communists were murderous or able to commit murder."

Staktopoulos ended his prologue at the beginning of the afternoon session and turned to tell the story of Polk's trip to Markos with as much detail as he could "so that Greece—my country—may cease being accused by all nations." The story is mostly that which we know from the revised confessions, except that here Staktopoulos adds a number of very curious details that seem to have come into the story in response to certain lingering questions from the courtroom debate, further revisions of the "official" text, it would seem, by those working behind the scenes to make the strongest case possible against the designated conspirators on the basis of Staktopoulos's already thoroughly revised confessions—and we learn subsequently that among these new details are a few that evidently surprised even the attorneys for the defense.

Staktopoulos's amended account begins with the news that on March 23 a woman came to his office to give him a note from Vasvanas arranging the meeting that sent him to Athens with a letter "to an American who wishes to go to Markos." This is the first mention of a woman messenger, perhaps inspired by the recently exposed Anna Molyvda connection. Then we learn that the mysterious "Nikos" of the Pontus Café meetings, identified in the revised confession of October 14 as "Eleftheriou," is now one "Varossianos," a leader of the KKE along with Mouzenidis. And we also learn that this Varossianos met with Staktopoulos on Friday evening at 8:00 P.M., before his phone call to Mamas at the Olympus-Naoussa restaurant, and asked Staktopoulos "whether I could hide Vasvanas in my house." Staktopoulos answered that he had no place to do so in his home but had a room in town where he could hide the andarte leader—and that is what he did late that evening, after Vasvanas personally asked him to do so in front of Polk during the rendezvous on Carolou Diehl Street. With this new bit of testimony, the problem of where Vasvanas stayed after coming into the city from the mountains was finally solved in the official account of things, but this detail also put Staktopoulos in the further jeopardy—as Anna Molyvda had put herself—of admitting to the crime of providing refuge for an andarte enemy of the state, a capital offense in those days, as Mouzenidis's "wife in hiding" had come to know fatally some months earlier.

Other new details emerged as Staktopoulos's account continued. Instead of sitting in the Luxembourg Café to await Polk's arrival as originally deposed (in the October 14 version, Polk was quoted as saying OK to that rendezvous "without asking me how to get to the Luxembourg"),[45] Staktopoulos tells the court that he offered to accompany Polk to the restaurant since the American didn't know the way there. In this revised version, he actually waited for his American colleague outside the pharmacy opposite the Astoria until Polk emerged at 8:05 P.M. on Saturday, carrying his small parcel, and the two of them, after taking an indirect route to the White Tower, got into a taxi together and went on to the Luxembourg. The point of this new information? It presumably served to make Staktopoulos's designated role seem both more realistically hospitable and more central, since he becomes Polk's escort not simply from the restaurant table to the waiting rowboat as in the original confession but from hotel to restaurant to waiting rowboat, and, as we learn next, to the caique hovering somewhere in Salonika Bay for the trip to Pieria.

It appears from the amended account that the first boatman, Mouzenidis, described in the October 1 confession as a man who did not say a word initially and who made Staktopoulos feel afraid, is a touch less silent here, because, after Polk calls up to his escort: "Come on, jump in," Mouzenidis says to Staktopoulos that "further on we would take two more persons from a caique," namely Vasvanas and the unknown man who ends up in the rowboat's bow. The sudden revelation that there was a waiting caique in the story presumably solves one of the crucial credibility problems in the original confession: five men in a boat rowing their way thirty nautical miles to the foot of Olympus on a rainy night. And to reinforce this detail, Staktopoulos now reports that just before Polk was shot, he told the American: "I shall leave you, because you will board a sailing boat." Whether or not the defendant realized it, this testimony, while helping the official solution to emerge from thorny territory, made the defendant vulnerable to further awkward questions about his presumably innocent involvement in what he said had occurred at sea.

Staktopoulos's account concludes with a more thorough narrative of his confusion and distress after the murder, including a trip to his room in town to ask Vasvanas "why he had involved me in this," but of course Vasvanas was nowhere to be found by that time. And then, Staktopoulos reached in his pocket for his billfold, his hand "touched Polk's identity card," and that caused him to return home, in great unease, to get his mother—as he had been ordered—to address the envelope that he had bought at a kiosk and that he mailed the next day in a box near the White Tower. No mention of his hand touching the Pan Am advertisement, or of his inexplicably including that in the envelope. And later in the week, on Saturday, he does an incriminating deed quite new to the text: he goes to his office at the *Makedonia*, searches among the photographic plates there to find the one picturing the incriminating envelope, and puts it in his pocket so that it will not appear in the paper his mother regularly reads.

The defendant's statement ends with his ultimate defense: had his companions told him that they intended to kill Polk, he would have let them know how wrong they were in calling on him for assistance. He wouldn't have denounced them, it is true, but he would have done his best to avoid being mixed up in the affair and he would have told Polk to postpone his trip "without letting him understand why." He wanted to express his sorrow to young William Polk, present in the courtroom, who lost a beloved brother, and to Mrs. Polk, who lost her son. Why hadn't he refused Vasvanas's proposal from the start? Because he was a Communist and had to help the Struggle for Democracy. And he wanted to help a colleague. Finally, he also "expected some material benefit, such as a position with a news agency." Who had ordered the murder of Polk? All Communists knew the answer to that but wouldn't tell. The order was given by the Greek Communist Party ("Mouzenidis and Vasvanas had no personal reasons to kill Polk"), as in the murder of Minister of Justice Ladas, but in the case of foreign victims, the "general line is received from outside," the Cominform in particular, though since Greece is not officially a member of the Cominform, in this instance from the Kremlin itself.

Staktopoulos was allowed to give a brief lecture on Russian history after the midafternoon recess and to offer his views on the Communist perception of the relation between Polk's murder and the Marshall Plan: aid to Greece would stop, the national army would have been deprived of war materiel, there would have been strikes, general misery, fertile soil for Communism to grow. The Communist radio now called him a traitor for disclosing the murder, but Greece was struggling for its independence and integrity. Though Polk's drama would pursue him the rest of his life, he wanted the court to know—and the text gives no evidence of irony here—that "in the Security Station where I was detained I awoke and became a Greek." He had told the truth, he had been sincere. "On you, the Court and Jury, depends my fate and that of my family."

But he still had questions to answer to before the court, some emerging from the latest amendments to his story. The president wanted to know, for example, why, if Staktopoulos was aware that the rowboat was taking Polk to a sailing caique, he was needed in the rowboat? Why didn't he simply tell his companions: "I have finished my job"? Staktopoulos had evidently not been adequately prepared by his sponsors to handle this question. "At any rate," he said, "that is how it happened.

I am not satanic." And another question: Was it so easy to board a sailing caique and take off at night, while the bay was patrolled? Answer: One Angelidis had managed to board a caique and go across to Olympus. Question: You say that Mouzenidis removed Polk's notebook and address book; was that because your name was written in it? Answer: "Maybe. But how Mouzenidis knew about it I am not in a position to tell you." Question: Why did you buy an envelope instead of using those your mother says you had at home, larger envelopes? Answer: "I cannot tell you, I was dizzy." Question: Why did you ask Mamas about Polk after the murder since you knew the latter was dead? Answer: "I don't know why. If Mamas had been clever, she would have noticed my hopeless position."

There were other questions from the attorney general and one or another of the judges, but the most pressing came from a juror, and it focused on the new information that the rowboat was heading out to meet a caique. Question: Since Polk was to be put on a sailing caique, why didn't either you or Polk say that he should not be blindfolded? Answer: I cannot say why. These people wanted to murder him. Question: You are an educated person, speak English, why didn't you go to the U.S. consulate after the crime and disclose it? You had the identity card in your pocket for two days, you had all that time to recover from the shock. No answer. Question: Did Mouzenidis speak English? Answer: No. Question: Then who told Mouzenidis that Polk's notebook contained names? Answer: Maybe they knew about it from Athens or what Polk carried with him. Question: Did you know ahead of time that the rowboat would be used to take you and Polk to the sailing boat? Answer: No. I was told that at the Luxembourg. Question: Why blindfold him? What could he see? The caique was on the open sea. Why tie up his hands and feet? Would they then lift him [bound and blindfolded] to put him on board the caique? All good questions that Staktopoulos evidently couldn't answer—good enough, in fact, to bring the whole of his revised testimony under a heavy shadow of suspicion. But they were questions that nobody raised again, in or out of court, secretly or publicly, either in Greece or in America.

The day's session ended with a final interrogation of Anna Staktopoulos. Juror: What happened, Mrs. Staktopoulos? Mrs. S: We were sitting in the garden. Gregory came and told me to write the address. I could not refuse him. I thought about it afterwards. Question: Is it then that he told you about the murder? Mrs. S: No, he did not tell me. I went to the desk in the room and I used the ink and pen and wrote: "To the Third Police Station, City." Question: Who wrote the numeral "3d"? Staktopoulos: I did, sir. Question (to Mrs. S): What happened afterwards? Mrs. S: I went to a neighbor's and had some coffee. I did not ask Gregory why he wanted me to write the address on the envelope. Question: Did you address another envelope? Mrs. S: No, I did not.

It seems that Mrs. Staktopoulos had not been coached much better than her son had been, because he was the one who had testified that she had asked him why she should address the envelope and had been told by him that the American lady Helen Mamas wanted her to do so. In any case the jury gave the old lady the benefit of the doubt. Not so in the case of her son Gregory.

There was a single afternoon session on the seventh day, given over to the attorney general's summation, which held only one surprise: his apparent generosity, as recorded by Raleigh Gibson,[46] in recommending a sentence of ten to twenty years imprisonment. Gibson's summary picks out the high points. The attorney general said that the circle of the case had not yet closed. The investigation would continue, especially regarding Staktopoulos's role in the fake Stalin interview, which might call for another trial. The attorney general was convinced, knowing the circumstances of the murder, that Staktopoulos had participated in it. But if the "hands which had murdered Polk were Greek, the conspirators were not Greeks." As far as the politics of the case was concerned, that was evidently enough said.

The defense attorneys had their day too, the eighth, which was devoted to five hours of summation by the two of them in turn.[47] Vafiadis had the floor first and quickly confirmed that the prosecution and defense were in agreement that the Communists had murdered Polk. After naming the illegal rightist bands who, "in the minds of prejudiced people," were thought for a while to have committed the crime, these Right extremists had to be excluded, because, "had the Right murdered Polk, it would not have sent the envelope but would have done its work so nicely that no traces of Polk would ever have been found." Besides, the murder was done in the "typical style" of the Communists by way of a bullet in the back of the victim's head. So the murder was committed on orders from Markos's headquarters to defame the Greek government by way of the claim that government agents had killed the American. The defense had asked for a postponement in order to get the testimony of Rea Polk, who couldn't have said "more than what the Court has already in its hands" but who could have helped the defense because she would have admitted in court that she was grateful Staktopoulos had disclosed "the real murderers of her husband," Vasvanas and Mouzenidis. The defendant himself was guilty "simply because his part was that of assisting his colleague Polk to go to the mountains." The press had played a dubious role in the case, judging the man before all the facts were in, influencing public opinion. Staktopoulos had been accused of murdering Major Meligris, but it had not yet been determined that such a major existed: a telegram had arrived from General Moutousis "saying that no such name is known."

At this point Vafiadis touches on the question of whether or not Staktopoulos's confession "is sincere," but finally skirts the issue. If we accept it as sincere, he declares, then the defendant merely happened to be there acting as interpreter when Mouzenidis and Vasvanas killed Polk; if we do not accept it, then "we should consider whether he, with others, killed Polk." In any case, the defense wants to register a complaint about Staktopoulos having been arrested on August 14 but not having been "brought to testify until October 1 and October 14." Why had that been done? "Because they wanted to deprive the detained from employing an attorney." Still, in Greece justice is above everything, though a small country. "If our foreign friends believe that unless we discover the murderers no aid would be given us," then "let them stop sending us their dollars." Greece will "honestly, heads up, carry out its traditions." It was a mistake for the Greek government to declare that it was a question of honor to discover the murderers. Greek justice would have carried out its duty without any such declarations.

Vafiadis now had to admit that the defendant had created problems by making "revelations" before the court of which "the defense had no previous knowledge," and this led him to ask that Staktopoulos "be examined for mental disarrangement." He listed some of the revelations: that the defendant hid Vasvanas in his room, that "Nikos is Varoussiades [sic]," that a woman had brought him a note prior to his departure for Athens. Staktopoulos contradicted himself, "believing his frank confession might lessen the degree of his guilt." No waiter at the Luxembourg Café testified that Staktopoulos went there, so it was apparently from somewhere else that he and Polk boarded the rowboat. That is still "a mystery." The defendant "is sincere on one single point": that Vasvanas and Mouzenidis "took Polk" and that he himself "did not previously know of the intention to commit this crime."

But Vafiadis felt he had to repeat that Staktopoulos's mental condition "is not satisfactory." The defendant tried to hide things on the one hand, while on the other he disclosed matters previously unknown to the defense. No one had testified that Staktopoulos and Polk were seen together, or that they ate lobster together, and that left a big question for the jury to think over. Another question was whether Mamas's refusal to express an opinion suggested that she was afraid she would later have to admit that she knew Polk's intentions. Then there was the question of whether Staktopoulos was mentally well or whether the threats he received had frightened him. Had the defendant revealed everything soon after the crime by going to the U.S. consulate, who could have assured him that he wouldn't be accused of conspiring in the crime? It was clear that the defendant was "either terrorized or mentally ill," because why mail the letter to the police—especially since nobody had seen him with Polk? The press had clearly influenced others so they were afraid to testify in Staktopoulos's behalf. Only one out of five character witnesses—Carl Compton—had had the courage to show up and say: "No I don't believe Staktopoulos could be a criminal—I have known him since he was a student." The jury, concluded Vafiadis, would finally have to judge the case according to its conscience and "the traditions of free Greek justice."

The one crucial question that Vafiadis couldn't ask rhetorically was why didn't the defense—this attorney in particular—having repeatedly visited the defendant in Security Police headquarters after October 14 and having been told in private by him (so he claims in his book) that he had been tortured to create his story in the first and second instance— why didn't the defense suggest that pressure from the Security Police might have brought on these new incriminating revelations along with the old and that Major Mouskoundis, the silent presence in the wings, be called on to face cross-examination in the name of free Greek justice? Apparently the Communist threat to the country made this obvious line of defense inconceivable, whatever the cost to the terrorized man in the dock. And another crucial question remained unanswered: Why didn't the assembled correspondents now, finally, with such evident manipulation of the defendant's confessions and the implausibility of certain facts blatantly revealed, begin to unmask the charade that had been going on in the courtroom in front of their eyes for so many days?

Vassilikos, the noted legal rhetorician, took over the afternoon session of the eighth day to create the broadest of smoke screens. The court recorder—or his English translator—tries nobly to sweeten the air by presenting the summary in a kind of shorthand: "Thanks the Court for the excellent way the proceedings were conducted. Recalls the day when Polk met his death, and stresses that the defense expresses sorrow to young Polk, and hopes that he will follow his brother's excellent career. Requests him to convey to his mother the sympathy of all Greeks. Remarks that he is sorry but cannot express same sentiments to Rea." We learn that Rea, as a Greek, insulted her country and betrayed its traditions when she forgot her oath to be present at the trial.

Vassilikos then extended his sorrow to the citizens of Abraham Lincoln and reminded the court that in 1821 little Greece sent a message to Everett in Boston requesting his support for Greek independence, as did Premier Kolokotronis; and President Monroe, "known for his doctrine of isolation," addressed the U.S. Congress to tell them that the Greek struggle for independence should draw the assistance of Americans, as did President Adams, which demonstrated the traditional friendship between America and Greece and the fact that material aid was not the sole aid from the U.S. And Vassilikos went on to name the Americans "who have fallen for Greece's independence." The Voice of Greece should now reach the most remote sections of the Universe with the news of the struggle for her freedom. The Greek people, working hard, had cultivated their infertile land and had spread civilization to the whole of humanity. Who could deny "that on this rock barbarians are crushed and exterminated?" More shorthand: "Praises old Greece. The battles of Salamis, Marathon, etc., and recalls Philippos, father of Alexander the Great, who fought not to conquer but to offer civilization. Names the Byzantine Generals and Emperors. Are we not the Greeks who 130 years ago were 1,000,000 and are now almost 8,000,000? But we shed much blood—very much indeed. Greeks without liberty cannot live. We, like David, stood up as [to] Goliath when aggressors from the North, came to invade Greece . . ." and on into a history lesson about World War II and the "obscure powers" that worked during the Occupation until one day they attempted "to enslave this people."

Vassilikos's statement continued with rhetorical vigor until the mid-afternoon recess, but beneath the rhetoric he was attempting to suggest that his client was more innocent than he was thought to be by the press and the public more generally—including, one assumes, most in the courtroom—while at the same time attempting to uphold the Greek process of justice and the particulars of what the inquiry, and the defense itself, had established. He agreed that the crime, as the attorney general had said, was organized and executed by the same obscure forces that had threatened the country during the German Occupation. In this context the Greek press was clearly prejudiced against his client, but the jury should listen not to "the noise of the Niagara Falls" but to their own hearts and consciences. He reminded the court that Pilate had made an unjust decision in the case of Christ and had released Barabbas. The jury was now faced with judging an innocent person. The indictment was a good one, but the defense believed "there is too much literature in it." Consul General Gibson had said that "freedom has been followed during the entire trial." Naturally, since Freedom was born under the skies of Greece, Freedom of Speech under Demosthenes and other philosophers who spoke freely in ancient times, and the defense would speak freely now: "The hands of Stahtopoulos are not stained by the blood of Polk." Public opinion was already against him and against a light punishment, but it was the jury's honest judgment that counted. His colleague had told the court during the morning session that Staktopoulos "was not normally examined." Vassilikos himself did not mean to insult the inquiry or the police, but "I referred to Stahtopoulos personally [sic]." The court recorder: "Gives history of [Staktopoulos's] arrest. Justifies Stahtopoulos for contradicting himself, and for his inadequate replies to questions put to him by the Court and the Jury. He will speak about four persons—Rea, Mamas, Hadjiargyris and Stahtopoulos—and will endeavor to place each one in position [with relation] to Polk's crime."

And, after the recess, that is essentially what Vassilikos did, the placing of each an attempt to save his client by showing him to be no more guilty than the three others who had so far been let off scot-free, the "pardon" granted them by the attorney general excusable only on the grounds that Constantinidis "has a Christian heart." First of all, Rea Polk: maybe a good wife but "a bad Greek," who deceived the court by pretending to be sick when a picture that Vassilikos had seen of her in a newspaper showed her to be happy. Instead of preventing Polk from making the trip north, she had helped her husband come into contact with Communists and—fatal woman—was thus liable for her husband's death and guilty of "false justifications" when she could have "enlightened not only justice but the whole world."

For her part, Helen Mamas, "the fruit of a Greek-American crossing," with Greek blood circulating in her veins, could tell the truth and ought to tell the truth but doesn't do so. Clever woman that she is, she took advantage of having a translator to work out her answers to questions, and while "her conscience inside burned" (didn't she drink eight glasses of water during her testimony?), she kept saying "no opinion." As far as Vassilikos is concerned, Helen Mamas was "the intermediary in the ring which linked up Polk and his murderers." And she represented those foreign correspondents who came to Greece and attempted to use illegal means to reach the mountains instead of supporting the policy of the U.S. government with respect to Greece. Mamas was caught lying in that she contradicted Matchen's testimony to the effect that she and Randall Coate were both visited by Polk with a request for help in finding a Communist contact. In short, "Mamas for me is a female Stahtopoulos." And Hadjiargyris is just as bad. He should thank God, said Vassilikos, that he found Christianity in the heart of the attorney general. During his five days at the trial, Hadjiargyris walked up and down the corridors out of fear and nervousness. Clearly Hadjiargyris had stolen the missing correspondence. It was only "the politeness of the Greek police" that kept them from confiscating Polk's correspondence from the start and thus discovering the culprits. Staktopoulos was merely a witness of the murder and not an accomplice in it, but, asked Vassilikos, who is really more guilty, the Staktopoulos of Salonika or the Staktopoulos of Athens, that is, Hadjiargyris?

Vassilikos concluded with a plea that in the case of his client the jury take all the extenuating circumstances into account: the refugee background of the two Staktopoulos defendants, the opinion of Carl Compton, the fact that on an important Communist mission only the chief of the unit really knows what is up and others involved merely follow orders in ignorance, the fact that certain of his client's "gestures" should be attributed to the automobile accident he had and to "mental disarrangement" occasioned by fear of threats from murderers, saboteurs, the OPLA organization, etc. And the man's failure to report the crime after it was committed should be attributed to shock, as was explained in the psychological findings of a French psychiatrist "to justify joy, sorrow, or something sudden—a shock," in this case the result of Staktopoulos's having witnessed the murder and having been threatened by the KKE. Staktopoulos did not know that a crime was to take place, and if he got into the affair, it was because Polk asked him to and because he had to obey orders. In any case, the defendant had now been purged, and "those who detained him during the period of the last 8 months are in a position to certify it." Vassilikos was even willing to say that Staktopoulos's having been crossed off the Communist list was real and not fictitious. He therefore requested that Staktopoulos be sentenced according to article 74, which would allow that the defendant did not know anything about the crime in advance. And if the jury for other reasons issued its verdict on other grounds, the defense could only "ask you to kindly be as lenient as possible and to consider also 'fair confusion.' "

The jury deliberated for three hours and fifteen minutes the following day over the nine "questions" presented to it, actually various ways of phrasing the degree of possible guilt of the two defendants, including, among other gradations, the contingencies of premeditation, of complicity before or after the fact, and of hiding the perpetrators in the Staktopoulos home. They emerged with a positive answer to only the fourth "question": "Is the said defendant Gregorios Stahtopoulos . . . guilty of having, himself and others moved by a common interest, decided in common the carrying out of the following punishable deed ['a manslaughter'] and on account of same, having agreed in common a mutual assistance, at the place and time aforesaid, carried with them unlawfully and without a permit of the competent authority in the town of Salonika a firearm, i.e., a revolver, full of gunpowder and bullets."[48] Staktopoulos was thus exonerated of premeditation and of hiding the perpetrators, but he was convicted of complicity in the crime and carrying arms. The jury's answer in the case of Anna Staktopoulos was "no" to one of the questions concerning her complicity and "no answer" to a second. There was "no answer" to the final question of whether the two defendants had carried out the acts of murder or complicity in murder as the result of "imbecility" or while "their mind was not entirely excluded but substantially disturbed and reduced."

On the jury's recommendation, Gregory Staktopoulos was sentenced to life imprisonment and Anna Staktopoulos was acquitted,[49] though the court decided that she was not due any compensation. Mouzenidis and Vasvanas were sentenced to death in absentia, their cases to be automatically reopened if one or the other were captured. Vassilikos was quoted as remarking at the final sessions that "the public will be surprised to learn the Jury's verdict for life sentence since the Attorney General asked a lesser punishment," and Attorney General Constantinidis then protested that "he never said such a thing" and that it was "the Jury and not he that pronounces the decision."[50] Winston Burdett reported that Staktopoulos "stood and wept quietly as the court announced the verdict."[51]

Gregory Staktopoulos testifying at the murder trial. The jury
is seated in the background on the upper level.

ΜΑΚΕΔΟΝΙΑ
Η ΠΡΩΤΗ ΠΡΩΙΝΗ ΕΦΗΜΕΡΙΣ ΕΝ ΘΕΣΣΑΛΟΝΙΚΗ.

ΟΚΤΩΒΡΙΟΥ 1948

Η ΚΟΜΙΝΦΟΡΜ ΕΣΚΟΤΩΣΕ ΤΟΝ ΤΖΩΡΤΖ ΠΟΛΚ

Κατάπληξιν προυκάλεσαν εἰς ὅλον τὸν κόσμον αἱ χθεσιναὶ ἀνακοινώσεις τῶν δύο ὑπουργῶν

Ο ΣΤΑΚΤΟΠΟΥΛΟΣ ΠΡΟΕΒΗ ΕΙΣ ΣΥΝΤΑΡΑΚΤΙΚΑΣ ΑΠΟΚΑΛΥΨΕΙΣ

κορσόνι τοῦ «Λουξεμβούργου» ἀναγνωρίζει τὸν Στακτόπουλον: Αὐτὸς εἶνε, λέγει. Τὸν γνώρισα! — Ἡ παγὶς τῆς κα
εως καὶ τοῦ πρωτοκόλλου. — Ὁμολογεῖ ἡ μήτερα. — Φέρτε μου μιὰ εἰκόνα νὰ ὁρκισθῶ! Θὰ τὰ πῶ ὅλα! Μὴν πειρε
κορίτσια μου. — Ἐν συνεχείᾳ ἀναγκάζεται νὰ ὁμολογήσῃ καὶ ὁ Στακτόπουλος. — Πῶς συνηντήθησαν εἰς τὸ «Λου
ον. — Ἡ ἐκτέλεσις ἔγινε ἕνα μίλλι ἀνοικτὰ ἀπὸ τὸ Καραμπουρνάκι. — Ὁ Μουζενίδης τὸν ἐπυροβόλησε ἀπὸ πίσω
εσωριάσθη εἰς τὴν βάρκαν. — Μετὰ τὸ ἔγκλημα ἀπεβιβάσθη εἰς τὴν πλὰζ Ντωβίλ. — Μετέβη εἰς τὴν οἰκίαν του, ἀλ
παντελόνι καὶ ἔπειτα μετέβη εἰς τὴν ἐργασίαν του ἕως τὸ πρωί. — Ἡ ἀπολογία ἀπετυπώθη εἰς δίσκον

ΑΠΛΕΤΟΝ ΦΩΣ ΕΙΣ ΤΟ ΜΥΣΤΗΡ

At the top, Minister of Justice Melas and Minister of Public Order Rendis meet
with the press to announce the "official solution." The *Makedonia* headline,
October 18, 1948, reads: "The Cominform Killed George Polk." In the lower photo
are the principal Salonika judicial authorities: Komotouros, Constantinidis,
and Moustakis.

Helen Mamas arrives to testify.

Polk's brother William recording statement by Rea Polk in lounge of La Guardia Airport as he leaves U.S. on April 5, 1949, eleven months after the murder. Below, Rendis and Melas arrive in Salonika.

General William J. "Wild Bill" Donovan (at top,
center) with William Polk listening to testimony
at the trial and, below, conferring with officials
at the trial.

At top, Salonika Chief of Police Xanthopoulos and his staff of senior police officers. Below, Vangelis Vasvanas (left) and Adam Mouzenidis—guerrilla leaders convicted of murder in absentia.

Gregory Staktopoulos waiting
for the courtroom to fill at
the trial. His mother, Anna,
is beside him, back turned.
Below, William Polk and
Consul General Raleigh
Gibson chat outside the
courtroom.

At the top, Staktopoulos during a trial intermission. Note Raleigh Gibson directly behind him. Below, facing questioners during the trial.

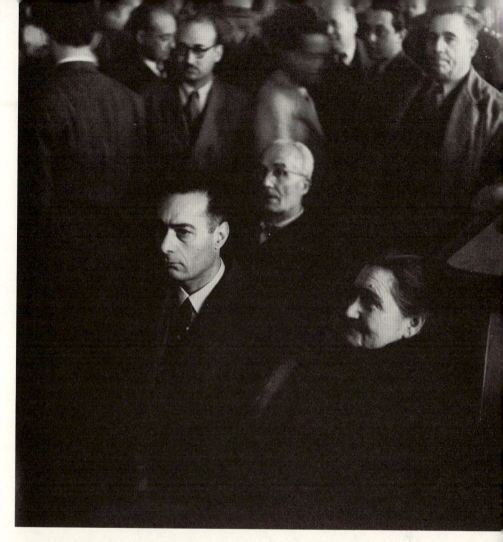

Gregory and Anna Staktopoulos in the dock.

Staktopoulos testifying on his own behalf, with picture of
Christ above the judges' bench in the background.

X The Whitewash

AT THE CONCLUSION of the trial on the afternoon of April 21, 1949, Raleigh Gibson took the first step toward establishing a perspective on the completed proceedings that would become the official response not only of the American government but of the designated representatives of the American press sent to observe the trial, as well as that of most local foreign journalists. Gibson issued the following statement at a press conference after the sentencing, as he recorded it in a cable to the secretary of state:

I have always had confidence that trial would prove to world how and by whom George Polk was murdered and this has been done. Judicial part of case was prepared with care and efficiency, and trial was one that can be remembered with pride. All judicial officials are to be complimented. Facts presented by judicial authorities were work of police officials of Salonika with cooperation of officials of Athens and Piraeus. Name of Major Mouskowdis [sic] must be especially mentioned and he must be complimented for intelligence, diligence, patience and brilliant work.[1]

We have seen that Gibson's ignorance of, or indifference to, what was going on behind the scenes at Security Police headquarters makes that statement an understandable conclusion to a long charade. What seems less understandable is the related misreading of the court proceedings in Salonika that emerges from two other statements that Gibson quotes in his cable, issued by observers who had attended the trial on behalf of two American press organizations, General Donovan representing the Overseas Writers Committee and William Polk and Constantine Poulos representing the Newsmen's Commission. Donovan is quoted as saying that he could not speak for the committee until he had handed in his report, but in his private capacity, speaking for himself, he "thought it proper ... to say that I attended every session of trial and found it honestly and efficiently conducted with fair and full opportunity to defense to present its case."[2]

William Polk and Constantine Poulos were a bit more equivocal, but less so than Raleigh Gibson had originally anticipated. They too said they were preparing a full report to be submitted to the Newsmen's

Commission, but "on this trial briefly" they could say that "we were impressed by case against Gregory Stahtopoulos and were convinced of his complicity in murder of George Polk. A defense attorney pointed out there are still many unanswered questions and much contradictory testimony. Until these questions are answered and these contradictions resolved, we agree with Attorney General that the investigation must continue and case cannot be considered closed."[3]

It seems that the press had largely come around to an acceptance of the official solution, which was sufficient for official purposes, but just two days earlier, following Staktopoulos's final testimony in court, Gibson had not been entirely sanguine about such acceptance, at least not by some correspondents, Polk and Poulos among them. He had sent in a lengthy confidential report to the secretary of state, justifying his "detailed examination" of press attitudes in a revealing prologue.[4] The Polk trial was peculiarly a newspaper trial, he said, not only because the victim and principal defendant were newspapermen but because much of the evidence being placed on record came from men and women of the fourth estate and "such links as are missing in the prosecution's case" might be found in the minds and records of certain journalists. And "in a very real sense," the Polk trial was "even directed at the press." The presentation of the case in court, though legally aimed at convincing a Greek jury that Gregory Staktopoulos and Anna Staktopoulos were guilty of murder, was "even more importantly an attempt to convince the American press, and through it the American people, that the murderers of an American newspaperman have been found and that the stain of that crime rests, not upon the present Greek Government, but upon the Communist Andartes and their masters in the Kremlin."

We have seen that this was indeed the attempt of prosecution and defense alike. But Gibson doesn't question the legitimacy of that mission or the assumptions behind it. And he goes on to suggest that "the honesty and completeness" with which the attendant correspondents report "what they see and hear" has "meaning above and beyond the normal requirements of impartial reporting," not, it seems, because the truth must come out whatever the political cost, and justice must be done whatever the presumed national interests of Greece and America, but because "only through them [the correspondents] can the Greek Government convince the American people that the conspiracy against Polk was indeed Communist planned and executed and that the Government to which the American people have granted their support is not a government which silences critics with shots in the back of the head." Apparently so convincing the American people is the "meaning above and beyond normal requirements" to which the attendant press should finally commit itself.

More often than not, in what follows, Gibson uses a correspondent's perspective on the Greek government case, the "official solution," as the measure of the correspondent's prejudice, as though the validity of that solution is to be taken for granted. Edgar Clark of United Press is described by Gibson as "possessing a cynical and iconoclastic personality," yet he "has appeared to show a greater degree of intelligent impartiality during the Polk trial than any other correspondent," owing, Gibson assumes, to his experience in Greece and other Balkan countries and his "understanding of the methods and procedures used by the Greek court."

One of Clark's "basic opinions of the trial" is that in all probability Staktopoulos "has agreed to cooperate fully in collaborating his confession . . . in exchange for the promise of a lenient sentence," and despite Clark's "belief in this 'deal' and the probable accuracy of that belief," this correspondent "considers that the trial is 'honest' and that the prosecution has already proved that Stahtopoulos took Polk to the boat and was in the boat when he was murdered." One might question the virtue of an "impartiality" that allows a trial to be considered "honest" when it involves a deal of the kind suggested; and one might have thought that a truly "intelligent impartiality" would have found implausible Staktopoulos's testimony to the murder of a voluntarily bound and blindfolded victim in a rowboat on its way to the foot of Olympus either directly or in league with a caique somehow hovering in Salonika Bay.

Other correspondents are pictured by Gibson as somewhat less "impartial." Sedgwick of the *New York Times* has a "strongly pro-Greek attitude" and a conviction that "much of the trial's American press coverage is leftist" and therefore naturally antagonistic to the present Greek government. But Gibson also tells us that despite the effect of Sedgwick's "favorite 'red herrings' " on his reporting and the "Sedgwickisms that creep into his copy," he is believed to cable a file that is "basically accurate and factual."

Barrett McGurn of the *New York Herald Tribune* has a problem at the other extreme, according to Gibson. McGurn's reporting carries "a surface gloss of impartiality," but this actually covers "the underlying negatives of a doubting Thomas." His constant qualifications create an impression of "uncertainty mingled with doubt as to the validity of the Government's case," and his attitude "mimics the violently suspicious attitude toward the Greek Government's handling of the Polk case which was fashionable in American press circles in the months follow-

ing the murder." Given the correspondent's youth and naiveté, concludes Gibson, the "continuation of this attitude past the point where
logic has begun to overrule fashion is not without possibility."

Winston Burdett and Alexander Kendrick of CBS appear to have skirted
the danger of going past the point where logic can overrule fashion and
are now pictured as being pretty much behind the government's case.
The consul general records—rather obtusely in the case of Burdett—that
"having for so long vetoed the possibility of a Communist plot as Government propaganda," the two, early on, "gave evidence of resisting the
reality of Communist responsibility for the death of Polk to the bitter
end, even if forced to admit that the prosecution's case was conclusive."
Now their original position has been modified to the extent of their
showing a "willingness to be convinced that the prosecution's case is
factual and true." Still, "they remain alert to any tendency which seems
to shadow the full legal honesty of the trial."

Gibson finds Burdett, though too easily influenced, the more intelligent and reasonable of the two. Fortunately, what may be "a feeling of
opposition to the conduct of the trial" in the "deeper levels of Burdett's
mind" has been kept under control during the early days of the trial,
"perhaps through the influence of General Donovan," perhaps—and here
one has to wonder what could have been moving on even the shallower
levels of Gibson's mind—"because of the obvious sincerity of the court
and the relative absence of disturbing developments." Kendrick is still
a potential problem: quicker of temper and less reasonable than Burdett,
he begins, says Gibson, with the assumption "that something is wrong
with the trial," and he believes that "the court expects every correspondent to assume a 100% pro-Greek and pro-Government attitude." Kendrick charged that the president of the court, in a private conversation,
"labeled all American correspondents crooks," and he assumes—Gibson
here adds "with perhaps some justification"—that any journalist not
sold on Greece and the prosecution's case is taken to be a Communist.
In any case Kendrick is subordinate to Burdett, a less important correspondent, and—Gibson concludes—Burdett's acceptance of the prosecution's case "has, in a measure, already been won, Burdett having admitted the weight of evidence presented in the court."

Constantine Poulos, William Polk's companion representing the
Overseas News Agency, has not yet shown his hand as clearly as Burdett
and other correspondents on the scene—still an "unknown ingredient"
in Gibson's book—but he is the loose gun that most worries the consul
general. Poulos arrived in Salonika with "a well-established reputation
as a 'leftist'" and as an opponent of the government's position in the

Polk case, but during the course of the trial "he has shown care in voicing his opinions," and "no overt word or act has yet been traced to him." Still, Gibson points out, he has been quick to raise carefully worded queries as to the honesty of the proceedings and the validity of the prosecution's case. It was Poulos who "voiced the strongest implications of 'jury packing' in the swift seven-minute designation of the trial jury," and it was Poulos who expressed an inability to see where the prosecution and the defense differed, "since both accepted the reality of a Communist conspiracy against Polk," thus making "the defense inoperative." Poulos also noted "the absence of 'workers' " on the jury, and he sparked objections to such "legal oddities" as the admission of hearsay and opinion in the court record—all of this, says Gibson, "despite his own obvious familiarity with the European legal viewpoint which they represent."

Gibson's comment here again reveals the bias of his persistent point of view regarding the trial and the proper role of the American press in covering it: the press is not to question legal oddities, irregularities, or the evident agreement before the fact of prosecution and defense, but to support, presumably in the national interest, the messy solution that was promoted (and to some degree shaped) at the trial in the name of justice. It was not clear at the time this cable was sent that Poulos would eventually accede to Gibson's view of what the national interest required in the way of press acquiescence, even to the extent of publicly stating that he was convinced of Staktopoulos's complicity in the murder. A thing that still much worried the consul general was Poulos's possible influence on young William Polk. Gibson reports that Poulos had been sitting with Polk throughout the trial and had given "every evidence of influencing the younger man to a marked degree." Young Polk had not yet been guilty of "any violent outburst," but he still showed "a continuing attitude of sullen resentment towards the entire proceedings," and if Poulos's influence could not yet be labeled dangerous, "it continues to give the appearance of an explosive cap in close proximity to a stick of dynamite." In view of Poulos's " 'leftist' " background, says the consul general, his actions "will bear close watching and careful attention."

Gibson's concern about William Polk's perspective on the trial was the subject of a special cable from the consul general to Washington, transmitted on the same day as his general summary of American press attitudes.[5] Attached to it was a copy of the letter of appeal signed by Norman Corwin, Ernest Hemingway, and Homer Bigart that was sent out in September on behalf of the group that Poulos and William Polk were representing in Greece, a letter that quotes General Donovan as having "accused the Greek government" of failing " 'to explore all the political possibilities' of the crime" and that calls for an independent investigation so that the George Polk story will not be allowed to die, since that would be "a victory for all those who believe a story can be killed by killing the man who gets it" and since the Polk murder "strikes at the work of every newsman trying to do an honest job anywhere in the world today."[6]

It is evident from this letter that Poulos and William Polk arrived in Greece with the charge to question what was going on in Salonika, even though one of the authorities cited in September to promote the charge, General Donovan, had changed his perspective in the meanwhile. It is equally evident from Gibson's cable that William Polk was not easily dislodged from his "sullen dissatisfaction with the proceedings" at the trial, despite what Gibson discerns—incorrectly, it turns out—as the "tempering effect on the influence of Poulos" that has resulted from "regular contact" in Salonika between William Polk and General Donovan. Even as late as April 19, the date of the cable, Gibson reports that William Polk still seems to feel that "the trial is 'staged' and that the evidence is insufficient to prove that George Polk was the victim of a Communist plot." Along with Poulos, he finds that the agreement between the prosecution and the defense attorneys "that Polk died as the victim of a Communist conspiracy" means that "there is no real defense operative at the trial" and that "political considerations are preventing a full and impartial hearing of all the facts in the case." His "negative attitude towards the defense," was evidently strengthened by its expressed satisfaction with the jury, whether "in its complement or its method of selection," an opinion that not only contradicted William Polk's conviction that the jury had been " 'packed' with conservative citizens on which the prosecution can rely for agreement," but that served as proof for Polk "that there is no real defense of Gregorios and Anna Stahtopoulos and that, therefore, there is no real trial of the case by American standards."

Another aspect of William Polk's attitude that seems to bother Gibson at this time is illustrated by young Polk's "marked efforts to keep Rea Polk's name and character spotlessly clean." The young man found it necessary to leave the courtroom "not during the detailed coroner's report on the condition of George Polk's waterlogged body, but at the mere mention by a witness that Rea Polk was considering or had decided upon separation from George Polk prior to his death." And he also tried to put on record a statement on Rea's nonappearance at the trial that "claimed competent medical authorities had ruled the trip and trial would be prejudicial to her delicate health," a claim that Gibson describes as "completely without official or legal basis." Since it was General Donovan who solicited the opinion of two medical authorities that Rea Polk "would not be able to meet the responsibility of testifying in a rational manner" and therefore could not have their consent to return to Greece,[7] the two Americans in Salonika working hardest to keep an unsteady craft from tipping over—Gibson and Donovan—were evidently not working hand in hand in this one regard.

But in the end, perhaps so as not to challenge openly what appears to have been a certain change of heart on Poulos's part, William Polk gave his name to the joint statement of April 21 in which he and the other representative of the Newsmen's Commission—itself representing five major press organizations with "approximately 10,000 working . . . members"—reported that they were not only impressed by the case against Gregory Staktopoulos but were convinced of his complicity in the murder, even if they also agreed with Attorney General Constantinidis that the case could not be considered closed.[8] Yet this statement was not their final comment in the affair. Three days later the two men visited Attorney General Constantinidis to complain about an article in a local newspaper calling Poulos a Communist, which the correspondent "disclaimed being."[9] William Polk, upset by news stories regarding Rea Polk's failure to return to Salonika for the trial, again requested that the attorney general include a statement in the court record regarding the reason for Rea Polk's not having appeared: physicians had been consulted, and they had agreed with both William Polk and his mother that, though Rea was not really ill, she "will fall ill if she returns for the trial."

It appears that Poulos now left the scene permanently, traveling with William Polk as far as Athens and then on to the U.S. by himself. His last comment on the Polk affair came a month later in an article he wrote for the *Nation* (May 28, 1949) in which he reaffirmed his belief that "on the basis of his own confession [Staktopoulos's] complicity was pretty well established." What was not established, he told his readers, was "the degree of his complicity." And he gave free voice to his many reservations about the trial: the evident agreement between prosecution and defense and even judges and jurors that there was no doubt that the perpetrators of the crime were Communists; the questionable validity of Anna Molyvda's testimony, mostly mumbled except for the crucial two lines about her meeting with Mouzenidis and Vasvanas which came out "clearly and loudly" and which were spoken with the charge of harboring a Communist criminal hanging over her head; the large issue of ex-Communist Zafiriou's reliability, which "was not questioned even once"; and some of the dubieties in Staktopoulos's confession, in particular the fact that nobody at the Astoria Hotel or at the Luxembourg Café—where Staktopoulos was well known—saw Polk and the Reuters stringer together at any time, including the night of May 8.

Poulos reported that he and William Polk were told by the owner of the café that he and his waiters "had informed the investigating authorities that Staktopoulos had lied in his confession," but neither the owner nor the waiters were called to testify at the trial by either the prosecution or the defense, and "when asked about this, the prosecutor shrugged it off, saying it was not important where Staktopoulos and Polk had their last dinner or exactly where they boarded the boat." Poulos concludes that in determining which parts of Staktopoulos's confession were true and which were not, obviously "one believes what one wants to believe and ignores the rest," though some parts "were proved to be false by several competent persons not in any way involved in the case, while parts accepted as true by the authorities, the court, and some observers were supported only by questionable witnesses whose lives or jobs were at stake."

In any case, Poulos apparently believed enough of Staktopoulos's confession to assume his complicity in the murder, and though Poulos senses coercion of Anna Molyvda, it seems not to have occurred to him that the whole of Staktopoulos's confession(s) could have also been occasioned by coercion. He clearly finds Staktopoulos suspect, no doubt in part because of the dubious biography of the Reuters stringer given out to him. He speaks of Staktopoulos as having been "one of the favored newspapermen in Salonika during the pre-war fascist dictatorship of Metaxas" (Staktopoulos was then a man in his late twenties and hardly established), who then worked for the German propaganda services (a new way of putting Staktopoulos's journalistic enterprise during this period), then, "according to testimony presented in court . . . supplied information to an Italian agent" (presumably meaning the red herring issue of his relations with his lady friend in Athens, Ms. Miha), then, as the Germans withdrew from Greece, joined "the powerful and then popular Greek Communist Party," subsequently worked for the British Information Service (Poulos here tells his readers that "it was obvious all through the trial that the complete truth about his relations with the British was being nervously concealed"), quit the Communist party in late 1946, "went to work for a conservative right-wing paper" (which is not an accurate description of the centrist-Venizelist *Makedonia*), and, finally, "to complete the cycle" and as "cross-examination by the prosecutor brought out at the trial, ... also served as an informer for the Special Security (anti-Communist) Police of Salonika." This biographical "cycle" makes Staktopoulos appear sinister indeed. But one can't help wondering why Poulos, besides interpreting some of these "data" incorrectly, gave more credence to what the trial brought up in connection with Staktopoulos's history than he did to other aspects of the trial, especially after Staktopoulos did his best to set the record straight by challenging those who accused him of various unproven activities, including that of arranging a homicide during the Occupation, and was never challenged or rebutted in turn.

Still, the fact is that Poulos came closer than any other correspondent at the trial to smelling out what was fishy about it; and his young companion, though under heavy pressure, continued the pursuit of truth as best he could after Poulos left the scene—alas, to little effect. We learn from a Gibson cable of April 30 that William Polk returned to Salonika on April 27 with the intention of interviewing several of the trial witnesses, Staktopoulos included.[10] He ended up doing so under peculiar circumstances. Constantinidis called at the consulate on the twenty-eighth to report that he had received a telegram from the minister of justice indicating that Poulos and Polk had received telephone threats while in Athens to the effect that "they would be killed by the rightists," and William Polk was therefore to be closely guarded during his Salonika visit and "not to be allowed to talk" to Staktopoulos, Anna Molyvdas, or Stelios Mouzenidis "except by permission of the Attorney General."

If we can believe another source, Kosta Hadjiargyris, William Polk was not allowed to see these three witnesses except in the presence of others, each of the three having been subject during the investigation to Major Mouskoundis's version of the third degree. Some two weeks after William Polk's return visit to Salonika, the second secretary of the American embassy in Athens, Robert G. Miner, reported that Hadjiargyris told him during a recent interview that Colonel Gordon of the British Police Mission "had supervised the whole questioning of Staktopoulos" (presumably by General Donovan as well as by young Polk)[11] and "had insisted that one of his men be present when William Polk talked to Staktopoulos."[12] In any case, Gibson records that William Polk was indeed closely guarded while in Salonika, and after an interview with the attorney general, "was allowed to see Stahtopoulos and other witnesses of the trial."[13] On April 29, just before returning to Athens, Polk called on Gibson to tell him that he had received complete cooperation from the attorney general, had talked to Staktopoulos and "other people connected with the trial," and "was convinced that Stahtopoulos was guilty of the murder of his brother, but . . . could not determine in his mind to what degree." As for "certain facts that had not been completely cleared at the trial," William Polk now felt that "time would give the complete picture." That appears to have given Raleigh Gibson an almost total diplomatic victory in handling the potential complication of American press coverage at the Polk trial.

It is unlikely that either William Polk or Kosta Hadjiargyris knew that the presence of observers at these interviews with trial witnesses remained a significant threat because all three of those named were still at risk of being tried for having admitted to hiding, or assisting someone in hiding, Communist enemies of the state, a capital crime. In the case of Staktopoulos specifically, Attorney General Constantinidis told Raleigh Gibson on April 26 that Major Mouskoundis "had been placed in charge of the investigation regarding the false radio story of an interview of Stalin's, as well as other Communist angles that had resulted in part from the testimony given in the Polk trial."[14] Constantinidis now indicated that he did not believe Staktopoulos would give detailed information regarding the Communist party, though he was still convinced that the man knew a great deal regarding its organization in northern Greece. Why he thought so at this late date, he did not say.

Regarding the possibility that Staktopoulos would receive a death sentence for giving refuge to Vasvanas, the attorney general "stated that since it only came from the confession and could not be proved, the death sentence would not be given" (Gibson's report does not specify that the "confession" in question here was the final version that Staktopoulos revised during the trial to include the announcement—surprising, we are given to believe, both to the prosecuting attorney and to the defense—that he had provided Vasvanas with a room for the night, while Mouzenidis was presumably being accommodated through the good offices of Anna Molyvda). But, said Constantinidis, there was still a possibility that Staktopoulos would be given a death sentence for his part in the false Stalin interview, "since treason could be charged." So the persistent threat hanging over Staktopoulos's head remained as sharp as it had been even after his having cooperated with the authorities to the limit of his capacities and been sentenced to life imprisonment for his effort. And now, with Mouskoundis in charge of the continuing investigation, there was no chance that Staktopoulos might see some relief ahead from the fear of surveillance and further punishment, especially since he was not sent to prison in keeping with his recent sentence but remained under Mouskoundis's custody at Security Police headquarters. And there he remained for the next four years, before being transferred first to the Salonika prison and then to the prison on Aegina island for another seven years, that is, until a commuted sentence in 1960—eleven years after the trial—allowed him to go home.

The effectiveness of Consul General Gibson's "diplomacy" was recognized and honored openly by General Donovan in a crucial "Informal Report on the Trial" that he sent his committee chairman, Walter Lippmann, as soon as the trial was over and that was excerpted in the Lippmann Report some three years later.[15] Donovan expresses the hope that the committee will write a note of appreciation to the consul general, "the kind of Consul we would like to believe always represents our country," because from the beginning he recognized the importance of "dealing with this case," has been "both the friend and advisor of the Greeks," and at the same time "has been a bridge of understanding between the Greek Government and the American correspondents." Most important of all, "without him and his efficiently run office there would never have been the relationship finally established with the Greek authorities." Without that relationship, one would want to add, there is at least an outside chance that the Lippmann Committee might have found a different perspective both before and after the trial and that justice might therefore have taken a different road in the Polk affair. At the very least, a whitewash of true history might have been prevented.

If Raleigh Gibson was the most influential figure in directing the local American press toward accepting the official Greek version of the Polk murder, General Donovan himself served as the key figure in neutralizing the American press so that the solution presented to the public in the spring of 1949 became the solution promulgated by the Lippmann Committee three years later, when the Polk affair had already lost sufficient momentum to remain more or less dormant until new questions began to be raised in both Greece and the United States some twenty-five years later. Donovan's "Informal Report" as the trial ended is the best source for demonstrating how his perspective—at least in the written record— had shifted since the distrustful and sometimes contentious summer days of 1948.

In addition to his already quoted remarks to the local press, Donovan tells Walter Lippmann in his report that "your committee can be certain that your original purpose has been realized," namely, " 'that no innocent man be "framed" and no guilty one be "whitewashed." ' " The "judges of Greece [he writes] have the confidence of the public," and "if the conduct of this trial is a fair example of other trials here, then that confidence is justified." The fact is that the "public" in Greece at that time was violently mixed politically, and to assume that there was a unified public confidence in any institution of government was either naive or disingenuous. In this particular regard, the extreme Left was roused to vituperation by one of the appointed judges, Papazisis, described by the guerrilla radio as a " 'pitch-black' monarchofascist criminal who has sent many innocent patriots before the execution squads," a "sadist" who made the people of Edessa "tremble at the sound of his name."[16]

Donovan's rhetoric in favor of the court officials was less hyperbolic, but he went in heavily for citing their military and other official credentials, spoke of the "courtesy" of the presiding judge, a man "not brilliant but thorough and painstaking," and described the defense attorneys as "both men of integrity." Vassilikos is cited as having a reputation for trial keenness and for oratory, which is "highly regarded in this country."[17] Donovan mentions that the attorneys together consumed twelve hours in summation. And he adds the grotesque comment: "In this area the relationship between Court and counsel is much as you will find in a community like Western New York or a city like Baltimore."

The remainder of his report on court behavior gently excuses some of the excesses and failures that the record amply illustrates. The "brushes between counsel and witnesses in which Court and jury often joined" are laid to the fact that "the Greeks are a contentious people"; these goings-on "enlivened" the proceedings and frequently made them "noisy," but never disorderly beyond control. The jury, "most active in their examination of witnesses"—in fact, "better in method and result than were the defense attorneys"—was "a fine example" of the important part a jury can take in such cases. Donovan does not add that without such activity there would have been virtually no cross-examination at all, and what there was did not sufficiently pursue the contradictions and implausibilities that should have brought Staktopoulos's "confessions" thoroughly into question.

Donovan's summary of the trial's substance is equally misleading. He indicates that the defense presented only two witnesses, Staktopoulos himself and Dr. Compton of Anatolia College, but he dismisses Anna Staktopoulos—and her revealing hesitations in court—with the parenthetical sentence: "(it was evident from the first that [Staktopoulos's] mother was out of the case)." In summarizing the prosecution's presentation, he picks out the former Communist Zafiriou as a chief witness, along with Stelios Mouzenidis, Anna Molyvda, a "chemist" (presumably the authority on ink), and two graphologists. Donovan gives Zafiriou this odd prominence because it was through him that the prosecution "showed several meetings with him [Zafiriou] and the defendant

Mouzenidis in the mountains where M[ouzenidis] told him he was going to Salonika on a dangerous mission."

The trial record in fact says no such thing. Zafiriou, described as "Surrendered Bandit Leader," reports that in March 1948 (the translation mistakenly has 1946), Mouzenidis told Zafiriou: "I'm going and wish to say good-bye." Zafiriou: "You don't look happy. Why?" Mouzenidis: "I am going on a mission which is a very difficult and dangerous one."[18] Fifteen days later he left for the Kroussia region. Zafiriou then learned from one Mrs. Ioannides—whom Mouzenidis had asked to take care of his wife and children—and from "other members at the headquarters" that Mouzenidis was killed at Kroussia. No mention of a mission to Salonika. It was only after Zafiriou's "surrendering" himself and arriving in Athens that he heard that "Ioannides and the guerrilla headquarters had organized Polk's murder and ordered Mouzenidis to come to Salonika to do the deed." This convinced him that the news of Mouzenidis's death at Kroussia was "planned to deceive those who would say that he was the killer when the Polk crime occurred," but the only evidence Zafiriou cites for this opinion in court is that "I am deeply convinced in my heart of it." Given the fact that he is testifying as a "Surrendered Bandit Leader," one can't help wondering what harsh pressures his heart might have been subject to at that time.

Donovan's summary of the prosecution's case then gives a sentence to Stelios Mouzenidis and another to Anna Molyvda, these, along with Zafiriou's testimony, providing "proof" that "tied into the Stakhtopoulos [sic] story." No questions raised about the story itself and the multiple variations in the confessions that created it. The report concludes with a one-sentence summary of the defense "to the effect that S[taktopoulos] did not know the true purpose of the journey, that (1) he was a Communist sent to perform the simple task of contacting Polk and acting as interpreter, (2) he wanted to help a fellow journalist realize his wish to reach the guerrillas." And the final issue that the defense presented the court: "Did Stakhtopoulos know or should he reasonably have known the purpose of the meeting?"—presumably with Mouzenidis and Vasvanas. Again, no comment on the fact that the prosecution and the defense shared the same assumptions about such a meeting and the Communist origins of the murder it promoted, assumptions that Donovan (and his assistant, Colonel Kellis) had ardently questioned eight months previously. No comment on the new implausibilities that had been brought into the record by the emendations that appeared in Staktopoulos's testimony before the court, a transcript of which, according to the Lippmann Report, General Donovan had gone over, as he had "examined in detail the voluminous records of the investigations preceding the trial."[19]

The Draft Report may provide a certain insight into Donovan's rationalization for ignoring the problems created by Staktopoulos's various confessions. The report points out some of the discrepancies between the October first and fourteenth versions of Staktopoulos's story (no mention of the discrepancy that appeared later that month—October 24—when Staktopoulos revised his confessions to eliminate the Athens meeting with Polk), and it finds the story itself "in many respects bizarre," demonstrating "a strange mixture of exhaustive memory for detail with respect to dates and time, and unexplained lapses of memory for names and the like." There is a suggestion that "Staktopoulos may have been coloring his statement in the light of facts which were already known" (i.e., the Murrow letter) when he quotes Polk's comment in the rowboat on being blindfolded, and the report also suggests that much of the bizarre nature of Staktopoulos's statements may have been owing to his "consistent attempt to picture himself as an unwilling tool of a murder he had no reason to anticipate." The report concludes that "essentially it is difficult to conceive of the story as a total fabrication in view of the fact that the witness would hardly have so testified, thereby subjecting himself to imprisonment or death had not the story been substantially true." Instead, he could have "stuck to his original statements that he knew nothing of the crime and had merely posted the letter as instructed." We learn that at the time the official solution was announced, Donovan "stressed the advisability of securing corroborative evidence so that the prosecution might rest on more than the confession of the defendants."[20] But there is no indication in the Draft Report that Donovan suspected that coercion, violent or otherwise, might have been exercised by the Security Police in obtaining the confessions or that the local authorities might have played a role in creating the story that became the basis for the official solution.

At what point Donovan decided to go along wholeheartedly with that solution, despite his early reservations about the way the investigation was being conducted, is not entirely clear from either his own papers or from the State Department archives. We have seen that by the time of his third visit to Salonika in early October 1948 he was ready to congratulate Major Mouskoundis on the Staktopoulos solution and to review the confessions uncritically. But there is evidence that he had already committed himself to the Mouskoundis-Constantinidis line by the time the issue of Colonel Kellis's transfer was brought to him by the Lippmann Committee in August 1948, when Donovan reported back that Kellis's return to Greece was unnecessary.

The account of this episode in the Lippmann Report, though the one occasion for criticism of the way American officials behaved in Greece, was not conclusive on the question of why or when Donovan changed from a negative to a positive stance regarding the course of the Salonika investigation. The Report tells us that "late in July 1949 [read 1948], without notice to General Donovan or the committee, Colonel Kellis was recalled to the United States. The Air Force wanted him for another assignment."[21] The committee ascertained that Kellis's recall had actually been suggested by "an official of the American Embassy in Athens [i.e., Karl Rankin] in a cable to the State Department." Kellis, we are told, "had been exploring certain leads pointing to the Right, or a terrorist organization of the Extreme Right, as the author of the crime," and since the committee and General Donovan thought it very important that all leads, "regardless of political embarrassment to anyone," be explored, the executive committee of the larger committee, working in Washington, "regarded this interference with Colonel Kellis's activities as a grave violation of Secretary Marshall's instructions" in that the Lippmann Committee had not been apprised "of the communications, both by cable and orally, leading to the recall" of its independent investigator.

Yet once the committee had "established the facts in this matter," a thing it accomplished "only by persistent investigation," it decided to postpone any action until General Donovan's return from Greece, presumably in August. It turned out, says the Report, that General Donovan "had taken occasion to impress on Greek officials the necessity of exploring fully the leads which pointed to the Right as well as those pointing toward the Left." Donovan advised the committee that he was satisfied that this would be done, especially since he had come to feel that certain key officials in the inquiry would not be displeased if the crime were found to have been committed by rightists. "As a result," the Report tells us, "plans for sending Colonel Kellis back to Greece were abandoned."

Another source, the notes that Colonel Kellis submitted to the CIA file on the Polk case in 1952 while he was working for the Agency, offers a rather different version of some aspects of this episode, as we have seen. Kellis records in these notes that he himself tried, after forty days on the job, to send a cable to Donovan through the embassy "notifying him of my desire to be relieved" of the assignment in Greece.[22] We are not told whether the cable went out, but Kellis says that he "later contacted General Donovan through other means" to pass on his request, and upon Donovan's return to Greece, presumably in July, "he [Donovan] allowed me [Kellis] to return to the U.S." This happened after Kellis had submitted to Donovan his confidential report listing the ten suspects—Staktopoulos among them—that Kellis had identified during his tour with the investigation and that Donovan "reviewed very carefully," finally asking "the Chief Investigator" (one assumes Major Mouskoundis) to concentrate on the Greek newspaperman who "within sixty days . . . confessed complicity in the crime."

The full implications of these and other of Kellis's notes for the CIA file will be reviewed in their proper chronological context (chapter 11), but if we take them to have a reasonable basis in truth, it would seem that Donovan helped to promote the Staktopoulos solution even before Staktopoulos was arrested on August 14, which would explain his immediately congenial meeting with Mouskoundis over the Staktopoulos confessions in October. In any case, well before the time of the trial, any sort of independent stance on Donovan's part vanished from the record, and there is evidence that he led the Lippmann Committee toward their acceptance of the official solution. The Report indicates that after the indictment of Staktopoulos and his mother, the committee "gave consideration to engaging a Greek lawyer to participate in the trial as counsel for Polk's mother or widow," a move that was permissible in Greek practice, but "General Donovan finally concluded . . . that this was unnecessary, especially since he was able to arrange to attend all sessions of the trial himself."[23] This "conclusion" on Donovan's part made him the sole representative of the Lippmann Committee at the trial, so that his estimate of what went on there became the principal source for the committee's conclusions as to justice in the Polk case. Besides the already quoted remarks on the efficiency and honesty of the way the trial was conducted, Donovan advised the committee "that, in his opinion, the evidence which caused the conviction of Stakhtopoulos [sic] would have led an American jury to a similar conclusion." And the Report adds: "General Donovan's judgments on all these essential points appear to have been shared by the American correspondents who covered the trial."[24]

By the end of the trial, this seems indeed to have been true of most, but not of William Polk; it was Donovan who was primarily responsible for frustrating his effort to question what seemed to be going on in front of his eyes, though he has admitted to being too inexperienced at the time and too ignorant of the country's procedures and ways to have understood fully the context of what he was seeing. In an article that appeared in the May 1977 issue of *More*, William Polk tells us that Donovan saw the issue in Greece as a simple one.[25] Greece was the current battleground in the undeclared war between the United States and the Soviet Union. He thought the Communists must have killed

George Polk "to use his death against America's Greek allies," a view of the murder in keeping with the Mouskoundis-Constantinidis line. And if it turned out that some other group had been responsible, whether a branch of the Greek government or a secret terrorist organization, that fact "would damage American will to stay the course against the Communists" and therefore the best thing that could be done, no matter who might prove to be guilty, "was to get the case behind us."

At the time, Polk reports, he thought Donovan's aim was to bury the issue decently. When he challenged him "on the lack of thoroughness of the investigation," Donovan became furious and asked him what he was trying to do. Polk told him that he was trying to find answers to the basic reporter's questions, the "who, why, and how, etc.," so that others might be deterred "from trying to kill reporting by killing reporters." Donovan saw this as "not only silly, but dangerous." Why was William asking such difficult questions and making things so complicated? Couldn't he see that they were in the middle of a war? "You are a smart young man from a good family," he quotes Donovan as saying. "If you keep on, you will ruin your career."

Polk tells us that at the time he was tired and terribly discouraged, "both young and way over my head in the macabre politics of 1949 Greece." Still, he could see that "things were not as they seemed and people were not what they said," and he felt that he could neither give in "to the helplessness of it all" nor "trade a brother for a better job." The implication is that he did his best to resist Donovan's pressure to whitewash the affair. In a recent interview (1987), he revealed that the confrontation described in the *More* article took place shortly after the trial ended, in front of the Grande Bretagne Hotel in Athens, where he was approached by Donovan and AP correspondent Socrates Chakalis (presumably the Athens AP journalist sometimes transliterated as Chakalis or Tsakalis) "and put to the wall" by Donovan, with words rather more aggressive than those quoted in the *More* article: "If you don't want to ruin your career," Donovan told him, "keep your mouth shut and your nose clean."[26]

William Polk also indicated in the same interview that he had come to dislike Donovan during the course of their brief association. He thought the man a bully, not so much The Last Hero (in keeping with the title of the generous 1982 biography of Donovan by Anthony Cave Brown) as The Last Jerk: often thickheaded, unsubtle, even "childish." Polk gave as an example the fact that, during the trial, Donovan not only made a point of sitting beside him (one assumes on the other side from Poulos), but when Polk brought out a rather primitive tape recorder of the only kind then available and turned it on to provide himself and posterity with a full record of the proceedings, Donovan took out a pencil and tapped it continually against the tabletop beside the recorder so long as it was working. "I ended up with a recording full of pencil tappings," said Polk, "and eventually threw the tape away as useless."

We also learn from the *More* article that Donovan scoffed at Polk's lack of knowledge of Greek politics and asked him during the Grande Bretagne encounter what political aspect of the case he thought had been missed during the investigation. When Polk mentioned the right-wing terrorist organization known as "X" ("Chi"), Donovan laughed sardonically and said there was no such organization—this though the Draft Report based on his knowledge of the case speaks of "the organization known as 'X,' an extremist Right Wing terrorist conspiratorial group allegedly with numerous sympathizers in the Greek army."[27] Chakalis laughed too: "X" was just "a myth in the minds of several critics of the Government." As Polk points out, the supposed myth later came to life quite dramatically under Grivas in the Cyprus guerrilla war and even later in the ranks of the Papadopoulos junta that took over Greece in April 1967.

In the 1987 interview, Polk disclosed what now seems an even more startling aspect of the political intrigue that he had found so unsettling in 1949. During the same posttrial visit to Athens, Minister of Justice Melas—presumably representing a liberal faction in the coalition government—told Polk that twenty to thirty years would probably have to go by before the young American would understand the "necessity" of what had taken place in the Salonika courtroom—the first indication William Polk had that what he now sees as a "phony" trial was indeed acknowledged to be something like that at the time by the leading political figure in the Greek judicial system.

As for General Donovan's influence on the course of events in the Polk affair, his most significant contribution appears to have been the authority he provided for the whitewash that the Lippmann Committee ended up giving the case in its 1952 Report. The most remarkable thing about the Report is that it took three years for it to appear.[28] The only excuse offered for the delay in the text itself was the committee's hope that in the years following the trial "the actual murderers" (the phrase that presumably distinguishes Vasvanas and Mouzenidis from Staktopoulos) might be arrested, tried, and convicted,"[29] as is possible under Greek law for those convicted in absentia—a rather lame excuse for the delay when the focus of the Report is on supporting the case against Gregory Staktopoulos, assumed to be at least a kind of solution to the

Polk case that the Lippmann Committee can now promulgate. From a February 1951 letter that Lippmann sent Eugene Meyer, a colleague on the committee—quoted in a seminal article on the Polk case by Yannis Roubatis and Elias Vlanton in the May 1977 issue of *More*—we learn that, as far as Lippmann himself was concerned, the Report "had been completed" by the date of his letter to Meyer; the problem lay elsewhere: "Bill Donovan—though he has made innumerable promises—has never produced his part of the report. What is more, he has discouraged Guy Martin [the committee's assistant counsel]."[30] We learn from the same letter that Ernest Lindley also "has never found the time to finish his part of it." Lippmann says that he hates "to leave a job of this kind in such a messy condition," but that is evidently what he had to do. The Report was submitted for publication in its less than complete form at some point during the weeks that followed (the published text is dated May 21, 1951).

The second thing that is remarkable about the Report—excluding its many appendixes—is its brevity: eight pages of text (reproduced in the Appendix to this volume) justified in the "Foreword" on the grounds that "a full accounting," including all the documentary material that came to the committee, would require "several volumes," and "even a summary" of the material and of all the actions and deliberations of the committee, its members, and its counsel, "would require a great deal of space."[31] Instead, what the committee offers is a "condensed report" (in an edition of only 2,000 copies, according to Roubatis and Vlanton) which it hopes will "satisfy the members of the American press and radio who supported this investigation" and also provide guidance if similar inquiries should be needed in the future." Granting it the greatest benefit of the doubt, it is unlikely that it did the first and scandalous if it did the second.

The Donovan papers tell us more than Lippmann apparently knew—or perhaps ever came to know—about Donovan's reluctance to contribute a full account both of his role in the affair and of how he viewed important aspects of the case. The first especially relevant document in this connection is a twelve-page double-spaced typescript entitled "Tentative Draft of the Polk Report," dated May 1949—in pencil, which casts some doubt on a dating that early—a document that is very close to the official Report as it appeared in 1952, with a few suggested deletions and revisions that were incorporated into the final text (the only substantial changes those that tended to make the departure of Colonel Kellis from the investigation appear somewhat less conspiratorial). The second, more important document is the Draft Report prepared at Donovan's request by Mary G. Jones, the full title of which appears as *"GEORGE POLK*/Re: Investigation of Death/Draft of Report on Polk Investigation by Mary G. Jones." The Draft Report is dated "10/50" (i.e., October 1950) and consists of some 140 double-spaced, typed pages divided into nine chapters (Introduction, The Overseas Writers Committee, Polk's Last Trip to Salonika, The Greek Government Organizes Its Investigation, Progress of the Investigation May–August 1948, The Detention and Arrest of Gregory Staktopoulos, The Indictment, The Trial and Conviction of Staktopoulos, Conclusion).

One can reasonably assume that this second document, based on information that must have been gathered for the most part by Donovan, was originally meant to serve as his contribution to the final Lippmann Report, and indeed some sentences from the longer document appear more or less verbatim in the eight pages that the committee finally published. But the full draft, which draws on whatever State Department dispatches (e.g., from the Athens embassy and the Salonika consulate to the secretary of state) and translated court records were made available to the general, is remarkably thorough, sometimes skeptical—as we have seen—and, though arriving in the end at the same conclusions as those that appear in the Lippmann Report, more candid in its commentary on questionable aspects of the case, including the character of some of the evidence and the deportment of both Greek and American officials. For example, the Draft Report states, with reference to Hadjiargyris, Rea Polk, Helen Mamas, and Daniel Thrapp, that "while none of these persons were apparently in any way involved in the crime nor were able to throw any light on the crime, the attitude of the Greek authorities towards them reflected in part their initial frustration as respects the guilty parties, their tendency to grasp at any straws and their innate suspicions of any person whose political views did not coincide directly with their own." But—the Draft Report continues—"this attitude of the Greek authorities underscored the wisdom of the determination of the Lippmann committee to assume an active role with respect to the investigation and demonstrated the effectiveness of the assistance which it was able to render in the course of the investigation."[32]

As this last claim suggests—and it is a claim that the record of the case does not support—where the Draft Report fails in candor, perhaps understandably, is in the image it gives of General Donovan's role in the affair as the Lippmann Committee's counsel, portraying him and other representatives of the press as applying essential pressure at certain moments to assure that the investigation moved forward with dispatch when it became stalled and that it finally reached the kind of just solution that the Lippmann Report itself promotes, sometimes with the same phrasing. We learn from the Draft Report that Staktopoulos was the "finger man" who led Polk into the trap that his murderers laid for him, that "no innocent man was framed," that the investigation, after some hesitation and delay, was "pursued with vigor and sincerity," that the trial of Staktopoulos and his mother was "fair" and was conducted "without prejudice to the defendants."[33] At the same time, the Draft Report states that "it is to be regretted perhaps that its [the trial's] emphasis was more on an attempt to justify the Greek investigatory authorities and Greek honor and less on an effort to check further into the actual facts surrounding the murder as related by Staktopoulos."[34]

The Draft Report concludes with a certain equivocation regarding the sometimes differing roles of American officials in Athens and the American press, but with little equivocation regarding the role of the Lippmann Committee and its counsel. We are told that the Lippmann Committee's "active role in the case, in addition to the help which it was able to render from time to time in uncovering of information and the checking of information volunteered by informants in Greece, was also responsible for the greater confidence displayed both by the Greek and the American public in the trial and conviction of Staktopoulos"[35]—which, unfortunately, does not now seem an exaggerated claim. On the delicate problem of the difference in approach between the American government officials and the American press (including the Lippmann Committee representatives) in dealing with the Greek government, we learn that the "difference in approach between the governments [sic] and the press was primarily one of emphasis."[36] To the press, the Greek government would be discredited if it failed to take "vigorous steps to uncover and apprehend the culprits even if they turned out to be connected with a group other than the Communists." To the State Department, any criticism of the Greek government tended to "reflect upon it despite the eventual result of the investigation and therefore should be avoided even though this might result in a less vigorous investigation."

The Draft Report finally suggests that it is difficult and maybe irrelevant "to assess the relative merits of the two positions."[37] We are told that "in general" the Lippmann Committee "enjoyed very cordial relations with the State Department and received sympathetic co-operation [sic] from most of the American officials abroad," and "General Donovan in his four trips to Greece was extended every facility by American diplomatic officials."[38] And the Draft Report concludes, "the eventual apprehension and conviction of Staktopoulos was the sole product of the Greek authorities," though the "perseverance of the Greek authorities in the investigation and the more thoroughly documented case presented against the defendants was undoubtedly attributable in large measure to the work of the Lippmann Committee and its counsel, General Donovan, as well as the press in general."[39]

Why did Donovan decide not to pass on the full document of the Draft Report to the Lippmann Committee? The most plausible answer is that Mary G. Jones's extensive draft revealed more than Donovan thought ought to be revealed about both the investigation and the trial. Though the general is pictured as exerting himself forcefully at certain moments to keep the investigation moving, he is also shown to have had his problems with certain Greek and American officials (though Raleigh Gibson gets an unqualified endorsement).

Since the Donovan papers do not actually provide evidence of Donovan's response to Mary G. Jones's draft (though we do have a letter from her that brings Theodore Lambron's comments and objections to his attention),[40] we have to work from the single fact that the document, with its mixture of candor and exoneration, was finally in large part suppressed. What was retained from it is all that appears in the "Tentative Draft of the Polk Report," which could be either a short preliminary draft that Mary G. Jones eventually drew upon—if we accept the penciled date of May 1949 as accurate—or a compilation of excerpts (the language often close and sometimes the same) from her much longer account of the case and its conclusion, in either case all that Donovan thought appropriate for the committee to include in its published Report. The assumption is that the general decided in the fall of 1950 that it was the better part of wisdom, with Staktopoulos beyond reach in prison (actually still at Security Police headquarters) and the trial long over, to avoid presenting any substantial issue in the committee's account of things that might bring the established solution of the Polk case into question.

What the eight pages of the published Report[41] in fact offer the reader is, first of all, a short history of the committee's activities in getting itself organized before General Donovan took over "a major part of the day-to-day work," then certain problems and "perplexing questions" that the committee had to face after it got itself organized, and finally the conclusions it came to, based in large part on what General Donovan derived from his four trips to Greece as the committee's counsel. We are told at the beginning of the section labeled "Conclusions" that in general the Committee "followed the practice of American newspapers when in any community there is a serious crime, with more than personal significance, which is not solved," namely, "to work with the authorities, to support them, to encourage those who are energetic, to put pressure on those who are slow, timid, or complacent, and to make an independent inquiry at the same time."

Presumably in keeping with this practice, the committee's "first step" was to meet with Secretary of State Marshall and to receive from him a promise that the committee would have "access to all official information in the case," for which purpose William O. Baxter of the State Department's Greek desk was designated to "maintain liaison" with the committee. Two members of the American embassy staff in Greece were assigned the task of following the Greek investigation on a daily basis, and similar instructions were sent to Mr. Raleigh Gibson, consul general in Salonika. The committee also learned from American authorities in Greece "that the British Police Mission, then engaged in training the Greek police in Scotland Yard methods, were actively cooperating with the Greek authorities in investigating the Polk murder." With the selection of General Donovan as counsel—"organizer and head of the wartime Office of Strategic Services, . . . qualified, preeminently by ability and prestige and uniquely by experience"—and with the subsequent appointment of Frederick Ayer, chief of Dwight Griswold's security division in Athens and former FBI officer, the committee's tie-in with the authorities both in the U.S. and in Greece was firmly established, for better or for worse.

With such a broad-based relationship to government—and former government—officials at a number of levels, it was predictable that the committee's effort "to make an independent inquiry" at the same time that it was resolved "to work with the authorities" would run into trouble. This came, the Report tells us, when the committee's "independent investigator," Colonel Kellis, left behind in Greece after Donovan's first visit there and engaged in exploring certain avenues that nobody else seemed to be exploring, was recalled to the U.S. after less than two months on the job, at the suggestion of "an official of the American Embassy in Athens [read Karl Rankin] in a cable to the State Department." The committee feels "compelled to report" that the work of this independent investigator was not only *not* facilitated but "in fact was frustrated" by "the Greek and American authorities." Still, the committee concludes, it "has no reason to believe and does not suggest that its independent investigator would eventually have produced evidence different from that which was presented at the Stakhtopoulos [as the name is spelled throughout][42] trial." What the committee does not feel compelled to report is that after Kellis left the scene and Donovan decided that the colonel was no longer needed in Greece, what "independent inquiry" remained under the committee's sponsorship had to emerge from the few communications he received via Theodore Lambron, from his own quick visits during the final phase of the investigation, and from his attendance at the trial, with the consequences we have seen.

General Donovan also became the key figure in coping with several other "perplexing questions" that confronted the committee. Hadjiargyris, "close friend of Polk's" but here unnamed, was one of these. He had expressed fear for his own life and had sought the aid of his American employer and several prominent American journalists to enable him to leave Greece. The problem was, says the Report, the Greek authorities regarded him as "a witness of potential importance" who had not satisfied them that he had disclosed all he knew about "Polk's underground contacts in Greece" (unspecified here or elsewhere). The committee "felt that it should take no step which might either frustrate the Greek official investigation or provide an excuse for failure to track down the murderers of Polk." So the question was turned over to General Donovan to handle. He was to present Hadjiargyris with a letter from his employer telling him that he must disclose all he knew before he would receive any assistance in leaving Greece. Donovan was then to interrogate the correspondent with a representative of the Greek government present if it so chose and the witness represented by counsel if he so chose; and if this interrogation provided information which might place the life of the witness in danger but did not implicate him in the murder, General Donovan and the committee "would use their best efforts to obtain a safe refuge for him in the United States or some other suitable place." Meanwhile, special police protection for the correspondent would be requested. The Report does not tell us whether the Greek government agreed to this procedure—hardly a normal mode at that time—or whether an interrogation of any serious kind took place, let alone what Donovan's determination of Hadjiargyris's situation turned out to be.

Then there was the problem of "potential sources of information who did not trust the Greek Government or particular prosecutors." Also, the committee was aware from the beginning "of the possibility that its pressure for the arrest and punishment of the murderers could result in a frame-up to satisfy the American demand for action." But the committee "invariably concluded that the proper course was to keep the primary responsibility fixed on the Greek Government, not only for a full, relentless and honest investigation and a fair trial but for the safety of those potential witnesses, who, rightly or wrongly, felt they were in danger." Though one could argue that this is not an unreasonable posture for an

American press association to assume in a dependent country, the committee's failure to assist their foreign colleagues in obtaining even minimal protection had ghastly consequences for Gregory Staktopoulos and much prolonged the torment of Kosta Hadjiargyris. The Report also tells us that General Donovan "had the opportunity to interrogate directly these possible sources of information," but we are not told if, when, how, or to what effect he availed himself of this opportunity. The Report provides little reassurance in this crucial area—anyway for those who have read *Yankee G-Man*—when it indicates that "on other occasions" during the early part of the official Greek investigation, "Mr. Ayer was present" when certain undesignated witnesses were interrogated.[43]

The conclusions expressed in the committee's Report can be easily predicted from the "practice" it chose to follow, from the collaborators it chose to work with, and from the way it chose to cope with the problems that arose. Under "Conclusions," it tells us that the committee "is able to report that the official investigation was, after some hesitation and delay, pursued with vigor by the Greek authorities and officers of the law"—though of course it cannot report that the committee never put itself in a position to know, and perhaps even to challenge, the quality of that vigorous pursuit after Staktopoulos was arrested and held at Security Police headquarters, over three months into the investigation. Earlier in the Report one learns that "it was . . . plain" the murder was the act of a gang that wished not to conceal but to draw attention to their crime, that "it was also established" that Polk "was attempting to reach the headquarters of the guerrilla forces" and this from Greek territory rather than from Yugoslavia (whether "he used the best judgment" in doing so was "arguable"), that Polk was "the victim of a plot to murder him with the deliberate intent of influencing the course of events in Greece," and, finally, since "it was evident that the crime was political" but not so evident whether the Right, the Communists, or "a terrorist gang operating independently, either from the Extreme Left or the Extreme Right" had perpetrated the crime, the committee "concluded that only a solution of the crime tested in open court could ever settle the case."

Its summary conclusion tells us that this has indeed happened. The committee is now "satisfied" not only that Staktopoulos and his mother received a fair trial but also that Staktopoulos "was in fact an accessory, that he was the 'finger man' who led Polk into the trap where his murderers were waiting for him." Whether Staktopoulos knew in advance that Polk was to be murdered "is another question on which the Greek jury, in convicting him of complicity, did not pass." Still, though Stakto-

poulos is "guilty of the charge on which he was convicted," the committee acknowledges that he was not the murderer. Those "tentatively
found guilty by the Greek jury," Vasvanas and Mouzenidis, have not
been found, though the civil war in Greece has been brought to an end
in the meanwhile. The reports that they "were killed before the end of
the Civil War" may be correct, or they "may have sought refuge in
another land." No mention of the fact that much effort was exerted by
the investigators in Greece to challenge repeated reports from guerrilla
sources that Mouzenidis was killed in battle some weeks before the
murder took place, and no mention of the opinion held by some that
both presumed murderers were so far up in the Communist hierarchy as
to be unlikely candidates for the roles they were given in Staktopoulos's
various confessions. As it turned out, Mouzenidis was never heard from
at any point, and Vasvanas, who followed the guerrillas out of Greece
and settled in Rumania, apparently attempted on several occasions in
later years to return to Greece in order to clear his name of involvement
in the Polk affair and finally died behind the iron curtain (as is documented in the chapter that follows).

The Report ends with rather pious sentiments—especially so when
seen as prefatory to the thin evidence it provides for its conclusions. The
committee hopes that the Polk case will not be forgotten, because the
safety of American correspondents working abroad in dangerous places
can best be ensured if it is known to all the world that they cannot be
attacked with impunity and that "the power and influence of the United
States Government, the concerted action of the press and radio, and an
aroused public opinion, will demand and will persist in demanding the
pursuit and punishment of the criminals." This in itself "cannot guarantee the safety of American correspondents, but it can act as a deterrent
against any who might otherwise think the risks were not too great."
End of statement.

What the Polk case unfortunately appears to have illustrated is that
in some "dangerous places," for example, Greece during its 1947–49
civil war, and at certain moments of arrogance in American history, for
example, the postwar period of incipient McCarthyism, representatives
of the press working in concert with the power and influence of the
United States government can help to effect exactly the kind of miscarriage of justice that the Lippmann Committee says it feared: "a frame-up
to satisfy the American demand for action." And an investigative committee of the press insufficiently vigilant in its work of surveillance or
without the heart to review even its own partial evidence with care and
skill—let alone all relevant evidence—can find itself whitewashing the
frame-up that has occurred.

How could a man of Walter Lippmann's reputation for seeing foreign affairs with clarity and wisdom and for telling things as he saw them have given himself to this Report? Ronald Steel offers an answer in his splendid biography of Lippmann, with the Polk affair specifically cited as a case in point: "Lippmann participated in the world as an 'insider.' . . . He operated entirely within the system. When, for example, he was appointed by a newsmen's committee to head the investigation of the murder of George Polk . . . he did not seriously question the State Department's contention that communist guerrillas were responsible— even though he privately recognized that discrepancies in the evidence pointed damningly toward the Greek government and the CIA."[44] The evidence for possible CIA involvement is obscure in the official record now in the public domain, because references to that government enterprise or its agents appear to have been excised from some documents, and other documents with such references withdrawn entirely from the Polk case files (the Agency was in any case in its infancy at the time of the murder, created by an act that Congress passed in 1947, hardly yet the fully active enterprise it was to become in Greece and elsewhere). But Lippmann's proclivity for operating "entirely within the system," whatever his private recognition of the truth, goes a long way toward explaining the way his committee was allowed to function and the conclusions it was allowed to promulgate in its Report.

The limited evidence offered by the committee for its conclusions— aside from the references to General Donovan's "Informal Report on the Trial . . ."—is anyway permitted to speak in large part for itself in the form of appendixes, without commentary or notes by those who prepared the Report. Along with the generous excerpts from Donovan's "Informal Report," the Overseas Writers resolution appointing the committee, and its Finance Committee's report, we are given a memorandum that Lippmann submitted to Secretary of State Marshall at the start of the committee's work; a memorandum on the May 24, 1948, conversation of the committee with Secretary Marshall; a commentary, solicited by Lippmann, on Staktopoulos's three early confessions (October 1, 2, and 14) written by E. M. Morgan, professor of criminal law at Harvard Law School and delivered on March 17, 1949 (misdated 1948); English translations of the three early confessions but not that of October 24, which eliminated Staktopoulos's proposed meeting with Polk in Athens, and not that of his amended testimony at the trial, with its news about his harboring Vasvanas and the waiting caique in Salonika Bay; a five-page document labeled "TELEGRAM FROM SALONIKA TO SECRETARY OF STATE," dated October 17, and misleadingly signed simply "GIBSON" (it is not in fact Gibson's account of the case at that point but his cabled translation of the official "communiqué" on the Polk case that was issued on that date by the ministers of justice and public order, in effect, what became accepted as the "official solution" in Greece); a transcript of a radio broadcast identified as "Columbia Broadcasting System Report No. 4 on the Murder of George Polk, Wednesday, April 27, 1949"; an undated document labeled "(Copy) *Confidential*/Report to Mr. Wells and Mr. Davidson Taylor from Winston Burdett and John Secondari," which turns out to be less than half of the report we have seen, which was submitted to CBS on June 15, 1948, by the two CBS representatives in Salonika (the sections left out are those subtitled "Police Reconstruction of the Crime," "Character of the Crime," "The Guilty Party," and "What the Police Have Done"); and, finally, two pages of "Remarks by Mr. Walter Lippmann" at the Overseas Writers Dinner on September 15, 1949, when a bowl was presented to General Donovan by the Lippmann Committee with an inscription "which records our recognition of your work in defense of the freedom of the press" and when a platter with a similar inscription was presented to the Lippmann Committee's assistant counsel, Guy Martin.

The two documents of particular interest are the commentary by the Harvard professor on Staktopoulos's confessions and some parts of the CBS broadcast directed by Edward R. Murrow. Professor Morgan's commentary—shared in by one Professor Maguire—begins with the revealing line: "Both Professor Maguire and I have read the so-called Confession of Gregorios Ioannou Stakhtopoulos" and proceeds from there to establish, item by item, the justification for the term "so-called."[45] The items may be summarized as follows:

(1) The papers submitted "do not contain a confession" but rather "an account of events" leading up to the murder, covering the murder, and following it, all "making clear the innocence of the witness and his ignorance of any evil plan. At most they make him an accessory after the fact."

(2) It is almost impossible to judge the credibility of Staktopoulos's statements "without the benefit of data concerning the persons and places mentioned therein," without knowing the method of the statements (were they, for example, uninterrupted narratives after preliminary questions?), without knowing whether the interrogators were friendly or hostile, and whether "there was any attempt to secure details which could be checked through other witnesses." Indeed, "the whole performance cried aloud for cross-examination."

(3) The statements "have mysterious persons who will not reveal their full names and who act in true mystery story fashion." The first four or

five pages of the October 14 statement are missing from that of October 1; "Kissos" becomes "Nikos"; the two or three rowboats at the Luxembourg Café dock vanish mysteriously; in the earlier statement Staktopoulos goes to Athens to see a young lady and meets neither Mamas nor Polk and in the later statement he tells of an interview with Polk in Athens. The commentary asks: Why these changes?

(4) In the earlier description of the meeting with the American correspondents in the Mediterranean Hotel, Staktopoulos "exhibits a remarkable memory for apparently unimportant details," then, in the later statement, acknowledges that part of his description of events at this meeting "was untrue, and gives a lame explanation."

(5) The whole performance impresses Morgan "as devised to describe actions prior to and at the event which are not subject to corroboration or denial by other available witnesses." The conspirators are described in statements "either so as to be impossible of identification, or, if identified, to be beyond probability of apprehension or possibly [sic] of prosecution"—with the exception of Mamas's conduct, which "was subject to check-up" and is "conceded to be false."

(6) The story of the murder that Staktopoulos offers "is fantastic." Polk "might well have consented to be blindfolded by people whom he believed friendly," but "no sane person would have consented to be bound hand and foot." It is "beyond comprehension" how "any man of common sense could have submitted" to such binding "without requiring at least a plausible excuse."

(7) The only "tangible pieces of evidence" are the Pan Am calendar, the identity card, and the envelope in which these were mailed. Professor Morgan assumes that the handwriting and the time of mailing "have been verified," but "how the witness came to have this is a story which depends for its credibility upon the uncorroborated word of the witness."

(8) Staktopoulos's answers to questions put to him in the October 2 supplement to his first statement "are far from satisfactory." The witness "is clearly trying to put responsibility for the whole affair on Mamas and her Communist associates." Staktopoulos's "responses to such slight cross-examination indicate the need for real cross-examination of the type common in Anglo-American practice."

Professor Morgan concludes that if Staktopoulos's statements are to be offered against him to show "that he had a part in the murder of Polk, he cannot very well explain them away." If they are also to be used as evidence of the guilt "of the persons named therein, and particularly of Vasvanas and Mouzenides [sic]," then "they are in my opinion so inherently weak as to be practically worthless unless they are corroborated by other credible evidence." Finally, if Staktopoulos "testifies orally on these matters, he may on proper examination tell a story which will carry a greater measure of persuasion than these writings."

What remains especially perceptive in Morgan's March review is his recognition that the story Staktopoulos tells in his statements—shrewdly called "the whole performance"—has been constructed so that it is not subject to corroboration or denial and so that the other figures involved in the conspiracy are so described as to be "impossible of identification, or, if identified, to be beyond the probability of apprehension." It could not have occurred to Morgan, however, as it might have to others with a chance to follow the circumstances of Staktopoulos's incarceration and to see him perform in court, what role the Security Police interrogators might have played in shaping Staktopoulos's seemingly self-protective strategy.

How the Lippmann Committee, made up of some of the most sophisticated journalists of that era[46] and avowedly aware that American pressure might result in a frame-up, could have failed to consider the possibility of a Security Police role remains a mystery—unless one chooses to see their apparent obtuseness as deliberate: the result of a decision against opening this hornet's nest and releasing the threat it held for the official solution that the committee endorsed in its Report. A second mystery is why the committee attached Professor Morgan's commentary to its Report, since the body of the Report makes no reference whatsoever to the professor's reservations regarding the Staktopoulos confessions, and there is no indication in the "Foreword" that this telling document is among the enclosures. At the very least, Morgan's judgment that Staktopoulos's uncorroborated statements are "so inherently weak as to be practically worthless" as evidence of the guilt of Vasvanas and Mouzenidis should have alerted those who prepared the Report to the need to provide corroborative evidence in convincing detail. Failing this, they had no warrant for declaring that Staktopoulos was not only an accessory to the murder but the "finger-man" for the "actual murderers," with only the names of Vasvanas and Mouzenidis offered as the possible killers—"tentatively found guilty by the Greek jury," though still missing some years after the trial ended.

The committee's failure in this connection is hardly mitigated by the remarks in the Report's final enclosure, remarks offered at the dinner in honor of General Donovan by the committee's chairman, the very man who had requested Professor Morgan's commentary. Walter Lippmann chose the occasion of the dinner (September 15, 1949), to announce that the Overseas Writers had "almost ready for publication a full account of the whole enterprise" of investigating the Polk affair, an enterprise "which has brought us to the point where we can say with entire conviction that the man who led George Polk into the trap, which resulted in his murder, has been arrested, convicted, and sentenced to life imprisonment."[47] And Lippmann adds that though this man is not himself the murderer, "we can at least say that one of the guilty men has been caught and that no innocent man has been made the scapegoat for a crime of which he is innocent."

After Professor Morgan's review of the partial evidence given him by the committee and after the committee's supposedly searching scrutiny of much else that was unavailable to Morgan in March 1949, what are the grounds for such "entire conviction," and where, even three years later, is "the full account" that would presumably present the necessary grounds? The full account in fact did not begin to appear until the scapegoat finally felt that he could speak out beyond intimidation, in his own words (and his own language), some twenty-five years later, his case aided by the book of a near scapegoat, Kosta Hadjiargyris, published in 1975.

The second telling enclosure that might have provided the committee additional early insight into the true course of events in Greece, a transcript of Edward R. Murrow's CBS broadcast one week after the trial, was also attached to the Report without comment or notes,[48] as though it was to be taken as simply further corroboration of the committee's ultimate conclusions. It does in fact appear to share these conclusions in large measure, but it also raises cause for doubt about the thoroughness of the investigation, the fairness of the trial, and the justice of the verdict. Murrow's sources have their limitations: Don Hollenbeck, who reports on the investigation, does so at second hand; Winston Burdett, who covers the trial, does so under the shadow of the prejudices we have seen; and Alexander Kendrick, who also covers the trial, presents his cabled views only by way of Murrow's concluding observations. Yet if the broadcast offers a mixed bag of data (some inaccurate), observations, and speculations, it nevertheless invokes certain pertinent questions and implications largely ignored in the body of the Lippmann Report.

Murrow opens the broadcast with a eulogy of his murdered colleague (a journalist "full of courage and an insatiable appetite for truth," a man with "the honesty and integrity, the reverence for fact and indifference to criticism which gave him the respect of the men in his trade"), then outlines the familiar events leading up to the murder, and finally turns the broadcast over to Hollenbeck to report on the investigation. Hollenbeck's summary account tells us that the "authority and responsibility for the solution of the crime" was in the hands of the Greek police, under the direction of Major Mouskoundis, and that both the CBS representatives (Burdett and Secondari) and the Overseas Writers Association representative (Donovan) "could act only as observers." But even as observers their "presence . . . did accomplish something" after it was found that Major Mouskoundis and the Greek police "were working one side of the street only." Strong representations were made to the major and to "high Greek officials—even to King Paul" that all political avenues should be explored as zealously as the Communist one. When the observers discovered that the police had failed to question "certain obvious witnesses, . . . some of those witnesses were then questioned." And General Donovan reported four months after the murder that, at "our insistence," the government of Greece was "compelled to take over the direction of the police inquiry at the highest level."

Soon after this "insistence," Hollenbeck tells his listeners, "things began to happen in the Polk case," namely, Staktopoulos, his mother, and "two fugitive Communists" were charged with the crime. Donovan is quoted as mentioning Minister of Public Order Rendis as the high official who "assumed personal responsibility for the conduct of the investigation"; no mention is made of Minister of Justice Melas—or of the conflict between the two ministries in which Donovan got embroiled. Hollenbeck's contribution to the broadcast ends with a brief outline of the case after the formal charges were published, including notes on the culprits (he has Staktopoulos wrongly employed by "one of Salonika's right-wing newspapers"—*Makedonia* being in fact a centrist, Venezelist paper), the guerrilla claim that both Mouzenidis and Vasvanas were dead at the time of the murder, and Staktopoulos's confession, which emerged "after a month of intensive questioning." He concludes: "Thus the government's case was made." No comment on the curious, sometimes absurd construction that this "intensive questioning" (actually six weeks long) finally produced.

Winston Burdett then takes over the broadcast to report on the trial. His account begins: "In many ways it was just an ordinary trial in a provincial criminal court of Greece." The jury of ten men was typical: "well-to-do citizens, selected according to Greek Law from the higher levels of Salonika's business and professional society." The presiding judge allowed Staktopoulos all the time he wanted to defend himself. The defense had ample opportunity to present its story. "Everyone from judges and prosecutor to jurors and defense attorneys had the right of cross-examination," and the defendant himself "took advantage of this right several times." Witnesses could expatiate "on almost anything they wished, with practically unlimited freedom." The jury was an active participant in most of the discussions, as were the three judges and "the three defense lawyers chosen by Staktopoulos himself" (the number here is misleading, as is the naive assumption regarding the defendant's choice). Burdett concludes that "the accused man got the kind of trial provided by Greek Law, an open trial, fairly conducted under the Greek rules," with no exceptions made in favor of any party.

Burdett then tells his listeners that the startling thing—anyway for "western observers"—was the fact that "under Greek Law there are no rules of evidence at all." Everything from "vague hearsay" to "personal opinion" is allowed to come out in court unchallenged. From the bench—which, in Donovan's words, deserved the confidence that the public gave it and which was presided over by a president who "kept the case moving and was meticulous in his attitude towards the defendants"[49]—"came a shower of leading questions" that Burdett says "would have made an American lawyer in an American court demand a mistrial then and there." Still, despite all that might have brought the proceedings into question among the American press representatives on the scene and that Burdett himself mocks at moments, the CBS correspondent finally passes the occasion off again as "just an ordinary Greek trial" that was made "extraordinary" not by the way it was set up and conducted or by the judgments it ultimately reached but by "the fact that it was a political event of first importance in Greece."

Burdett illustrates the political character of the event by reporting that everybody seemed to accept a single political thesis from the outset, the judges often seemed more determined to prove this thesis "than to determine the exact degree of guilt of the accused man," no witness was prepared to suggest that someone other than the Communists might have been behind the murder, and all but one American—who "had nothing to fear from Greek opinion"—refused to testify on Staktopoulos's behalf (the four Greek character witnesses were "all ill on that particular day"). Burdett suggests that they may have felt that the trial was about something bigger than Staktopoulos and that "issues like Communism and patriotic devotion were also involved." It does not seem to occur to him—as it apparently did not to any press representative quoted in the archives—that intimidation by the authorities may have been more to the point than even patriotic devotion, as was surely the case with the principal witness and others held by the Security Police.

Burdett goes on to say that the essential question about the trial for the outside world "is very simple," namely: "What facts did it establish about Polk's murder?" He seems to imply that the answer to this is to be found entirely in Staktopoulos's "story," which he "stood before his judges for six hours to tell." For Burdett, the story held "no surprises, no sensational revelations"—though one presumes he was familiar with the confessions of October 1, 2, 14, and 24 of the previous year, where the story was rather different in significant details. Or, if he was not familiar with all of the earlier versions, he could have indicated just what he knew and didn't know by the time the committee got around to publishing his part in the broadcast three years later, especially since he was the representative of the American press in Salonika with the longest history of involvement in the case and had taken an active part in the early phases of the investigation. As it is, his account sticks strictly to the script of Staktopoulos's testimony in court and not only does not highlight the various inconsistencies and changes in the tale that might suggest a forced "construction" but makes the story presented in court sound more plausible than it possibly could to those familiar with the early texts, where, among other details, a meeting between Staktopoulos and Polk in Athens has been fully outlined and then excised; where Vasvanas and Mouzenidis are both more crudely mysterious—and less hospitably treated by Staktopoulos; and where we do not see a caique hovering in Salonika Bay to facilitate the difficult sea voyage to the foot of Olympus.

At no point does Burdett question the validity of Staktopoulos's story in an essential way. He does raise the question of how "believable" were the two "key witnesses" produced by "the Greek State" to corroborate that story, the brother and sister-in-law of Mouzenidis, also whether the two spoke "freely or under coercion," but he answers his own question by stating blandly that General Donovan "asked to speak to these two witnesses privately," was readily granted his request by the Greek attorney general, and after "talking with them through an American interpreter," reported that he "was satisfied that they had spoken freely and without pressure." He then suddenly adds: "Generally, American observers were convinced that Stakhtopoulos was no mere scapegoat of the Greek police"—as though the thought in fact may have occurred to him and others present. He goes on to say that, throughout the trial, Staktopoulos "was fighting to cover and minimize his own role in Polk's death," again as though some role by Staktopoulos in the murder had been proven beyond doubt and was to be taken for granted. In the case of Mother Staktopoulos, her testimony was "nailed down" by two hand-writing experts who said the writing on the incriminating envelope "was hers beyond all possibility of doubt." Burdett then adds, almost as a non sequitur in the case of Mother Staktopoulos: "The jury acquitted the old woman, cleared Stakhtopoulos of the charge of premeditation, but found him guilty as an accessory after the fact."

Burdett's summary makes no mention of Mother Staktopoulos's revealing hesitation in court, but he is bothered enough about Staktopoulos's story to suggest that it is still not the complete story. There are lingering questions that he shares with his listeners. For a start, how was the plot organized? What exactly were the roles of the men named by Staktopoulos and those left unnamed? Did Polk and Staktopoulos really take a taxi to the Luxembourg Café when no taxi driver was found who remembered them, and did they really dine in public at the Luxembourg when the proprietor does not remember seeing them there that night and did not serve lobster on May 8? Why did the rowboat return to shore to let Staktopoulos off while Polk's bound and bleeding body was still aboard? Burdett's answer: "The Greeks are poor cross-examiners and nobody thought of asking Stakhtopoulos about that." In any case, he finds that "these are the main gaps in the story," and it remains "an unfinished story" until they have been filled. But the more important questions raised by Professor Morgan's review of the confessions are not asked here, nor is there any suggestion that the official solution may in fact be a sham. Burdett's account is clearly intended in the end to support Murrow's conclusion to the broadcast: "There is general agreement that Stakhtopoulos was deeply implicated in the murder of George Polk. But, as we have related to you tonight, there are many unsolved questions surrounding this case. It may be that the full story will never be told; but the investigation continues."

Alexander Kendrick's contribution to the broadcast focused on what he perceived to be a different area of intimidation clearly manifest at the trial: that exercised by the Greek press against foreign correspondents in Greece, American correspondents in particular. He reported that the trial "ended with a series of vitriolic attacks by Greek rightist newspapers against these foreign correspondents, calling them spies, communist dupes, fellow-travelers, drunkards, liars, barflies." He felt that it was sometimes hard to figure out if the trial was for the murder of Polk or simply of Polk himself for having tried to report "the Greek story objectively." The jurors couldn't understand what purpose an American correspondent might have had in wanting to go to Markos's headquarters, surely a suspect purpose in the midst of a civil war in which there was no middle ground. They thought Polk might be "a 'Confused Liberal,' or a man of little judgment," possibly under Communist influence, by which the court meant "the Greek assistants [to] American correspondents" who "provide them with information on internal affairs, on political developments, on economic questions," for example, Polk's assistant, Kosta Hadjiargyris, who was "interrogated for five hours."

The attitude of suspicion toward American correspondents stemmed, according to Kendrick, from the fact that they had reported "the dark side of the Greek crisis, as well as the official communiques . . . the essential instability of the Greek Government, and its unrepresentative character." Kendrick felt that with the murder of Polk and its aftermath, the hostility of officials would be more pronounced, the news sources would shy away, the police would be more curious, the attempts to plant information would increase, Greek associates would become more afraid to work for foreign journalists. But Murrow, in reporting these views, tried to end his broadcast on a positive note: whatever else the Polk trial accomplishes, it "can erect a red light for American policymakers, make them ask themselves why they and the Greeks should be afraid of American correspondents; and whether honesty and integrity in American reporting are not after all laudable war aims also—no matter what kind of war is being fought."

One can't help wondering what must have gone through Winston Burdett's mind as he heard Kendrick's implicit defense of Kosta Hadjiargyris, the man Burdett had thought—less than a year previously—ought to be given the third degree.[50] Kendrick's citation was in any case timely and no doubt gave Hadjiargyris heart at a crucial moment—assuming he was made aware of it—because Hadjiargyris's troubles were not yet over. We learn from a cable and its enclosures sent by Harold B. Minor, the new chargé in Athens, that Hadjiargyris felt himself much threatened by what he perceived to be a new investigation devoted solely to [his] involvement in the crime" that Minister of Justice Melas had requested the Salonika court to undertake at the conclusion of the Polk trial[51] and what Hadjiargyris also perceived to be the "irresponsible behavior of certain Greek officials, most particularly Mr. George Melas."[52] Hadjiargyris fought back, first of all by sending a long letter to Attorney General Constantinidis informing him "in writing of certain data about the Polk case" which he had "transmitted" to Constantinidis verbally during the Staktopoulos trial but which, on the attorney general's advice—"whose correctness I fully realised"—he did not mention in court or mentioned "only fleetingly."[53]

The letter was sent on May 3. Ten days later, Hadjiargyris called on Robert G. Miner, second secretary of the American embassy, to deliver a copy of the letter and to discuss his current predicament in view of his reputation having been injured by imputations made in the Staktopoulos indictment and during the trial, and in view of his position as correspondent for the *Christian Science Monitor* having been "jeopardize[d]."[54] He informed Miner that copies of the letter were sent at the same time to Chief of Police Evert and his assistant Panopoulos, to Minister of the Interior Rendis, to the editor of the *Christian Science Monitor*, to the British ambassador, and to Walter Lippmann, among others. Hadjiargyris said that if "the investigation continues with no prospect of clearing him in the near future," he intended to publish a letter in the Greek press asserting his innocence and demanding that Constantinidis make the document he had sent him public—presumably to the world at large, since it was already public in a number of high and not-so-high places.

What Hadjiargyris puts in writing to Constantinidis is first his conviction that the murder was planned not in Athens but in Salonika and, second, his deep suspicion that Randall Coate (whom he insists on calling "Coates") was the person who put Polk in contact with those who did him in. He begins by stating that he believes "the Staktopoulos trial closed satisfactorily from the point of view of national interest," and "despite the lies of Staktopoulos there can be no doubt that he is somehow involved in the crime." In short, he does not here challenge the primary assumptions of the official solution to the degree that he later does in his 1975 book. His purpose, he says, is not to reverse the judgment at the trial but to "defend my honor to the end, come what may," his "silence in Salonika" having been "more than enough so far as my duty to my country is concerned."

His defense turns on "reconciling" three "irreconcilables," namely, that Polk left Athens without any clear intention of going to interview Markos or even of going to Salonika specifically; that the organization and execution of the crime in Salonika "appeared to have occurred in the astonishingly short space of 36 hours"; that several days before Polk's arrival in Salonika the police were informed (from British sources, Hadjiargyris was told) that Vasvanas was coming to the city "for terrorist acts." Two "utterly divergent" conclusions were reached on the basis of these "irreconcilables": that "Athens witnesses" and more particularly Hadjiargyris himself lied about Polk's intentions and were therefore involved in the crime in some way, or that "the crime was organized in Salonika by a right-wing organization," since the Communists could not have "decided and executed" it in such a short period of time. Hadjiargyris tells the attorney general—rather unconvincingly—that the second conclusion was refuted "by the fact that, though considered a Communist by certain extremist circles in Athens, Polk was nevertheless not very widely known, certainly less widely known than Bigart or Thrapp." The first conclusion is not only refuted by the testimony of the Hadjiargyris couple, but "is contrary to all known facts," for example, those that point to Polk's having originally planned to take his young wife on a vacation trip to Kavalla and his having decided to stay in Salonika on the spur of the moment, then, "finding himself alone on a general information journey," deciding suddenly to try to make a last effort "to secure a real contact with the Communists" despite his "sick condition" (i.e., the painful recurring complications from his nose injury).

It is at this point that Hadjiargyris feels the investigation made "its supreme error" by insisting that a political murder could not have been decided upon and organized in thirty-six hours. He argues that indeed it could have been, especially if one discarded "the unnecessary presumption" that it was Polk the individual who was murdered after long preparation rather than the next foreign correspondent who came along with the intention of visiting Markos—a "desire" that Hadjiargyris tells us "had always been actively shared by the majority of correspondents on passage through Greece." The implication is that, from the murderers' perspective, Polk, representing " 'X' Foreign Correspondent," happened to be in the right place at the right time. The rest of Hadjiargyris's letter is directed toward showing that at the time of Polk's arrival in Salonika there was already in place "an organization of a mixed nature in which Communists and at least one British official were meeting at different points for different reasons," an organization that could "at any time be transformed into a trap for the murder of any foreign correspondent," which made it entirely unnecessary for the Communists to "undertake the highly risky and complicated job of setting up in Athens and Salonika yet another parallel organization and trap," in particular one involving the assistance of Kosta Hadjiargyris.

The "British official" designated by Hadjiargyris is the man who "for a considerable time" carried out "contact work between correspondents and Salonika Communists," namely, "the Press Officer of the British Embassy," Randall Coate. Hadjiargyris here offers much of the same information to support this claim that he offers in his 1975 book. As he related "en passant" in court, during December 1947, Coate sent Reuters correspondent Bigio an invitation from Markos "to both of them to visit guerrilla general headquarters" a few days after Bigio "had expressed such a desire" to Mr. Coate. The British embassy persuaded Bigio to abandon his plan "but no measure was taken against Mr. Coates." Hadjiargyris also "noted" in court that from the day of his deposition, "the chief delegate of the British Police Mission followed the entire proceedings of the court" (perhaps also to the point here is William Polk's recent remark that "there were eleven British observers at the trial in various disguises").[55] Then Hadjiargyris reminded Constantinidis that he had verbally mentioned Thrapp's having reported confidentially to United Press, and thence to CBS, that he "had one British and one Greek contact with the Communists in Salonika," and Winston Burdett subsequently told Hadjiargyris that Coate was this British contact. The purpose of Thrapp's having made these contacts: a trip by caique to the Pieria region in April 1948, "foiled partly on the advice of Mr. Gibson" but mainly because Thrapp was transferred outside Greece. Then there was Polk's meeting with Coate (contrary to the testimony of other witnesses, Hadjiargyris says that Coate was "the first person whom Polk saw in Salonika," and "on the noon of May 7th") during which "he put the question of establishing a contact with the Communists." There was also the fact of Coate's departure from Salonika six days after the murder and two days before the discovery of Polk's body, followed by the transfer of his secretary ten days later, so that since then "there has been no British Information Service officer in Salonika" (another inaccuracy, according to British sources of the period, which indicate that Coate was replaced by one Cockell).[56]

Hadjiargyris then goes into Coate's history in Greece: an Intelligence Service liaison with the resistance movements; considered "an intelligence service man" by the Americans even while serving as British Information Officer; a man who "in his talks . . . was more anxious to receive than to give information." Mr. Sorkin, former U.S. Information Service representative in Salonika, thought Coate "one of the best informed men in Salonika," and Mr. A.G.R. Rouse, former chief of the British Information Department in Athens, told Hadjiargyris that Coate was "the best informed man in Macedonia." And there were the visits to Salonika by Robert Low of *Time* and Mary Barber to secure a photograph of Markos for *Time*'s cover, and Stephen Barber's successful trip from Salonika to visit the Vitsi guerrillas, these contacts with Communist sources presumably aided by Randall Coate.

Hadjiargyris concludes that the only argument in favor of the "official theory" regarding an Athenian connection to the murder is Staktopoulos's confession, which "has made inconsistency into a rule" and one part of which—Staktopoulos's claim "to have carried out indirect negotiations with Polk in Athens on March 28th, 1948"—Hadjiargyris himself demonstrated, by concrete evidence submitted to the investigating magistrates on April 19, 1949, to be "an inspired lie." Thus, says Hadjiargyris, the three "irreconcilables" that he cited "get reconciled by the knowledge that an organization preexisted in Salonika," previously labeled by him "a permanent and effective contact organization," one capable of murdering a foreign correspondent when it chose to do so. Hadjiargyris ends his long argument by stating that William Polk has given him permission to make any use he might care to of "the following sentence which slipped from Staktopoulos' lips when Mr. Polk interviewed him in his cell: 'It was a trap set for the first correspondent who came along.' " Whether this "slipped" sentence is anything more than an "inspired" guess on Staktopoulos's part, Hadjiargyris's letter does not say.

In this semipublic correspondence with Constantinidis, Hadjiargyris pulls his punches here and there, as we learn from remarks that he made to Robert G. Miner of the American embassy on delivering the document. It was not only Constantinidis's "advice" that kept him from disclosing all his "facts" in court, but also Hadjiargyris's "desire to avoid destroying or throwing serious doubt upon the Government's case." And he "wished to avoid implicating the British if possible." His sending a copy of his document to the British embassy now was not for purposes of blackmail but because he knew that Chief of Police Evert would turn his copy over to the British anyway and "Hadjiargyris thought it preferable" that the British "be provided with a good translation." Regarding the material missing from Polk's CBS file, Hadjiargyris told Miner that Stephen Barber had removed the missing documents because "they showed that Steve Barber had suggested that Coates was the man to put Polk in touch with the Communists." He added that Staktopoulos had at one time been an employee of Coate's. And he pointed out the specific weak points in the government's case: the conflicting testimony given by Staktopoulos in his various confessions—especially regarding his Athens trip—the failure to find the taxi driver who took Polk and Staktopoulos to the "supposed dinner" at the Luxembourg Café and the failure of the waiters there to recall seeing the two men, the "lack of explanation" for the return of Polk's identity card and the "unexplained absence" of Polk's other identity cards and notebook.

Miner reported of the interview that "he [Hadjiargyris] thinks Staktopoulos is taking the rap for someone else, that he is too weak a person ever to have been entrusted with the kind of mission he confessed to"; that it is "highly unlikely" that Mouzenidis, a member of the Central Committee of the Greek Communist Party, would have been given the kind of mission "alleged" in Staktopoulos's confession; and finally, that Hadjiargyris believes that Coate "was in the boat at the time of the murder and indeed may have pulled the trigger," though Hadjiargyris's views regarding the motivation are "obscure," having to do with the British being "incensed at the US for the latter's Palestine policy" and therefore wishing "to make trouble for the US in another part of the same theatre, namely Greece." In support of this theory, Hadjiargyris saw the great outcry in the British press about the executions that followed the assassination of Minister of Justice Ladas in May 1948 as having the same purpose.

The response of the British to all this appears to have been typical: total silence. Hadjiargyris reported to Miner that he had informed one Colonel Hobbs of the British Military Mission about the contents of his Constantinidis letter before sending it to British Ambassador Sir Clifford Norton, and Hobbs subsequently told Hadjiargyris that Sir Clifford "would talk to him, Hadjiargyris, about it." When nothing happened after a lapse of several days, Hadjiargyris delivered the letter. We learn from a second Miner memorandum that Hadjiargyris subsequently visited Hobbs, who promised to bring the matter before the counselor of the British embassy and "communicate later with Hadjiargyris."[57] When Hadjiargyris had still heard nothing by May 16, he told Miner that "he intends to make no more approaches to the British on this subject."

Hadjiargyris did not know—nor did Miner—that behind the scenes the British were far from silent on the subject. We learn from a "confidential" memorandum and a "secret" addendum to it now in the public domain in England, that the British had been aware of—as they put it—"the attempt of Hadjiargyris to pin the responsibility for the crime on the British" as far back as August 31, 1948, a matter referred to in "Reilly's Top Secret letter to Wallinger" of that date.[58] On May 12, 1949, one John Roper of the British embassy in Athens sent Sir Anthony Rumbold of the Foreign Office a copy of Hadjiargyris's letter to Public Prosecutor Constantinidis with a note indicating that "we think that at one time Mr. Hadjiargyris hoped to blackmail this Embassy into using its influence to get him whitewashed." Mr. Roper continues: "Perhaps he still hopes to do so. In any case the Ambassador thinks that we should take no notice of the present letter, poor stuff as it is. You may, however, like to have a copy of it and to let Tony Rouse [the A.G.R. Rouse mentioned in Hadjiargyris's letter] know of the charges contained in it."

Sir Anthony apparently did just that, because Rouse responded in detail—if secretly—on May 23, 1949.[59] Yes, he had of course heard of "Coate's alleged connexion" with the Polk affair. It had been in the local press, and Coate himself "admitted that he had been approached by Polk in this connexion, but maintained that he had declined to give him any assistance or information." In his "explanation" to Rouse—presumably his chief at that time—Coate said that Polk had made similar approaches to a number of people in Salonika, both official and unofficial. Rouse does not find it surprising that Polk should have contacted Coate in this instance since "most foreign correspondents made their number with him," he being one of two information officers in Salonika "with greater experience in local affairs" than his American colleague, an official who "was appointed long after him without previous knowledge of the area." On more than one occasion Rouse himself had been asked by foreign correspondents for assistance in "similar undertakings to that envisaged by Polk." Then comes the significant caveat: "Although I have no hesitation in discounting these fantastic allegations, I appreciate that certain circumstances tended to lend credence to them."

These "circumstances" include the transfer of Coate and his secretary shortly after the murder—though that was in fact "purely coincidental" since "Personnel Department had been considering these transfers long before Polk had even arrived in the country"; and it was not true, as Hadjiargyris claimed in his letter, that after Coate's departure there was no British Information Service officer in Salonika, one Cockell having replaced Coate. But there was also the circumstance of Coate's "alleged intelligence activities," this "also credible, as owing to his wartime work in this region, he was inclined to pay too much attention to such matters." Rouse reports that "in point of fact I had to reprimand him on this score as far back as 1946," yet "I know that he continued to take more interest than he should have done in gathering information as opposed to producing it"—though Rouse felt that he had to point out a particular problem in Greece: "The Greek translation of the word 'information' implies 'intelligence'," a confusion that the Communist paper *Rizospastis* had used in one instance to promote a misconception involving Rouse himself.

There were other "unfortunate" factors for the record. One was that an assistant of Coate's named Stappard, still working for the consulate general, "was inclined to dabble in spurious intelligence work, having also been 'in the mountains' with ELAS," and it had been necessary that he too be reprimanded at one time for "some case which, if I remember rightly, was connected with the Jugoslav Consulate in Salonika." Added to this was the fact that Staktopoulos once worked for AGIS (the Anglo-Greek Information Service), forerunner to the present Information Service. Though Coate was not with AGIS at the time Staktopoulos worked for them, as Hadjiargyris had suggested, Rouse believes Stappard was. Finally, Rouse reports that he thinks Coate did in fact obtain a letter of invitation from Markos's headquarters "whilst accompanying the first Balkan Commission which made contact with the rebels" and had forwarded the letter to Bigio, the Reuters correspondent. But Rouse also thinks "that it was an open invitation to any correspondent to visit the guerrillas."

Rouse concludes his commentary by indicating that the "above factors would lend evidence to the alleged complicity of Coate" and that Coate himself "aggravated matters by interesting himself unduly in intelligence activities," which was "one of the reasons for my asking for his transfer" long before the Polk case ever arose. At the same time, Rouse says, "I need hardly add that I exonerate Coate and refute [Hadjiargyris's] charges" in his letter to Constantinidis. He adds that Hadjiargyris is "not only a dangerous man but a frightened one and will go to any lengths to extricate himself from suspicion."

Meanwhile, Raleigh Gibson was expressing similar sentiments to his superiors at the Department of State, after meeting with Attorney General Constantinidis on May 26 to discuss the Hadjiargyris letter.[60] Gibson tells the secretary of state that it appears "Hadjiargyris is extremely frightened at the continuation of the inquiries, or that he has become mentally deranged," because Gibson can't think of any other reason for Hadjiargyris's statement that Randall Coate "was in the boat at the time of the murder and indeed may have pulled the trigger." Gibson's principal British contact, Sir Charles Wickham of the British Police and Prisons Mission, informed him that he considered Hadjiargyris's letter "nothing but blackmail," and he did not feel that the letter brought out "anything especially detrimental to the findings of the court." At the same time, he told Gibson that he felt the action of Salonika officials in continuing the inquiries "was not wise," and Gibson adds that it is his belief the British "can only be embarrassed in that Coates' [sic] connection with its intelligence service may be brought out." He also adds that Coate had requested a transfer to Oslo as early as October 1947, and the order for him "to proceed as soon as convenient" was received on April 23, 1948, this information presumably obtained from Sir Charles.

Regarding the other implications of Hadjiargyris's letter, Gibson agrees with the general view—shared also by Constantinidis—that the letter was written mainly to prove that "it was not necessary for George Polk to have had a previous contact in Athens" and by "this fact to clear Hadjiargyris of any connection with the case." In response to the "weak points in the Government's case" that Hadjiargyris brought out in his conversation with Robert G. Miner, Gibson can say only that "these were accepted at the time of the trial by the majority of the newspaper men attending." As for Staktopoulos's confession (presumably the version offered in court), Gibson says that the witness did change it "on a number of points," but this was due to "continued questioning" and Staktopoulos's desire not to implicate himself in the murder except as an innocent participant. Then he adds the curious remark: "The prosecution did not endeavor to secure further facts regarding Staktopoulos' trip to Athens, but accepted the statement as made." Indeed so, but Gibson evidently does not see that as grounds for bringing the whole series of confessions into question.

One thing does bother him, though. The prosecution "failed to use Stahtopoulos' statement that the dinner with Polk did not take place at the Luxembourg" but at his own home (as Gibson had reported before the trial, on April 10),[61] and Gibson feels that the attorney general's explanation of this failure in the memorandum of their conversation that he attaches to the cable "is rather weak," especially since Staktopoulos's attitude "all during the trial appeared to be one of complete cooperation on points that would not implicate him," which suggests that "the truth regarding the dinner could have been obtained at the trial." However, says Gibson, "this point does not affect the findings of the Court."

It might well have done so were the consul general ready to probe more deeply into the question of Staktopoulos's confessions, as he had not been prepared to do for many months. The attorney general's response to Gibson's question regarding the setting of the last dinner was to say that Staktopoulos "was continually changing and adding to his original confession," but his testimony "before the Attorney General" was "the official one to be used at the trial."[62] This might have suggested to Gibson that earlier "official" testimony on record had been changed as seemed necessary in order make the prosecution's case in court more credible, and whether or not Constantinidis was allowed to be privy to the process of such change, the attorney general clearly had chosen to go along with the dubious product that emerged from Security Police headquarters in various shapes. Constantinidis also said that Staktopoulos's statement about the dinner not having taken place at the Luxembourg "was not made under oath" and for this reason was not used at the trial. Under what circumstances it was made, Constantinidis evidently did not say nor did Gibson ask. The attorney general added that Staktopoulos "was always adding new information to his confession," and it was even possible that he had given information to his lawyers regarding the murder "that the authorities did not know," as he had done in testifying to giving Vasvanas refuge. Of course in Greece as elsewhere, there are authorities and authorities, as Gibson should have known, Major Mouskoundis and the Security Police being the missing link here.

Regarding Hadjiargyris's statement that the attorney general had advised him not to disclose certain information at the trial, Constantinidis asserted that the name of Coate had not come up in their conversation. Regarding what had come up, all of it meant to convince the jury that Hadjiargyris did not know of Polk's plans to visit Markos, he had told Hadjiargyris that he "would not be believed and there was no reason that he should give such information to the Court." The attorney general had a few additional points to make about Hadjiargyris. He considered the *Christian Science Monitor* correspondent "no less satanic" than Staktopoulos. He asked: Was there any portion of truth in his letter that demanded an investigation? He found "no data to prove" Hadjiargyris's statements. Staktopoulos, Mouzenidis, and Vasvanas were all connected with the murder plot, and Hadjiargyris "does not reject the statement of Stahtopoulos [*sic*]" that they were. Now Hadjiargyris "may be trying to involve Coates as the fourth person to have participated in the murder," but in this connection the attorney general referred to a letter addressed to the minister of justice by the American embassy in Athens quoting a statement made by Coate in Oslo "regarding Polk's call on him in Salonika." Coate had stated: "I may have been the last person to see Polk. I remember he asked me to help him make a trip to the mountains. I refused to be of any service to him, since I noted that Polk was an inexperienced person and did not appear too serious."

The other questions raised by Hadjiargyris's letter are more lightly dismissed. Constantinidis revealed that Mrs. Barber "admitted going to Polk's office at Rea's request" and delivered certain files to her, but "it was difficult to decide whether the missing files were of any real value." For his part, Gibson tells the secretary of state that the failure to find the boat used for the murder can probably be explained by the investigation having fallen off after Staktopoulos's confession was obtained, and the return of the identity card was probably for the purpose of identifying the body if it did not wash ashore for some time and might therefore not be in a condition that would make identification easy. In any case, both the consul general and the attorney general appear to have agreed that if the Hadjiargyris letter were to be published in the Greek press, it would not receive extensive publicity except in the Communist newspapers, and—in Gibson's words—"will not affect public opinion in Greece or abroad," especially so because, as the attorney general pointed out, "Hadjiargyris admits that from all angles Stahtopoulos is connected in some way with the murder, whether contacts were made in Athens or Salonika." Still, Gibson thinks that the Salonika officials "are too open in their desire to implicate Hadjiargyris," to the extent that "it would appear that personal feeling has entered the case."

That is the last official communication on the subject in the State Department file. It seems that British and American pressure was sufficient in the end to cool the local enthusiasm for further pursuit of Kosta Hadjiargyris. He was eventually allowed to leave the country, and he settled in England for some years before returning to Athens to work as a journalist and to write his book on the Polk affair. In the weeks following the trial, the Greek press, which we are told had treated the end of the trial as an anticlimax,[63] appears to have continued in that mode, while the Communist press offered its usual mixture of bad rhetoric, hyperbole, unproven accusation, and occasional hard questioning: Staktopoulos was a British agent; why should the Communists want to kill Polk, a "leftist journalist," when they gladly accepted visits from "rightists" like Bigart and Mathews?[64] Consul General Gibson, "whose participation in the whole frame up is well known," in stating that the trial was fair and that the Polk case was therefore closed, expressed the fear of the Americans and the Monarchofascists that the investigation might continue; and now that it is all over, Staktopoulos will either be set free in a few months or, "if he becomes dangerous, will commit suicide in the Paparigas fashion [i.e., be assassinated]."[65]

Staktopoulos was in fact permitted to be forgotten month by month in a corner of the Security Police headquarters. William Polk, who had visited him there just after the trial—during which he had appeared to be "under sedation" so that "he did not stand or speak quite like a fully sober man"—saw him again at Security Police headquarters two years later, "and he seemed more coherent."[66] Polk adds: "As far as I could see or hear, he was not ill-treated. Even then, he was, from time to time, let out for strolls on the streets."

XI | Toward a Resolution

IN ATTEMPTING TO RESOLVE certain of the ambiguities that still characterize the Polk affair—ambiguities that served the needs of some and that
frustrated others—one has to begin by stating that the hard facts and the
concrete evidence in the murder case remain almost as limited as they
were in 1949. What we know is that the hands and the feet of the clothed
corpse were loosely bound, that an autopsy revealed that the victim died
from drowning after being shot in the back of the head, that the victim's
stomach contained a mostly undigested meal of lobster, peas, some meat
and some alcohol, that money and documents were found on the body
but several personal items—a notebook and appointment book—were
not among the effects offered as evidence by the investigators. We also
know that before recovering the corpus delicti, the police received an
unstamped, rather awkwardly addressed envelope containing an advertisement for Pan American Airways—described by some as a "calendar
card"—and a press identity card belonging to George Polk.

No other tangible evidence was produced during the investigation or
at the trial, unless one counts the personal belongings and correspondence that Polk left behind in his Athens apartment and his Salonika
hotel room—or didn't leave behind, as in the case of the pajamas that a
maid in Athens thought was in his Salonika baggage and the material
found to be missing from the files in his Athens study. The intangible
evidence consisted of confessions and depositions obtained from witnesses during the eleven months before the trial, from testimony presented in court, and, finally, from testimony offered some years after the
event. What one might call circumstantial evidence emerged from
George Polk's actions before his disappearance and the reported actions
of others both immediately before and immediately after his disappearance. Other circumstances that might be taken to have a bearing on the
resolution of lingering questions are those of the political climate in
Greece at the time of the murder and the existence of a civil war.

The most important testimony that emerged in the years after the
trial is that of Gregory Staktopoulos's insistence that he was tortured by

the Security Police in order to confess to a totally fabricated story—actually, a series of stories—that implicated both him and others in the murder, all of whom were in fact innocent of any involvement whatsoever. He first presented his claim to complete innocence in letters to the Greek press from his Salonika prison that were published in 1956 (one of these was addressed to William Polk and another to "Greek Justice"), but his principal effort at clearing his name came in an unsuccessful appeal to the Greek Supreme Court filed in 1977.[1] In connection with this appeal, his lawyer, Stelios Papathemelis (a centrist member of Parliament at the time),[2] introduced new information that had been partially revealed in a 1966 Salonika news story and that the lawyer tracked down to its source in preparation for the appeal. Papathemelis claimed that the envelope containing the Pan American advertisement and identity card was addressed by one Savvas Karamichalis, a Salonika grocer, at the request of one Evthimios (shortened to Thimios) Bamias, an illiterate small-time merchant in the Salonika harbor area who had found the items in some sort of wallet on the quay near the Trianon café, not far from the White Tower, and had brought them to Karamichalis's store.[3]

Bamias told Papathemelis that, at the time of the discovery, he had been nervous about getting involved in any sort of police investigation and didn't want to identify himself as the one who had found these items, especially after Karamichalis indicated that they belonged to a foreigner, so he had gone out and bought an envelope and had asked Karamichalis to address it for him, then had mailed it in to the police without a return address or a stamp. Since Karamichalis was long since dead by the time of the 1977 appeal, Papathemelis presented Karamichalis's son and widow to testify, along with Bamias himself, that they had been witnesses to Karamichalis's having addressed the envelope.[4] And the lawyer also produced handwriting experts to verify that the handwriting on the envelope was indeed that of Karamichalis, though the experts had to use photographs of the original for their work because the envelope had been transferred in the meanwhile to the hands of the Supreme Court, where it "disappeared."[5] In any case, the Supreme Court turned down the appeal in 1979 by a vote of five to two.

One way of approaching the complex issues raised by a suspect investigation, a sometimes farcical trial, and a rejected appeal that introduced new testimony is to attempt an answer to some of the lingering doubts that these aspects of the Polk affair failed to resolve, and to do so by questioning certain of the assumptions behind the evidence that was allowed to stand. Regarding the envelope, is it likely that a man who loved his mother would ask her to address an envelope that he knew would incriminate her in a serious crime that she had no part in when he could have just as easily addressed the envelope himself? Presumably not. Therefore, one might better assume that someone other than Mother Staktopoulos addressed the envelope. If the motive for mailing in the envelope was to identify a body that might eventually surface either as that of George Polk or in an unidentifiable condition, why enclose a completely irrelevant Pan Am advertisement? No reason. Therefore, one might better assume that the two items were in fact mailed in by somebody who did not entirely understand the insignificance of the one while perhaps understanding some aspect of the significance of the other (it bore a foreign name and a photograph), a circumstance that does not seem appropriate to the case of Reuters stringer Staktopoulos nor to a deliberate attempt to establish identification. The inclusion of the Pan Am advertisement-calendar card, almost totally forgotten in the formal and informal discussion of the case, suggests that the person who mailed the envelope to the Third Police Precinct did not know exactly what he was mailing, and this in turn points at least to the possibility of an accidental discovery of these two items.

Regarding the question of whether or not Polk allowed himself to be blindfolded and his hands and feet bound before he was murdered, one can assume that he was both sane and wary enough not to permit any such thing while he still had his senses. Therefore, the body must have been bound after the murder. And since no blindfold turned up at any point, one can ascribe the presumption of blindfolding to literary license influenced by Polk's letter to Murrow, which in turn suggests that much literary invention—some of it quite implausible—went into the confessions that became the basis for the official solution to the case. Since no taxi driver remembered taking Staktopoulos and Polk to the Luxembourg Café and no waiter remembered seeing them there, let alone serving them an uncharacteristic meal of lobster and peas,[6] one can assume that this meal in the Luxembourg was an aspect of the invention that went into the official Staktopoulos text. And the same can be said for the proposed rowboat trip to Pieria and the foot of Olympus, not only because no rowboat was found but because the distance made that mode of transportation very unlikely.

The appearance of a waiting caique so late in the story creates further doubt that there was a planned journey by sea, and the news that Vasvanas was put up by Staktopoulos in Salonika, also a late addition to the story, seemed so suspect at the time that even Attorney General Constantinidis decided this potentially fatal criminal offense had to be buried on the lame excuse that Staktopoulos's testimony in this regard had not been taken under oath. In fact, the presence in Salonika of both the designated murderers who were convicted in absentia rested on the testimony of witnesses who had to be considered unreliable because they were subject to police intimidation both before and after they testified in court; and there is still no firm evidence that Adam Mouzenidis was alive either at the time of the murder or subsequently.[7] Vasvanas, who eventually ended up in Rumania, was reported by Papathemelis and other sources to have sought repatriation as late as 1979 to clear his name in the Polk affair but apparently died before that possibility could be realized.[8]

There are several lingering questions about the behavior of both Polk and Staktopoulos at the time of the murder that appear to challenge the logic of certain fundamental assumptions that remained unchallenged by those who accepted the prosecution's argument and the court's verdict. If Polk had any sort of specific plan to visit Markos in his mind before he reached Salonika, why did he spend so much effort looking for a possible contact after he reached the city and why did he do so without making the slightest attempt to conceal his intention? His behavior in this respect tends to support Hadjiargyris's view that the idea of arranging an interview with Markos—however long-standing the ambition—occurred to him as a possibility on this occasion when he decided to get off the plane at Salonika airport. And if Staktopoulos, for his part, was as involved in the arrangements for the trip to Markos as his confessions suggested and was also subsequently a witness to Polk's murder, is it likely that the Reuters stringer would have approached Rea Polk on two occasions during the days after the CBS correspondent disappeared to ask for her help in writing a story about her missing husband, as she indicated Staktopoulos did in her conversations with William E. Colby? It would seem that such potentially incriminating, blatantly insensitive, and professionally irrelevant action by someone who had actually witnessed the murder of Rea's husband must be seen as implausible however one might view the character of the man in question and whether or not one ascribes the story on Polk that did in fact appear in the Sunday edition of *Makedonia* to the Reuters stringer. Staktopoulos remembers asking Rea if she had any news of her husband, and William E. Colby reported Rea's having described two meetings with Staktopoulos during which a possible story about Polk's disappearance was discussed. Rea does not now remember those meetings, as she does not recall the Colby conversations, though she does remember talking at some length to General Donovan after she reached the United States in 1948. A record of Colby's notes on his conversations with Rea, which he acknowledged having sent Donovan in September 1948,[9] is now available both among the Donovan papers and in the State Department archives.

A final unresolved question: If the dinner meeting that Polk arranged for Saturday evening was meant to lead directly to a trip by rowboat or caique or some other means into guerrilla territory, why did he leave behind so much in both personal effects and professional equipment that he—or any other reporter on such a mission—would normally have taken with him? This aspect of the circumstantial evidence suggests that his dinner meeting, and any meeting later that evening, were seen by him as an opportunity to discuss and plan a possible trip rather than as the starting point for the trip itself, and this in turn creates enough further doubt about the official account of events that evening to encourage ample disbelief in what was served up at the trial.

What the evidence—tangible, circumstantial, lately revealed—and various rational assumptions based on this evidence suggest is a rather different scenario from that which American officials and much of the American press took to be plausible in 1949. The following seems more plausible. Polk arrived in Salonika without any specific plan in mind for his last visit to the northern regions, but once there, openly and aggressively pursued the possibility of arranging an interview with Markos, while also considering a possible story on the "child abduction question." At some point during his two days in the city, more likely on Saturday than Friday, he met somebody who offered to bring him into contact with others whom Polk presumed might be able to arrange a trip to Markos's headquarters or some kind of encounter with leaders on the guerrilla side of the civil war.

Polk went to dinner on Saturday evening with this purpose in mind, and whether or not he considered the occasion to have its dangers, the quantity of mostly undigested food left in his stomach suggests that he found the occasion exciting enough to eat more quickly and voraciously than was his habit. In any case, he surely did not expect to be killed during dinner, and though there is at least one report from the Astoria Hotel staff suggesting that he returned briefly to his room before vanishing into the night and then returned again after midnight, he did not pack all that one might assume he would consider appropriate for a trip to gather news in remote guerrilla territory. It is of course possible that he was prepared to travel outside of Salonika in one direction or another with only the clothes on his back if that seemed to him essential for getting his mission under way, and he may indeed have been persuaded that this is what he had to do on that Saturday evening, but it is more likely that he met his death during or immediately after a meeting intended for planning a trip rather than for actually setting out to sea.

Regarding his last meal, it appears most plausible that the dinner he attended was not in a public place but in a private home. That does not necessarily mean that the murder occurred there; the dinner may have been preliminary to Polk's meeting one or more persons who would presumably facilitate his encounter with the guerrilla leadership, or, as he put it in the letter to Murrow that he wrote on Saturday afternoon, help him, "with a contact through a contact, . . . to get in touch with persons who count." It is highly unlikely that we will ever know where the dinner took place, but there are hints in the evidence that allow some speculation. For one, a dinner of lobster and peas in 1948 has the ring of a meal served up by a non-Greek household, most aptly American or British. Staktopoulos quotes a sworn deposition made by Colonel James Kellis before the Greek consul general in New York in 1978 to the effect that Kellis himself questioned the waiters at the Luxembourg Café, showing them Polk's photograph, and found no one there who recognized Polk as a client of the restaurant, but during his investigation of the restaurant issue he learned from a policeman that remnants of lobster shells had been found in Randall Coate's apartment not far from the Salonika waterfront, and this news had made him wonder if Polk's last meal may not have been at Randall Coate's table.[10] Kellis also testified that Coate had later made "an explicit statement," during his tour in Norway, that he was "the last foreigner to meet Polk before his death."

If so, one wonders how Coate could have known that to be true unless he was responsible for introducing Polk to those nonforeigners (i.e., Greeks) who did Polk in. A Salonika journalist who once worked for Coate, Christos Lambrinos, did not preclude this possibility, even a deliberate introduction to people who could have been some kind of threat to Polk, though he doubts that Coate was involved in the murder itself. Lambrinos reported that Coate had become rather bitter about the fact that the Americans were replacing the British as the primary foreign power active in Greece, and when the journalist decided to work for the newly arrived Americans at a significantly higher salary than he was receiving from the British, Coate said to him: "How easily you Greeks give up your old friends and latch on to new ones."[11] The same source suggested that one of Coate's secretaries had a similar complaint about Coate after he left town for Norway. Lambrinos also said that Coate and

Staktopoulos knew each other well, and he thought that Staktopoulos may have worked for Coate at one point (Coate's chief, A.G.R. Rouse, indicates otherwise, as we have seen). But Lambrinos said emphatically that some time before Polk reached Salonika on his fatal trip north, he had been at a party given for Coate in anticipation of the British information officer's departure for Norway, news that appears to confirm the report by Coate's superior, Rouse, that the transfer was requested by Rouse "long before this [the Polk] case ever arose."

Coate's superiors were apparently convinced that the British information officer was not culpable in an incriminating way (if the secret communications between them on the subject—now in the public domain—can be taken at face value), and they allowed Coate to continue in government service without any evident penalty. But of course Coate's involvement, outside the declared meeting with Polk in his office, may have been simply to bring Polk in touch with others who then acted entirely on their own—and presumably without Coate's knowledge—in staging an "assassination" of the CBS correspondent. Without further evidence in this connection—and Coate's continuing silence has to be seen as characteristic of British officials with a history of service in intelligence—it seems only reasonable to give him the benefit of the doubt.

In any case, whether or not Polk was introduced to his assassins somehow under Coate's auspices, what seems most plausible is that Polk did in fact eat in private on Saturday evening, met those whom he presumed to be of possible help to him either at dinner or at another meeting soon after, was shot by one or another of these "contacts" from behind without expectation or warning, lost that section of his wallet containing the press identity card and the Pan Am advertisement either while his body was being searched or while he was being transported to some point on the Salonika waterfront in anticipation of being dropped with bound hands and feet into Salonika Bay.

Was Gregory Staktopoulos among those whom Polk met on Saturday evening, whether at dinner or elsewhere? No hard evidence exists pointing to that conclusion, and the softer evidence of his various confessions turned so mushy in the end as to be discardable. There is only one small opening for doubt about the extent of Staktopoulos's connection with Polk in the book that the Reuters stringer published in 1984, where the overwhelming impression one receives is that of a man doing his best to be as honest as his intelligence permits, while also making little attempt to hide the passion he feels about his unjust suffering at the hands of the Security Police and the Greek legal system. Staktopoulos reports that early in his interrogation by the Security Police he was asked if he "saw the foreign journalists who came to Salonika."[12] Yes, Staktopoulos had replied to his interrogators, those who came to him with an introduction from the Athens office of Reuters, headed in those days by Bitsio and Modiano. These two "had sent me Homer Bigart and Thrapp, whom, though, I was unfortunately unable to assist." And he goes on to say that it was his custom to publish a notice of the arrival in Salonika of foreign journalists, which he did in the case of those two, as he did in the case of George Polk, whom he met only once in his life for five minutes in the Mediterranean Hotel.

What Staktopoulos does not tell us in his book is exactly what sort of assistance Bigart and Thrapp wanted from him, and in view of Thrapp's role in the Polk affair, which included his statement in Rome about having had one British and one Greek "contact" during his own trip to Salonika to explore the possibility of visiting Markos, and in view of Bigart's actually having reached the guerrilla leader's headquarters that summer, Staktopoulos's reference to these two American correspondents in his book might have been less succinct and more thoroughly explicated to avoid the possibility of suspicion by those searching his account of things for a final answer. Staktopoulos also indicated in his 1986 interview—this in passing—that he had "escorted Bigart" around Salonika on one occasion, but again, the occasion remained unspecified, and the reference was offered quite casually, as though it had no particular relation to the Polk affair. And Bigart himself does not remember ever meeting Staktopoulos.[13]

There is in any case no evidence at all that the Athens office of Reuters asked Staktopoulos to assist Polk one way or another, and in a 1977 interview Thrapp indicated that to the best of his recollection he did not and would not have mentioned Staktopoulos's name to anyone when asked at the time of the investigation about his Greek "contact" in Salonika.[14] Without any hard evidence, even after so many years, that Staktopoulos met Polk other than on the one occasion he acknowledges, he, like Randall Coate, must be given the full benefit of whatever small doubt may remain. Even if one chooses to believe, in the face of what seems most reasonable, that Staktopoulos somehow helped Polk to get in touch with those Polk was seeking out, one would have to challenge both the account in William E. Colby's notes and Staktopoulos's own account of his behavior after Polk's disappearance, especially his approach to Rea Polk in connection with a story he wanted to write about her missing husband, which surely suggests that he did not know that whatever contact he may have had with Polk would lead to murder.

The ultimate fact we are left with is that Polk was indeed murdered by somebody that Saturday evening, and given the bullet fired from behind, the loose binding of hands and feet after the fact, the notebook and appointment book that were missing from the personal effects that he carried with him to his death, and the cash that remained undisturbed in his pockets, it seems the murder was meant to appear to be an assassination motivated by politics. It is very likely that it was so. The remaining question is: whose politics? Greek officials were quick to say that a bullet fired from behind the victim's head was a Communist mode of assassination, but nobody—including the Americans on the scene—apparently considered the possibility that this mode was adopted by others of a different political persuasion precisely in order to make the murder appear a Communist crime. And no other facts emerged during the investigation that pointed indisputably to a Communist conspiracy to assassinate Polk or any other American correspondent. On the contrary, what emerged during the period of the investigation was evidence that the Communist guerrillas were eager to appear hospitable toward Westerners whom they felt might serve their propaganda interests. At the same time, no facts emerged during the investigation that pointed indisputably to a conspiracy to do Polk in by either the Right or the government then in power.

When the Lippmann Committee and its counsel chose to hold to the view—as expressed in their Report—"that the mystery could not be solved deductively—that is to say, by attempting to decide who had the most to gain by the murder of Polk" but chose instead to conclude "that only a solution of the crime tested in open court could ever settle the case,"[15] they chose a dangerous and ultimately mistaken course, at least on the journey that was meant to lead to an honest rather than merely expedient resolution. The truth is that an attempt to decide who had the most to gain by the murder of George Polk—or anyway who thought they had most to gain—was a surer path toward a solution to the mystery than the open, and quite capricious, trial that the committee and its counsel not only promoted but finally vindicated.

What speaks most forcefully against the conclusion reached by the trial prosecutors, defense lawyers, and almost all Greek and American officials involved in the case, namely that the crime was committed by the Left in order to discredit the Right, remains the fact that—as Roubatis and Vlanton were the first to suggest—Communists committing a murder in Salonika would find it extremely difficult to pin that murder on the Right when an ardently anti-Communist government was in charge of the investigation, a government that was likely—as proved to be the case—to do everything in its power to cast the blame for the crime back on the Communists.[16] And the chance of a guerrilla contingent carrying out a crime of that kind undetected in the heart of a city on edge to protect itself against Communist infiltration was anyway slight. Both the logistical and the political difficulties indicate that the Communists were likely to lose more than they might gain from murdering Polk in sight of the Salonika waterfront at a time when Polk was eager to travel to guerrilla headquarters, and the experience of others who did reach guerrilla territory during the late stages of the civil war—Bigart, Graessner, McShane, BBC correspondent Kenneth Matthews[17]—demonstrates that the Communists hoped to gain at least a strong propaganda advantage from encounters with Westerners who arrived in their midst, whether voluntarily or otherwise, and therefore handled the arrivals with some care.

It is not easy to argue that agencies of the Right, whether civilian, military, or paramilitary, stood to gain much of political value by arranging the murder of an American correspondent in Salonika, but given the civil war context, they would not have been in danger of losing as much as the Communists were likely to lose by a crime of that kind, since official agencies partial to the Right were at least partly in command of what for them was home territory, and unofficial agencies of the Right could count on more sympathy in high places than the Communists could possibly hope for from any quarter—as the trial itself demonstrated. And the Draft Report tells us that "Minister Rendis admitted to General Donovan that it would be almost impossible for him to interrogate or arrest any members of the Military Police [the right-wing agency that Rea Polk, among others, suspected of being behind the murder] . . . unless he had almost conclusive proof of their complicity,"[18] which, given the civil war context and the role of the armed forces then in command of the Salonika region, would probably have been almost impossible as well. Also, given the civil war context, and particularly what we have seen to be the hostility of much of the Greek press toward American correspondents thought to be critical of the Greek government (Bigart and Thrapp specific cases in point), it is not difficult to imagine that some agency of the Right in Salonika, official or secret, faced with the news that an aggressive American correspondent who had been critical of the Greek government in some of his dispatches was going around town trying to make contact with sources that would send him to interview the rebel general Markos, might have thought they had a duty to stop the correspondent from doing so, especially after the hullabaloo that Thrapp's recent visit to the city had occasioned.

One can imagine a Saturday evening meeting set up initially to discourage Polk from going on with his mission—as he had apparently been discouraged from doing by most of those he sought out for help during his two days in the city—a meeting that turned into an "assassination" when it became clear that Polk was obstinate in his ambition. Some have imagined a like meeting with possible Communist contacts that turned into an assassination when those Polk was meeting got cold feet because they felt the American correspondent could not be relied on to keep the encounter secret or to serve their purposes by way of the Markos interview or for some other reason. And one theory that still circulates among repatriated former guerrillas is that Polk was done in either by a double agent acting in concert with a Communist delegation sent into the city to contact the CBS correspondent or by a faction of the Communist guerrillas sympathetic to Zachariadis and unsympathetic to Markos. But the possibility of a Communist assassination by whatever agency assumes more free movement in Salonika by Communist conspirators, both before and after the murder, than seems plausible at that time, especially after the miserable failure of the effort by local investigative authorities to make a Communist presence there appear in fact plausible. One can conclude that some agency of the Right would have fewer logistical and political difficulties in staging an "assassination" and, in the heated war climate of those days, could well have persuaded itself that it was performing a reasonable—if not downright patriotic—act by preventing Polk, and thereby discouraging others of his inclination, from interviewing the enemy. As it turned out, Homer Bigart was not intimidated in this way, but it may be to the point that the "enemy" chose to arrange his trip to interview Markos not in Salonika but in Belgrade.

One of the strangest aspects of the Polk affair is the lack of solid evidence regarding possible participation by either Left or Right that turned up not only during the investigation but in the decades since. It is therefore easy to suspect that any tracks pointing to one or another group or agency were quickly covered over and have remained hidden ever since. Again the suspicion has to be that any such tracks led to the Right rather than the Left, because it was clearly to the advantage of the Salonika investigators, given their preconceptions and political biases, to reveal whatever they could that might indicate a Communist conspiracy and to hide anything precise pointing toward the Right, whether that turned out to be an agency of the police, or a branch of the military, or one or another of the secret organizations, such as "X," known to exist in Salonika at the time. And the same can be said about a possible British involvement in what occurred, whether it consisted of a more or less innocent introduction by Randall Coate to those who did Polk in—or by his assistant, Stappard, who remained at the British consulate general in Salonika—or something more sinister. British police representatives were there from start to finish to help cover up what might be necessary, and there were American officials in the wings with the kind of predisposition that suggests they might have been willing to aid their allies in this if called on to do so. But there is little at this point beyond speculative hunches to support the notion of an early British cover-up of whatever involvement their local officials may have had in the Polk affair, and in the case of the Greek officials on the scene at the start, one gets the impression not so much of men moving in concert to hide known facts as of men fumbling around to find anything they can that will support a preconceived theory. Their failure to do that—or anything else substantial—after more than two months of effort is what finally led to the Staktopoulos solution, concocted, it now seems, not only to satisfy their preconceptions but to satisfy their new American patrons, after having struggled in both subtle and unsubtle ways against heavy pressure from that sometimes overbearing source.

What we emerge with beyond the borders of speculation after so many years is firm grounds for believing that the murder did not happen as the "official solution" would have it. Most of what Gregory Staktopoulos presented in his confessions now appears to be pure fabrication, and those who still want to hold to the view that Staktopoulos was involved at least to the degree of having introduced Polk to those who murdered him would have to find culprits more credible than those Staktopoulos initially identified and would have to offer a political motive more convincing than the one he offered under the shadow of Security Police headquarters. We also have firm grounds for believing that the Lippmann Committee failed in its mission as this was outlined in its Report. It did not succeed in conducting "an independent inquiry,"[19] and since it did not do so, it had no business assuming much of what it assumed and arriving at the conclusions it reached. There is also evidence that its stated decision "to work with the authorities, to support them, to encourage those who are energetic, to put pressure on those who are slow, timid, or complacent"[20] helped to promote—in a significant sense—the opposite of what the committee's counsel identified as the committee's "original purpose," namely, "that no innocent man be 'framed' and no guilty one be 'whitewashed.' "[21] There is now little doubt that Staktopoulos was framed rather than justly tried, and there is little doubt that the framing, and those who participated in it, whether knowingly or otherwise, were grandly whitewashed, in part through the committee's own Report.

There is one aspect of the Report that proved prophetic. Though it seems clear that General Donovan, and perhaps some committee members, were, in the end, moved most by the disposition to get the case behind them once and for all whatever the remaining questions—no doubt Raleigh Gibson's disposition as well—the Report tells us that the committee "hopes that the case will not be forgotten."[22] Indeed it was not. The first who tried to see that this did not happen was I. F. Stone in 1952 through a series of five articles in the *Daily Compass* that commented scathingly on what the Lippmann Committee had offered the American public at that time.[23] Under the headline "I. F. Stone Exposes Polk Murder Case Whitewash," the series opens with the statement that the character of certain disclosures in the Lippmann Committee's published report and the long delay in making these disclosures "indicate that the investigating committee weakly allowed the American and Greek authorities to pull the wool over the eyes of the American public, and that it was willing to hold back vital information rather than go to bat with these authorities on behalf of justice for their dead colleague." Working only from the committee's Report, Stone of course could not speak with conviction about the specific miscarriage of justice in the case of the Reuters stringer who was in his fourth year at Salonika Security Police headquarters as Stone's text went to press.

The most shocking of the committee's disclosures, according to Stone, is the Colonel Kellis episode. Donovan's excuse for not requesting Kellis's return to Greece after his recall on the grounds that the general had—as the Report put it—"taken occasion to impress on Greek officials the necessity of exploring fully the leads which pointed to the Right as well as those pointing toward the Left" and had been "satisfied that this would be done" seems to Stone a "bill of goods" that had been sold him by Greek officials and that Donovan in turn sold the Lippmann Committee.[24] Stone would no doubt have seen the episode as even more scandalous had he known that the Report misdates Colonel Kellis's recall as "late in July 1949" rather than 1948, so that while Stone thinks Kellis was removed from the scene after being in Greece only a little over a year, Kellis in fact left Greece after little over six weeks there. And what would have struck Stone as more scandalous still are the implications of Kellis's CIA notes on the episode indicating that he let Donovan know of his wish to be relieved of his assignment before Donovan's return to

Greece in late July, a return that was soon followed by what appears to
have been Donovan's acceding to—and, if we are to believe Kellis's
notes, aiding in—the Staktopoulos solution, this as early as nine months
before the trial.

In his commentary on the Kellis episode, Stone asks why the committee held back from the public the knowledge of Kellis's recall for three—
in fact, four—years. Was it out of fear that there would be an outcry if
it became known that the American embassy in Athens had helped the
Greek government get rid of the one man investigating clues that led to
the Right? He quotes what he calls the committee's "pompous" conclusion that the safety of American correspondents working abroad in dangerous places can be best insured if it is known to all the world that these
correspondents cannot be attacked with impunity and that the power
and influence of the American government, the concerted action of the
press and radio, and an aroused public opinion "will demand and will
persist in demanding the pursuit and punishment of the criminals," to
which Stone adds the acid comment that instead of arousing public
opinion, the Lippmann Committee "weakly helped hush up facts which
would have embarrassed the Greek and American governments and
forced a fuller investigation." What insight there is in this conclusion
would seem to apply even more forcefully to the committee's counsel,
though Stone could not have deduced that from the committee's Report
alone.

During the rest of his series, Stone takes up some of the questions
raised by Professor Morgan's commentary on the Staktopoulos confession and goes on to argue that the Lippmann Committee, made up in
Lippmann's own words of "men whose profession it is to have few
illusions," showed in its own account of the Polk case that it had allowed itself—"gracefully" for "men with few illusions"—to be "gulled
by the Greek and American governments." Like "the lady in the bar-
room story," the committee "raped awful easy," and through "the feeble
bit of whitewash" that it published as its Report can be seen "advance
warnings enough to have set a cub reporter on guard, much less top men
of a profession supposed to have 'few illusions.'" He finds a double
crime revealed between the lines of the Report: the murder of the "de-
cent young man, an honorable reporter" (as he calls Polk at one point)
and the crime of the Greek and American governments "in preventing
a real investigation" of the murder and "in making an accomplice of this
bunch of journalistic stuffed shirts"—and he adds: "I do not believe they
deserve a more polite characterization" (the following names are listed
at the end of the "Foreword" to the Report, which of course does not

necessarily mean that all were fully aware of what their names were being given to: Ernest K. Lindley, Joseph C. Harsch, Paul Wooton, Peter Edson, Eric Sevareid, Harold Hinton, Phelps Adams, Wallace R. Deuel, James L. Reston, and Blair Moody).

Rankin's early cable to the secretary of state dated May 21, 1948, which was "paraphrased" in an addendum to the Report,[25] becomes the principal basis for Stone's insight into the official American impulse to go along with the governing theory proposed by Greek officials from the start of their investigation. This cable—as recorded in the Report—has Rankin stating that although Attorney General Constantinidis is anxious to believe that the murder "was not committed by anyone from the Right Wing" and is "trying to convince himself that suspicion does not lie in that direction, . . . I do not think that he will suppress any information leading in that direction." The excerpt from the cable concludes with the further statement that "I personally feel that the investigation is being handled efficiently." The original of the cable was in fact submitted initially by Raleigh Gibson from the Salonika consulate, and what the Lippmann Committee was given by the State Department to paraphrase turns out to be the copy of Gibson's cable that Rankin signed and submitted from the embassy in Athens; so the first-person opinions in it, though obviously shared by Rankin, belong in the first instance to Gibson (the original actually says: "My personal opinion is that the investigation is being efficiently handled by the police and national security").[26]

Had I. F. Stone been aware of this double submission by Gibson and Rankin, it would only have added strength to his argument, since it illustrates the evident collusion—certainly the reciprocity of views— among American diplomatic officials in the two major Greek cities as the Polk affair unfolded. In any case, he concludes his commentary on this issue by indicating that the Lippmann Committee's acquiescence in the Greek government's theory regarding the murder and its reluctance to challenge the effort of American officials in Greece not only to bring the committee into line with the official theory but to arrange the recall of its own independent investigator (that is, Kellis) and in the end to "keep quiet about American official connivance in the hush-up" and to withhold publication of Professor E. M. Morgan's expert analysis of the "dubious confession" for three years should, in Stone's opinion, "provide journalism schools with a model lesson in how to be a willing sucker instead of a real reporter."

When Stone comes to the subject of the trial, he sees that occasion as "a subtle piece of flim-flam" on the basis of the documentation that the committee itself offered, even if this documentation contradicted Donovan's view that the trial was efficiently and honestly conducted and the committee's own view that Staktopoulos and his mother "received a fair trial." Where Stone misses the mark a bit is in his use of Murrow's CBS broadcast of April 27, 1949, to challenge the committee's conclusion.[27] Though we have seen that the two correspondents he quotes from, Winston Burdett and Alexander Kendrick, were in fact critical of much that went on at the trial, Burdett was the one who ended up reporting that General Donovan "was satisfied" that the witnesses he interviewed "had spoken freely and without pressure," and he also reported that "generally, American observers were convinced" that Staktopoulos "was no mere scapegoat of the Greek police," which is presumably why he could imply that if "the whole truth about Polk's death has not yet been told," some part of the truth came out of the trial. And Murrow himself follows his presentation of Kendrick's criticism by declaring that "there is general agreement that Stakhtopoulos [*sic*] was deeply implicated in the murder of George Polk." One doubts that I. F. Stone would have shared that general agreement had he been among the observers at the trial and had he been privy to the range of communications between officials in Greece and the Department of State—or even to the Lippmann Committee's share of those communications.

Stone's sharpest irony is reserved for General Donovan. He finds it "extraordinary" how much this "experienced and able trial lawyer" managed not to see in the Salonika courtroom. While Donovan was supposed to be investigating the murder of Polk on behalf of "a committee of distinguished American newspapermen," he succeeded in overlooking "the most important aspect of the trial from the standpoint of American foreign correspondents," namely, the implicit and explicit attacks on those correspondents that Kendrick reported. Why had Donovan failed in his charge in this and other ways? Stone suggests that given the general's close links with the U.S. government and the State Department, he was "hardly the ideal choice as an independent counsel and investigator." Not that "he did or would sabotage" the inquiry, in fact, he "seems to have begun with as sour a view of the Greek government's activities in the Polk murder as most working newspapermen," but the implication is that in the end he was "too easily reachable by government officials, . . . too susceptible to considerations of high policy." Stone shrewdly sees this as the committee's principal weakness as well: "to stand up for justice would have been to clash with the powers that be, to risk one's own liaison with that nice warm intimate world of State Department contacts, to invite suspicion upon oneself."

The committee's failure to tell the American public all it could have told and its having issued a report only after a delay of three years, "in the midst of the summer doldrums, with the murder almost forgotten, . . . as if deliberately to attract as little attention as possible, like shame-faced men walking rapidly away from a crime they should have averted," leads Stone to a final piece of eloquent outrage. Under the Report's "unctuous phrases" and "amid [its] smugly self-serving declarations," he feels that one may still reconstruct the way the committee and General Donovan and the State Department "helped the Greek government hush up pertinent facts on the murder of a newspaper colleague," but "it would take the bitter pen of a Juvenal adequately to sum up this typical example of a spectacle familiar in every age and society—the readiness of the respectable to gloss over the worst crimes rather than risk their own standing in the circles of wealth and power."

Still, despite the hush-up and the gloss over, the Polk affair in fact continued to remain alive during the decades that followed, because two of its victims, Gregory Staktopoulos and Kosta Hadjiargyris, remained alive, if wounded, and in the end neither could let the case rest where it had presumably been buried. And they got help from others, both in Greece and in the United States. Four years after I. F. Stone's blistering series—which few appear to have noticed—Staktopoulos smuggled the letters proclaiming his innocence out of Salonika prison, and when his claim was published in the Greek newspaper *Apoyevmatini*, the debate in Greece about who was really responsible for Polk's murder caught fire again. In his letter to "Greek Justice," Staktopoulos stated that he did not murder Polk, was in no way involved in the murder, did not have the slightest knowledge about the affair.[28] What he had confessed to had no relation to reality, and he had been compelled to say what he had said, under direction, for reasons of national interest, even in the courtroom. Neither he nor his mother had addressed the famous envelope, as God was his witness. He knew Vasvanas and Mouzenidis only by sight, had not met with them, or talked to them, or seen them during the period in question. He requested a new trial, at which he would tell the real truth, and those who heard him then would fully believe in his inno-cence. Besides, he remarked, the disclosures of the honorable chief of police, Ioannis Panopoulos (actually, head of the directorate of the Greek police in the Ministry of Public Order), that had brought the official solution into question, were themselves grounds for a new trial. Stakto-poulos wrote William Polk much the same, though he added a reference to an article that had appeared in *Apoyevmatini* the previous month (March 1956) which suggested that the British had planned, organized, and carried out the murder of George Polk. And Staktopoulos underlined his desire to "restore his honor, the most precious thing on earth."

In the covering letter to his journalist colleague Vassos Tsimbidaros, the Reuters stringer said that after his "confession" he understood how confessing worked in Communist countries, and he appealed to the judicial authorities of his country and "our great friends and allies the Americans" to protect his life and the lives of his sisters. Later that year, with the help of his original lawyer, Economou, Staktopoulos's sentence was reduced from life imprisonment to twenty years.

It was the first sign of hope that had come Staktopoulos's way since he was returned to the hands of the Security Police after the trial ended. He tells us in his book that they had not treated him too badly during the four years they had him under guard at the headquarters. He was taken out occasionally to a café for a coffee or a meal, once traveled in Mouskoundis's Jeep as far as Serres, was allowed to watch the guards playing cards and backgammon in their central meeting place, was even encouraged to join them—but he had no heart for it. He was always watched, even when his mother and sisters came to visit. When William Polk visited him, the room was full of police. He doesn't remember what he was asked or how he replied, but after Polk's brother left, he was told to put what he had said in writing and hand it over to Major Mouskoundis. He doesn't remember what he wrote out, but it clearly didn't please Mouskoundis, because he was put in a basement cell for a while, he thinks until the danger of further visits by foreigners had disappeared. And when his mother died early during his tour at the headquarters, he wasn't allowed to attend the funeral, though he was taken out once to visit her grave.

His morale became a problem for the Security Police. He sat mostly with his head hung low, didn't eat enough, slept badly, especially after his mother died. He smoked eighty cigarettes a day, of an inferior brand. He talked rarely. The Security Police decided to put him to work translating again, but the texts were all boring police documents. Two officers came to him for English lessons. He didn't prove good at that, couldn't get his mind into it: he wanted to die, and they wanted him to teach English! A "cousin" of the head man arrived from Athens to examine him, ask him questions, see if had gone out of his mind or was on the way there. He was never given a report on the issue.

Finally, with the persistent help of his sisters, especially Adriani, and supported by his old lawyer, Economou, he asked to be transferred from Security Police headquarters to the Seven Towers prison in Salonika, and he was given a hearing. Constantinidis had been replaced by Sakelariou, and the latter was shocked to find that Staktopoulos was still being held illegally by the Security Police. Mouskoundis argued that this unusual action was merely to protect Staktopoulos from possible Communist reprisal for what he had confessed to. The argument didn't hold, and the transfer order was set in motion. From that moment on, Staktopoulos became terrified that there would be more torture now, then new charges he would have to confess to, some new murder he hadn't committed or the old Stalin interview charge, but he didn't see Mouskoundis again before leaving the headquarters, and the last he heard of him was well after he was safely in the main Salonika prison, where news reached him some years later that his former tormentor had died. Staktopoulos refused to believe it, though it was true: How could Mouskoundis die while his victim was still alive to talk? The possibility of his talking had been the one thing they had warned him about before he left Security Police headquarters: if Staktopoulos knew what was good for him and his family, he would keep his mouth shut. And even the new attorney general, Sakelariou, had told him that his sisters could visit him freely in his new cell but no messages were to go out.

The messages went out nevertheless, first an appeal for a pardon that was evidently ignored, and after some four years of adjusting to the new prison, where he was given more work therapy and at one point regular psychiatric care, the several letters for publication that were smuggled out by a frightened Adriani, still persistent in her good offices. Though the press attention this caused appears to have resulted in a lighter sentence, it also appears to have caused his transfer to the prison on Aegina island, which brought him new despair, because he was afraid that regular visits by his sisters would stop. The place was really a sanatorium for unhealthy or mad convicts. And indeed he felt himself going mad while there. He became obsessed with the charade that he had been a part of, and his mind, in turning it over and over, became quite unsettled.

But there were things in the new prison that he feels helped him to survive. They put him on a diet that included milk every morning, yogurt at noon, and meat four times a week. He managed to keep himself in cigarettes, a pack a day, by selling the milk and yogurt for a drachma and the meat for a drachma and a half. And he befriended a professional thief who would bring him two cigarettes—one to smoke and one for behind his ear—whenever he ran out completely. Adriani showed up regularly to offer comfort, his other sister less often because she had married in the meanwhile. And the prison officials made efforts to get him back in touch with humanity by giving him work first in the library, where he was in charge of checking out books to other inmates, then as a kind of clerk in the administrative section with a typewriter to play with.

All this did him good by slow degrees, anyway kept him from going mad. But he can't remember laughing even once the whole time he was in that prison. In 1958 his lawyer Economou filed another petition for pardon which was rejected, but he was able to get his sentence reduced to seventeen years in 1960, so that in August of that year, with time credit for good behavior, he was finally released to go home. Staktopoulos tells us that he had entered Security Police headquarters a young-looking thirty-eight-year-old in 1948 and emerged from Aegina prison at the age of fifty, hair white, a "human mess."[29] By that time Major Mouskoundis was dead, and Attorney General Constantinidis, having failed to reach the Supreme Court in Athens, was doomed to serve out his career in the provincial town of Larissa.

Once out of prison, Staktopoulos decided that it was the better part of valor to keep his lips sealed, but the case had a way of coming into public view again every now and then. In 1965, the newspaper *Athinaiki*, which called itself "independent" and was generally considered centrist, offered a six-part series on the Polk affair that was rather hard on Staktopoulos.[30] Whom had he really been serving? the paper asked. What other convicted criminal had been given the privilege of spending four years at Security Police headquarters in a well-furnished room instead of in a prison cell? And being assigned to the "reform" rather than "criminal" section of the Seven Towers prison? And petitioning for a pardon so soon after his incarceration and so regularly thereafter? What convicted criminal had ever managed to do that before? And out on a life sentence after only twelve years? Yet for all his good treatment, said the paper, the man complains that the authorities have not fulfilled their responsibility, while he has entirely fulfilled his. Even the greatest skeptics are ready to believe that he was in reality a miserable agent of somebody else. But of whom exactly? Surely of outside influences, the foreign finger, surely the British Intelligence Service working in concert with the American authorities, in particular with General Donovan and the American consul general in Salonika. In the end, concludes the paper, it will out, all of it.

A year later (March 7, 1966) came the story in a Salonika newspaper, *Makedoniki Ora*, about "E. M. (full name available to the Attorney General on request)" having been the one who found Polk's identity card and the Pan American advertisement while walking along the quay near the Trianon Café and having taken these to "S. K." for advice. According to the news story, some days after mailing the items in to the police, the two men learned about Polk's murder and decided, in order to avoid being drawn into the affair, especially given the troubled times, not to report their role in the discovery. This, the article tells its readers, raises many questions. Since Staktopoulos and his mother knew that they hadn't mailed in the identity card, what caused them to confess falsely, and in view of the false confessions, what value is there in the fiction that Staktopoulos and the police created regarding the presumed murderers Vasvanas and Mouzenidis? Finally, who in fact dropped the identity card that was found by E. M. near the Trianon Café and why did the person who dropped it think it necessary to remove it from Polk's corpse?

These are all questions that the article feels need to be answered more fully, especially since their review of the case (not always fully accurate) reveals many peculiarities: the immediate assumption by certain local officials that the Communists were responsible; Rea Polk's initial calmness, which was then succeeded, after the body was discovered, by her crying out heart-breakingly to Raleigh Gibson that "nationalists" had murdered her husband; then the files found to be missing from Polk's office covering exactly the period of his Middle East research into the Anglo-American dispute over oil in that region; and just when the report appeared that Polk's identity card had been found, a "British agent of the Intelligence Service assigned to the British Consulate in Salonika, . . . Randall Coates [sic]," Staktopoulos's "chief at the British Information Service," suddenly left town for Athens and flew out to Norway on May 15. Then, the next day, Polk's body was found 400 meters from Coate's apartment, the body bound in a way that was "unique in Greek criminal records," the stomach full of lobster and peas, a meal "especially dear to the British." A meeting between Polk and Coate had been verified by both Greek and American sources, and it was reported that Athens Chief of Police Panopoulos, meeting General Donovan at the home of Minister of Public Order Rendis, told this representative of the American press that " 'lobster and peas had been eaten at Coates' house during the evening of the murder and that it was not impossible the murder had taken place there.' "

The article goes on to report that Panopoulos testified in connection with a 1956 court case that the Polk murder had not occurred as it was shown to have occurred at the Salonika trial and that he himself had discovered how it had taken place, but Panopoulos didn't elaborate on the matter at that time and has been silent since.[31] And, continues the article, there had been others who had raised questions, had said they would tell all, Donovan for one, but he too had been given instructions, had been threatened, was silenced in the end. Then there were the newspaper reports that British Intelligence had been behind the whole thing, had planned it all in Athens. And hadn't William Polk, the victim's brother, told the press after the trial that there were still many unanswered questions and much contradictory testimony, and until these matters were resolved, the investigation ought to go on? Finally, there was the statement by "Sir William," head of the British Police Mission in Athens, to Minister of Justice Melas in April 1949, to the effect that it would be very difficult, if not impossible, ever to find the culprits, not only because the murder was political but because enough time had passed before the body was discovered to allow those who had committed the crime to cover their tracks.

Indeed so, concludes the article: the agents of the murder had done their work well; they were in a safe place abroad. But today's revelations in *Makedoniki Ora*, backed up by witnesses, surely indicated that a retrial was called for. The government had an obligation to order one, so that the true murderers could be identified, along with the motives of those who chose to depict the affair as other than it was in reality, and along with the identity of those who actually aided the murderers. Most of all, an answer was needed to the question of how the Greek authorities could have gone along with the version of the murder that they did accept (i.e., one that named only Greeks as the culprits). Was it preferable to foist a repulsive crime of that kind onto their own people? In order to benefit whom? And why?

In the same month that *Makedoniki Ora* brought news of witnesses willing to testify that the Pan Am advertisement and Polk's identity card had been found by a passerby walking along the Salonika quay, Kosta Hadjiargyris published a series of articles on the Polk affair in the Athenian newspaper *Ethnos*, excerpts from the book he intended to publish in 1967 and which in fact finally appeared, with the results of broader research, in 1975. He reported that the delay, which served his text in the end, was caused by the bad times that had come to Greece. In April 1967, Colonel George Papadopoulos and a clique of extreme Right officers had taken over the country following a military coup, and for the next seven years this junta ruled dictatorially, with harsh measures against all overt opposition, including many well-documented instances of torture by the Military Police (ESA) of that era. The climate was hardly an appropriate one for reopening the Polk case file. That presumably had to wait until democracy was restored and all vestiges of censorship and other remnants of the junta tyranny were removed.

In 1976, a year after Hadjiargyris's detailed account of Staktopoulos's ordeal at Security Police headquarters and his well-researched questioning of the process that had sent Staktopoulos to jail for twelve years, Staktopoulos himself decided to break his long silence by publishing an interview in a leading Athenian daily, *Ta Nea*, during the course of which he recanted the confessions that had led to the convictions at the trial and declared that he had been framed so that liberal American journalists opposed to the established government in Greece would stop sending dispatches home that favored the Communists and so that public opinion in the United States would swing decisively against the guerrilla forces.[32] Then, in January 1977, with the support of Stelios Papathemelis and others, he told the press that fear had kept his mouth sealed all these years but that now he wanted to tell the full story as it had happened—the torture, the way the confessions were forced out of him, the imprisonment for four years under constant surveillance at Security Police headquarters—and to appeal to the Greek Supreme Court for a retrial that would clear his name.

This did not prove easy. The immediate problem was that the two officials who had been responsible for taking the formal version of Staktopoulos's confession in the Salonika Security Police headquarters during October 1949 and for preparing the original indictment, Christos Moustakis and Christos Komotouros, had prospered over the years and were now both members of the Greek Supreme Court.[33] Papathemelis, acting as Staktopoulos's lawyer, decided to wait until their term was up, some months in the future. In the meanwhile he went to work on the information that had been brought to light by *Makedoniki Ora* some ten years earlier. By December 1978, with Staktopoulos beside him, he was able to hold a press conference to introduce the opinion of the handwriting experts he had consulted, all members of the Greek Graphological Institute, to the effect that the handwriting on the famous envelope sent to the Third Police Precinct was not that of Anna Staktopoulos.

Papathemelis told the press that he was prepared to demonstrate, with scientific authority supporting him, that the envelope in question had in fact been addressed by Savvas Karamichalis, who, though now deceased, had left behind sufficient samples of his handwriting for purposes of identification. He was also prepared to challenge the report by the handwriting experts Poulantzas and Kouyias that had served as the basis for the charges against Anna Staktopoulos and had been presented in court as the significant tangible evidence providing credibility for Staktopoulos's confessions. Papathemelis also told the press that he had tried to get Professor Poulantzas to appear in public and to respond to the new evidence that challenged the professor's original finding, but Poulantzas had answered the deputy's telephone "invitation" by swearing in language that was unprintable and by hanging up on him. In his written response to the press, Poulantzas indicated that comment by him at this time would be entirely out of order since any new evidence had to be submitted to the Supreme Court and examined there, as was scheduled to happen on March 10, 1979.

The newspaper accounts of this press conference show that the discussion was not confined to questions of handwriting only but touched on other lingering issues, including Athens Chief of Police Panopoulos's questioning of the official solution and the implications of a new obstacle reported by Papathemelis: the CIA had a collection of sixty-six detailed documents relating to the case but had permitted researchers to review only six of these, the others being kept out of circulation because their contents was considered vital to American security interests. Staktopoulos was also pressed by reporters to elaborate on the history of his involvement in the case, and that brought him no comfort. As one paper put it (*Thessaloniki*, December 7, 1978), the "tortured journalist's exposition" before his colleagues created "a tragic image of the affair." His "explanations were offered sometimes with tears, sometimes with shouting and emotional outbursts as the terrible days he and his family had known came to life in front of him." He reported that he had been told continually that he had offered great service to his country. The paper concludes that "the questions raised again by this shocking story" may find their answers in the retrial that must surely take place "on behalf of justice and the truth."

But that was not to happen, even after a second public discussion of the new evidence in February 1979 and the testimony of two handwriting experts, Valindras and Halkias, that the envelope was indeed the work of Savvas Karamichalis and not of Anna Staktopoulos.[34] (When Papathemelis was asked from the floor about the delay of over ten years before the new evidence had been pursued by anybody, he invoked the problem presented by the 1967–74 dictatorship.) The Supreme Court reviewed Staktopoulos's appeal in March 1979, and rejected it in June 1979, with two out of the seven judges dissenting. Papathemelis's first reaction was that, given the constitution of the Supreme Court at the time—military judges from the years of the dictatorship and judges of the Moustakis-Komotouros faction—it would have been surprising if the appeal had been accepted. Its having been rejected was "self-explanatory."[35]

Several weeks later, Papathemelis gave a more substantial response in an article for the press.[36] As he saw it, there had been two tenable options open to the Supreme Court: to accept the legitimacy and validity of the new evidence or to order further proof. Instead, he asserted, the court chose to offer a series of arguments based on old evidence, with the aim of propping up a desired conclusion. Papathemelis then illustrated the false logic that the court had used in effecting its aim, citing a series of examples from the majority opinion, followed by his parenthetical comments: (1) lobster and peas were found in Polk's stomach; Staktopoulos confessed to eating lobster and peas; therefore, his confession is true and the accused is guilty (comment: What value could that conclusion have when the confession, often revised, came six months after the lobster was identified by the autopsy?); (2) an inkwell was found (if in fact it was found) in Staktopoulos's home; the ink was the same as that on the incriminating envelope; therefore, Staktopoulos's mother addressed the envelope (comment: though thousands of others in Salonika had the same ink); (3) the accused confessed that he had deposited the envelope in a mailbox near the White Tower at 10:30; the envelope was picked up there by a post office employee at 11:00; therefore, his confession is true (comment: as though somebody else couldn't have deposited the envelope in the box).

Along with this false logic, the court failed according to Papathemelis in not having heard the testimony of any witnesses, in not having taken into account the latest scientific theories regarding confessions and the role that despair can play in a man who sees no escape, in not having considered American (that is, Professor Morgan's) published reservations regarding the confessions, and in not having taken into account the "transgression" of elements outside the system of justice and even outside Greece, as was demonstrated in certain State Department archives (presumably those excerpts published by Roubatis and Vlanton in the May 1977 issue of *More*, and more amply by Yannis Voultepsis in a series that appeared in the Athenian journal *Epikaira* during October 1977). These factors, said Papathemelis, plus the appeal for a retrial by Evangelos Vasvanas (once the government allowed him to be repatriated) and that by the family of the deceased Mouzenidis ought to be enough to open the Polk file again at any moment. The praiseworthy vote of the two dissenting judges had prepared the way for the final elucidation of the crime—though, he concludes, history is on "our side," without need for legal confirmation, and in its own chosen time history will give justice the opportunity to take stock of truth.

Perhaps to help history on its way, Gregory Staktopoulos, despite the rejected appeal and health problems, managed to get his own final word on the Polk affair into the record through the book he published in 1984, at a time when the case had again begun to drift toward oblivion, along with many of those who had taken part in it. Since the Lippmann Report was less than the final word from American sources, history also received some help from at least one of the "foreign fingers" thought to have been a conspirator in the case. The first postdictatorship contribution from America came in the form of a lengthy 1975 review of Hadjiargyris's book by Professor Stephen G. Xydis of Hunter College, CUNY, a version of which appeared in the annual *Southeastern Europe/L'Europe du Sud-Est* (vol. 2, no. 2 [1975]: 194–98) and in a Greek version published as a series in the Athenian newspaper *Kathimerini*.[37] Since Xydis's speculation regarding the Polk affair still has currency among a number of those interested in the case, especially in Greece, and since it has not been fully examined in the light of developments during the past decade, it merits some reconsideration here.

Professor Xydis offers his readers a history of the case that draws mostly on Hadjiargyris's account in the 1975 book under review by him, and his interpretation of the affair closely follows Hadjiargyris's line, namely, that the key figure in the case is Randall Coate (or, as both Xydis and Hadjiargyris insist on calling him in the face of ample contrary evidence, Randall Coats). This causes Xydis to distort the case a bit, for example, when he pictures Coate as leaving Salonika for Athens on Thursday, May 13, "without any advance notice" (p. 18). As we have seen, there is now some evidence that Coate's transfer was solicited well in advance of Polk's arrival in Salonika and that a farewell party for Coate had already been scheduled at the time of Polk's fatal visit. Xydis's account of the missing CBS file also rather oversimplifies that issue, more so than Hadjiargyris himself does, and he suggests that Rea Polk's explanation of "why she never informed the investigation about her having had this particular file taken out of her husband's office" is "rather lame" (p. 20), though in other instances Xydis gives proper weight to the "third degree" treatment that witnesses either underwent (Anna Molyvda and Stelios Mouzenidis in particular) or feared they would undergo (which appears to be Rea Polk's less than lame grounds for keeping certain information from the police, especially after her early harsh sessions with her interrogators).

Without having had access to the relevant State Department archives, Xydis isn't entirely accurate about the timing of Donovan's visits to Greece, and he has to rely on what Hadjiargyris offers in characterizing

Donovan's influence in the affair. Xydis tells his readers, for example, that "it was toward the end of Donovan's second visit to Greece that Stakhtopoulos [*sic*] was held" (p. 25) when in fact it was toward the end of Donovan's second visit that the general was objecting strongly to the slow pace the investigation had taken and was recommending that a judicial committee enter the inquiry—though, if we can believe Kellis's CIA notes, Donovan also had Staktopoulos's name in hand as a suspect at that time, and it may have come as no surprise to him when the Reuters correspondent was arrested several weeks after Donovan's departure from Greece.

Xydis offers as fact an account of how Staktopoulos was chosen as scapegoat based on a quotation by Hadjiargyris of an evidently unpublished conversation that the Athens police chief for the Ministry of Public Order, Ioannis ("Yannis") Panopoulos, was reported to have had in 1956 with an Athenian lawyer named Dimosthenis Mirasyetzi who was interested in the case.[38] According to the Hadjiargyris quotation, Panopoulos told the lawyer that Staktopoulos was arrested and tried because somebody had to be arrested and tried as the guilty party. The Americans had requested that by cable. Minister of Public Order Rendis called a meeting of the council dealing with the Polk case and reported that the U.S. government categorically demanded that somebody be found guilty, and it had given Prime Minister Sophoulis a quick deadline for doing so, warning him that otherwise aid to Greece would have to be cut. The council had come to a decision. During the hasty exchange of views that followed, the name of Staktopoulos inevitably came up as the most appropriate choice for the role of victim, though—says Panopoulos—he wasn't the likeliest candidate, since he wasn't one of those who would agree to confess to everything for a little money, be sentenced to death, then show up six months later with a new name and a passport for America. But he was "relatively" the most appropriate candidate.

Perhaps all too plausible, especially given Donovan's distress during these days and his close links to official Washington, but Hadjiargyris's word that this is what Panopoulos said in conversation with a third party about what had happened at a meeting eight years previously cannot legitimately be considered, either by the professor or his readers, as proof positive of the way things actually happened. And one would have to say the same about Professor Xydis's less plausible reconstruction of both the murder and its origins, which Hadjiargyris himself, though generally appreciative of the professor's support for his views, finds quite unacceptable when he comments on it in a postscript to the second edition of his book.

Xydis begins his reconstruction by suggesting that Hadjiargyris took "an improbable leap" (p. 35) when he proposed not only that the crime might have been committed on land in a house near the waterfront but actually in Randall Coate's own house on Niki Boulevard near the Trianon Café, opposite which the body was found. "A more likely hypothesis," Xydis believes, is that Polk boarded a caique that was supposedly to take him across Salonika Bay to the mountains of central Greece, and that he did so not on Saturday night but on Sunday morning, spent that morning and early afternoon on board, ate his last "exotic" meal there, was shot in the head out of hearing of land, was then trussed up so that he would be sure to drown if still alive and was either dumped overboard from the caique or more likely from a rowboat that carried him closer in toward the quay, bundled up both so that transport would be easier and so that "there would be less of a splash" (p. 37) when he was dropped overboard. If Polk was blindfolded—and Xydis suggests that the blindfolding may be a myth—this may have been done to keep Polk from seeing that at the end he was not heading toward Olympus but toward the Salonika waterfront.

This hypothesis derives from Xydis's acceptance of the testimony by the Astoria Hotel doorman that after Polk returned to the hotel on Saturday night at 11:00 and hurriedly went out ten minutes later, he then returned to the hotel again at 12:45 A.M. presumably to spend the night, which would explain why Donald Matchen was told, when he phoned the hotel on Sunday morning, that Polk had left at 8:00 A.M., as it might also explain why Polk's three-day alarm clock, which presumably woke him Sunday morning, was still running when Rea Polk reached Salonika on Wednesday. Given the coroner's report that Polk had shaved eight to ten hours before his death, that would place his last meal, Xydis tells us, sometime after the noon hour and the murder between 3:30 and 5:30 on Sunday afternoon, hence his hypothesis about the hovering caique. The problem with that hypothesis, as Hadjiargyris points out in his postscript, is the new questions it raises: Where exactly was this caique and rowboat that were never discovered? Where did they go? Why were they never seen by anybody though they were presumably on the move in broad daylight: not spotted by the Salonika coast guard nor the military authorities on watch there nor anybody else in or near the Bay? Had the caique been the ghostly Flying Dutchman, says Hadjiargyris, somebody surely would have noticed it.

But it is Professor Xydis's new theory about exactly who was behind the murder that disturbs Hadjiargyris most, not without reason. Xydis accepts Hadjiargyris's basic contention that British Intelligence was behind the murder and that it was an anti-American act, not one that was "within the overarching framework of the most intimate British-American relations as conducted by London at the time" (i.e., not one planned at the highest levels) but also not one that the British considered a blunder since the British government "continued availing itself" of Coate's services for some years after the event (p. 38). So far perhaps so good. What Xydis now argues is that Hadjiargyris hasn't properly answered "which particular section of SIS [British Secret Intelligence Service] might have carried out such an anti-American, anti-Greek operation," and he finds that there is a simpler explanation behind the whole enterprise than that provided by Hadjiargyris's "broad and rambling tour d'horizon of the international situation in the Eastern Mediterranean and the Middle East at the time," even if focused mainly on "the extremely turbulent state of affairs then prevailing in Palestine" (pp. 37–38). Even so far perhaps so good. But Xydis's simpler explanation, what Hadjiargyris calls "a daring leap of logic" that serves to introduce the professor's "own *deus ex machina*," is that Kim Philby, master double agent then assigned to Istanbul, planned the operation and had it carried out by Randall Coate. As head of the British Intelligence station in Turkey, argues Xydis, it must have been Philby "who supervised the counter-espionage operations of British SIS agents in northern Greece, among whom was Coats" (p. 40).

How so? Xydis accepts Hadjiargyris's contention that Randall Coate's task in Salonika was "not merely to facilitate visits of foreign correspondents to Markos's headquarters in northern Greece," but also, working for SIS, to spy on the Greek Communist Party in that region, to gather information about "leading elements" in the guerrilla movement, to reach "conclusions about the objectives of Soviet policy in Greece," and also to "spring traps for the KKE and exploit them for the purposes of British policy in Greece" (pp. 38–39). If Coate was engaged in these kinds of intelligence activities, then "he must have been working for the particular section of SIS that was responsible for anti-communist and anti-Soviet espionage and for counter-espionage in particular," which meant that he worked for the same section of SIS that Philby supervised from Istanbul. Why would Philby want Polk murdered? As a double agent he was secretly serving Soviet interests by this plot. Xydis tells us that "from Moscow's viewpoint, Polk's murder in 1948 not only was consistent with Soviet objectives of stirring up conflicts within the 'capitalist camp,' " but it also "served to 'sharpen the contradictions' between the 'socialist' and 'capitalist' camps," and, further, "in the context of intra-communist conflicts," served as "a blow directed against Markos and his

guerrilla operation" after Stalin decided that—as he told a group of Yugoslav officials visiting Moscow—"the Greek guerrilla struggle had no
chances of success and therefore should fold up" (p. 42). Finally, says
Xydis, Staktopoulos's "cruel fate" could be viewed as Stalin's revenge
against him for the "obscure role" that Staktopoulos played, according
to the murder inquiry (though later dropped by Constantinidis as a possible charge), in providing his newspaper with the broadcast text of the
fictitious Stalin interview that presumably embarrassed Moscow—
though Xydis suggests in a parenthesis, inexplicably, that the interview
too may have been another Philby intrigue.

In his postscript, Hadjiargyris raises pertinent questions about this
new theory (questions that Xydis, who died in 1977, evidently did not
have occasion or time to answer). Why did Coate's superiors keep their
faith in him for so many years instead of suspecting him of being a
double agent working for some other country's secret intelligence service (since they themselves presumably hadn't issued an order for the
murder of Polk to be carried out via Philby)? Or why didn't they suspect
Philby of having acted outrageously on his own initiative when Coate
revealed Philby as the source of his orders, as he surely would have had
to do? And in any case would the Russians have permitted one of their
top spies, still undiscovered, to expose himself dangerously, as Philby
would have been exposed, simply to get rid of a single American correspondent, however potentially damaging to American-Greek relations?
Philby was surely too valuable to them to be put at risk for such a
limited aim.

Hadjiargyris concludes that Xydis's theory presupposes a carefully
planned plot based on some prearranged contact between Polk and the
Philby-Coate axis when all the evidence, including Polk's visit to Coate
in Salonika, suggests that "Polk's effort [to reach Markos] was a matter
of chance, unplanned" (p. 344). What Hadjiargyris cannot bring himself
to consider is the possibility that Coate was not in fact an official British
spy working for clearly defined British interests and their designated
anti-American policies but a kind of "loose gun" who was bent on gathering information and contacts on his own, against the wishes of his
superiors—as one of his superiors in fact indicated in a secret exchange
with the Foreign Office—and if at all involved in the Polk affair may
have been so without anything as criminal as murder in mind.

The most substantial help that American sources provided in clarifying the affair, after I. F. Stone's early series, came with the Roubatis-
Vlanton article that appeared in the May 1977 issue of *More*.[39] These two
journalists were able to bring together sources from both Greece and the

United States, including newspaper articles from both countries, the Lippmann Report, Hadjiargyris's book, some of the State Department archives then open to the public, and a number of interviews with individuals involved in the affair. They reach much the same conclusion as I. F. Stone did regarding the role of the Lippmann Committee and its counsel in promoting the official solution, and they provide a generally accurate image of the role played by American officials and some of the American press. They also give much attention to the various arguments—Hadjiargyris's in particular—regarding the possible involvement of Randall Coate (whose name they get right but whose position is described, without any indicated source, as "a British intelligence officer operating under cover of the British Information Office in Salonika which he headed").

Theirs is the most complete short history of the case to date, but it has its limitations. For a start, the language of the piece sometimes reveals a certain political bias that makes the reader wary of possible distortion as they outline their argument (for example, Hungary and Czechoslovakia are described as having "come under Soviet influence" by 1948, which is putting it rather mildly, while at the same time Washington was "solidifying its post-war empire," which is putting it rather strongly).[40] But the more serious problem is the kind of oversimplification, or truncation of time, in presenting evidence, which again leads to a degree of distortion, no doubt at least in part the result of the authors' having to deal with an immensely complicated history in the space allowed by a single article, long as it is. Donovan's extended—and shifting—role in dealing with the Salonika authorities is given two sentences and is highlighted by a single quotation (his remark to Mouskoundis that "an arrest was desired") from a cable sent on July 27, six weeks after his first visit to Greece. The result is that Donovan's part in the inquiry is made to seem more arbitrary and uncomplicated than it actually was, at least during the early stages of the investigation. And Polk is described as having been "critical of the right-wing government, not of the Left" when in fact he had been worried about a dictatorship at either extreme, and in his *Harper's* article not only generally supported the American aid program but thought the exercise of American pressure in bringing down the Tsaldaris government to make way for Sophoulis's coalition government "a triumph for the Griswold Mission's farsighted, practical thinking."

In the case of Raleigh Gibson, the oversimplification of the consul general's perspective on the case is the result of the authors' using a text offered in the Lippmann Report as their source rather than the relevant original document in the State Department archives. Roubatis and Vlanton quote Gibson as cabling the secretary of state to say: "My personal opinion is that Polk's murder was planned by the Cominform and was carried out by the Communist Party of Greece in order to throw the blame of the murder on the right, thus to defame Greece abroad and to stop the application of the Marshall Plan to Greece."[41] This quotation is in fact a version of the American consulate's translation of part of Gregory Staktopoulos's revised confession of October 14, a concluding statement by the accused which Gibson indeed transmitted to the Department of State but which the Lippmann Report inaccurately ascribes to Gibson by placing the consul general's name at the end of Staktopoulos's text.[42]

In general, Roubatis and Vlanton make rather arbitrary use of the documents that were available to them in the State Department archives, quoting bits and pieces here and there, sometimes misleadingly out of context and without sufficient concern for the chronology of the excerpts. The July 27 quote by Donovan calling for an arrest is followed by the statement: "The only problem was finding a suitable suspect. The Communists fit the bill"[43]—and to illustrate the latter conclusion, the authors quote a May 25 remark by Dwight Griswold, followed by a May 21 cable by Gibson, without any attention to the history of the debate about possible suspects (e.g., Rea Polk and Kosta Hadjiargyris) that is illustrated by cables submitted to Washington during the two months between late May and late July. In the case of Staktopoulos's various confessions, so rich in implications regarding the creativity of Mouskoundis and other Greek officials, Roubatis and Vlanton virtually ignore the archives and again summarize this aspect of the affair in two sentences.

What gets more than ample space in their article is the role of Colonel James Kellis, who emerges in their brief history as the one American investigator who appeared to be on the right track until he was derailed by Karl Rankin. On the basis of an interview with Kellis, we are told that the colonel became convinced—"and still is convinced today" (i.e., in 1977)—that the extreme Right was responsible for Polk's death. What purpose would have been served if the Communists had killed him? Kellis is reported to have asked. And the more Kellis looked into the case, "the more contradictions he found in the police theories of the murder." Then, "a number of independent sources," including Minister of Public Order Rendis and "two British intelligence officers" told Kellis that the Right had killed Polk.[44] But a little later in the article we also learn that "Kellis believes, to this day, that the British were involved."[45]

He is reported to have said in "a recent interview" that "wittingly, or unwittingly, Coate had Polk transferred to other people, not the Communists, who killed him," and Kellis recalled a conversation with Sir Charles Wickham in a Salonika bar during which Sir Charles "told him, half jokingly, 'we have a habit of throwing people in the bay if they get too independent.' " Kellis gives the impression that he thought half such a joke was half too much.

In any case, as early as mid-June of 1948, Kellis had reported to Guy Martin, the assistant counsel to the Lippmann Committee, that up to that moment he had "sincerely believed that the Communists were behind the murder" but now (June 18) he "was not too certain," and he was having a *crise de conscience* because "many of our officials here were concerned that if the extreme Right committed this murder and were discovered that this may upset our aid program to Greece." Difficult days; what was he to do? "I was debating the question whether if we do expose the right, such an act would harm our national interest." But Kellis had to conclude that "as we stand now, we believe our evidence does not support the police theory that the commies committed the murder." Roubatis and Vlanton then conclude that "Kellis was asking too may uncomfortable questions. . . . Something had to be done to cut off this line of inquiry." So Karl Rankin sent his July 17 cable stating that "Embassy believes sooner Kellis removed from scene the better."[46]

The trouble here is again the loose handling of dates. Kellis was in Greece a full month between his letter to Guy Martin and Karl Rankin's cable to the State Department suggesting his recall. What happened during that month? From the Roubatis-Vlanton account, based on a memorandum that Ernest Lindley sent Walter Lippmann and an open letter that Kellis published in a number of Greek newspapers almost thirty years later (March 8, 1977), we get the impression that Kellis was constantly frustrated by others, local American officials in particular, who were not as keen as he was about conducting a vigorous and impartial investigation, which presumably meant tracking down suspects of whatever political persuasion. In his open letter, Kellis goes so far as to make what Roubatis and Vlanton call a "remarkable admission": "I believed then, and I still hold to this opinion, that we should have conducted an honest, penetrating and impartial investigation. Unfortunately, my colleagues in this investigation had a different view and their position prevailed."[47] And the open letter continues: "In this instance, we violated some basic precepts which affected Greece and America. . . . Also, my impression of the direction of the investigation was that it violated the basic rules of evidence, law and morality."

In a piece entitled "Death in Salonika Bay: Who Pulled the Trigger" that Kellis published in the *New York Times* after the *More* article appeared,[48] we learn that Kellis not only challenged "many inconsistencies and discrepancies" which he found in Major Mouskoundis's "story," but "collected other information which contradicted the official investigation and reported to General Donovan that I believed there was an attempted right-wing cover-up." Then Karl Rankin stepped in and "admonished me: 'I don't see why you are breaking your back trying to uncover who killed this correspondent. If you, as a military officer, or I, as a diplomat, were killed, none of these people would give a damn.' " Kellis tells us that he left Rankin's office "disheartened by his [Rankin's] lack of principles and courage" and "more than ever convinced that the American, British and Greek authorities in Greece were determined to hide the truth." He could not accept the Rankin-Mouskoundis argument that there was need to pin the murder on the Communists so that public opinion in America would remain favorable to the Greek government and vital American assistance would continue. His experience had convinced him that the essential thing was for America, "through whatever influence we exercised in Greece, to remove from both the Government and the military corrupt and inept officials in order to gain the people's support." And George Polk "had been making the same point" before he was murdered. In any case, Kellis's "insistence that I would not be a party to a cover-up led to my removal from the investigation and my reassignment to Washington." Upon his removal, Major Mouskoundis "and some Government officials decided it was time to act. They arrested a Reuters news agency correspondent, Gregoris Stactopoulos [*sic*]. . . ." And what followed from that was torture, the confessions, the trial, etcetera.

The difficulty here is that the State Department archives, though indicating that Kellis indeed challenged Mouskoundis's story at times, never show him presenting any precise evidence of other possibilities. He clearly did not buy the official solution whole as it was outlined in the beginning, but nowhere do we see him offering another solution. In the two letters from Kellis to Donovan which survive among the Donovan papers, the one dated June 19, 1948, and the other June 28, 1948—that is, written by Kellis during the month between his letter to Guy Martin and the Rankin cable suggesting his recall—there is little evidence of his providing any information much different from what the other investigators were offering during this period or of his challenging significantly the various directions that the investigation took during the month of June. On the contrary, the letter of June 19 appears to support Mouskoundis's creation of a major role for Colonel Vasvanas ("Moskoundis [sic] and the police at Salonika informed us that Col. Vasvanas of the Communists irregulars . . . was in Salonika at the time Polk was murdered. I made several trips to Kozani and from sources inside the army intelligence and the gendarmerie I was able to verify this information"). Kellis remains "polite and pleasant" in all his contacts with Mavrokordatos and Rendis in Athens as "the only way to gain their confidence and cooperation," and he seems fully in league with his American colleagues on the scene in Salonika ("Mr. Burdett, Mr. Secondari and Mr. Ayer are working as hard if not harder than I do, in this case. It is a difficult case and there are many obstacles to overcome . . .").

In the June 28 letter, we again find Kellis supporting Mouskoundis as "one darn good policeman" who is "not backed with an efficient organization," nor proper laboratory facilities, nor an effective "net of informants," but who is trying to solve "a difficult crime with few clues left behind" as best he can. Kellis tells Donovan that "it would not be fair to look upon the Greek authorities with a critical eye while we overlook our shortcomings." What he appears to have in mind is the problem of the American press. He tells Donovan that "we came here with the idea that we do have the support of the U.S. press," and "for a while" the Greek police "thought that they would be immune from unfair criticism from the U.S. Press" and would be free to proceed with the investigation "without any outside influences," but "they soon realized that this is not true." There was the threat by more than one U.S. correspondent to write caustic dispatches if Rea Polk's passport were withdrawn. And the problem of Hadjiargyris still being a correspondent for a reputable U.S. newspaper. And correspondent Thrapp's reluctance to furnish information. All of this had contributed to the slow progress of the investigation. On the other hand, the U.S. embassy, the Mission to Greece, and the U.S. consulate at Salonika "have been extremely cooperative."

Kellis concludes his report by indicating that if the Communists are involved in the crime, "as the police seem to believe," then "we will have to let them do the best they can under the circumstances and try to solve it their own way." If "the extreme right," either as an organization or as individuals, is involved, then "the discovery of the criminals would be just as difficult." Pressure could be brought on the police "to suppress the investigation." But Kellis feels he has to state, "in all fairness," that he has not yet detected any such pressure "from above." He has contacted "many persons outside the government (many of them

British Intelligence Officers)," and though some of them "would certainly like to see Tsaldaris and his friends crucified," nobody has so far offered "any concrete evidence."

One hardly gets the image of a man in conflict with the authorities—whatever the authorities—in these two letters. Despite Kellis's telling Roubatis and Vlanton that he was put under surveillance after leaving the investigation and that efforts were made to discredit him (as a " 'leftist,' " we learn from a letter he sent Ernest K. Lindley in 1956),[49] the fact is that he was subsequently given a tour of duty with the CIA—from 1950 to 1954 according to Roubatis and Vlanton, although in the letter to Lindley, Kellis speaks of completing his "3 years overseas tour with NATO" in June 1956). The fact is also that during his CIA service (in 1952), Kellis recorded notes for the CIA file on the Polk case[50] that suggest a rather different history of his involvement in the investigation from what the *More* article proposes, one that contradicts the impression left with Roubatis and Vlanton that "Kellis's leads were apparently never followed up by the Lippmann Committee"[51] (the notes, as part of a secret CIA memorandum, were not declassified and released for publication until 1979, two years after the Roubatis-Vlanton article appeared).

We can see from the published text of the once-secret CIA notes that they were heavily censored to remove names and other evidently too sensitive material at the time of their publication, but what text we are given provides a contradictory picture of Kellis's role in the investigation and, at the same time, an unambiguous image of his close, thoroughly loyal relation to Donovan in the Polk affair. Kellis reports that he was reluctant to accept the Donovan assignment because he knew the Polk case was "politically a 'loaded affair' " and that he would be hurt by it, but his loyalty to General Donovan "demanded that I take the risk," even after he was advised against it by "certain high officials" in the air force who detected that the "Greek Government and the American Embassy in Athens were, to say the least, viewing the Correspondents Association's participation in the investigation with considerable displeasure."

We are told that after Kellis landed in Greece with Donovan on June 10, 1948, the general ordered him "to supervise the investigation and insure that 'a vigorous, impartial and penetrating investigation is carried out,' " but with Tsaldaris, the American embassy, and some correspondents on his neck, Kellis felt "like a pinch hitter with the bases loaded and two strikes against me." He adds: "Needless to say, I plunged into the job without any hesitation." But during his forty-five-day stay in Greece he encountered "much direct and indirect sabotage by [deletion] certain members of the American Embassy." He found it regrettable that the chargé d'affaires and the two men in the embassy monitoring the Polk case "took a negative position." And he reports a slightly different version of the conversation with Rankin that he quoted in the *New York Times*, the chargé here telling him: "Why are you killing yourself over the Polk case? If you or I were killed, like the Consul General in Jerusalem [Tom Wasson], nobody would care." Kellis adds: "Obviously the Charge d'Affaires was willing to forfeit many principles over which many Americans died in the past and are willing to die today. Freedom of the press was a light matter for him."

Indeed, as State Department archives amply testify. So far so good. But now come those several revelations that paint a rather different portrait of Kellis's contribution to the investigation and its ultimate outcome than we get from what he told Roubatis and Vlanton and from what he told the readers of the *New York Times*. After his "40 days of hard work" had produced the list of ten suspects that included not only the Reuters stringer Staktopoulos but "some officials of the Greek Government," Kellis decided, in view of the obstacles he had encountered so far, to visit the chargé d'affaires "and ask for permission to send a cable to General Donovan through the Embassy notifying him of my desire to be relieved from this investigation." We are not told whether or not the permission was granted, but, as we have seen, Kellis reported that he later "contacted General Donovan through other means" and on Donovan's return to Greece, the general "allowed me to return to the U.S."

From this account one has to conclude that Kellis was not removed from the investigation because he refused to be party to a cover-up, as he reported in the *New York Times*, but himself asked to be removed— perhaps after confronting what he considered too many obstacles—and was granted his request by none other than the man who had arranged his assignment to Greece. We also learn that though there had been "many charges and countercharges during the course of the investigation," some substantiated and some not, "the fact remains that at the initial stage of the investigation, the Greek authorities were negligent and to some degree so were the American authorities." But, says Kellis, Donovan had gotten things moving on the right track. When he arrived in Greece "he shook many of these people out of their lethargy and caused them to move." And then comes what we have seen to be the largest revelation of all: it was General Donovan who selected Gregory Staktopoulos's name from the list of Kellis's ten suspects and asked "the Chief Greek Investigator" to concentrate on that suspect, a move that led "within sixty days" to Staktopoulos's confession of complicity in the crime. And this revelation is followed by Kellis's image of his ultimate contribution, at least for CIA records: "It is possible that if it were not for my basic investigation and its screening and evaluation by General Donovan that [*sic*] this crime might never have been solved."

No modest claim, especially since few over the years have come to regard the case as truly solved, but the immodesty of it isn't what gives pause. How does one reconcile Kellis's complimentary remarks regarding Mouskoundis and his American colleagues in his letters to Donovan, and his putting the finger on Staktopoulos (whether or not Donovan then followed up on his lead), with his supposedly remarkable admission in his open letter to the Greek press that his "colleagues in this investigation" had a different view from his "and their position prevailed"? And how does one reconcile his dubieties about the extreme Right having committed the crime in his June 28 letter and his subsequent putting the finger on Staktopoulos with his later claim, in the interview with Roubatis and Vlanton, that he became convinced "then," and is still convinced in 1977, "that the extreme Right was responsible for Polk's death?"[52] His next to last CIA note suggests a possible answer to this second question at least: "We reviewed everything carefully and investigated in all directions. We could not overlook any group, party or individual. To point out how complex things can be in determining the political motivation behind the Polk murder, one need only look at the convicted accomplice. This man was a crypto-Communist, he was an agent of the British Intelligence Service and was also a member of a Greek Rightist organization." It would appear that, politically, Gregory Staktopoulos was anything you chose to make him—though Kellis is the only important investigator in the Polk affair to have indicated that the Reuters stringer belonged to some rightist organization, here and elsewhere left unnamed. The CIA notes end with the statement, again contradicting later statements, that "upon completion of my 45 days in Greece I returned at my own initiative to the United States."

This document, written in 1952 and first brought into the open in 1979, is the last word on the Polk case that we have from American sources. If we are to take it for something approaching the whole truth, it pinpoints Kellis, by his own admission, as the American investigator who fairly early on identified Gregory Staktopoulos as one of the key suspects in the case and Donovan as the one who selected Staktopoulos as the suspect most worthy of Major Mouskoundis's concerted attention—though there is no evidence that either Donovan or Kellis knew the cruel form that such attention could take at Security Police headquarters. Kellis's list and Donovan's subsequent choice from it would explain why the general did not think it necessary for Kellis to return to Greece after Kellis had completed his forty-five days of investigation and had submitted his confidential report to Donovan, especially if Kellis himself had requested that he be allowed to return to the States and had finally done so—as he put it—at his own initiative. It would also explain why Donovan was so ready to accept the official solution not long after Kellis's return to the States and so many months before the trial, and why Donovan remained committed to the solution through the trial and its aftermath. Kellis's notes also bring into question the Roubatis and Vlanton comment that "Kellis' leads were apparently never followed up by the Lippmann Committee." It would seem that one lead was followed up by General Donovan—in fact, became the unhappy resource for the official solution presented in the October 17 indictment.[53]

What Kellis's notes do not serve to answer is the contradiction between the colonel's self-image in 1952 as a man whose "basic investigation" promoted a solution without which the crime "might never have been solved" and the colonel's self-image in 1977 as a man believing that "we should have conducted an honest and penetrating and impartial investigation," a belief in conflict with that of "colleagues" who not only thought otherwise but who finally prevailed. It would seem from the CIA notes that colleague Donovan's position, inspired by Kellis's research, was what finally prevailed. And if Kellis was correct in his impression, expressed in the same open letter, that "the direction of the investigation . . . violated the basic rules of evidence, law and morality," his CIA notes suggest that he and Donovan both contributed to that violation by the pressure they put on Major Mouskoundis generally and by their promotion of the Staktopoulos solution specifically. Finally, how does one reconcile Kellis's 1977 statement in the *New York Times* that his insistence on not being party to a cover-up led to his removal from the investigation and his reassignment to Washington with his 1952 note indicating that he asked to be relieved from the investigation himself and that it was in part his investigative work before leaving and Donovan's decision after he left that led to the Staktopoulos solution? The *Times* article implies that the Staktopoulos solution, with all its ghastly consequences, was the result of a decision to act on the part of Major Mouskoundis and "some Government officials"—presumably Greek government officials—and that this decision was made "upon my removal." Perhaps so, but are we then simply to brush aside Kellis's list of ten suspects and Donovan's choice of one for Mouskoundis "to concentrate on," however little either American may have guessed what those ominous words came to mean in the hands of the Salonika Security Police?

Kellis ends his *Times* article by telling his readers that he could not accept then or now "that we could support national interest by disregarding moral principles" as some in Greece had recommended during his forty-five days there in 1948, because, as he told some Greek reporters who interviewed him on the Polk case in 1977, "compromises on pragmatic grounds eventually turn to haunt us." It now seems that his secret 1952 notes on his role in the Polk investigation may be a certain case in point. But can one take these notes for the gospel truth? Or are they at least in part an early effort by Kellis to make himself out to have been one of the few who were on the right track in an investigation that appeared to be getting nowhere initially—perhaps by the conscious design of others—and in this way to get his share of credit for the presumed solution of the case during the period that solution was recognized to be valid, as his later effort was the same kind of thing on a different track during a period when that official solution was generally taken to be an instance of rigged justice?

One of the difficulties in trying to reach a resolution in the Polk affair is created by exactly this kind of documentation. Is one to give full credence to notes written secretly for a CIA file by a man then working for the CIA, notes published with excisions so long after the fact? And is one to give any more credence to contradictory statements by the same man twenty-five years later when those statements are made in personal interviews and open letters or articles published in the press? As with all texts in conflict, the reader finally has to make his own choice on the basis of whatever he can bring to bear in deciphering and judging those texts. Historians generally prefer to consider texts written close to the event as more reliable than those written long after the event, when memory, and its capacity for self-serving distortion, may have greater sway. In this instance, Kellis's 1948 letters to Donovan seem the most reliable and objective source. Both the 1952 CIA notes and the commentary twenty-five years later, though in conflict, appear to have a more or less equal measure of self-congratulatory subtext.

The one resolution in this area that appears unchallengeable is that the Lippmann Committee's independent investigator and its counsel cannot have it both ways. Either Colonel Kellis and General Donovan recommended Staktopoulos at a crucial moment and thereby contributed to the Staktopoulos solution, or Major Mouskoundis created the solution—possibly on orders from others—and then successfully sold that solution to General Donovan, who in turn sold it to the Lippmann Committee and presumably to Colonel Kellis also, because, even if we discount the colonel's claim to have spotted Staktopoulos as a suspect, there is nothing on record to show that Kellis questioned the conclusion reached in the 1952 Lippmann Report regarding Staktopoulos's guilt until Kellis chose to comment on the case twenty-five years later. Since Colonel Kellis, along with General Donovan and Major Mouskoundis, is no longer with us, such texts as we now have are all that he, or two of those he worked with most intimately in 1948, can provide for our illumination.

XII Epilogue: The Context of Injustice

IN HIS 1977 ADDENDUM to the *More* article on the Polk affair, William Polk remarks that "whoever killed my brother will turn out to be less important than the attempt to find out."[1] It would seem more accurate to say that, at this late date, the question of who killed George Polk will turn out to be historically less important than the evident attempt that was made to pin the crime on an appropriate scapegoat and then to whitewash what had been done. We have seen other examples of the same enterprise on the domestic front since World War II. What makes the Polk case valuable for the student of American history (and perhaps of Greek history) is that the attempt here came on the international front very early in America's career as a world power and, more significant, it appears to have involved an unusually complicated collusion between three nations, two of these at different stages of a patron-client relationship with the third but all three sharing what they perceived to be a common enemy. Also valuable for the student of American history was this equally unusual example of evident collusion between the U.S. government's executive branch and the fourth estate, which was supposed to be among the agencies within the American system that acted as a check on excessive authority, not to say hubris, on the part of the executive branch.

The specifics are what make the case provocative, though complicated. On the level of action, what appears to have happened is that after a slow investigation of several months that was not turning up leads in any direction, whether or not all possible directions were being explored, officials on the American side, working primarily through representatives of the American press, persuaded—through one or another form of pressure—officials on the Greek side that it was important to the progress of American-Greek relations, and some think of American-British relations, that a culprit be arrested and put on trial for the murder of George Polk. Gregory Staktopoulos, once a member of the Communist party, was then chosen as the best candidate among several other suspects under investigation—Rea Polk and Kosta Hadjiargyris at one time among these—and after forty-five days of secret interrogation by the

Security Police in Salonika, was shown to have confessed not to the murder of George Polk but to having witnessed the murder at the hands of two Communist leaders absent from the region at the time they were accused and absent ever since.

Some six months later Staktopoulos was tried on the basis of highly questionable evidence in a court case that barely examined that evidence, was convicted of complicity in a crime he had confessed to merely observing, was sentenced to life imprisonment, was then confined illegally for four years under the surveillance of those who had elicited his confession. At the time there was virtually no recorded objection from the authorities of any of the three nations that had been involved in the investigation of the Polk case regarding the way Staktopoulos's role in the affair was handled and only sporadic objection from others since. American press witnesses at the trial, though sometimes critical of both the aura and the process revealed in the courtroom, generally ended up accepting the verdict that Staktopoulos had been implicated in the crime, and this view was reaffirmed three years later in the official report of the Lippmann Committee, which had made itself the principal representative of the American press. The case remained virtually dead in both Greece and America for the next fourteen years and was not significantly reviewed until twenty-five years later.

On the level of authority, it was necessary for a variety of agencies and persons to end up in some sort of collusion in order for the Staktopoulos solution to survive as it did. On the Greek side: cabinet ministers representing competing political constituencies in a newly formed coalition government (Rendis, Melas); professionals in the civil service working as police investigators more or less independently (Mouskoundis, Xanthopoulos, Evert) or directly under the Ministry of Public Order (Panopoulos); various officials working within the Greek judicial system (Constantinidis, Moustakis, Komotouros). On the American side: diplomatic officials, career or otherwise, in Greece (Gibson, Rankin, Ayer, Griswold, Grady); officials of the State Department or other governmental agency in the U.S. (Baxter, Lovett); representatives of the American press assigned to work on the case in Greece (Burdett, Secondari, Donovan, Kellis, Lambron); representatives of the American press working in the U.S. (Lippmann, Lindley). On the British side: police advisers in Greece (Wickham, Martin); diplomatic officials in Greece (Rouse, Roper). These are among the investigators and the authorities behind them who are actually named in various dispatches and documents and who either helped to create the Staktopoulos solution or ended up accepting it in due course. But there is some evidence that others were also involved in one way or another behind the scenes, perhaps on the British side and surely on the American side, where there is the occasional reference to officials working for the CIA in the Athens embassy who were meant—and still are meant—to remain nameless.

What made it possible for these disparate authorities to end up working together to promote a ghastly solution to an embarrassing crime and then to whitewash that solution so that it could remain more or less concealed for many years? Part of the answer has to be that there was a shared perception in each country of what the national interest was in the face of a common enemy. In the case of Greece, in the midst of a civil war, it was perceived by officials at whatever level to be in the national interest to designate the Communists as the culprits, and it was also perceived by them to be in the national interest to find a victim who would satisfy American demands so that the aid program against the common enemy would not be threatened.

In the case of the Americans, at the start of the investigation it was also perceived by most officials to be in the national interest to designate the Communists as the culprits, and it was understood to be important to work hand in hand with Greek officials in finding a satisfactory solution to the crime so that the new relationship between the two countries would not be threatened. It was also understood by American officials to be in the national interest to keep the American press from interfering with this objective. The British appear to have determined that their national interest was that of working on a daily basis to support both the official Greek and the official American point of view in the case so long as they themselves were not implicated and so long as they were not represented as a principal in the action, especially while one of their local officials was under some suspicion and especially during a period when they were withdrawing from Greece on their own initiative.

An early complication in the case from the official point of view was the presence of American press representatives in Greece—first Burdett and Secondari, then Kellis and Donovan—who were permitted by Washington to take an active part in the investigation, if generally under the eye of the local American authorities. The first two appear to have been effectively neutralized by Frederick Ayer and Raleigh Gibson so that they were prepared, after initial reluctance, to go along with the direction the investigators seemed to be heading in the early stages under Major Mouskoundis (e.g., toward implicating Rea Polk and Kosta Hadjiargyris) and not to complain too harshly about the slow pace of the investigation during the weeks after they arrived on the scene. Kellis and Donovan proved to be less pliable at first, Kellis rather incoherently pursuing various candidates for suspicion—the Left, the Right, the British, a journalist he evidently thought had served all three, and even, it seems, certain officials of the Greek government—and Donovan, frustrated for some weeks by what he saw as the lack of effective research and precision on the part of the Greek authorities, finally calling for an arrest of some kind (whether he did this mostly on his own initiative or with the active encouragement of American officials in Greece and Washington remains unclear, though one Greek official, Panopoulos, was reported to have said that a demand for an arrest also came directly from Washington to the Greek prime minister).[2]

The work of Kellis and Donovan appears to have resulted, by the month of August 1948, in a decision by certain of the Greek authorities to focus their hopes for a solution on getting Gregory Staktopoulos to confess to complicity in a crime committed by absent Communist leaders. The process took forty-five days, during which apparently few questions were asked about what was going on at Security Police headquarters by either Greek, American, or British officials on the scene, and the solution proved to be one that all parties could ultimately accept: Greek officials in Salonika and Athens; American officials in Salonika, Athens, and Washington; British officials wherever they showed themselves; and key representatives of the American press still active in the case.

Another part of the answer to how all this could have come about resides in the confluence of preconceptions and prejudices that the various agencies brought to the Polk affair. On the Greek side, most of those involved identified patriotism with anti-Communism, an easy identification in the black-and-white aura of the civil war; and, similarly, on the American side, most officials identified their national interest with anti-Communism, also easy in the cold war, pre-McCarthy aura of 1948–49. And the cold war had begun some time since to affect the British in a related way, though there was perhaps more division on their home front than even Truman experienced when he put the Truman Doctrine before the American people in March 1947. The cold war had also served to justify the institutionalization of secrecy in government, what in the U.S. had originally been thought a temporary if necessary instrument of World War II. General Donovan himself said in May 1948: "Whether we like it or not, we have many enemies in the world today and we must know exactly what they are doing. . . . We must counter Soviet subversive attacks and help to build resistance in countries Russia attempts to subjugate."[3] By that time the CIA, which Donovan had helped to define, had been solidly established by Congress, and the idea of service in undercover ways was not only respectable in America, but such service was sought by talented graduates of the best universities, some of whom might have entered the career Foreign Service in an earlier era.

In Greece, secrecy was institutionalized down to the most local level by 1948, in particular within the complex police and military network that operated during the civil war, and secret interrogation as a police method, with its ample capacities for violence, if perhaps not routine in all areas, was hardly confined to the Salonika Security Police under Major Mouskoundis. The secret interrogation of suspected or confirmed Communists during this period was, in any case, rarely a gentlemanly exercise. And the tradition of third degree methods sometimes degenerating into torture was revived with a vengeance during the 1967–74 dictatorship, in one instance, the Ann Chapman murder case, evidently resulting again in the conviction of a scapegoat on the basis of a forced confession that was later recanted.[4]

What appears to have happened in the Polk case is that men from different countries who were established anti-Communists and also fully devoted to undercover work (Mouskoundis, Donovan, and quite likely whoever represented the British along with Wickham and Martin) came together at the right time to promote a solution, in the communal national interest, that was created in detail secretly (the quality of violence required probably also secret to most) and that called for an agreement among all that there would not only have to be much willing suspension of disbelief for the solution to stand but also much willing suspension of civil rights and a cooperative press to make it stick.

Officials on all sides appear to have had little difficulty living with what was required. Donovan became the key figure in bringing the nonofficial agency of the American press into line with what appears to have been largely Mouskoundis's creation. Donovan succeeded in doing so finally because those he worked for were pliable, for the reasons that both I. F. Stone and Ronald Steel have suggested: a propensity on the part of certain established members of the press to work within the system and to avoid the kind of challenge to government operations, especially those supported by the State Department, that might appear to undercut what was regarded as essential policy or that might threaten certain of their vital sources.

The key press representatives that Donovan had to convince were Walter Lippmann and Ernest K. Lindley, the latter president of the Overseas Writers during 1948–49 and the former chairman of its special Committee of Inquiry, in short, the two men most in command of the American press exploration of the Polk affair, an exploration which Lippmann had made sure would be restricted in the first instance to the Overseas Writers Committee, at least as far as official sanction was concerned.[5] We have seen Ronald Steel's use of Lippmann's role in the Polk affair to illustrate Lippmann's commitment to operating "entirely within the system" and Lippmann's consequent refusal to question the State Department's contention that the Communist guerrillas were responsible for Polk's murder "even though he privately recognized that discrepancies in the evidence pointed damningly toward the Greek government and the CIA."[6] We have also seen Lippmann's eulogy of General Donovan at the Overseas Writers dinner in September 1949, where he found that he could say "with entire conviction" that the man who led George Polk into the trap that resulted in his murder had been "arrested, convicted and sentenced to life imprisonment," as he could also say "on behalf of men whose profession it is to have few illusions" that "in this undertaking we have learned that your [Donovan's] sense of justice is equal to your courage."[7]

The case of Ernest K. Lindley is not as rich in irony, but it has its measure of it. Though he appeared in Athens at one point to challenge Karl Rankin's myopic and monolithic view of the case, he seems to have been as reluctant as Lippmann was to challenge the official solution once it became official on both sides of the Atlantic. Roubatis and Vlanton portray Lindley as an apologist for the State Department;[8] true or not, he was clearly an apologist for General Donovan, and by extension, for Donovan's handling of his assignment as counsel for the Overseas Writers. When the magazine *More*, in a 1977 poll of Lippmann Committee members, asked Lindley if he believed "that the original inquiry was conducted in a thorough and just manner" and whether new evidence (unspecified) warranted a reexamination of the case, Lindley gave them the following statement:

The Overseas Writers report was based on the findings of its counsel, William J. Donovan, a lawyer and public servant of the highest distinction and probity, who, as organizer and head of the OSS, had been the highest-ranking intelligence officer in this country during World War II. Both Walter Lippmann . . . and I . . . had known him personally for years. We both regarded him as the person best qualified to serve as our counsel, which he did without compensation and at his own expense, as a generous service to the American press. The inquiry proceeded without prejudgement as to the political affiliation of the murderer or murderers of George Polk. We successfully resisted attempts by politically motivated persons and groups in the United States to share control of the inquiry. General Donovan was assisted by, among others, one of his former Lieutenants [Col. Kellis] who had served with the Greek guerrillas. In the end, General Donovan concluded that the Greek trial, which he attended, was fairly conducted and that its verdict was justified. It would take solid evidence to convince me that General Donovan's seasoned, impartial judgement was wrong.[9]

Lindley's assumption in 1948 that the highest-ranking intelligence officer of World War II, "seasoned" by service in the OSS, would be the best-qualified person to serve a major American press organization as counsel in a politically complicated inquiry was surely a bit naive, however well he knew the man personally. But it was either disingenuous or thickheaded for Lindley to speak so unequivocally in 1977 of Donovan's "impartial judgement" about the Polk trial verdict after evidence to the contrary had long been on record and after thirty years of covert government operations, including Watergate, should have created grounds for a degree of doubt. One would like to think that Walter Lippmann was also merely naive in his 1948 assumption that his committee's working hand in hand with the State Department and their official representatives in Greece—Rankin, Gibson, and Ayer in particular—would help the American press get to the truth; but Ronald Steel's analysis suggests a broader, and in this instance more dangerous, flaw than naiveté in Lippmann's commitment to operating "entirely within the system."

On the other hand, from the complaint in the committee's Report, one has every reason to think that Lippmann hardly expected representatives of the American government abroad to hinder the so-called independent investigator he sent to Greece on behalf of the Overseas Writers, with Secretary of State George Marshall's blessing. But had Lippmann been privy to the confidential communications between Athens and Washington in the months before the murder, he would have seen a pattern of suspicion and hostility in the encounters between the fourth estate and American officials in Greece—from Lincoln MacVeagh to Karl Rankin—that would have perhaps made him less eager to claim that other representatives of the American press bent on their own independent investigation "would interfere with the inquiry" that his committee had in progress (Lippmann had in mind specifically the team of John Donovan, Constantine Poulos, and William Polk designated by the Newsmen's Commission to Investigate the Murder of George Polk, which had approached him for assistance in late September 1948 and which was rebuffed by him in early October).[10]

Another aspect of the collusion between disparate agencies which brought about the Staktopoulos solution and allowed it to survive, that between Greek and American investigators, did not take shape easily, but once it did, the collusion here again worked as efficiently as was required. The broader problems of the new relationship between the two countries had its influence in creating tensions initially. Greece, a nation proud under any circumstances, had done more than its share as an ally of Britain and America during the war, especially in defeating the

Italian army during the Italian campaign, and its officials rightfully felt that they had some claim to being treated as equals, however limited their nation's power and however impoverished its circumstances. What complicated the issue was the civil war, considered so threatening by those running the country that almost any compromise seemed appropriate in order to ensure the continuation of American military and economic aid, which was regarded as vital for Greece's survival after the British decision to withdraw from Greece.

On the American side, there was a tension between what American officials perceived as a need to work amicably with those in Greece who were devoted anti-Communists and the need to see to it that the American aid program was not sabotaged by inefficiency, corruption, or both overt and covert political opposition. During the early months of the investigation, one can discern the sporadic outbreak of the conflict between pride and necessity in the behavior of Greek officials, both in the case of Athenian political figures such as Melas and in the case of Salonika investigators such as Mouskoundis, Xanthopoulos, and Constantinidis. The Americans—General Donovan and Raleigh Gibson in particular—were sometimes too much on their backs, and they clearly resented it. As for the Americans, diplomacy sometimes came into conflict with a sense of mission, and this led to arrogant demands.

There also appeared to be a general feeling among American officials and even some press representatives that they were in possession of the principles that truly counted, while they perceived Greek officials, however devotedly anti-Communist, to be often antidemocratic and often corrupt by American standards. Even Kellis, presumed by so many to have been the most independent and objective of the American investigators, takes a high moral tone in this connection, telling his *New York Times* readers that his experience with the guerrillas in World War II had convinced him that it was necessary for the Americans, through whatever influence they exercised in Greece, "to remove from both the Government and the military corrupt and inept officials in order to gain the people's support," a lesson that he saw carrying over to Vietnam.[11] And George Polk himself seemed in favor of American Mission officials carrying as big a stick as might prove necessary for the promotion of their interests.

In the Greek context, and perhaps whenever a patron nation thinks in terms of removing officials from the government of its client ally for whatever reason, it is not certain that such thinking, let alone any subsequent action, will promote a favorable image among the people of that ally, and in the long run, such efforts at domestic interference are surely doomed to make more enemies than friends. But in 1948, the possibilities for such arrogant exercise were large because of the disparity in power between the two countries and the desperate need on the part of the poorer of the two. It appears in the Polk affair that after late July of 1948, Greek pride gave way to necessary compromise, both in Salonika and in Athens, and from that point on, the two nations worked in relative harmony to present a culprit who would presumably satisfy American public opinion so that the American aid program would not be threatened in any way and the war against the common enemy would be brought to a conclusion.

There are those who would argue that such expediency was essential in the context, but there are others who would say that American public opinion—and long-range American policy—would have been better served not by the crude Staktopoulos solution but by an honest admission that the case could simply not be solved on the basis of the evidence in hand. That unsettled resolution would also have prevented a cruel miscarriage of justice that, given a reasonably civilized world, surely cannot be seen to have served any humane principle.

Appendix: The Polk Report, May 21, 1951

THE FOLLOWING MATERIAL, the principal text of the "Lippmann Report," is excerpted from the 76-page document published under the title *The George Polk Case: Report of the Overseas Writers of the Special Committee to Inquire Into the Murder at Salonika, Greece, May 16, 1948, of Columbia Broadcasting System Correspondent George Polk.*

As soon as the main facts about the murder of George Polk became known, the peculiar importance of the case was appreciated by the American press and radio. Polk was murdered deliberately and for political reasons while he was working as a foreign correspondent on a story of great interest to the American people.

That much seemed evident and is now undisputed. His body was found floating in the harbor of Salonika on May 16, 1948. His arms and legs had been bound with rope, and he had been shot in the back of the head. The coroner estimated that the body had been in the water about seven days. Except for some papers, Polk had not been robbed. His identity card was mailed to the Salonika police. It was, therefore, plain that the murder was the act not of an individual assassin but of a gang, and that the murderers wished not to conceal but to draw attention to the crime.

It was also established that Polk was murdered while he was attempting to reach the headquarters of the guerrilla forces. There is no doubt that Polk's purpose was to obtain news and information to be broadcast and published. The committee is satisfied that Polk's efforts to make contact with Markos and to cross the lines of the Greek civil war were the actions of a bold, enterprising and adventurous American reporter determined to see for himself and to report what he saw. Whether he used the best judgment in seeking to reach the guerrillas from Greek territory rather than through Yugoslavia is arguable. But it does not alter the fact that his errand was legitimate and that he was the victim of a plot to murder him with the deliberate intent of influencing the course of events in Greece.

Many other American correspondents have lost their lives while they were at work. But so far as we know, Polk is the first American correspondent abroad who was murdered for political reasons. It was, therefore, the plain duty and interest of his colleagues to act. It was their duty and interest to do what they could to make known to the world their determination to use the power of the American press and radio to protect the security of American correspondents. For obviously the freedom of the press would be a mockery if journalists can be murdered with impunity.

The problem of the committee was to decide how the power of the American press and radio could be exerted most effectively and wisely on behalf of the security of American correspondents. The Polk case posed this problem in an extraordinarily difficult form. For Polk was murdered in a distant land torn by civil war—a civil war which in its turn was an episode in a world wide conflict.

Moreover, we must, in order to give a true account of the work of the committee, note that Polk was a severe critic of the Greek Government, and that, therefore, though it was evident that the crime was political, it was not self-evident what the political motive was.

The Greek Government asserted from the beginning that Polk had been murdered by the Communists in order to discredit the Greek Government in the eyes of the American people. The Communists asserted from the beginning that he had been murdered by agents of the Right, because they wished to silence a dangerous critic and to discourage other American reporters. It was also possible, in the view of the committee and its counsel, that the crime was the work of a terrorist gang operating independently, either from the Extreme Left or from the Extreme Right.

The committee and its counsel held to the view that the mystery could not be solved deductively—that is to say, by attempting to decide who had the most to gain by the murder of Polk. The committee concluded that only a solution of the crime tested in open court could ever settle the case. Therefore, though they examined all the theories, they were resolved not to tie themselves to any of them.

The committee's first step was to ask for an appointment with the Secretary of State. At the interview, which took place in Secretary Marshall's office on Monday, May 24, 1948, it transpired that American officials in Greece had reported to the Department that the murder had occurred and that the Greek authorities were investigating it and had expressed the opinion that the investigation was being properly conducted at that stage. No representations had been made to the Greek Government, however, nor were any then contemplated. Secretary Marshall, when he had acquainted himself with the facts, instructed our Embassy in Greece to designate a qualified member of its staff to follow developments closely and to express informally to the Greek Government the deep concern of the State Department, of the American press and radio, and of the American public in general, that the crime should be solved and its perpetrators punished. He also directed the Embassy to keep the State Department informed in detail of all developments, promised the committee access to all official information in the case, and designated Mr. William O. Baxter, of the Greek desk, to maintain liaison with the committee. (The text of the memorandum which formed the basis of the conference with Secretary Marshall is printed in the appendix.) Two members of the staff of the American Embassy in Greece were designated to follow the Greek investigation daily. Similar instructions were sent to Mr. Raleigh Gibson, Consul-General in Salonika. The American authorities in Greece reported also that the British Police Mission, then engaged in training the Greek police in Scotland Yard methods, were actively cooperating with the Greek authorities in investigating the Polk murder.

The committee also discussed in a preliminary way with Secretary Marshall two other possible courses of action: (1) the assignment to Greece of trained American police investigators to check on the Greek official inquiries and (2) an independent American "undercover" investigation of the murder. The committee made no specific proposals along either of these lines, as it had not yet had the opportunity to obtain the views of General William J. Donovan, who only that day had been asked and had consented to serve as its counsel. It had been with these possibilities in mind, however, that the committee had sought the aid of the organizer and head of the wartime Office of Strategic Services. It felt that General Donovan was qualified, pre-eminently by ability and prestige and uniquely by experience, to give it advice and assistance.

On May 26, a subcommittee conferred with Mr. Dwight P. Griswold, Administrator of American Aid to Greece, who was then in Washington. He, like Secretary Marshall, was cooperative. He suggested that the chief of his own security division for the past year, Mr. Frederick Ayer, might be of service. Mr. Ayer, a former officer of the Federal Bureau of Investigation, was then training his successor, preparatory to his own return to the United States. As a result of the meeting with Mr. Griswold, Mr. Ayer was relieved of all other duties and his return to the United States was deferred. For the next two months, he gave full time to the Polk inquiry.

The committee apprised the chairman of the Foreign Relations Committee, Senator Arthur H. Vandenberg, and the chairman of the Foreign Affairs Committee, Rep. Charles A. Eaton, of its objectives and initial activities. Both immediately offered their full support. Senator Vandenberg asked Senator Henry Cabot Lodge, Jr., to interest himself in the matter in behalf of the Foreign Relations Committee. A former journalist, Senator Lodge on his own initiative, prior to the formation of the Overseas Writers Committee, had written to the State Department requesting full information about the investigation of Polk's death.

The Greek Ambassador to the United States, Mr. Vassili D. Dendramis, was informed of the creation of the committee, and an appointment with him was arranged for June 3, when General Donovan could be present. Meanwhile, on May 28, Ambassador Dendramis had delivered to the Secretary of State a note from his Government, setting forth the steps taken in investigating the murder and promising that "justice will be done, regardless of what the investigation may disclose."

From June 3, a major part of the day-to-day work of the committee was assumed by General Donovan, as its counsel. He himself made four trips to Greece. Mr. Guy Martin, of the Washington office of his law firm, regularly read and made digests of the official reports from Greece to the State Department. To facilitate close cooperation with General Donovan and his staff, an executive committee was formed, comprising Messrs. Walter Lippmann, Marquis Childs, Ernest K. Lindley, Joseph Harsch, Benjamin M. McKelway, and Phelps Adams.

It would prolong this report unduly to describe all the questions of policy and procedure which arose. A brief summary of a few of them may be of value, however, if only for the information of any group which may be called upon to undertake a similar task in the future.

One of the first of several perplexing questions was raised by a Greek correspondent for an American newspaper. He had been a close friend of Polk's and had many American friends. He expressed fear that his own life was in danger and sought the aid of his American employer and several prominent American journalists to enable him to leave Greece. The Greek authorities, however, regarded him as a witness of potential importance and were not satisfied that he had disclosed all that he knew about Polk's underground contacts in Greece and the events leading up to Polk's trip to Salonika.

The committee felt that it should take no step which might either frustrate the Greek official investigation or provide an excuse for failure to track down the murderers of Polk. At the same time, it had no way of knowing that this correspondent's fears for his life were not well based.

The committee's answer to this dilemma was, briefly, this: (1) The American employer of the correspondent wrote him that he must disclose all that he knew pertaining to the affairs and connections of Polk before he would receive any assistance in leaving Greece; (2) this letter was to be presented to the correspondent personally by General Donovan; (3) General Donovan himself was to interrogate the correspondent, although a representative of the Greek Government could be present and the witness might be represented by counsel if he chose; (4) if the interrogation provided information which might place the life of the witness in danger but did not implicate him in the murder, then General Donovan and the committee would use their best efforts to obtain a safe refuge for him in the United States or some other suitable place. In addition, the Greek Government was requested to provide special police protection to this correspondent: in effect, it was notified that his safety was a matter of special concern to the American press and radio.

Similar problems arose with respect to other persons in Greece and were handled in a similar way. One of these individuals was Polk's young Greek widow, Rea. When General Donovan had satisfied himself that she had told the Greek authorities all she knew, the committee supported her request to leave Greece. She came to the United States with the understanding that she would return to Greece when needed as a trial witness. When the time arrived for her to go back, she was under medical supervision and her doctors advised General Donovan and the committee that she could not stand the ordeal. Fortunately, the Greek prosecutors concluded that her testimony was not essential to the trial of Gregory Stakhtopoulos.

The committee gave much thought to the problems presented by potential sources of information who did not trust the Greek Government or particular Greek prosecutors. It was also aware from the beginning of the possibility that its pressure for the arrest and punishment of the murderers could result in a frame-up to satisfy the American demand for action. In the end it invariably concluded that the proper course was to keep the primary responsibility fixed on the Greek Government, not only for a full, relentless, and honest investigation and a fair trial but for the safety of those potential witnesses, who, rightly or wrongly, felt they were in danger. General Donovan had the opportunity to interrogate directly these possible sources of information, and on other occasions during the early part of the Greek official investigation, Mr. Ayer was present.

The committee considered from time to time the offer of a reward for information leading to the arrest and prosecution of the murderers. The Greek Government had announced a reward of 25 million drachmas (approximately $2,500.00). One of the dangers inherent in a larger reward was that it would lead to a frame-up or false conviction. Also, in connection with a reward, there is always the question of whether it shall be given to an accomplice. On General Donovan's advice, the committee withheld an offer of a reward until September 24, 1948, when it announced one of $10,000. No one qualified for, or claimed, this reward as a result of the trial and conviction of Stakhtopoulos as an accessory. The offer was not formally renewed after his conviction but it was not immediately withdrawn. The financial underwriters of the committee's inquiry agreed to extend their pledges in sufficient amount to cover a claim for the reward in connection with the arrest and trial of the actual murderers. General Donovan advised the committee some months ago that, in his judgment, its offer of a reward could be considered expired.

One of the most difficult questions presented to the committee was to what extent it should undertake an independent investigation of the murder. It seemed evident that nothing was to be gained by sending a special journalistic board of inquiry to Greece. American correspondents in Greece were following closely developments and the Columbia Broadcasting System had sent two able correspondents to Greece to give full time to the case. An alternative was to send undercover investigators, but properly trained and reliable operatives who knew the Greek language and the tangled skeins of Greek factionalism were rare.

General Donovan, however, arranged with the United States Air Force to borrow temporarily the services of Lieutenant Colonel G. L. James Kellis. An American citizen of Greek extraction, Kellis had made a brilliant record during the war as an o.s.s. officer. He had, among other exploits, gone into

Greece during the German occupation, established contact with the Greek underground leaders of ELAS, and directed important sabotage operations. General Donovan took Colonel Kellis with him on his first trip to Greece as counsel for the committee, on June 10, 1948, and left him there when he returned to the United States.

Late in July 1949, without notice to General Donovan or the committee, Colonel Kellis was recalled to the United States. The Air Force wanted him for another assignment. The executive committee in Washington ascertained, however, that his recall had been suggested by an official of the American Embassy in Athens in a cable to the State Department. Colonel Kellis had been exploring certain leads pointing to the Right, or a terrorist organization of the Extreme Right, as the author of the crime. At that time, he was, to the best knowledge of this committee, the only investigator who was testing that theory of the crime. The committee and General Donovan regarded it as very important that all leads in what was then still an unsolved mystery be thoroughly explored, regardless of political embarrassment to anyone. It was primarily for the purpose of pursuing lines of investigation that the Greek authorities might neglect that General Donovan took Colonel Kellis to Greece.

The executive committee regarded this interference with Colonel Kellis's activities as a grave violation of Secretary Marshall's instructions in not apprising the committee of the communications, both by cable and orally, leading to the recall of the committee's independent investigator. The executive committee established the facts in this matter only by persistent investigation. In repsonse to the executive committee's protests, the Air Force consented to Colonel Kellis's return to Athens if General Donovan wanted him and the State Department promised to see that he received thereafter the full cooperation of the American authorities in Greece. A decision was postponed until General Donovan's return from Greece. General Donovan had taken occasion to impress on Greek officials the necessity of exploring fully the leads which pointed to the Right as well as those pointing toward the Left. He advised the committee that he was satisfied that this would be done and that, from a political viewpoint, certain key officials in the inquiry would not be displeased if the crime were found to have been committed by Rightists. As a result, plans for sending Colonel Kellis back to Greece were abandoned.

The committee and its counsel obtained iron-clad assurances from the Greek authorities that if or when a trial was held it would be a civil trial, not a court-martial, and that it would be public so that it could be fully covered by the American press and radio. After the indictment of Stakhtopoulos and his mother, it gave consideration to engaging a Greek lawyer to participate in the trial as counsel for Polk's mother or widow. This is permissible in Greek practice. General Donovan finally concluded, however, that this was unnecessary, especially since he was able to arrange to attend all sessions of the trial himself.

The indictment, brought March 14, 1949, charged the following persons with various degrees of complicity in the murder of Polk: Evangelos Vasvanas, Adam Mouzenides, Gregorios Stakhtopoulos and the latter's mother, Anna Stakhtopoulos. Stakhtopoulos and his mother were already under arrest. Warrants were issued for the arrest of Vasvanas and Mouzenides, both Communists in the guerrilla forces of General Markos, but they were never apprehended.

The trial was held in Salonika, April, 1949, before three judges and a jury of twelve. The Stakhtopouloses were represented by counsel and the procedures conformed to the requirements of Greek law and judicial practice. Gregorios Stakhtopoulos was convicted on one count of complicity in the murder and sentenced to life imprisonment. His mother was acquitted. The jury found Vasvanas and Mouzenides guilty of the actual murder. Under Greek law, such verdicts may be brought even when the accused are not present. If subsequently arrested, however, they may request and receive a new trial.

General Donovan attended all the sessions of the trial with a reliable interpreter of his own selection. He also had the advice of a Greek lawyer. He went over the transcript of the trial, as he had examined in detail the voluminous records of the investigations preceding the trial. General Donovan advised the committee that the trial was "efficiently and honestly conducted with fair and full opportunity to the defense to present its case" in a judicial atmosphere with none of the trappings or atmosphere of a cause célèbre. He also advised the committee that, in his opinion, the evidence which caused the conviction of Stakhtopoulos would have led an American jury to a similar conclusion. General Donovan's judgments on all these essential points appear to have been shared by the American correspondents who covered the trial.

CONCLUSIONS

As this outline of its activities may suggest, the committee in general followed the practice of American newspapers when in any community there is a serious crime, with more than personal significance, which is not solved. It is common practice in cases of this sort to work with the authorities, to support them, to encourage those who are energetic, to put pressure on those who are slow, timid, or complacent, and to make an independent inquiry at the same time.

The committee is able to report that the official investigation was, after some hesitation and delay, pursued with vigor by the Greek authorities and officers of the law. It is able to report also that in its work it received the cooperation and support of the Secretary of State and many American officials in Washington and in Greece. It is compelled to report, however, that the work of its own independent investigator in Greece was not facilitated, that in fact was frustrated, by the Greek and American authorities. The committee knew very well that even in an American community, far more so in a foreign country, the odds are against the private solution of a mysterious crime. It has no reason to believe and does not suggest that its independent investigator would eventually have produced evidence different from that which was presented at the Stakhtopoulos trial. But it does suggest that doubts in some minds would have been more quickly, if not more firmly, resolved if the committee's investigator had received the full cooperation of the American and Greek authorities.

The committee is satisfied that Stakhtopoulos and his mother received a fair trial. Moreover, it is satisfied that Stakhtopoulos was in fact an accessory, that he was the "finger man" who led Polk into the trap where his murderers were waiting for him. (Whether Stakhtopoulos knew in advance that Polk was to be murdered is another question on which the Greek jury, in convicting him of complicity, did not pass.)

But Stakhtopoulos, though guilty of the charge on which he was convicted, was not the murderer. The committee has delayed its report and dissolution in the hope that the actual murderers might be arrested, tried, and convicted. But, though the Greek civil war has been brought to an end, Vasvanas and Mouzenides, who were tentatively found guilty by the Greek jury, have not been found, and no new evidence implicating others has been brought to light. The reports received by Greek police that Vasvanas and Mouzenides were killed before the end of the Civil War may be correct, or they may have sought refuge in another land.

The committee hopes that the case will not be forgotten. For the safety of American correspondents working abroad in dangerous places can best be insured if it is known to all the world that they cannot be attacked with impunity—that the power and influence of the United States government, that the concerted action of the press and radio, and an aroused public opinion, will demand and will persist in demanding the pursuit and punishment of the criminals. That in itself cannot guarantee the safety of American correspondents, but it can act as a deterrent against any who might otherwise think the risks were not too great.

Notes

CHAPTER I. PROLOGUE

1. Confidential report transmitted by the American consulate in Salonika to the Department of State, now in the U.S. National Archives, No. 89 (May 25, 1948), 368.113 Polk, George, encl. 1, pp. 2–4. The State Department documents having to do with the Polk case in the National Archives Building are filed either under "368.113 Polk, George" or, much more frequently, under "811.91268," followed by a number designating the date (e.g., "/5-2548" for May 25, 1948). In citing the first source, I have generally given the full reference number, as above. In citing the second often repeated source, I have restricted my references to the document number, the date number, the enclosure number (when relevant), and page numbers when such citation seems called for by the document's length and the specificity of the quotation from it and when its pages are actually numbered. Many of the State Department documents cited in the chapters that follow are simply single or double-paged cables.

2. John O. Iatrides, "Civil War, 1945–1949: National and International Aspects," in *Greece in the 1940s*, ed. John O. Iatrides (Hanover, N.H.: University Press of New England, 1981), p. 391n.87.

3. Brenda L. Marder, *Stewards of the Land: The American Farm School and Modern Greece* (Boulder, Colo.: East European Quarterly, 1979), pp. 213–16.

4. Gregory Staktopoulos, *Ipothesi Polk: I Prosopiki mou martiria (Polk Affair: My Personal Testimony)* (Athens: Gnosi, 1984) [referred to subsequently as "Staktopoulos"].

5. Kosta Hadjiargyris, *I Ipothesi Polk: O Rolos ton Xenon Ipirision stin Ellada (The Polk Affair: The Role of the Foreign Agencies in Greece)* (Athens: Gutenberg, 1975) [referred to subsequently as "Hadjiargyris"].

6. *Daily Compass*, August 6–11.

7. "Who Killed George Polk?" *More: The Media Magazine*, May 1977, pp. 12–23.

8. As quoted by Theodore Draper in his article, "American Hubris: From Truman to the Persian Gulf," *New York Review of Books*, July 16, 1987, p. 42.

CHAPTER II. THE VICTIM

1. Interview in 1987 with Louis Buol, the Swiss vice-consul in Salonika at the time of Polk investigation.

2. No. 89 (May 25, 1948), 368.113 Polk, George, encl. 1.

3. The *New York Herald Tribune* of May 17 so designates Condon's first name. The name appears as "Wade" in the Burdett-Secondari report to CBS discussed below and simply by the initial "W" in several State Department documents.

4. No. 203 (May 16, 1948), 368.113 Polk, George.

5. No. 88, 5-2548, p. 3. (See chapter 1, n. 1, for an explanation of the mode of citation here and elsewhere when the basic file number in the National Archives is 811.91268).

6. No. 196, 5-1248.

7. No. 822 (May 17, 1948), 368.113 Polk, George.

8. Hadjiargyris, p. 23.

9. No. 145, 7-2748, encl. 1, pp. 7–8.

10. *More*, May 1977, p. 22; p. 23n.49.

11. Copy of note by A.G.R. Rouse (R 5102/10139/19 G) marked SECRET. Public Record Office, ref. Fo371/78404 6159.

12. No. 112, 6-1548, pp. 3–8.

13. The reference is to the U.S. military attaché, Colonel Allen C. Miller II.

14. No. 99, 6-748, encl. 1, p. 2.

15. Ibid., p. 1.

16. No. 112, 6-1548, pp. 8–16.

17. Based on several interviews with Rea Polk during 1986 and 1987.

18. No. 88, 5-2548, encl. 3.

19. Ibid., encl. 5.

20. No. 217, 5-2148.

21. 5-2148 (unnumbered, May 21, 9 P.M.).

22. *Washington Post*, May 20 and 22. (The latter is discussed first.)

23. 3:2. The numerals indicate the relevant chapter and page(s) in the Draft Report. This source is to be found in the archives that General Donovan left in the hands of his law firm, Donovan, Leisure, Newton & Lombard (subsequently referred to here as "Donovan Papers"). Mary G. Jones verified in a phone conversation with the author (1988) that she was asked by General Donovan to prepare this long report but she could not comment on its contents or speculate on General Donovan's decision not to make it public at the time she turned it over to him.

24. May 17, 1948.

25. No. 822 (May 17, 1948), 368.113 Polk, George.

26. May 17, 1948.

27. May 18, 1948.

28. May 17, 1948.

29. No. 88, 5-2548, encl. 7.

30. Ibid., encl. 6.

31. No. 236, 5-2748.

32. No. 244, 5-2948.

33. No. 248, 6-148.

CHAPTER III: THE WAR AND THE PRESS

1. Dominique Eudes, *The Kapetanios: Partisans and Civil War in Greece, 1943–1949*, trans. John Howe (New York: Monthly Review Press, 1972), p. 318.

2. Based on personal interviews, 1986.

3. The EAM (National Liberation Front) was created in September 1941 by the KKE (Greek Communist Party) and a number of small political groups of the center-left as a resistance movement whose military force was called ELAS (National Popular Liberation Army).

4. See Theodore Draper, "Neoconservative History," *New York Review of Books*, January 16, 1986, p. 6 and n. 2.

5. Iatrides, in *Greece in the 1940s*, p. 391n.87.

6. Draft Report, 3:1–2.

7. 11-2647, Dec. 3.

8. No. 3188, 10-1046; no. 1733, 12-1746; no. 3454, 12-2146.

9. Lawrence Wittner, "American Policy toward Greece, 1944–1949: Prelude to Civil War," in *Greece in the 1940s*, ed. John O. Iatrides, pp. 231–32, and n. 25.

10. George Th. Mavrogordatos, "The 1946 Election and Plebiscite: Prelude to Civil War," in *Greece in the 1940s*, p. 384n.55.

11. Quoted by Theodore Draper in "American Hubris: From Truman to the Persian Gulf," p. 41.

12. No. 413, 4-748.

13. Wittner, in *Greece in the 1940s*, p. 237.

14. Ibid.

15. Iatrides, in *Greece in the 1940s*, p. 214.

16. See pp. 59–61 below and Rankin's discussion with Lindley on pp. 149–50.

17. Phone conversation with the author, 1987 (though Bigart thought it was his Republican colleague Geoffrey Parsons who finally persuaded the *Herald Tribune* to allow the dispatches to appear).

18. No. 1169, 6-2648.

19. AMAG [American Mission for Aid to Greece] 1242, 6-2848.

20. *Memoirs of a Mountain War, Greece: 1944–1949* (London: Longman, 1972), pp. 141–43.

21. 4-1948 (April 19); also, no. 476, 4-2248, encl. 1.

22. Wittner, in *Greece in the 1940s*, p. 236.

23. Based on personal interviews with former Communist guerrillas in Salonika, 1986.

24. Wittner, in *Greece in the 1940s*, p. 236.

CHAPTER IV. THE ATHENS CONNECTION

1. *The George Polk Case: Report of the Overseas Writers of the Special Committee to Inquire Into the Murder at Salonika, Greece, May 16, 1948, of Columbia Broadcasting System Correspondent* GEORGE POLK, p. 21 [referred to subsequently as "Lippmann Report." Page references to this document are to the original, not to the excerpt printed in the Appendix to this book.]

2. Edman and Marcy were originally "designated follow Polk investigation" in a cable from Rankin dated May 21 (no. 884, 5-2148), but the only reference to their specific duties appears in another cable from Rankin sent on June 2 (no. 957, 6-248, erroneously dated May 2) which indicates that Edman would continue to handle the "press aspect" but that Marcy's function of reporting to the department would presumably be supplemented by Ayer's reporting to the department also via the Athens embassy and the Salonika consulate, a decision reached after a meeting with AMAG at which it was decided that Ayer would "devote full time to the case."

3. Office Memorandum from Baxter to the Secretary, May 27, 1948, 5-2748.

4. No. 210, 5-2048; no. 217, 5-2148.

5. No. 210, 5-2048.

6. No. 965, 6-248 (Report No. 1).

7. No. 890, 5-2248.

8. No. 626, 5-1948.

9. No. 890, 5-2248.

10. Tel. no. 22-733 [the only identification number, appearing opposite the address—35, Asklipiou Street, /Athens—and the date.]

11. Hadjiargyris.

12. (Chicago: Henry Regnery Co.). See esp. pp. 270–99.

13. *New York Times*, January 5, 1974.

14. Information from various personal interviews.

15. No. 661, 6-1848.

16. No. 1460, 7-3048.

17. Identified in the State Department archive by the title alone: "WINSTON BURDETT FROM ROME—REPORT ON MURDER OF GEORGE POLK 7/31/48."

18. No. 1281, 7-848.

19. January, 5, 1974.

20. No. 92, 4-2149.

21. No. 112, 6-1548.

22. No. 965, 6-248.

23. No. 1043, 6-948.

24. Interview with the author, 1986.

25. Ibid.

26. Hadjiargyris, pp. 59–60. I have not been able to track down this journal.

27. No. 1043, 6-948.

28. *More*, p. 21 and n. 44.

29. No. 661, 6-1848.

30. No. 1043, 6-948.

31. No. 112, 6-1548, encl., p. 16.

32. No. 1043, 6-948.

33. No. 112, 6-1548.

34. No. 120, 6-2348, encl. 2.

35. As we shall see below in chapter 10 (p. 311), Attorney General Constantinidis also reported—in this instance to Raleigh Gibson—that Mrs. Barber had admitted going to Polk's office at Rea's request and subsequently delivering certain files to Rea.

36. No. 88, 5-2548, encl. 1a.

37. Subsequently a distinguished Athenian journalist.

38. No. 145, 7-2748, encl. 1, pp. 7–8.

39. Information given the author by Prof. John O. Iatrides.

40. No. 1102, 6-1748 (Report No. 9).

41. No. 86, 6-648, encl. (Office Memorandum: Jack D. Neal to W. O. Baxter, marked SECRET).

42. No. 265, 6-1348 (Report No. 7).

43. No. 1119, 6-1948 (Report No. 11).

44. No. 265, 6-1348 (Report No. 7).

45. Though Mouskoundis expressed his reluctance in this regard with specific reference to Hadjiargyris into late July, as reported by Attorney General

Constantinidis to Raleigh Gibson on
July 31 (no. 152, 8-1048, encl. 1, p. 1).

46. No. 110, 6-1448, encl. 1, p. 2.

CHAPTER V. THE SALONIKA CONTACT

1. Interview with the author, 1986.
2. *More*, May 1977, p. 14.
3. The Draft Report tells us in a note
(2:4, n. x) that "Kellis had made a brilliant record during the war as an oss officer. He had among other exploits, gone
into Greece during the German occupation, established contact with the Greek
underground leaders of ELAS and directed
important sabotage operations."
4. Lippmann Report, p. 1.
5. Ibid., p. 20.
6. Ibid., p. 21.
7. The Draft Report (2:12) underlines
this development when it tells us that
the Lippmann Committee's decision to
avoid an independent inquiry and to be
represented in Greece by General Donovan "was welcomed on all sides" and
that the State Department, in a note addressed to its representatives in Greece,
"declared that while General Donovan
was not being sent to Greece as an official governmental representative, nevertheless he went 'with the blessing of the
State Department.'"
8. No. 1071, 6-1348.
9. No. 110, 6-1448, encl. 1.
10. 4:6.
11. Ibid., 6–7.
12. No. 110, 6–1448, encl. 2.
13. No. 275, 6-2448.
14. No. 1177, 6-2648.
15. No. 1179, 6-2648.
16. No. 1183, 6-2748.
17. No. 1212, 6-3048.
18. Interview with the author, 1986.
Among the Donovan papers there is a
"Memorandum," dated April 9, 1949,
and signed by William J. Donovan, that
indicates the two doctors in question
were Dr. Louis Brush of New York City
and "Dr. Nelson, physician in charge at
Barnard College." When Donovan talked
to these doctors regarding the possibility
of Rea's returning to Greece to testify at
the trial, "they said they were putting
this girl to bed at once and that they considered that her nervous condition was
such that she would not be able to meet

the responsibility of testifying in a rational manner," and, though Rea herself
"was anxious to go," the two doctors
"could not give their consent."
19. No. 127, 6-2848, encl. 1.
20. No. 140, 7-1948.
21. Ibid., encl.
22. No. 1460, 7-3048.
23. No. 145, 7-2748, encl. 1.
24. Ibid.
25. Donovan's attempt is recorded in
Department of State, "Memorandum of
Conversation," June 29, 1948, 6-2948.
26. No. 1281, 7-848.
27. No. 145, 7-2748, encl. 2.
28. Ibid., encl. 3.
29. *More*, pp. 16 and 23n.12 [1355, 7,
17, 48].
30. Donovan papers (in cap. script).
31. 368.113-Polk, George/8-548.
32. *Declassified Documents Quarterly*, Catalogue 5, 1979 (with reference
to CIA, December 3, 1952).
33. Donovan papers. The discussion
of Kellis is under "P.S." on p. 2.
34. *New York Times*, September 17,
1977.
35. *More*, p. 21.
36. P. 9.
37. *Declassified Documents Quarterly*, CIA, December 3, 1952.
38. No. 1451, 7-2948.
39. Donovan papers, headed "COLUMBIA
BROADCASTING SYSTEM/CBS REPORT . . . ,"
p. 20.
40. No. 1451, 7-2948.
41. Donovan papers, "MEMORANDUM FOR
THE AMERICAN EMBASSY/FROM William J.
Donovan," pp. 1–2.
42. No. 1451, 7-2948.
43. No. 340, 9-2348.
44. Donovan's own view of the cause
for the failure of his proposal is suggested by the Draft Report (5:13–14),
where we are told that Prime Minister
Sophoulis, Venizelos, and Rendis were
all favorably disposed toward the creation of a Special Judicial Commission
should the investigation appear "doomed
to collapse," but the idea was opposed

47. No. 102, 6-948, also encl. 1, p. 1.
48. No. 265, 6-1348 (Report No. 7).
49. No. 266, 6-1448 (Report No. 8).

by Melas, whose objections "may have been directed less to the substance of the proposal than to his own irritation that he, rather than Minister Rendis, was not consulted first." In any case, "it was clear" that the Greek officials, "as a whole," were reluctant to take the initiative in urging such a commission "without some indication from the American diplomatic officials in Greece as to their endorsement of the proposal. No such endorsement was ever forthcoming."

45. In a letter from the general (unsigned) to Eugene Meyer, dated November 9, 1948, among the Donovan papers, Lambron is described as "our man in Greece." See also No. 1613, 8-1848 (August 18, 1948), where Lambron is referred to as "Donovan's deputy." In a footnote to the Draft Report (2:4a, n. xx), Lambron appears as "Dr. Lambron," an American citizen of Greek extraction, who was studying medicine in Greece at the time of the investigation. We learn that "by reason of his thirteen years residence in Greece, he was eminently qualified to act for the [Lippmann] Committee not only by virtue of his linguistic

fluency but also by reason of his knowledge of the members of the Greek political parties and in general of the Greek mentality." A certain insight into Lambron's own "mentality" can be gained from his criticism of the Draft Report: see below, chapter 10, n. 29.

46. Donovan papers, "Athens, Greece,/7 September 1948," addressed to "Dear General."

47. Ibid., "Athens, Greece/14 September 1948," addressed to "Dear General."

48. No. 1460, 7-3048.

49. No. 152, 8-1048.

50. No. 145, 7-2748, encl. 3.

51. No. 102, 6-948, encl. 1.

52. No. 112, 6-1548.

53. No. 134, 7-748.

54. No. 1281, 7-848.

55. See above, chapter 4, p. 82.

56. Donovan papers, memorandum to General Donovan from Mary G. Jones re *Report on Polk Investigation*, October 16, 1950, p. 2.

57. "WINSTON BURDETT FROM ROME . . . 7/31/48."

58. No. 157, 8-1748.

CHAPTER VI. THE ACCUSED

1. Christos Lambrinos in a 1986 interview with the author.

2. A Salonika journalist who wished to remain nameless, in a 1986 interview with the author.

3. In Staktopoulos.

4. Interviews with the author, 1986 and 1987.

5. The September 28 memorandum is an "Office Memorandum" on Donovan, Leisure stationary, headed "Mr. William J. Donovan /W. E. Colby / George Polk." The September 30 memorandum is headed "General Donovan / W. E. Colby /POLK INVESTIGATION." The embassy document, no. 8, 1-449, encl. 1, is discussed in detail below, pp. 205–6.

6. In an October 1987 phone conversation with the author, William E. Colby confirmed that he had met with Rea on several occasions during the summer of 1948. See also a letter from Davidson Taylor to Colby, dated July 7, 1948, among the Donovan papers.

7. Newspaper archive, Municipal Library, Salonika.

8. No. 862, 8-1948, encl. 1, as translated for the embassy by C. Economides.

9. No. 1573, 8-1248.

10. No. 157, 8-1748.

11. No. 1676, 8-2648.

12. For Donovan's perception of the failure of his Special Judicial Commission proposal and of Melas's role in its rejection, see above, p. 374, n. 44.

13. No. 1728, 9-248.

14. No. 157, 8-1748.

15. No. 1732, 9-248.

16. No. 880, 8-2648, encl. 1.

17. No. 1251, 7-448.

18. On July 25.

19. No. 169, 8-3148, encl. 1.

20. No. 323, 9-148.

21. No. 327, 9-448.

22. P. 294: "In his [Mouskoundis's] opinion, the handwriting was that of Gregory's mother—and his opinion was confirmed by experts. We even sent the documents later to a laboratory but they

could not positively associate the two handwritings" (i.e., that on the supposedly incriminating envelope and that of Gregory's mother, Anna). In this connection, the Donovan papers include a curious document that appears nowhere else in the record, originally forwarded to Donovan in Athens by Colby on August 7, 1948, a report—also dated August 7—that the general had solicited from one Miss Klara Goldzieher-Roman of International Valley, South Kortright, Delaware County, N.Y., and that came to the following conclusions, among others: the handwriting on the supposedly incriminating envelope is that of "an average person of Greek nationality who attended Greek schools ... is not literate and did not write frequently ... a man not over the thirties" with a constitution that is basically strong, though at the time of writing "he was not in good health and he was also in a bad nervous condition," though he has "a great will-

power" which "gave him the endurance to write these few words in a rather steady way," the whole giving Miss Goldzieher-Roman "the vague feeling that this man has something to do with aviation."

23. 6:4.
24. No. 174, 9-1148, encl.
25. No. 1814, 9-1348. A copy of the broadcast is among the Donovan papers.
26. No. 1302, 9-1048.
27. No. 1879, 9-2048.
28. No. 181, 9-2348, encl.
29. No. 340, 9-2348.
30. No. 343, 9-2848.
31. No. 344, 9-2948.
32. No. 188, 9-3048.
33. Interview with the author, 1986.
34. Interview with the author, 1986.
35. Interview with the author, 1986.
36. What follows is based on an interview with the author in the summer of 1986.

CHAPTER VII. THE CONFESSIONS

1. No. 196, 10-1848, encl. (English text); no. 205, 10-2948 (Greek text).The quotations offered from this Greek text and others that follow are in my translation whenever the official translation seems to me inadequate, as it generally does.
2. Ibid., encl. pp. 10ff.
3. No. 206, 10-2948.
4. Interview with Louis Buol, 1986.
5. Interview with the author, 1986.
6. No. 203, 10-2148, encl. 1 (Greek text); encl. 2 (English text).

7. No. 351, 10-648.
8. No. 352, 10-848.
9. No. 204, 10-2148, encl. 1 (English text); encl. 2 (Greek text).
10. No. 359, 10-1748.
11. No. 354, 10-948.
12. No. 2112, 10-2048.
13. No. 211, 11-1348, encl. 1, pp. 3–4.
14. No. 62, 4-2749, encl. 1.
15. For Carl Compton's view of the Polk affair some thirty years after his testimony at the trial, see below, chapter 9, n. 44.

CHAPTER VIII. THE OFFICIAL SOLUTION

1. No. 354, 10-948.
2. No. 1437, 10-748.
3. Ibid.
4. "General Donovan reviewed very carefully all of the ten suspects that I had submitted to him in my confidential report, and asked the Chief Greek Investigator to concentrate on one, a Greek newspaperman. Within sixty days this newspaperman confessed complicity in the crime." Declassified Documents Quarterly, CIA, December 3, 1952.
5. No. 192, 10-1384, encl. 2.

6. Ibid., encl. 1.
7. "Memorandum of Conversation, October 18, 1948," 10-1848.
8. See New York Times, October 19, 1948. According to the Draft Report (6: 15–16), Donovan's public position after the official announcement, namely "that final judgement on the Greek case could not come until after a full and fair trial on the facts had been held," was not only endorsed by the Lippmann Committee but was "the position" taken by the "American press."

9. *Herald Tribune*, October 19;
Times, October 20.
10. October 19.
11. No. 2119, 10–2048.
12. "Memorandum of Conversation, October 26, 1948," 10-2648.
13. No. 2145, 10-2348.
14. No. 365, 10-2848.
15. *New York Times*, October 16, 1948.
16. No. 215, 11-1848.
17. No. 219, 11-2748, encl. 2.
18. No. 219, 11-2748.
19. No. 227, 12-1748, encl.
20. No. 1, 1-349.
21. Ibid., encl.
22. No. 1240, 12-2348.
23. See above, pp. 58–62.
24. Letter to the author.
25. Phone interview, 1987.
26. The embassy document is no. 8, 1-449.

27. Ibid., encl. 1.
28. Staktopoulos, p. 54.
29. Hadjiargyris, p. 120.
30. No. 8, 1-449: N.B. "Copy to American Consulate, Salonika."
31. No. 51, 1-949.
32. No. 79, 1-1349.
33. No. 6, 1-1749, encl.
34. No. 15, 2-1649, encl.
35. No. 16, 2-1649, encl.
36. No. 30, 2-1649.
37. 868.00B/2-1749.
38. No. 365, 10-2848.
39. No. 22, 3-349.
40. No. 28, 3-1149.
41. No. 47, 3-1549.
42. No. 69, 4-1047.
43. No. 38, 4-249, encl.
44. No. 43, 4-749, encl.
45. No. 48, 3-1549.
46. See above, p. 110 and chapter 5, n. 18.

CHAPTER IX. THE TRIAL

1. No. 53, 4-1949.
2. No. 57, 4-1949.
3. No. 88, 5-2548, encl. 1a.
4. 7:6. The discussion of the indictment takes up the sixteen pages of the Draft Report that follow.
5. No. 92, 4-2149.
6. Lippmann Report, p. 59.
7. No. 49, 4-1349.
8. No. 72, 4-1249.
9. No. 49, 4-1349.
10. No. 72, 4-1249.
11. 8:5–8
12. Lippmann Report, p. 59.
13. No. 71, 4-1249, and no. 49, 4-1349.
14. No. 49, 4-1349.
15. Ibid., encl.
16. The possibility of Adam Mouzenidis having stayed at the YMCA in Salonika is difficult to take seriously since the building is in the heart of a city that was heavily policed at the time, with frequent police ID checks, and since Adam Mouzenidis was well known in Salonika.
17. No. 73, 4-1249.
18. No. 6, 1-1749.
19. No. 50, 4-1949, encl. 1.
20. Ibid., encl. 2.
21. The Draft Report (8:14–15) tells

us that after Helen Mamas challenged Stavridis's claim that she had asked him whether "Gregory" was at the UNSCOB meeting on the afternoon of May 7 and whether he would tell Staktopoulos that Polk wanted to see him, Stavrides "also stated that Rea Polk had been present at this meeting and this statement was never challenged although it was clear that Mrs. Polk could not have attended the meeting since she was not in Salonika at the time" (i.e., on May 7, having reached the city on May 12).
22. No. 75, 4-1449.
23. No. 51, 4-1649, encl. 1.
24. Ibid.
25. No. 78, 4-1449.
26. Ibid.
27. No. 51, 4-1649, encl. 1, p. 12.
28. No. 80, 4-1549.
29. The Draft Report (7:12) gives a similar account of Hadjiargyris's performance: his testimony and interrogation "consumed almost four hours," but despite the continuous barrage of questions from judge, jurors, and counsel, Hadjiargyris adhered to his previous statements that he knew nothing of Polk's plans to contact the guerrilla headquarters, that he doubted that Polk had arranged his contact from Athens, and

that he knew nothing about the stolen correspondence file."

30. No. 51, 4-1649, encl. 2, p. 3.
31. No. 80, 4-1549.
32. Staktopoulos, p. 108.
33. No. 52, 4-1649, encl.
34. No. 82, 4-1549.
35. No. 52, 4-1649, encl., p. 2.
36. Ibid., p. 7.
37. Ibid., p. 8.
38. No. 61, 4-2749, encl. 1, pp. 1ff.
39. Ibid., p. 6.
40. Ibid., p. 1.
41. Ibid., encl. 2, pp. 1–2.
42. The relevant document is among the Donovan papers; see Notes, pp. 375–76n.22.
43. No. 62, 4-2749, encl. 1.
44. In a memoir of his years at Anatolia College that Carl Compton wrote between 1980 and 1982, when he was close to ninety years old (*The Morning Cometh: 45 Years with Antolia College,* ed. John O. Iatrides and William R. Compton [New York: Caratzas, 1986]), the author provides an account of the Polk affair (pp. 98–99) that not only assumes Staktopoulos's testimony at the trial regarding his involvement in the case to have been accurate but adds several curious—and subsequently unsupported—details that perhaps serve to illustrate some of the rumors and hypotheses that were current at the time of the trial among local observers (though one must here take into account the lapse of time between the events narrated and Carl Compton's remembrance of them some thirty years later). For example, Compton tells his readers that Helen Mamas, a former teacher at Anatolia College turned journalist, "sent [George Polk] to Gregory Stacktopoulos [*sic*], a

graduate of Anatolia," and, through Staktopoulos and "a supporter of the guerrillas" known to the Reuters stringer, "an arrangement was made" for the interview with Markos. The three men then had dinner at a seaside restaurant, were picked up by a boat, and "were told that they would row across the bay to a point where an escort would be waiting for them, with horses, to lead them to the guerrillas' secret headquarters." Polk was then shot in the boat, his body was thrown overboard, and Staktopoulos "was given Polk's passport and other papers with orders to mail them to the police." The rest of the account more or less follows the official one, though we learn that after much delay an envelope "with the same texture and the same handwriting" as that used for the mailing in of "Polk's papers" reached the hands of the police, and the handwriting on this second envelope "was easily traced to Mrs. Staktopoulos," who was then arrested. "Gregory then went to the police, told the whole story, and took his mother's place in jail." Compton concludes that, of the various reasons offered for the murder, the "most generally accepted theory" was that the guerrillas committed the murder in order "to cause trouble for the Greek government." The editors add a note at this point outlining Staktopoulos's claim to have been a scapegoat, as presented in his 1984 book.

45. No. 204, 10-2148, encl. 1, p. 7.
46. No. 88, 4-2049.
47. No. 64, 4-2749, encl.
48. No. 68, 4-2749, encl., p. 1.
49. No. 92, 4-2149.
50. No. 65, 4-2749, encl.
51. Lippmann Report, p. 63.

CHAPTER X. THE WHITEWASH

1. No. 92, 4-2149.
2. Ibid.
3. Ibid.
4. No. 57, 4-1949.
5. No. 56, 4-1949.
6. Ibid., encl.
7. See above, chapter 5, n. 18.
8. No. 92, 4-2149.
9. No. 70, 4-3049, encl.

10. No. 70, 4-3049.
11. We learn from the Draft Report (8:9–10) that after the testimony in court of Stylianos Mouzenidis (Adam's brother) and Anna Molyvda (Adam's sister-in-law), "General Donovan asked and received permission to interrogate the pair outside the courtroom in order to ascertain for himself whether they had tes-

tified under duress. As a result of this interview, General Donovan declared that
he was satisfied that they had testified
voluntarily and in all sincerity." Nothing is said about the circumstances
under which this interview—presumably
involving an interpreter—was conducted
or on what basis General Donovan arrived at his conclusion.

12. No. 361, 5-1749, "Memorandum
of Conversation."

13. No. 70, 4-3049.

14. Ibid., encl.

15. Donovan's "Informal Report on
the Trial" appears on pp. 12–14.

16. No. 59, 4-2049.

17. In the Draft Report (8:6), Theo-
doros Economou is listed as one of the
three attorneys representing Staktopoulos and his mother, but in fact Economou does not appear anywhere in the
trial transcript, and Staktopoulos reports
in his book (p. 114) that Economou withdrew from the case shortly before the
trial because he could not agree to a defense strategy based on an acknowledgment of Staktopoulos's guilt, as recommended by Vassilikos.

18. No. 49, 4-1349, encl.

19. P. 10.

20. 6:12–14.

21. P. 9.

22. *Declassified Document Quarterly*, CIA, December 3, 1952.

23. P. 10.

24. Ibid.

25. P. 29.

26. Personal interview, Vence, France,
June 6, 1987.

27. The Draft Report (3:3–4) also
speaks of Salonika as not only "the center of Communist operations and intrigue" but "the operating headquarters
of other extremist factions in Greece" as
well. Along with the "X" organization,
it mentions the Greek Military Police as
"the other important organization" con-
stituting "the largest and most powerful
secret police body in Greece."

28. The text is dated May 21, 1951.
Roubatis and Vlanton indicate the date
of publication as July 1952 (*More*, p. 19).

29. P. 11.

30. P. 19.

31. P. 2.

32. 4:21.

33. 9:9–10.

34. One such "fact" that the Draft Report cites (8:18) is Staktopoulos's late
emendation of his testimony when he
"informed the Court that he had hidden
Vasvanas in his room on the night preceding the crime." The Draft Report
comments that "defense attorneys made
no move to interrogate him," though the
judge and jurors "questioned him at
some length primarily as respects his
protestations that he had no knowledge
of the real intentions of the murderers."
Why Donovan and Gibson made no attempt to follow up the implications of
this late emendation, the Draft Report
does not say.

35. 9:4.

36. 9:6–7.

37. 9:7.

38. 9:9.

39. 9:7.

40. The letter is in the form of a
memorandum from Mary G. Jones to
General Donovan headed "Report on
Polk Investigation," and it is dated October 16, 1950. Lambron is referred to as
"Lambrun," and his objections are summarized as follows: first, he felt that the
chapter on the indictment "put the
Greek authorities in a very unfavorable
light," a thing that he feared "might be
used by communist propaganda as a
means of slurring the investigation"
(Mary G. Jones did not agree "that one
should be influenced by this, provided
that the report is a fair presentation");
second, Lambron thought "that Mr.
Ayer was cast perhaps in too favorable a
light" (as we have seen, this document
quotes Lambron as saying that he felt
Ayer's "contribution to the investigation
had been nil"); and, third, Lambron
thought "that Mr. Hadjiargyris was depicted in too sympathetic a light," in particular because the Draft Report left the
reader with the impression that the
Greek authorities had no reasonable
grounds for their suspicion of Hadjiargyris (Mary G. Jones responds to this criticism of the draft by stating that "since
no facts exist which would evidence a
basis for their suspicion other than the
surmise that he [Hadjiargyris] might

have had leftist or communist leanings, I see no point in indicating this type of surmise in our report").

41. Pp. 4–11.

42. The various names that are given Staktopoulos in the documents having to do with the Lippmann Committee's report may offer a clue to their chronological order. Only Mary G. Jones's long report of October 1950 gives the name correctly as "Staktopoulos," which suggests that by that date those who had been involved in the case had finally gotten the name right. What one assumes are earlier and greatly abridged drafts give the name first in the unpublished "Tentative Draft . . ." (dated May 1949 in pencil) as "Stahtopoulos" and then in the published version as "Stakhtopoulos."

43. See chapter 3.

44. *Walter Lippmann and the American Century* (Boston: Atlantic Monthly Press, 1980), p. 487.

45. Pp. 24ff.

46. The committee members are listed in the Lippmann Report on p. iv.

47. P. 75.

48. Pp. 56–66.

49. Lippmann Report, p. 12.

50. See chapter 3.

51. No. 361, 5-1749, "Memorandum of Conversation" (May 13, 1949). The conversation was with Robert G. Minor, second secretary of the American embassy.

52. Ibid., "COPY (Copy of covering note to the British Ambassador)."

53. Ibid., "To: Mr. P. Constantinidis."

54. Ibid., "Memorandum of Conversation" (May 13).

55. In the personal interview cited above.

56. Copy of note by A.G.R. Rouse "(R 5102/10139/19 G)." Public Record Office, ref. FO371/78404 6159.

57. No. 361, 5-1749, "Memorandum of Conversation" (May 16).

58. Public Record Office, ref. FO 371/78404 6159 ("*Confidential*/British Embassy Athens, May 12th, 1949").

59. Ibid., note by A.G.R. Rouse.

60. No. 81, 6-149.

61. No. 69, 4-1049.

62. No. 81, 6-149, encl.

63. No. 806, 4-2249.

64. No. 59, 4-2049.

65. No. 67, 4-2749.

66. *More*, p. 29.

CHAPTER XI. TOWARD A RESOLUTION

1. Staktopoulos, pp. 241–47; 369ff.

2. In 1987 he was appointed Minister of Northern Greece (subsequently called Minister of Macedonia and Thrace).

3. Staktopoulos, p. 362ff.

4. In an interview with the author (August 1988), Papathemelis indicated that Bamias had been reluctant to talk about the Polk case even as late as 1977 and, an old man at that time, had not always been coherent or consistent in what he had to say. Papathemelis was able to follow up on the Karamichalis aspect of the new evidence by way of Karamichalis's son, who, once condemned to death himself as a Communist andarte, was persuaded to cooperate with Staktopoulos's lawyer through the intervention of Leonidas Kirkos (head of the Greek Communist Party, Interior). When Papathemelis was shown a series of notes—names, dates, etc.—by Karamichalis on the back of a family photograph, the law-

yer not only saw the similarity between Karamichalis's script and the handwriting on the envelope addressed to the Third Police Precinct but also noticed that, in one of his notes, Karamichalis had added a numeral in parenthesis following a number written out in script in the same manner as the address appearing on the envelope. This convinced him that he was on the right track.

5. According to Papathemelis's postscript to Staktopoulos's book (p. 413), the original handwriting experts used the same "official photographs" rather than the original envelope in arriving at their conclusions about the handwriting.

6. The Draft Report (5:2) tells us that two waterfront restaurants were found that served lobster on Saturday, May 8, but none that served lobster and peas.

7. In his 1988 interview with the author, Papathemelis reported that Stelios Mouzenidis had told him that he and

Anna Molyvda had been tortured before they testified at the Polk trial and also that Stelios Mouzenidis claimed to have attended a memorial service for his brother—one announced in the press (unspecified) at the time—some weeks before Polk was murdered. Papathemelis also reported that he had heard that Mouzenidis was selected at one point by the police as a potential suspect because he was a "Professor of English," which made the presence of Staktopoulos as interpreter redundant.

8. See the commentary by Stelios Papathemelis in the Salonika newspaper *Thessaloniki*, July 13, 1979, column 2. Papathemelis told the author that he talked to Vasvanas over the phone at one point in the late 1970s and that Vasvanas not only denied having been involved in the Polk murder, but said that he learned about it some time after the fact because he was in the mountains with his andarte unit at the time of the murder. Indeed, he had tried to return to Greece to clear his name, but his application was made during a period when few former andartes were allowed back from behind the iron curtain, and he died before he could fulfill his wish.

9. Telephone conversation with the author, 1987.

10. Staktopoulos, p. 373.

11. Interview with the author, April 28, 1986. Lambrinos died in 1988.

12. Staktopoulos, p. 45.

13. Telephone conversation with the author, 1987.

14. *More*, May 1977, p. 17.

15. P. 5.

16. *More*, p. 20.

17. See *Memoirs of a Mountain War: Greece 1944–1949* (London: Longman, 1972), pp. 214ff.

18. 4:5.

19. P. 11.

20. Ibid.

21. P. 12.

22. P. 11.

23. August 6–10, 1952.

24. That Donovan was not entirely naive about what the Greek authorities could and could not do in coping with a lead that pointed to the Right is suggested by the Draft Report's revelation that Minister Rendis admitted to him

that it would be almost impossible for Rendis to interrogate or arrest any members of the Military Police unless there was almost conclusive proof of their complicity (see above n. 18).

25. Pp. 22–23.

26. The Gibson cable is numbered 217, 5-2148 ("From: Salonika /May 21, 9 P.M."); the Rankin cable is unnumbered, 5-2148 ("From: Athens /May 21, 9 P.M.").

27. Lippmann Report, pp. 56–66.

28. Staktopoulos, pp. 244ff.

29. Ibid., pp. 310–11.

30. May 3–8, 1965.

31. The Panopoulos episode is dealt with more precisely by Hadjiargyris in his book (pp. 110–11), as we shall see below.

32. June 7, 1976 (see also Staktopoulos, p. 354).

33. Papathemelis told the author that at the time of the Colonels' dictatorship, a colleague of his had reported a conversation he had with Moustakis during which the Supreme Court justice had suggested that if the colleague performed "properly," he too might reach the prominence that Komotouros and Moustakis himself had reached after their performance in the Polk affair.

34. See the account in *Thessaloniki*, February 24, 1979.

35. *Ellinikos Vorras*, June 28, 1979. In his 1988 interview with the author, Papathemelis indicated that sitting justices of the Supreme Court in Greece have much influence on the election of their colleagues, who are chosen by senior members of the judiciary.

36. *Thessaloniki*, July 13, 1979. Papathemelis's argument here is again outlined in his postscript to Staktopoulos's book.

37. The quotations from the Xydis review that follow are from a more detailed typescript copy loaned to the author by Professor John O. Iatrides.

38. Hadjiargyris, pp. 110–11.

39. Pp. 12–23.

40. Pp. 13–14.

41. P. 20.

42. P. 55. Cf. no. 204, 10-2148, encl. 1, p. 7.

43. P. 16.

44. Ibid.

45. P. 22.

46. P. 16. The relevant cable is no longer in the State Department files on the Polk case, nor is it any longer catalogued by the National Archives, but Roubatis and Vlanton have a copy of the text in their files. There are two cables relating to Kellis's role that appear in other sections of the State Department files (why they were not included in the selection of material having to do with the Polk case remains a mystery, but I am grateful to Professor John Iatrides for bringing them to my attention). In the first, we see that Karl Rankin was concerned about Kellis's presence in Athens as early as June 14, when he sent a cable to the secretary of state (868.00/6-1448) stating that the embassy had "endeavored comply with DEPTEL 724, June 5, enjoining secrecy concerning Kellis visit Athens," but Kellis's arrival in Athens on the same plane with Donovan and his having acted as Donovan's interpreter during interviews with Sophoulis and Tsaldaris "have left no doubt in Greek minds as to occasion his visit." In fact Tsaldaris "has queried Embassy re Kellis, including his alleged erstwhile EAM liaison activities and fact he is remaining here after Donovan's departure." This matter, says Rankin, "liable cause unfortunate impression." The second cable, filed under 103.ECA 02/7-1248, is signed by Secretary of State Marshall over William O. Baxter's initials and addressed to AMEMBASSY ATHENS. It suggests that by July 14, the date of the cable, the State Department had already been in touch with the air force regarding Kellis's transfer: "Air Force informally indicated it will permit Kellis to remain in Greece until Gen. Donovan's forthcoming visit and will then insist on his immediate return Washington." The word "insist" suggests that the State Department expected some resistance to the transfer on Donovan's part when he returned to Greece in late July. If there was resistance, it proved to be short-lived—and whether there was remains an open question (see above, pp. 121–23 and below, pp. 344ff.).

47. Pp. 21–22.

48. September 17, 1977.

49. May 23, 1956; copy in Walter Lippmann Papers, Sterling Memorial Library, Yale University.

50. *The Declassified Documents Quarterly*, CIA, December 3, 1952.

51. P. 17.

52. P. 16.

53. By way of the following description, the Draft Report (6:3) gives us some indication of what Donovan was told about Staktopoulos's six weeks of detention at Security Police headquarters between August 14 and his "confession" of October 1: "Staktopoulos was kept in a special room at Security Police headquarters rather than in the City prison and a doctor was assigned to him to make regular checks on his health. Reportedly Staktopoulos suffered from a weak heart and it is improbable that undue pressure could have been exercised on him without jeopardizing his health. At the same time there was no doubt that his interrogation was steady and intensive, going on daily and lasting generally for about four hours from 9:00 P.M. to 1:00 A.M. Immediately after each session he was requested to write out what he had testified to verbally. In this manner the police were able to confront him with his own discrepancies and to seek explanation." There is no record of General Donovan's ever having asked to see these written statements by Staktopoulos or his ever having interviewed the doctor who was presumed to be in constant attendance. Compare Staktopoulos's rather different account of the supervision, medical and otherwise, that he received at Security Police headquarters, chapter 6 above, especially p. 143.

CHAPTER XII. EPILOGUE

1. P. 29.

2. Hadjiargyris, p. 111.

3. Quoted by Roubatis and Vlanton, *More*, p. 16.

4. As described by Richard Cottrell in his book *Blood on Their Hands: The Killing of Ann Chapman* (London: Grafton Books, 1987), Ann Chapman, a

twenty-five-year-old freelance journalist for the BBC's Radio London, was strangled in the St. Nicholas district of Vouliagmeni, Athens, in October 1971. She had gone to Greece on an expenses-paid trip intended to promote tourism in Greece under the Colonels' dictatorship, although she is reported to have told her mother before boarding her flight to Greece that "I have a big story which is going to make my name for me" (p. 20). Some thought that she planned to make contact with the resistance movement in Greece; some in the resistance movement apparently feared that she was a British agent or spy (p. 59). In any case, a man named Nicholas Moundis, a former prison guard with a record as a sex offender, was finally brought to trial in 1973 and was convicted of manslaughter in the course of attempted rape on the basis of a confession that he later recanted with the claim that it had been extracted from him after torture by the police who had detained him. He was sentenced to life imprisonment. The case was reopened by petition from Ann Chapman's father, Edward, to the European Parliament in 1983, and a finding by Richard Cottrell that Ann had not been killed by Moundis but was the victim of " 'agents acting illegally under the authority of the military regime' " (p. 8) was unanimously supported by the Parliament in May 1984. Moundis was released from prison by presidential edict (although not officially pardoned) after serving eleven years of his sentence.

5. The Draft Report (1:5) tells us that the Newsmen's Commission to Investigate the Murder of George Polk "advocated the establishment by Congress of an American Investigating Body," and the commission also "proposed that an investigation team be sent to Greece," but "neither of its proposals came to fruition." What the Draft Report fails to point out is that the Lippmann Committee, through its chairman, actively opposed the Newsmen's Commission effort to send a team to Greece during the course of the investigation, in particular at the time the official solution was taking final shape in late September 1948.

Donovan, Kellis, Burdett, Secondari, and Lambron remained the sole group designated to represent the American press while the investigation was in progress both before and after the Staktopoulos solution was promulgated. In this connection, see n. 10 below.

6. *Walter Lippmann and the American Century*, p. 487.

7. Lippmann Report, pp. 75–76.

8. *More*, p. 19. Also p. 23, n. 35.

9. Ibid., p. 24.

10. The letter of solicitation to Lippmann from the Newsmen's Commission was dated September 20, 1948, and was signed by Irving Gilman, who reported that the team of newsmen was "ready to go to Greece to make an on-the-spot investigation into the murder of George Polk." He hoped that the Overseas Writers might make a contribution to the fund being raised for this purpose or arrange a loan or "perhaps even [underwrite] our appeal," since, said Gilman, "I am sure you will agree with us that it is of the utmost importance to get this team to Greece as soon as possible and to keep the case of George Polk alive in the public mind." Lippmann, replying two weeks later (on October 4), indicated that "we would have no authority to spend any of the funds raised for our committee, except on investigation for which we ourselves took full responsibility," and in any case he felt that he "must go further" and point out that "our committee does not agree that it is important to get this team [i.e., the Newsmen's Commission team] to Greece as soon as possible, and in fact believe that it would interfere with the inquiry which is now taking place there. The presence of two American investigating parties in Greece at the same time would only serve those officials who may not wish to pursue the inquiry," and since "General Donovan is about to go to Greece for the third time, I should consider it most unfortunate if another American investigating team arrived there in the near future." Lippmann adds: "In view of the fact that your decision to appoint a team to go to Greece implies that you have reason to

think that you could solve the mystery better than the investigators who are already there, I should like to ask you whether you have any clues, contacts or evidence on the case which are not in our possession and if you have, whether you will place them at the disposal of General Donovan and our committee" (Walter Lippmann Papers, Sterling Memorial Library, Yale University). Eight days after this letter was mailed, General Donovan, Winston Burdett, and Theodore Lambron, accompanied by Raleigh Gibson, interviewed Major Mouskoundis in Salonika and received the details of the official Staktopoulos solution (No. 192, 10-1348, encl. 1).

11. September 17, 1977.

Index

Acheson, Dean, 55
Acropolis, 96
Adams, Phelps, 327, 365
"Aghios Nicolaos," 161, 162, 172, 182, 185, 199
Ahmed, Dr., 20, 21, 127, 133, 161
Albania, 44, 46
American aid program, 17, 47–48, 55, 66, 161, 356, 361, 362. *See also* American Mission; Griswold, Dwight; Truman Doctrine
American Farm School, 5, 6–8
American Mission, 45, 46, 49, 60, 343, 361. *See also* Griswold, Dwight
American press, 71, 72, 90, 97; accepts official solution, 268, 355; concerned about handling of case, 9, 101, 106–7, 356–57; Donovan and, 192, 197, 277, 383n.5; Draft Report on, 287; Gibson views on, 271; on jury selection, 229; Kellis views on, 347; Kendrick on treatment of, 301–2; Lindley defends, 148; MacVeagh's distress over conduct of, 51–54; and miscarriage of justice, 292; observers at trial, 223; official Greek fear of criticism from, 128; and possible arrest of Rea Polk or Hadjiargyris, 107; Rankin's concern about, 56–58, 150; relations with diplomatic establishment, 102, 104; reports of mistreatment, 101. *See also* Burdett-Secondari report; Lippmann Committee
Angelakoudis, Mr., 245–46
Anglo-Greek Information Service, 254, 308
Apoyevmatini, 329
Astoria Café, 161, 185, 193
Astoria Hotel, 15, 22, 23, 28, 108, 115, 134, 161, 184, 187, 199, 274, 340
Athenian connection. *See* Hadjiargyris, Kosta; Polk, Rea
Athinaiki, 332
Autopsy report (coroner's report), 14–15, 24, 172, 187, 225, 226, 313, 337, 340;

and William Polk, 272; Vassilikos on excellence of, 240
Avyeris (friend of Staktopoulos), 136, 137
Ayer, Frederick, 9, 367; assigned to case, 71, 289, 356, 365; background, 76–77; on Barber episode, 96–97; on Communists' role, 84, 99; frustrated by restrictions, 80; and Gibson, 81–82; on Greek judicial process, 90; Lambron on, 379–80n.40; leaves investigation, 113; meets Donovan, 102, 103; meets Rea Polk, 78; and Mouskoundis, 83, 97, 112; opinions on contribution of, 129; and questioning of Rea Polk, 108–9; relations with Burdett and Secondari, 83–84, 85, 90, 91; on security police behavior, 81, 152; and Staktopoulos, 82, 128; and Staktopoulos solution, 82; suspects Rea Polk and Hadjiargyris, 76, 78–80, 82, 104, 127; takes charge of investigation, 77; on "third degree" interrogation, 80; and *Yankee G-Man*, 76, 82, 83

Bailey, Hugh, 115
Bamias, Evthimios, 314, 380n.4
Barber, Mary, 93–97, 100, 187, 246, 248, 254, 305, 311
Barber, Stephen, 93, 96, 97, 187, 245, 246, 254, 305, 306
Baxter, William O., 71, 102, 214, 215, 289, 364
Beatty, Morgan, 101
Bigart, Homer: on Americans in Greece, 66; desires independent investigation, 271–72; on Greek army, 57; Griswold views on, 62–64, 67; Hadjiargyris's presumed influence on, 88; Markos trip, 55, 58–62, 150, 183, 204, 228, 248, 322, 323; Polk's views on, 35; Rankin views on, 55–56, 150; and Staktopoulos, 320
Bigio (Reuters correspondent), 304–5
British Broadcasting Corporation, 89

Vermillion, Robert, 53
Virginia Military Institute, 36
Vlanton, Elias, 10, 12, 285, 321, 337, 342–45, 349, 351, 359
Vorras, 254
Voulgaris, Admiral, 89
Voultepsis, Yannis, 337
Voutsi, Maria. *See* Vroutsi, Despina
Voutyras, Michael, 179, 181
Voyadjis, Anastasios, 160, 167, 177, 181, 185
Vroutsi, Despina, 92, 244–45

Wickham, Sir Charles, 33, 96, 309, 345, 358
Wittner, Lawrence, 57, 63, 65

Wooton, Paul, 327

"X" (Chi), 26–27, 284, 323; "X-ites" (Chi-ites), 84
Xanthopoulos, Apostolos, 107, 120, 146, 231, 361
Xydis, Stephen G., 338–42

Yankee G-Man, 76, 82, 83, 291
"Yannis," 183, 189, 247
Yugoslavia, 44, 59, 62

Zachariadis, Nikos, 45, 46, 47, 117, 323
Zafiriou, 231, 274, 278–79
Zionists, 32
Zotos, 235, 239